Classroom Teaching Skills: A Handbook

Classroom Teaching

JAMES M. COOPER, GENERAL EDITOR
University of Houston

JOHN HANSEN
Florida State University

PETER H. MARTORELLA
Temple University

GRETA G. MORINE-DERSHIMER
San Jose State University

DAVID SADKER
American University

MYRA SADKER
American University

ROBERT SHOSTAK
Florida International University

SANDRA SOKOLOVE
Wheaton College

TERRY TENBRINK
University of Missouri

WILFORD A. WEBER
University of Houston

Skills A Handbook

D.C. HEATH AND COMPANY
Lexington, Massachusetts   Toronto

TO OUR STUDENTS

because those who can, teach;
and those who teach, learn.

Contents

Teaching Concepts   *194*

PETER H. MARTORELLA

 **Interpersonal Communication Skills**   *238*

SANDRA SOKOLOVE, MYRA SADKER, AND DAVID SADKER

 Classroom Management   *284*

WILFORD A. WEBER

Observation Skills

JOHN HANSEN

Evaluation

TERRY TENBRINK

Preface

Margaret Mead once said, "No man will ever again die in the same world in which he was born." Her theme of change certainly applies to the field of teacher education. At one time in the not-too-distant past, teacher education consisted of a few courses on education theory, some courses on methods, and a topping of student teaching. Except for the student teaching, and maybe a little observation experience, the program consisted of campus-based courses.

Teacher education today differs considerably from the above description. Programs are much more field-oriented than ever before, requiring prospective teachers to spend more time working with children in schools. The emphasis now on practical experience with children should not be interpreted as a movement away from theory. Rather, educational theory is being integrated with practice. This integration recognizes that theory, to be internalized, must be learned in the context in which it is to be applied. In the past, prospective teachers were expected to translate theory into practice with little help. Usually they were unsuccessful. Today with the help of newly developed curriculum materials, teacher educators help trainees apply the theory in field contexts and provide them with feedback on their efforts.

This *Handbook* and its accompanying *Workbook* attempt to help teacher educators meld theory with practice. The books conceptualize the teacher as a decision maker — one who makes planning, implementing, evaluation, and management decisions as part of the instructional role. In order to make and carry out these decisions the teacher needs certain teaching skills. The conceptual framework of the teacher as a decision maker is presented in Chapter One. Each subsequent chapter addresses a particular skill by first discussing the theory behind the skill, then giving the reader practice situations where the skill can be applied and feedback received. Because each chapter presents specific learning objectives as well as mastery tests, the reader receives immediate feedback on this learning.

After students have completed the *Handbook* and *Workbook* chapters, the instructor may want to set up microteaching experiences that will enable them to practice the skills with actual learners. Ultimate acquisition of the skill must, of course, take place in actual classroom situations.

From the outset our goal has been to produce instructional materials that are (1) important, (2) flexible, (3) readable, and (4) scholarly. A word about each of these features follows.

First, the *importance* of the teaching skills contained in these books has been dramatically demonstrated during the past decade by the millions of dollars spent on researching them and the multitude of books and articles published on each one. There has been, however, a puzzling hesitation to draw together and theoretically integrate existing knowledge of them into a single, comprehensive set of instructional materials. Our own decision to attempt such a major publishing venture was based to some extent on formal and informal market research conducted from the spring of 1972 up to the present. Feedback has consistently confirmed a key point: students emphatically want to master practical teaching skills that will enable them to cope successfully with their classroom responsibilities. Consequently, it is our belief that these instructional materials, dedicated as they are to the mastery of basic teaching skills, will be retained and used by most students as an ongoing, self-evaluation tool — to be referred to both during and after their field experiences.

Our second goal, to produce a highly *flexible* text, has been met in two ways. First, the content itself — the skills — is ubiquitous, reaching into virtually every course in the teacher-training curriculum. Second, both the *Handbook* and the *Workbook* have been designed as self-contained teacher education materials, thus permitting their use in a variety of capacities in all parts of the curriculum. Instructors may choose to focus on particular chapters for one course and different chapters for another course. How the books are used will depend on the structure and organization of a given teacher education program.

Our third goal, *readability*, has been achieved by a rewrite editor who spent several hundred hours smoothing out and simplifying the manuscripts of the various authors. While each author's unique writing style has been consciously preserved, the level and structure of writing has been adjusted to conform to preplanned standards. In each chapter we have tried to present a relatively simple, jargon-free presentation within a four-step, self-teaching format including (1) a statement of objectives, (2) a presentation of written information, (3) practice exercises with answers, and (4) a mastery test with answer key.

Finally, our goal of developing materials representative of the best current *scholarship* has been met by experienced authors, each a recognized authority regarding the particular skill he or she is writing about. In most instances the authors have field-tested their materials extensively with teacher education students. Further information on each author is presented on the following pages.

James M. Cooper
University of Houston

About the Authors

James M. Cooper is Professor of Curriculum and Instruction at the University of Houston. He received his Ph.D. in education from Stanford University in 1967. He is coauthor with Kevin Ryan of *Those Who Can, Teach*, a first-experience book for prospective teachers, and *Kaleidoscope: Readings in Education*. He has also written books and articles in the areas of competency-based teacher education, microteaching, and differentiated staffing. He was Director of one of the USOE Model Elementary Teacher Education Programs at the University of Massachusetts and later was Associate Dean for Graduate Studies in the College of Education at the University of Houston.

John H. Hansen is Director of a teacher corps project and Program Leader in Childhood Education at the Florida State University. He has studied and worked in Minnesota, Wisconsin, Illinois, Nebraska, Oregon, Rio de Janeiro, and Florida. His collegiate education culminated in three degrees from the University of Wisconsin-Madison. Professionally, he has been a supervisor of student teachers, director of field experiences for a teacher education program, chairman — department of curriculum and instruction, and consultant in changing teacher behavior. For two years, he served as a consultant to the Brazilian Ministry of Education and Culture in the areas of teacher education and curriculum development. His published works include a book on middle schools, numerous materials on observation, and articles and monographs on teacher education.

Greta Morine-Dershimer has taught in elementary and junior high schools for ten years, and has been training preservice and in service teachers for ten years. She received her Ed.D. from Teachers College, Columbia University in 1965 in curriculum research and theory development. Her major areas of interest have been in developing teacher decision-making processes and teaching strategies for concept learning. Her major publications include *Discovering Your Language* (a seventh grade linguistics textbook coauthored with Neil Postman and Harold Morine), *Discovery: A Challenge to Teachers*

(coauthored with Harold Morine), *Creating the School: An Introduction to Education* (coauthored with Bruce Joyce), and "Teaching," a chapter in the 1974 *N.S.S.E. Yearbook* on the elementary school in the United States. In her work at the Far West Laboratory she has developed a series of films on "responsive teaching" to train teachers in the use of concept-learning strategies (coproduced with Ned Flanders) and a set of films on changing sex role stereotyping in schools (coproduced with Gloria Golden and Lisa Hunter).

Peter H. Martorella is Professor of Curriculum and Instruction at Temple University. He received his Ph.D. degree from Ohio State University in 1966 and later completed a post-doctoral fellowship at the University of Washington. The author of two books on concept learning, *Concept Learning in the Social Studies: Models for Structural Curriculum* and *Concept Learning: Designs for Instruction* (Intext), he also has written two texts in the area of social studies, *Elementary Social Studies as a Learning System* and *Social Studies Strategies: Theory into Practice* (Harper and Row). He has been a public school teacher at the elementary, junior high school, and senior high school levels in New York, Ohio, and California.

David Sadker is Associate Professor and Director of Teacher Education Programs at The American University in Washington, D. C. He has lectured extensively on sex-role stereotyping, particularly as it applies to male stereotypes. He has published numerous articles in *Phi Delta Kappan*, *Social Education*, *Journal of Teacher Education*, *Elementary School Journal*, and a variety of other educational journals. His latest publication — coauthored with his wife, Myra — is a text on children's literature entitled, *Now Upon a Time: A Contemporary View of Children's Literature* (Harper and Row).

Myra Sadker is Associate Professor of Education at American University in Washington, D. C. She is coauthor of *Sexism in School and Society* (Harper and Row) and coauthor of *Now Upon a Time: A Contemporary Approach to Children's Literature* (Harper and Row). She has published in many educational journals, including *Phi Delta Kappan*, *National Elementary Principal*, *Instructor*, *Educational Leadership*, *Social Education*, *Elementary English*, and *Journal of Teacher Education*.

Sandra Sokolove is Assistant Professor of Education at Wheaton College in Massachusetts. She received her Ed.D. degree from the University of Massachusetts in 1975. Her professional interest and early writing have focussed on humanistic education and interpersonal communication.

Robert Shostak is Chairman of the Division of Secondary Education and Coordinator of the English Education program at Florida International University. He taught high school English for six years before moving to the State University of New York at Albany, where he joined the English Education staff in the School of Education. During the next eight years he taught English methods courses and supervised student teachers, and spent almost two years planning and implementing the University's first program for economically disadvantaged students. In 1971 he joined the planning staff at Florida International University to develop that state's first performance-based teacher education program. He received his bachelor's degree in humanities from Colgate University, a master's degree in teaching English from the State University of New York at Albany, and a Ph.D. in curriculum and instruction from the University of Connecticut. He is the author of *World Literature: Four Representative Types*, as well as a number of articles in professional journals.

Terry D. TenBrink is Professor of Educational Psychology at the University of Missouri. He received his Ph.D. in educational psychology from Michigan State University in 1968, where his studies emphasized learning theory, evaluation, measurement, and research design. His teaching experience spans elementary, junior high school, high school, and college students, and he has been principal of an elementary school. He stays in touch with the classroom through numerous consulting activities in public schools and in adult education, and by teaching courses in evaluation, learning, human development, and general educational psychology at the University of Missouri. He has published numerous journal articles and is engaged in continuing research on the conditions under which learning occurs efficiently. In 1974 his textbook *Evaluation: A Practical Guide for Teachers* was published by McGraw-Hill.

Wilford A. Weber is Professor of Education in the College of Education of the University of Houston. He holds a B.A. in psychology from Muhlenberg College and an Ed.D. in educational psychology from Temple University. He has taught at Syracuse University and directed a number of funded projects, and has authored more than fifty papers, articles, chapters, monographs, and books concerned with teacher education, instructional systems design, and classroom management. His interest in classroom management stems from his experience as a teacher of court-committed juvenile delinquents.

JAMES M. COOPER

The Teacher as a Decision Maker

What Is a Teacher?

At first glance such a question seems obvious. A teacher is a person charged with the responsibility of helping others to learn and to behave in new and different ways. But who is excluded from this definition? Parents? Band directors? Drill sergeants? Boy scout leaders? At some time or another we all teach and, in turn, are taught.

We generally reserve the term "teacher," however, for persons whose primary professional or occupational function is to help others learn and develop in new ways. While education, learning, and teaching can, and do, take place in many different settings, most societies realize that education is too important to be left to chance. Consequently, they establish schools to facilitate learning and to help people live better and happier lives. Schools are created to provide a certain type of educational experience, which can be called the curriculum. Teachers are trained and hired by societies to help fulfill the purposes of the curriculum. Teachers, in the formal educative process of schooling, are social agents hired by society to help facilitate the intellectual, personal, and social development of those members of society who attend schools.

Until modern times teachers themselves had very little formal schooling; often they knew barely more than their students. As late as 1864 an Illinois teacher described the image of the teacher as "someone who can parse and cypher; has little brains and less money; is feeble minded, unable to grapple with real men and women in the stirring employments of life, but on that account admirably fitted to associate with childish intellects." [1] Needless to say, this early-day image of the teacher has changed considerably for the better. Today teachers are better educated, earn more money, and are more highly respected members of society than their nineteenth century counterparts. Society requires its teachers to obtain a college education and specific training as teachers. This increase in the educational level of teachers is recognition that if teachers are to facilitate the intellectual, personal, and social development of their students, then they must be much better educated than ever before.

Effective Teaching

Possession of a college degree does not in any way ensure that teachers will be effective. But what is an effective teacher? What is a good teacher? Are they the same?

Good teaching is very difficult to define because the term "good" is so value-laden. What appears to be good teaching to one person may be considered poor teaching by another, because each one values different outcomes or methods. One teacher may run the classroom in a very organized, highly structured manner, emphasizing the intellectual content of the academic disciplines. Another may run the class in a less structured environment, allowing the students much more freedom to choose subject matter and activities that interest them personally. One observer, because of his value system, may identify the first teacher as a "good" teacher, while he criticizes the second teacher for running "too loose a ship." Another observer may come to the opposite conclusion with respect to which teacher is better, again, because of a different set of values.

While it remains difficult to agree on what "good" teaching is, "effective" teaching can be demonstrated. *The effective teacher is one who is able to bring about intended learning outcomes.* The nature of the learning is still most important, but two different teachers, as in the example above, may strive for and achieve very different outcomes and both be judged effective. The two critical dimensions of effective teaching are *intent* and *achievement*.

Without intent student achievement becomes random and accidental, rather than controlled and predictable. However, intent is not enough by itself. If students do not achieve their intended learning goals (even if the failure is due to variables beyond the control of their teacher), the teacher cannot truly be called effective.

While effective teachers are defined as teachers who can demonstrate the ability to bring about intended learning outcomes, what enables them to achieve desired results with students? Have you ever stopped to think about what, if anything, makes teachers different from other well-educated adults? What should effective, professional teachers know, believe, or be able to do that distinguishes them from other people? Think about these questions seriously because they are central questions, the answers to which should be at the heart of your teacher education program.

Some people will state that the crucial dimension is the teacher's personality. Teachers, they will say, should be friendly, cheerful, sympathetic, morally virtuous, enthusiastic, and humorous. In a massive study, David Ryans concluded that effective teachers are fair, democratic, responsive, understanding, kindly, stimulating, original, alert, attractive, responsible, steady, poised, and confident. Ineffective teachers were described as partial, autocratic, aloof, restricted, harsh, dull, stereotyped, apathetic, unimpressive, evasive, erratic, excitable, and uncertain.[2] But as two well-known educators once remarked, ". . . what conceivable human interaction is not the better if the people involved are friendly, cheerful, sympathetic, and virtuous rather than the opposite"?[3] These characteristics, then, while desirable in teachers, are not uniquely desirable to that group alone.

It might be difficult to reach a consensus on exactly what knowledge and skills are unique to the teaching profession, but most educators would agree that special skills and knowledge are necessary and do exist. Certainly teachers must be familiar with children and their developmental stages. They must know something about events and happenings outside the classroom and school. They must possess enough command of the subject they are going to teach to be able to differentiate what is important and central from what is incidental and peripheral. They must have a philosophy of education to help guide them in their role as teachers. They must know how human beings learn and how to create environments which facilitate learning.

General Areas of Teacher Competence

B. O. Smith has suggested that a well-trained teacher should be prepared in four areas of teacher competence to be effective in bringing about intended learning outcomes.

1. Command of theoretical knowledge about learning and human behavior.
2. Display of attitudes that foster learning and genuine human relationships.
3. Command of knowledge in the subject matter to be taught.
4. Control of technical skills of teaching that facilitate student learning.

1. Command of Theoretical Knowledge About Learning and Human Behavior.   For years education has been criticized for its "folkways" practices. Educational recipes and standardized procedures were formally and informally passed on to new teachers to help them survive in classrooms. While this practice still exists, many scientific concepts from psychology, anthropology, sociology, linguistics, cybernetics, and related disciplines are now available to help teachers interpret the complex reality of their classrooms. Those teachers who lack the theoretical background and understanding provided by such scientifically derived concepts can only interpret the events of their classrooms according to popularly held beliefs or common sense. Although common sense often serves us well, there is ample evidence that teachers who habitually rely on it will too often misinterpret the events in their classrooms.

Beginning teachers frequently face the difficult situation of receiving different, contradictory messages from their professors and from the teachers with whom they work. While their professors are apt to focus on theoretical knowledge, the experienced teacher may often advise them, "Forget the fancy theoretical stuff and listen to me. I'll tell you what works in real life." This "folkways" approach to education may be in conflict with what the new teacher has learned and create a dilemma about how to handle an actual situation.

The problem confronting student teachers is not that the theories put before them are unworkable, but that they simply haven't internalized those theories to the point where they can be used to interpret and solve practical problems. They have not been provided with sufficient opportunities to apply the knowledge, to translate it from theory into practice and thereby master it.

An example of a theoretical concept that is derived from psychology and that has enormous implications for teachers is the concept of "reinforcement." From their educational psychology courses most teachers know that a behavior that is reinforced will be strengthened and is likely to be repeated. Nevertheless, these same student teachers often respond to a disruptive pupil by calling his or her actions to the attention of the class. If the pupil is misbehaving because of a need to be recognized, the student teacher, by publicly acknowledging the misbehavior, is actually reinforcing it. When the pupil continues to act up periodically, the student teacher doesn't understand why. Although a student teacher may have intellectually grasped a concept such as "reinforcement," this understanding is not synonymous with internalizing or mastering the concept. Mastery requires practical application to concrete situations.

Because theoretical knowledge can be used to interpret situations and solve problems, many classroom events that might otherwise go unnoticed or remain inexplicable can be recognized and resolved by applying theories and concepts of human behavior. This is not an easy task. It requires understanding, insight, practice, and feedback from colleagues and professors. Proficiency will not be achieved as a result of formal training alone; it is a lifelong process involving both formal training and an unending program of on-the-job self-improvement.

2. Display of Attitudes that Foster Learning and Genuine Human Relationships. The second area of competence identified as essential for effective teaching has to do with attitudes. An attitude is a predisposition to act in a positive or negative way toward persons, ideas, or events. Most educators are convinced that teacher attitudes are a very important dimension in the teaching process. Attitudes have a direct effect on our behavior; they determine how we view ourselves and interact with others.

The major categories of attitudes that affect teaching behavior are: (a) teachers' attitudes toward themselves; (b) teachers' attitudes toward children; (c) teachers' attitudes toward peers and parents; and (d) teachers' attitudes toward the subject matter.

(a) *Teachers' attitudes toward themselves.* There is evidence from psychology that persons who deny or cannot cope with their own emotions are likely to be incapable of respecting and coping with the feelings of others. If teachers are to understand and sympathize with their students' feelings, they must recognize and understand their own feelings. Many colleges are responding to this need by including counseling sessions, sensitivity training, and awareness experiences as part of their teacher education programs. These experiences emphasize introspection, self-evaluation, and feedback from other participants. The goal is to help prospective teachers learn more about themselves, their attitudes, and how others perceive them.

(b) *Teachers' attitudes toward children.* Most teachers occasionally harbor attitudes or feelings toward students that are detrimental to their teaching effectiveness. Strong likes and dislikes of particular pupils, biases toward or against particular ethnic groups, low learning expectations for poverty-level children, and biases toward or against certain kinds of student behavior, all can reduce teaching effectiveness. Self-awareness of such attitudes toward individual pupils or classes of children is necessary if teachers are to cope with their own feelings and beliefs. If teachers possess empathy for their students and value them as unique individuals, they will be more effective and will derive more satisfaction from their teaching.

(c) *Teachers' attitudes toward peers and parents.* Teachers do not exist in isolated classrooms. They interact with fellow teachers and administrators and often have sensitive dealings with parents. Sometimes they can be very effective in dealing with children, but because of negative attitudes toward the adults they encounter, their professional life is unsuccessful. This is a rare instance, however, for most people have similar attitudes toward all persons, adult and child, possessing similar characteristics. Many of the comments already made regarding teachers' attitudes toward themselves and children also apply to their attitudes toward peers and parents.

(d) *Teachers' attitudes toward subject matter.* The message, in one word, is ENTHUSIASM! Just as students are very perceptive in discovering the teacher's attitude toward them, they are also sensitive to the teacher's attitude toward the subject matter. Teachers who are not enthusiastic about what they teach can hardly hope to instill enthusiastic responses in their pupils. The best way to ensure such enthusiasm is for teachers to plan their instruction around subject matter that is of high interest to them. From whom do you think you would learn more — an enthusiastic teacher dealing with an esoteric topic, such as cave paintings of primitive man, or an uninspired teacher dealing with contemporary political history? As a teacher, you should not allow yourself to be pressured into teaching something that you care little about. After all, if you don't care about the subject matter, how can you ever hope to motivate your students into learning about it?

3. Command of Knowledge in the Subject Matter To Be Taught. Command of the subject matter to be taught is an obvious necessity for any teacher. But taking courses in biology or history or mathematics is not sufficient. A teacher's subject matter preparation really has two aspects: (1) a study of the subject matter itself, and (2) a judicious selection of the material that can be transmitted successfully to the student.

College courses taken in disciplines like mathematics or English help teachers acquire an understanding of the disciplines, their basic concepts, and their modes of inquiry; but college courses are not directed toward what should be taught to elementary or secondary school students. What should be taught is obviously much less extensive and advanced than the content of the college courses and requires that teachers know the school curriculum as well.

Teachers must, therefore, rethink much of the content of a particular discipline as it relates to the lives of their pupils. To be effective communicators, teachers need an understanding of both children and subject matter and, beyond that, special training in linking the two.

As B. O. Smith states:

> . . . the teacher should know the content he is to teach as well as that of the disciplines from which his instructional subject matter may be taken. The first is necessary for teaching anything at all. The second applies a depth of knowledge essential to the teacher's feelings of intellectual security and his ability to handle instructional content with greater understanding.[4]

4. Control of Technical Skills of Teaching that Facilitate Student Learning. The fourth area of competence required of effective teachers is possession of a repertoire of teaching skills. Such a repertoire is necessary if teachers are to be effective with students who have varied backgrounds and learning aptitudes. Teacher education programs must, therefore, include a training component focusing on the acquisition of specific teaching skills. No program can afford to concentrate so exclusively on the acquisition of knowledge that it ignores or slights the "practice" dimension of teaching. Whereas the knowledge components involved in teacher preparation focus on the contexts or situations that confront teachers, the skills component focuses directly on the trainees — on the observation, analysis, and modification of their teaching behavior.

THE TEACHER AS DECISION MAKER

We have examined briefly four general areas of competence in which teachers must develop proficiency to be effective. While this examination is useful for obtaining an overview of the basic components of a well-designed teacher education program, it does not provide any guidelines on what a teacher actually does when teaching. A model of the teacher and of the instructional process can provide some guidelines to help teachers better understand what they should be doing when they teach. For this purpose, we shall examine the model of the teacher as a decision maker.

First consider the following situation: You are a middle school social studies teacher. You want to teach your students what a protective tariff is. What decisions must you make before this can be accomplished? First, *you have to decide exactly what you want them to know about protective tariffs.* You probably will want them to know how protective tariffs differ from revenue tariffs, why countries impose protective tariffs, how other countries are likely to respond, and who benefits and who suffers when protective tariffs are imposed.

Second, *you must decide what student behavior you will accept as evidence that the students understand protective tariffs and their ramifications.* Will they have to repeat a definition from memory? Will they have to give examples? Will they have to analyze a hypothetical situation and describe the pros and cons of imposing a protective tariff?

Third, *you will have to plan a strategy for obtaining the desired pupil learning.* Will you have the students do some reading? Will you lecture to them? Will you show them some audiovisual materials? How many examples will you need to show them? What provisions will you make for those students who don't understand? How much time will you allot for this learning activity?

Fourth, *as you teach the lesson, you will have to decide, based on student reactions, which parts of your strategy to adjust.* Are the students responding in the manner you thought? Are there any new classroom developments that will force you to change your tactics or the decisions you had previously made?

Fifth, *you will need to evaluate the impact and outcomes of your teaching.* Have the students satisfactorily demonstrated that they understand what protective tariffs are? If not, what is the deficiency in their understanding? What can you do about it? How effective were the strategies you used to teach the concept?

All these questions require decisions from alternative choices. Even the initial decision to teach the concept of protective tariffs required a choice from other social studies concepts. As this example demonstrates, the teacher is constantly making decisions with regard to student learning and appropriate instructional strategies.

What kinds of decisions? In the example of the protective tariff, you would have to decide how the students would best learn the characteristics of protective tariffs, based on their previous learning experiences. If you had decided to lecture, you would be predicting that, given the particular students and the available material, they would learn best through a lecture method.

Suppose that midway through the lecture you pick up cues from the students that they are not really understanding the concept of a protective tariff. It may be that they weren't ready to understand the concept, or it might be that your lecture was ineffective. Now you have to decide whether to continue, try a different strategy, or reintroduce the concept later.

The various steps of this decision-making model are depicted in Figure 1.1.

Within the instructional role teachers must make decisions related to the three basic teaching functions shown in Figure 1.1: (1) planning, (2) implementation, and (3) evaluation.

The *planning* function requires that teachers make decisions about their students' needs, the most appropriate goals and objectives to help meet those needs, the motivation necessary to attain their goals and objectives, and the instructional modes and teaching strategies most suited to the attainment of those goals and objectives. The planning function usually occurs when teachers are alone and have time to consider long- and short-range plans, the students' progress toward achieving objectives, the availability of materials, the time requirements of particular activities, and other such issues. Some teaching skills that support the planning function include observing pupil behavior, diagnosing pupil needs, setting goals and objectives, sequencing goals and objectives, and determining appropriate learning activities related to the objectives.

The *implementation* function requires that teachers implement the decisions that were made in the planning stage, particularly those related to instructional modes, teaching strategies, and learning activities. While much of the planning function is accomplished when teachers are alone, the implementation function occurs when teachers are interacting with students. Teaching skills that support the implementation function include presenting and explaining, listening, introducing, demonstrating, eliciting student responses, and achieving closure.

The *evaluation* function requires decisions about the suitability of chosen objectives as well as the teaching strategies keyed to those objectives and, ultimately, whether or not the students are achieving what the teacher intended. To make the necessary decisions, teachers must determine what kind of information they need and then gather it. Teaching skills that support the evaluation function include specifying the learning objectives to be evaluated; describing the information needed to make such evaluation; obtaining, analyzing, and recording that information; and forming judgments.

The *feedback* dimension of the decision-making model simply means that you examine the results of your teaching and then decide how adequately you handled each of these three teaching functions. On the basis of this examination you determine whether you have succeeded in attaining your objectives or whether you need to make new plans or try different implementation strategies. Feedback, then, is the new information you process into your decision making in order to adjust your planning, implementation, or evaluation functions or to continue on the same basis. It is the decision-making system's way of correcting itself.

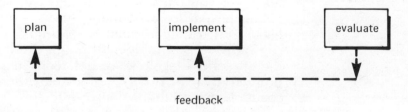

FIGURE 1.1   Model of the teacher as decision maker.

The model of the teacher as a decision maker has been introduced as a way of conceptualizing the instructional role of the teacher. Admittedly, this conceptualization is a simplification of what actually occurs in teaching, but that is why models are useful. They allow us to see the forest without being confused by the trees.

This particular model represents a theory of teaching and makes several basic assumptions. First, the model assumes that teaching is goal directed, that is, that some change in the students' thinking or behavior is sought. Second, the model assumes that teachers are active shapers of their own behavior. They make plans, implement them, and continually adjust to new information concerning the effects of their actions. Third, the model assumes that teaching is basically a rational process that can be improved by examining its components in an analytical manner. It assumes teachers can control the feedback process by selecting both the amount and kind of feedback to use. Fourth, the model assumes that teachers, by their actions, can influence students to change their own behavior in desired ways. Stated another way, the model assumes that teaching behavior can affect student behavior and learning.

There are other models that depict the teacher's role differently and are based on different assumptions about effective teaching. However, this model was selected as the organizing rubric of this book because of the model's simplicity and its power to capture the essence of what teachers do in the instructional process. Teachers are professionals who are educated and trained to make and implement decisions.

The four general areas of teacher competence, identified by Smith and discussed earlier, represent the broad categories of preparation that teachers need in order to make intelligent, effective decisions. Thus, competence in theoretical knowledge about learning, attitudes that foster learning and positive human relationships, knowledge in the subject matter to be taught, and a repertoire of teaching skills provide teachers with the tools necessary to make and implement professional judgments and decisions. Figure 1.2 depicts this relationship.

As you think about Figure 1.2, it should become obvious to you that people may strive toward mastery of the decision-making model without ever achieving it. To achieve mastery would require total command of the four general areas of competence and the ability to apply expertly the knowledge, attitudes, and skills acquired in each instructional decision. But, even if decision making cannot be mastered, teachers can become increasingly competent at it and, consequently, become increasingly effective with their students.

How Are Teaching Skills Acquired?

This Handbook and its supporting Workbook are designed to equip you with a repertoire of teaching skills crucial to the decision-making process. Without such a repertoire of skills, your decision-making alternatives are severely reduced.

What teaching skills have had the most beneficial impact on student learning? To answer that question conclusively is impossible. While much educational research has been directed toward answering this question, the results to date are either too tentative, varied, or of little practical value to help educators design training programs. Re-

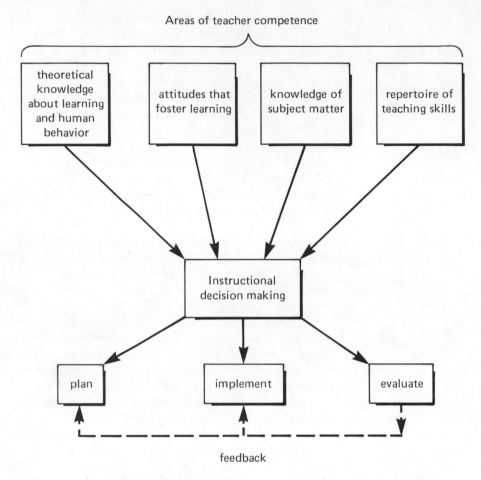

FIGURE 1.2   Relationship of teacher-competence areas to process of instructional decision making.

search studies may soon prove helpful in the design of such programs, but at present their value is limited.

The skills chosen for this Handbook are skills supported by many teacher educators on the basis of their own teaching experience and their diagnosis of the teacher's role as a decision maker. These skills are complex, not simple, ones. Their acquisition requires both careful study and diligent practice. The Handbook and the accompanying Workbook are designed to get you thinking about the skills, to understand their purpose and how they fit into the instructional act, and to start you practicing their application in analytical, simulated, or classroom situations. It will be up to you and your instructors to provide opportunities where you can practice the skills in more complex and realistic situations, eventually practicing them in a classroom context with actual students.

How does one go about learning complex teaching skills so that they become part of one's "natural" teaching style? Bryce Hudgins has described very well a three-stage process of complex skill acquisition.[5] The first phase is a *cognitive* one. The learner must form a cognitive map of the skill he is to learn. He should know the purpose of the skill and how it will benefit him. Further, this cognitive phase helps the learner to isolate the various skill elements, their sequencing, and the nature of the final performance. As Hudgins says, ". . . this is a time when the learning of the student can be facilitated by assisting him to form a concept of what is contained in the skill, how its elements fit together, and how his present knowledge and experience can contribute (that is, transfer positively) to what he is to learn." [6]

The second phase for complex skill acquisition is *practice*. We have all heard the old saying, "Practice makes perfect." While this statement may not take into account many other requisites, it is certainly true that complex skills cannot be learned without a good deal of practice. The seemingly effortless motion of an Olympic swimmer is not acquired without thousands of miles of practice swimming. Similarly, the skill of driving a car is not learned without a lot of practice. So too, with complex teaching skills. Both Hudgins and B. O. Smith agree that the amount of practice devoted to the acquisition of teaching skills in most teacher education programs is so small that it is ridiculous to expect teachers to demonstrate these skills at even passable levels.

The third phase for acquiring a complex skill is *knowledge of results*. Practice will not really make perfect unless the persons trying to acquire the skill receive feedback regarding their performance. This point has been repeatedly demonstrated in psychological experiments where subjects are given great amounts of practice in a given skill but are deprived of any feedback regarding their performance. Without such feedback their performance does not improve, while other subjects, whose practice of the same skill includes feedback, do improve upon their initial performance.

Since learning complex teaching skills requires (1) *cognitive understanding*, (2) *practice*, and (3) *knowledge of performance* (feedback), any teacher-training materials aimed at developing such skills should incorporate these three conditions into their design. This Handbook and its accompanying Workbook have such a design. The Handbook is also self-contained; that is, you can acquire conceptual aspects of a particular skill without reliance on outside instructors, materials, or the availability of a group of students to teach. There will be times, however, when you will be asked to work with some of your peers and provide feedback to one another.

You might be asking yourself the question, "Can complex teaching skills really be mastered in the absence of pupils to be taught?" Ultimately, no, but there are various intermediate stages that are helpful to go through as you acquire skills. Hudgins has presented these stages in Figure 1.3.* Stage 1 involves a conceptual understanding of the skill, its elements, their sequence, and the nature of the final performance. Usually this first stage is accomplished by reading about the skill and its elements and/or by seeing the skill demonstrated and having its various elements explained. It does not normally involve practice.

Stage 2 is accomplished through self-contained training materials directed at each of the major elements comprising a model of the skill. Appropriate feedback must also be provided for each of the elements within the model. The training materials should themselves be prepared in accordance with the elements of the model.

* From Bryce B. Hudgins, "Self-Contained Training Materials for Teacher Education: A Derivation from Research on the Learning of Complex Skills," Report 5, National Center for the Development of Training Materials in Teacher Education (Bloomington, Indiana: School of Education, Indiana University), 1974, p. 23. Reprinted by permission.

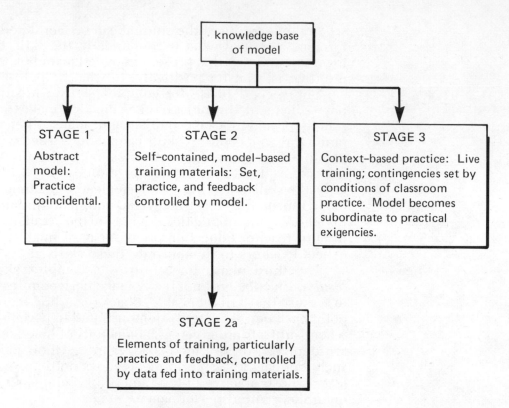

FIGURE 1.3   Self-contained training materials in a teacher-training sequence. Figure shows (1) the dependence of training materials upon an adequate knowledge base for the model and (2) the position of the materials as the reality dimension of training is varied.

Stage 2a requires that the practice exercises contained in the training materials be developed around actual data obtained from studies of real children. In other words, practice situations, drawn from actual data, should be used in order to make them as realistic as possible and, hopefully, highly transferable to actual classrooms.

Stage 3 represents actual classroom situations where the skill can be practiced with actual students. This is the context where the teacher tries to "put it all together" and receives feedback on his or her performance. The importance of Stages 2 and 2a becomes apparent when one thinks of moving directly from Stage 1 to Stage 3. Reading about the skill and then immediately practicing it in a real classroom is analogous to reading a manual on how to operate an automobile and then taking it out into heavy traffic to practice. Obviously, no responsible driver educator would use this procedure. Instead, he would require the learners to practice various elements in simulated or controlled situations before allowing them to take a car out alone.

Because teacher education has lacked the training materials needed to develop basic teaching skills, beginning teachers have traditionally been asked to move directly from Stage 1 to Stage 3. Sometimes the teacher has succeeded in spite of these circumstances, but in many instances the results have been disastrous. Although ultimately you must exercise these skills with actual students in real teaching situations, your probability of success will be greatly increased if you first develop a thorough understanding of the skill and its elements, if you have controlled practice situations which are reality-based, and if you receive feedback in order to adjust your performance in necessary ways.

HANDBOOK'S DESIGN

The purpose of this Handbook and the accompanying Workbook is to help you develop competence in selected teaching skills that are basic to implementing the decision-making model. To acquire these complex teaching skills, you will need to follow Hudgins's three-stage model. Accordingly, the Handbook and the Workbook both incorporate Hudgins's model of complex skill acquisition in their design.

Each chapter in the Handbook focuses on a particular teaching skill. Within each chapter a cognitive map of the skill you are to acquire is provided. This cognitive map includes the purpose of the skill, its various elements and their sequencing, and the nature of the final performance.

Each chapter consists of self-contained materials that require practice and provide you with feedback on your efforts. While the chapters in the Handbook provide some practice and feedback, the Workbook is designed explicitly for that purpose by providing additional and more complex application situations. The Workbook chapters also offer suggestions on how you can further develop the skills in microteaching or real teaching situations. If circumstances permit it, your instructor may also provide you with opportunities to practice these skills in classroom contexts.

To develop a smoothness and a high level of competence in teaching skills, far more practice is necessary than can be provided in these two books. Further, if you are an elementary school teacher, many of these skills must be practiced within the context of different subject matter areas. Your competence in questioning skills, for example, is partially a product of your knowledge of the subject about which you are asking questions. Using our previous example, if you know little about protective tariffs, you are not likely to ask stimulating and provocative questions about that topic.

Format of Each Chapter

Each chapter is written with a common format that contains (1) a set of objectives, (2) a rationale, (3) learning materials and activities, and (4) mastery tests.

1. Objectives. The objectives, stated in terms of learner outcomes, specify the competency or competencies you will be expected to demonstrate. Wherever it is appropriate, the objectives will be arranged in a learning hierarchy, leading you from relatively simple objectives to more complex ones. The Handbook emphasizes conceptual understanding and appreciation of the skills, while the Workbook, building on that knowledge, emphasizes performance and application objectives.

2. Rationale. The rationale describes the purpose and importance of the objectives within the chapter. It attempts to explain why you should want to spend your time acquiring the competencies the chapter is designed to produce. The rationale is considered very important because if you are not convinced that the particular skill you are being asked to develop is important to effective teaching, then it is unlikely that you will be willing to spend the time and effort needed to acquire competence in that skill.

3. Reading Materials and Activities.   Each objective has an accompanying set of reading materials written specifically for that objective. In addition, some of the authors have provided backup activities for those who want additional work on a particular objective. The nature of the reading materials and activities varies depending on the specific objective for which they were constructed.

4. Mastery Tests.   Each chapter contains mastery tests with answer keys to enable you to assess whether or not you have achieved the objectives. These mastery tests assess your learning after you have completed the reading and backup activities related to each objective. This technique allows you to discover immediately after completing each section whether or not you have met the objective satisfactorily. In addition, at the end of some of the chapters there are final mastery tests that serve as a last check on your achievement.

This format (objectives, rationale, learning activities, and mastery tests) has been successfully tested in hundreds of teacher education programs. It is a very efficient design because all the materials are geared to help students achieve the stated objectives. Extraneous and inconsequential materials are eliminated, allowing students to make best use of their time. If used properly, the format increases the probability that you will be able to acquire a beginning level of competency in these basic teaching skills.

Description of the Skills

Skills were included in this Handbook on the basis of their importance in implementing the decision-making model of instruction. While other skills might have been included, those that were selected are among the most crucial to the model.

As you will recall, the three basic elements of the decision-making model are *to plan, to implement,* and *to evaluate.* Each skill is important in carrying out at least one of these three functions. Some skills are useful for more than one function. The nine skills that comprise this book are:

Plan
1. Planning
2. Writing instructional objectives

Implement
3. Presentation skills
4. Questioning
5. Teaching concepts
6. Interpersonal communication
7. Classroom management

Evaluate
8. Observation
9. Evaluation

1. Planning is perhaps the most important function a teacher performs since the whole decision-making model is based on this skill. In Chapter 2 Greta Morine-Dershimer emphasizes the need to generate

alternatives in the planning process. On the basis of a research study she conducted in California, Morine-Dershimer concludes that a consideration of alternatives is *the* basic skill to be learned in instructional planning. Unless alternatives have been considered, no decision has truly been made.

The chapter focuses on four basic questions to be asked in planning:

1. What are some alternative goals or purposes to be achieved through this instruction?
2. What are some alternative ways of determining where pupils stand in relation to a given goal?
3. What are some alternative procedures for helping pupils to achieve a stated goal?
4. What are some alternative methods to determine whether a given procedure was effective?

These four questions are the major focus in Morine-Dershimer's chapter, but each of the other chapters in the book addresses one or more of these questions as well.

2. Writing instructional objectives is a basic planning skill. By specifying instructional objectives, teachers define their purposes in terms that are clear and understandable. In Chapter 3 Terry TenBrink makes the distinction between well-written and poorly written objectives. Furthermore, opportunities are provided within the chapter (1) to rewrite poorly written objectives and (2) to write objectives for a specified unit of instruction. Well-written instructional objectives enable teachers to plan and implement their instructional strategies. The success of teachers' implementation skills greatly depends on the thoughtfulness and clarity of their instructional objectives.

3. In Chapter 4 Robert Shostak presents three basic presentation skills — set induction, stimulus variation, and closure — which research studies have demonstrated to be important components of effective presentations. Set induction refers to teacher-initiated actions or statements that are designed to establish a communicative link between the experiences of students and the objectives of the lesson. Stimulus variation is a teacher action that attempts to vary a classroom presentation in order to maintain high student interest. Closure refers to those teacher actions or statements designed to bring a lesson presentation to an appropriate conclusion. The effective use of these three skills will help establish and maintain student interest in the lesson and will ensure that the main parts of the lesson have been learned.

4. Probably no teaching behavior has been studied as much as questioning. This is not surprising since most educators agree that questioning strategies and techniques are key tools in the teacher's repertoire of interactive teaching skills. In Chapter 5 Myra and David Sadker chose Bloom's *Taxonomy of Educational Objectives: Cognitive Domain* as their system for classifying questions, since Bloom's *Taxonomy* is the most widely used cognitive classification system in education. They designed their chapter (1) to classify and construct questions according to the six levels of Bloom's *Taxonomy* and (2) to describe the nature and dynamics of three teaching techniques (wait time, probing questions, and reinforcement) that can increase the quantity and quality of student responses. If the skills presented in this

chapter are utilized in teaching, the net effect will be students who are more active participants in the learning process.

5. How people learn concepts and how teachers can facilitate student acquisition of concepts are the focus of Chapter 6. Concepts, as used in the chapter, are: (1) categories into which our experiences are organized and (2) the larger network of intellectual relationships brought about as a result of the categorization process. As Peter Martorella points out, our view of reality depends on our conceptual network. A primary task of every teacher is to help students gain an understanding of the world both by teaching new concepts and by fitting new phenomena into already existing concepts. Without mutual understanding of concepts and their meanings, communication with one another would be impossible.

6. "He knows his subject matter, but he just can't seem to relate to his students." At one time or another most of us have had a teacher who would fit this description. While much of a teacher's success in relating to students is difficult to explain and even more difficult to teach, some specific behaviors that stimulate personal inquiry can be taught and should contribute positively to the affective climate of the classroom. In Chapter 7 Sandra Sokolove, Myra Sadker, and David Sadker have defined interpersonal communication skills as a series of specific behaviors that stimulate personal inquiry — inquiry that leads to greater self-knowledge and eventually to more precise and meaningful communication. Teachers who successfully employ the skills of *attending behavior, active listening, reflection, inventory questioning,* and *encouraging alternative behaviors* will help their students to gain greater self-knowledge and become more effective communicators — two vital steps toward better human relations.

7. No problem concerns beginning teachers more than the problem of classroom management. Most new teachers are afraid of not being able to control their students and are aware that lack of control will impede effective instruction. Furthermore, few areas in teacher education curriculums have been neglected as much as classroom management. The major reason for this neglect has been that, until recently, educators had a poor systematic understanding of classroom dynamics. Recently, however, our knowledge in this area has expanded to the point where systematic instruction in classroom management is now possible.

In Chapter 8 Will Weber emphasizes that teachers need to establish and maintain proper learning environments. While the purpose of teaching is to stimulate desired student learning, the purpose of classroom management is to establish the conditions that best promote student learning. Classroom management skills are necessary for effective teaching to occur, but they do not guarantee such behavior. Weber examines three different philosophical positions regarding classroom management — behavior modification, establishing a proper socio-emotional climate, and group processes — and provides numerous opportunities for diagnosing classroom situations according to each of these three viewpoints.

8. One fact every teacher quickly learns is that classroom life is fast-paced and changes constantly. An effective teacher must be able to (1) observe these changes accurately, (2) process the information, and (3) make decisions about what to do next. No one can accurately observe and register everything that goes on in a typical classroom. However, effective observers selectively filter out those events that are of little use and record only the data that are relevant to their purposes.

Chapter 9 provides various ways to observe, record, and analyze teacher and student classroom behaviors. John Hansen's use of informal observation methods does not require any complicated, predetermined observational system. The techniques are relatively simple to use, while generating a great deal of information.

9. Evaluation and knowledge of results are essential if teachers are to improve their teaching effectiveness. The critical nature of evaluation is rarely disputed; nevertheless, few teachers receive adequate training in evaluation concepts and procedures. Terry TenBrink's chapter on evaluation focuses on critical components of the evaluation process. His basic position is that educational evaluation is useful only to the extent that it helps educators make decisions. (Again, the emphasis is on the teacher as a decision maker.)

TenBrink perceives evaluation as a four-stage process: (1) preparing for evaluation, (2) obtaining needed information, (3) forming judgments, and (4) using judgments in making decisions and preparing evaluation reports. Throughout the chapter examples of problems and decisions that teachers are likely to face are used. This practical emphasis should make evaluation concepts and procedures for making better instructional decisions easier to understand and apply.

NOTES

1. Myron Brenton, *What's Happened to Teacher?* (New York: Coward-McCann, 1970), p. 71.

2. David Ryans, *Characteristics of Teachers* (Washington, D.C.: American Council on Education, 1960).

3. J. W. Getzels and P. W. Jackson, "The Teacher's Personality and Characteristics," in *Handbook of Research on Teaching*, ed. N. L. Gage (Chicago: Rand McNally, 1963), p. 574.

4. B. O. Smith, *Teachers for the Real World* (Washington, D.C.: American Association of Colleges for Teacher Education, 1969), p. 122.

5. Bryce B. Hudgins, "Self-Contained Training Materials for Teacher Education: A Derivation from Research on the Learning of Complex Skills," Report 5, National Center for the Development of Training Materials in Teacher Education (Bloomington, Indiana: School of Education, Indiana University), 1974.

6. *Ibid.*, pp. 5–6.

ADDITIONAL READINGS

Hudgins, Bryce B. *The Instructional Process*. Chicago: Rand McNally, 1971.

McDonald, Frederick J. *Educational Psychology*, 2nd ed. Belmont, California: Wadsworth Publishing Co., 1965, pp. 48–69.

Mosston, Muska. *Teaching: From Command to Discovery*. Belmont, California: Wadsworth Publishing Co., 1972.

Shavelson, Richard J. "What Is *The* Basic Teaching Skill?" *Journal of Teacher Education* 24 (Summer 1973): 144–149.

Smith, B. O., et al. *Teachers for the Real World*. Washington, D.C.: American Association of Colleges for Teacher Education, 1969.

Elizabeth Hamlin, Dietz/Hamlin.

GRETA MORINE-DERSHIMER

Instructional Planning

Objectives*

1 Given a set of objectives, to identify the content focus, the "actor," and the specificity of the designated learning outcome.

2 Given a set of alternative diagnostic procedures, to identify the diagnostic question being asked in each case.

3 Given a set of instructional procedures, to identify in each case the skills practiced, the materials used, and the provisions for pupil ideas, individual differences, and evaluative feedback.

4 Given two alternative lesson plans for teaching the same content, to identify the differences and similarities between the two plans in terms of their: (a) specific objective, (b) diagnostic procedure, (c) instructional materials, (d) skills to be practiced, (e) group or individual skill practice, (f) provision for pupil ideas, (g) provision for individual differences, and (h) provision for written feedback.

Planning is a central skill for teachers because it incorporates so many other teaching skills. Teachers build their instructional plans around goals or purposes, but, in order to make these goals specific, they must develop skill in writing instructional objectives (see Chapter 3). The instructional procedures they formulate to pursue their objectives should be keyed to their diagnoses of student needs, which, in turn, are keyed to their classroom observation abilities (see Chapter 9). In order to provide instructional variety within an appropriate learning environment, they must decide how to present information (see Chapter 4), when and how to question students (see Chapter 5), and how to manage their classrooms (see Chapter 8). Finally, they must decide how to evaluate the effectiveness of their instruction (see Chapter 10).

Many people believe that planning is one of the most important skills a teacher can have and that teachers who plan better must also teach better. Some people think that planning is something teachers do in the quiet of their classrooms — before pupils arrive for the day or after they leave for the night. Others may suspect that many teachers never really plan at all, except to write down the page numbers of the textbook to be covered each day. The truth, of course, is that none of these views is completely accurate.

* These objectives should enable you to identify or *differentiate* among (1) instructional objectives, (2) diagnostic procedures, (3) instructional and evaluative procedures, and (4) finished plans. Ultimately, you should be able to *generate alternatives* at each step in the planning process, but first a knowledge base from which such active decision making can proceed must be established.

The myths about teacher planning are legion. Unfortunately, they are influential in determining what prospective teachers learn about the process of planning. Which of the following statements are myths, and which are probably accurate descriptions of the reality of teacher planning?

A little goes a long way.

Everybody's doing it.

Try it — you'll like it.

Plans are made to be broken.

A plan a day keeps disaster away.

Catch as catch can isn't much of a plan.

A plan of beauty is a joy forever.

Good plans, like good times, grow better in the sharing.

Don't look back!

If you're expecting a quick check on how well you identify myths about teaching, you're going to be disappointed. The surprising fact is that very few studies of teacher planning have been conducted; and those that have are more apt to deal with the effects of writing behavioral objectives or the kinds of decisions teachers make when they begin to plan a lesson, rather than with what planning is or what teachers do with their plans.

One fairly recent study of teacher planning, which was carried out with forty elementary school teachers in California,[1] does give some description of the reality of planning. These teachers were asked to write down their lesson plans for two lessons that were to be videotaped or audiotaped by special observers. Then they were interviewed about their general planning procedures. In another portion of the study, the same teachers took records of a group of children and planned how to begin a reading program for the class. The data obtained from teacher responses to these tasks were analyzed to determine how teachers actually planned, what kinds of things they considered in planning, and what types of information they used in deciding what and how to teach.

One fact was clearly established. All forty teachers said they planned regularly for lessons. "Regularly" rarely meant writing a lesson plan for every lesson. Teachers almost unanimously indicated that they usually jotted down a few notes in a lesson plan book and only wrote more extensive plans when they were dealing with content or materials that were new to them. However, teachers were just as unanimous in declaring that writing detailed lesson plans was a necessity for a novice teacher, and they recommended the procedure highly for student teachers.

It was found that a number of teachers developed their plans for the special lessons in the study over a period of days. They would get an idea for a set of procedures or materials; then later on, while driving to work or shaving, another version of the lesson would occur to them, and they would revise their plans. For many teachers, planning was something going on in their heads at various odd moments and was clearly not confined to a quiet, empty classroom.

Plans Are Not Made To Be Broken — Just Revised

Teachers often say that it is important to be alert to opportunities, ready to grasp the "teachable moment" and use it to advantage. In fact, one argument that some teachers give for not writing lesson plans is that they want to feel free to react spontaneously as instructional opportunities arise.

The results of the California study of teacher planning showed that few teachers actually made drastic changes in their planned lessons once they were underway, regardless of whether the original plans were written out in detail or were largely mental notes. Teachers did make adjustments in their plans as they interacted with pupils, but the large majority of these revisions were small procedural refinements, such as having a child come to the board to write down an idea instead of writing it down oneself. Another frequent revision was to drop out a step in the procedures toward the end of the lesson because time was running out. Only in a very few instances did teachers change their lesson plans to incorporate a new topic or procedure suggested by a pupil during the course of the lesson.

Good Plans Are Often Shared

Several teachers who taught particularly interesting lessons told interviewers that they had discussed their lessons with other teachers beforehand and incorporated some of their ideas. One teacher "commissioned" a friend to draw a picture, around which class discussion was built. Another teacher sought advice from a math specialist while trying to decide what the major objective of her lesson should be. In general, teachers indicated that they would like to have more opportunity to share ideas for lessons and materials with their fellow teachers.

The Value of Looking Back

Teachers in the California study consistently agreed that they made a point of thinking back over a lesson they had just taught to consider how they might have changed their plans to improve the lesson. They felt that this process was useful in helping them to plan later lessons more effectively.

Most teachers, when asked to evaluate their plan after they had finished teaching a lesson, said that they thought their original plan was sound and that, if they had to reteach the lesson, they would approach it in basically the same way. However, they noted that if they used the same lesson plan with another group of children, the lesson would probably turn out a bit differently, because the children's responses would be different. In other words, teachers believed that good plans could and should be reused, but they definitely did not think that reusing a lesson plan meant *repeating* the same lesson.

Do Better Planners Make Better Teachers?

Among other things, the California study looked for relationships between the kinds of planning teachers did and the average amount of learning their pupils achieved in special two-week units. No simple relationships were found. At this point we cannot say that a teacher who states behavioral objectives achieves more pupil learning than a teacher who states general goals for a lesson. We have not demonstrated that teachers who plan lessons in detail are more effective than teachers who write sketchy plans or who have no written plans at all. In short, we do not really know what a *better* plan is, in terms of pupil learning, except for the fact that teachers whose pupils learned more made fewer general or broad statements in their lesson plans. That is, their statements tended to be specific.

We do know, in addition, that teachers think ahead, that they consider planning to be an essential activity, and that designing a lesson is, for many teachers, one of the most interesting parts of teaching. We also know that a great deal of variety exists in the way that teachers approach planning. One important aspect of developing skill in planning is discovering what kind of planning works best for you. This chapter is designed to assist you in that process.

WHAT'S IN A PLAN?

Despite the scarcity of educational research on teacher planning, several useful concepts can help you improve your planning skills. These concepts come from two sources — general knowledge about the decision-making process and professional knowledge about the instructional process.

One of the primary tasks of the teacher is to make planning decisions. These decisions range from such seemingly simple matters as organizing the seating arrangement of the classroom to more complex problems such as determining what it is that children need to learn. Planning decisions are of two basic types: long-range decisions that may stand relatively unchanged for several months or a full year, and short-term decisions that determine what will go on for a given day or just a given hour. Both simple and complex planning decisions, and both short-term and long-range planning decisions, involve essentially the same process.

Specific Steps in Planning

The basic planning process involves (1) having some goal or purpose in mind, (2) finding out where pupils are in relation to this goal, (3) devising some instructional procedures to move pupils toward the goal, and (4) determining how to tell whether or not the procedures work. All teachers use this simple four-step process when they plan, but they do not always emphasize every step equally. The goal or purpose may be rather vague at times. A very general description of pupil background or needs may be considered sufficient. The instructional procedures to be used may be just barely sketched in. The method for evaluating the procedures may not be stated at all; it may exist only in the teacher's head.

The reason that many teachers skim over certain steps in the planning process is that planning has become a habit with them. Although good habits are essential to orderly functioning and achievement, if all teacher actions were habitual, the job would become unbearably dull and routine. It is important, therefore, not to let the instructional planning process become too routine. One thing that educational research *has* demonstrated is that teachers who *vary* their instruction have students who learn more and like school better.[2]

Generating Alternatives

One good way to keep planning from becoming too habitual is to consider alternatives continually. The teachers in the California study of planning demonstrated in several ways that, as they planned, they worked at generating alternatives. The new idea for a lesson that was thought of while shaving or driving to work, the procedural refinement made during the instructional process, the solicitation of ideas from a colleague, and the lesson review are all examples of teachers actively seeking alternatives.

Consideration of alternatives is *the* basic skill to be learned in instructional planning, for unless alternatives have been considered, no decision has truly been made. Furthermore, thinking of alternatives helps teachers to be more specific about their actual plans, for each alternative provides a comparison and defines more precisely what the final plan will be. But what kinds of alternatives should teachers consider when planning? A good starting point is provided by the four steps of the planning process itself. The basic questions to be asked are:

1. What are some alternative objectives to be achieved through this instruction?
2. What are some alternative ways of finding out where pupils stand in relation to a given objective?
3. What are some alternative procedures for helping pupils to achieve a stated objective?
4. What are some alternative methods for determining whether a given procedure was effective?

Making Choices

At some point in the planning process the teacher must settle on one of several alternatives and move to implement the plan. Teachers are always making choices, but the choices are only explicit if the alternatives have been stated. A teacher who never considers existing alternatives has chosen to follow an established routine, even though the choice was not made consciously.

An interesting by-product of choosing among alternatives is that it can help the teacher to clarify his or her own preferences. Suppose that every time you chose between two alternatives you had to explain your choice. Over a period of time the reasons you gave for certain choices would begin to form patterns.

Some teachers may consistently pick the same instructional procedures, because they can predict pupil responses, while others may vary their procedures, because variety appeals to them and helps them stay interested and alert. Some teachers may regularly decide to use the method that requires the least preparation, because there is never enough time to get all the work done, while others may spend a great deal of extra time in preparation, simply because they enjoy this aspect of teaching.

The choices that you make stem from your concerns and interests, and by studying your choice patterns you can gain needed insight into your own style of instructional planning. As you work through this chapter, you will be asked to reflect on these choices at several points.

The procedures for using this chapter are fairly simple. A series of tasks will be presented, corresponding to the first three objectives stated at the opening of the chapter.

Each task will involve the following steps:

1. Read the task and the alternative responses that have been developed by others.
2. Select the two alternatives you prefer.
3. Generate a third alternative of your own.
4. Compare your three alternatives to determine how they are alike and how they differ.
5. Choose one of the three alternatives and indicate why you selected it.
6. Compare your choice and reasons for selection with those of other students.
7. Make a record of the new ideas you developed as you worked through the task.
8. Take a mastery test to determine how well you understand the ideas presented in the task.

For each task there are some open-ended response forms that invite you to develop your own ideas and to practice using the concepts presented. These response forms are meant to be learning activities, not tests. At the end of each task there is a mastery test.

When you have completed the three tasks, you will be asked to select a new topic and subject area and to plan two alternative lessons on that topic. You may then decide to teach these two lessons to two different groups of children and to study the responses of pupils to each plan. The final test of competency in planning, as with all teaching competencies, is based on what children learn as a result of the teacher's efforts.

Objective 1

Given a set of objectives, to identify the content focus, the "actor," and the specificity of the designated learning outcome.

LEARNING ACTIVITY 1

Teachers seldom begin to plan lessons in a vacuum. They have textbooks and other instructional materials that suggest the content, goals, and procedures of instruction. They have state and local curriculum guides to assist them in making decisions about what is to be taught. For this task you will be given a lesson topic and some suggested goals or objectives similar to the kind found in a teacher's guide for a textbook.

The lesson topic used here is one that can be used at a variety of age levels, from first or second grade through junior high or high school. Pupils at different age levels will respond differently, and the appropriateness of particular objectives will vary from grade to grade. You may find it useful to select a particular grade level that interests you and to plan for children of that age as you work through each task. Study the information on the following pages. Be sure you understand the possible content to be covered and the possible objectives to be achieved. Then fill out Response Form I, which directly follows the lesson.

LESSON TOPIC: EXPANDED SENTENCES

In this lesson you will be teaching one aspect of language comprehension, the skills of understanding and constructing expanded sentences. How you teach the principle of expanded sentences is left to your judgment. The following paragraphs describe what is meant by "expanded sentences," suggest some possible objectives for a lesson, and give some examples of how this principle can be communicated to children.

When a sentence is expanded, the meaning of the sentence (statement, question, or command) in its simple form is altered by adding any one of a variety of modifiers. Expansions can be made on any sentence, although the simplest illustrations begin with basic noun–verb constructions. The expansions of a sentence can be either further expanded or gradually "contracted" in order to demonstrate the effect of additional words. For example, the sentence "She climbed the tree" may be expanded to "She climbed the big apple tree" or contracted to "She climbed." Both modifications illustrate the effect of expansion.

The expanded-sentences material is drawn from work in the area of structural linguistics, which focuses on the "transformation" of sentences, that is, the ways in which changes in sentence structure affect changes in meaning. These principles of transformation are somewhat atypical of the subject matter covered in the regular curriculum. You should feel free, therefore, to experiment using any material and examples you wish.

Some rules of sentence expansion which may emerge in the course of a lesson include:

1. Adding words to a sentence is one way to change the meaning of a sentence (or, adding more information changes the meaning of a sentence).
2. All sentences can be expanded; no sentence is too long to be expanded.
3. You can expand (change the meaning of) a sentence by describing each thing in more detail (use of adjectives and adverbs).
4. You can expand a sentence by talking about more kinds of actions (additions of verbs).
5. You can expand a sentence by saying *when* (or *where*) something happened.
6. You can expand a sentence by saying *what* (addition of direct or indirect objects).
7. You can expand a sentence by adding phrases as well as single adjectives or adverbs.
8. You can expand a sentence by adding clauses.

You may select one or more or any combination of the above rules as objectives for the lesson, or you may think up your own. Other kinds of objectives, not built around rule identification, might be:

9. Pupils can identify expanded sentences from a list containing both simple and expanded sentences.
10. Given a set of simple sentences, pupils can expand them in at least one (or two, or three) way(s).
11. Given an expanded sentence, pupils can reduce it to a simple sentence by removing the appropriate words.

Different objectives may be appropriate to different groups of pupils, depending on grade level and general ability. You should select objectives you feel comfortable with for your class and arrange the lesson accordingly.

Some examples of expanded sentences which you might want to use in your lesson are given below. You may use these and/or others that you may think up; the only real restriction on use is that the vocabulary be appropriate to the grade level of the pupils for whom you are planning the lesson.

Examples of Expanded Sentences

The snow covers the streets.
The *dirty* snow covers the streets. (adjective expansion)
The dirty snow covers the *cold*, *dark* streets. (adjective expansion)

The birds fly.
The *green* birds fly. (adjective expansion)
The *big*, *mean*, green birds fly *south today*. (adjective and adverb expansion — where, when)

The children ran.
The children ran *to school*. (adverb expansion — where)
The children ran *and skipped* to school. (verb expansion)

The monkey ate.
The monkey ate *a sandwich*. (direct object expansion — what)
The *big*, *hairy* monkey ate a *turkey* sandwich *very fast*. (adjective and adverb expansion)

The robin sang.
The *red* robin sang *in the tree*. (adjective and adverbial phrase expansion — where)
Yesterday the red robin sang *happily* in the tree. (adverb expansion — when and how)

Danny cooked.
Danny cooked *dinner*. (direct object expansion — what)
Danny cooked dinner *because his mother was sick*. (clause expansion)

These sample sentence expansions suggest the kinds of changes that can be made using the sentence expansion rules. Others should be easy to think up. You might plan to ask the pupils to suggest other simple or expanded sentences to work on.

RESPONSE FORM I

Directions: Please work alone to answer these questions. Later you may want to compare your responses with others.

1. What grade level are you planning for?

    _____

2. Select two alternative objectives for this lesson from among those suggested in the sample lesson topic presented earlier. Write these objectives below.

    _____

    _____

    _____

    _____

    _____

3. Think of another possible objective *not* suggested in the instructions to teachers for this lesson. Write it below.

    _____

    _____

    _____

    _____

    _____

4. Compare the three objectives you have written down. How are they alike?

    _____

    _____

    _____

    _____

    _____

5. Compare your objectives with the following ones formulated by classroom teachers:

    Teacher A (Elementary)
    1. Given a set of simple sentences, pupils can expand them in at least one, two, or three ways.
    2. Given an expanded sentence, pupils can remove the appropriate word(s) to produce a simple sentence from it.

    Teacher B (Elementary)
    1. Children will learn that they can make a sentence more interesting or more dramatic by adding descriptive words or words that tell when or where something happened.

Teacher C (Elementary)
1. To tell pupils the meaning of nouns, verbs, and adjectives.
2. To show pupils you can change the meaning of a sentence by talking about more kinds of actions (verbs).

Teacher D (Elementary)
1. Students will demonstrate an understanding of a simple sentence.
2. Students will expand a simple sentence.
3. Students will realize that the image created by an expanded sentence is limited by the reader's/listener's experience.

Teacher E (Secondary)
1. Given a set of simple sentences and a group of logical connectives (and, but, because, although, therefore, etc.), students will expand each sentence in at least four different ways, while maintaining logical sense.

Teacher F (Secondary)
1. Pupils will compare sentences written by Ernest Hemingway and Kurt Vonnegut to determine the effects of contracted and expanded sentences on the reader.

Teacher G (Secondary)
1. To show pupils how to expand sentences by adding phrases in both the adjective and adverb positions.

_____

_____

_____

_____

_____

_____

Comparison of Teacher-Selected Objectives

The sets of objectives selected by teachers differ from each other in terms of what is to be learned or, in other words, *their content focus.* Teachers A and E focused on the *operation* of expanding and contracting sentences, that is, the process of doing it. Teachers B and F focused on the *application* of sentence expansion, that is, how it can be used for some purpose. Teachers C and G focused on *factual knowledge* related to sentence expansion, that is, what kinds of words are being added. Teacher D focused on student understanding of the *process of communication*, that is, what affects the message a sentence is sending.

The objectives also differ with regard to *who is to be the "actor."* For example, Teachers C and G phrased their statements in terms of what the *teacher* will do, while the other sets of objectives state what the *pupils* will do or learn. In addition, the objectives vary in their degree of *specificity*. For example, it is relatively easy to note whether pupils can expand a sentence in two or three different ways. You can just give them a sentence and ask them to write some expanded versions. But how can a teacher be sure that children have "learned" that an expanded sentence is more interesting? Does "learn" mean that a child *says* a particular sentence is more interesting? Or does it mean that a child will use expanded sentences more frequently the next time he or she writes a story? Explicitly stated objectives can help the teacher to evaluate pupil achievement more accurately.

All the objectives presented above are worthwhile for a single short lesson. All of them can serve as a guide to the teacher in deciding what procedures to use in teaching sentence expansion. Some of them may be similar to the objectives you yourself selected and stated. With these sets of objectives as additional information, perhaps you can now reexamine your own objectives from a new perspective. Go on to Response Form II and follow the directions given there.

RESPONSE FORM II

Directions: Answer questions 1 to 4 on your own. Then, if possible, form a discussion group to answer questions 5 and 6. This exercise will give you an opportunity to practice analyzing objectives. A mastery test will follow.

1. Review your objectives from Response Form I to determine the general learning emphasis (operation, application, factual knowledge, etc.).

   (a) Do your objectives differ in their general emphasis or are they similar?

   _____

   _____

   (b) What is (are) the general emphasis (emphases) you have taken?

   _____

   _____

   _____

   _____

2. Consider the terms in which you have stated your objectives.

   (a) Did you phrase your objectives in terms of teacher behavior or pupil behavior?

   _____

   _____

   (b) Do your objectives differ from each other in this respect?

   _____

   _____

3. How easily could your objectives be evaluated? Are they stated in a way that specifically suggests how you might measure pupil achievement?

   _____

If not, can you rephrase them to be more specific in this respect?

_____

_____

_____

_____

4. Reconsider the three objectives you originally stated, and select *one* of them as the basis of a lesson plan. Write the objective below.

_____

_____

_____

What are your reasons for selecting this particular objective?

_____

_____

_____

5. If possible, compare the objective you have chosen to those chosen by other students. What have they emphasized in their objectives?

_____

_____

_____

What seems to be the most "popular" emphasis?

_____

How much variation in emphasis is there among the group?

_____

6. Compare your reason for selecting a particular objective with the reasons given by other students. What seems to be the most "popular" reason?

_____

_____

_____

7. Now that you have heard several other objectives stated, can you generate one or two additional alternative objectives which might be used to plan lessons on the topic of sentence expansion? If so, list them here.

_____

_____

_____

_____

8. What new ideas have you developed while thinking through the problem of identifying objectives for a lesson? List these below.

_____

_____

_____

_____

_____

_____

9. What questions do you still have about identifying goals and objectives for a lesson?

_____

_____

_____

One Step at a Time

Selecting objectives for a lesson is one of the first steps in planning, and it is obviously a very important step, since other plans must follow from the objectives. Later, as you work through Chapter 3 on writing instructional objectives, you will have an opportunity to develop further skill in stating objectives. For the present, you can check your mastery of the concepts developed in this learning activity.

Mastery Test

OBJECTIVE 1 Given a set of objectives, to identify the content focus, the "actor," and the specificity of the designated learning outcome.

Study each of the following objectives. Identify the content focus (operation, application, factual knowledge), the identified "actor" (pupil or teacher), and the specificity of expected learning outcome (vague, specific, or detailed).

1. Given ten problems on addition of three one-digit numerals, pupils will complete them with an accuracy of 80 percent or higher.

   Content focus: operation application facts other
   Identified actor: teacher pupil not specified
   Learning outcome: vague specific detailed

2. To compare articles from three different newspapers dealing with the same event and to decide which newspaper you would rather subscribe to.

Content focus: operation   application   facts   other

Identified actor: teacher   pupil   not specified

Learning outcome: vague   specific   detailed

3. To demonstrate to pupils that hot air expands, by performing two simple experiments.

Content focus: operation   application   facts   other

Identified actor: teacher   pupil   not specified

Learning outcome: vague   specific   detailed

4. Pupils will learn the rules of softball well enough to umpire a game.

Content focus: operation   application   facts   other

Identified actor: teacher   pupil   not specified

Learning outcome: vague   specific   detailed

ANSWER KEY
Mastery Test, Objective 1

1. *Content focus:* operation
   Identified actor: pupil
   Learning outcome: detailed

2. *Content focus:* application
   Identified actor: not specified
   Learning outcome: specific

3. *Content focus:* facts
   Identified actor: teacher
   Learning outcome: vague

4. *Content focus:* application
   Identified actor: pupil
   Learning outcome: specific

If you were accurate in three out of four responses for each category (e.g., content focus), you have demonstrated comprehension of the ideas presented in Learning Activity 1. You are ready to proceed to Learning Activity 2.

If you missed more than one out of four responses to a given category, you might find it helpful to pick a topic and write an objective according to specification (e.g., operation, pupil, specific; or facts, pupil, specific). Check the completed objective with your instructor or a fellow student. Then proceed to Learning Activity 2.

Objective 2

Given a set of alternative diagnostic procedures, to identify the diagnostic question being asked in each case.

LEARNING ACTIVITY 2

There are many ways of determining pupil "starting points" for a particular topic. Most individualized or programmed curriculum materials provide diagnostic tests or pretests for a variety of basic skills. Teachers can use these to match students with appropriate instructional materials.

Sometimes teachers develop and administer their own simple pretests on a concept or topic they plan to teach. The teacher might then divide the class into groups on the basis of the test results, teaching different aspects of the topic to different groups.

Some teachers plan lessons so that the initial part of the lesson gives them information about what the pupils already know. Then they adapt the rest of the lesson to fit student needs. (You will see an example of this later on in the activity.) Generally, if this approach is taken, the teacher will "predict" the probable attainment of pupils and plan two or three possible activities that fit these predictions.

Other teachers do not worry about diagnosing pupil attainment of a concept or skill before they teach it. They assume that all children will benefit from a lesson, even though some may already know the material and others may not be quite ready to grasp it. Educators are less sympathetic to this point of view than they used to be several years ago. There is increasing pressure to adapt instruction to the actual needs of pupils, and to do so requires some knowledge of what pupils already know or can do.

Standardized achievement tests are not really useful to the teacher in deciding what pupils know about a specific topic. They can only give a general picture of pupil attainment. For example, it is not safe to assume that because a pupil has a low score on a reading achievement test, he or she will necessarily lack knowledge or skill in every aspect of reading dealt with at that grade level.

The teacher's job, then, is to learn what children know in relation to the specific content being taught. This must be done frequently, and it cannot be too time-consuming a process, because diagnosing pupil attainment is only the *beginning* of the instructional process.

To get a better understanding of this process, study the teacher plans below, then fill out Response Form III, which follows.

When elementary classroom teachers were given the task of planning a lesson on sentence expansion for their own pupils, they devised several different ways of diagnosing pupil knowledge in relation to this topic. Here are some of the procedures that teachers planned to use in relation to the specific objective: *Pupils will expand a simple sentence in at least two ways.*

Teacher A   Ask pupils to give an example of a simple sentence; have each pupil write his/her example on a piece of paper. Then walk around and read their examples; have students read some examples aloud and write these on the chalkboard.

Teacher B   Give pupils a worksheet and have them do the first two examples individually. Observe their responses. Worksheet will read:

    1. Sam ran.

       Sam ran _____.

    2. The man swam.

       The _____ man swam.

       The _____ man _____ swam.

Teacher C   Put a simple sentence and an expanded sentence up on a chart.

       Birds fly.

       The graceful birds fly swiftly in the sky.

Ask children to tell how the sentences are *similar* and *different*.

Teacher D   Ask pupils:

What is a sentence?
What does a sentence consist of?
What does a subject consist of?
What does a predicate consist of?

Put a simple sentence on the board:
She climbed.

Ask pupils:
Is this a sentence?
Does it contain both parts of a sentence?

Secondary teachers who were planning lessons on sentence expansion also devised different ways of diagnosing pupil knowledge. Here are two procedures that teachers planned to use in relation to the objective: *Given a set of simple sentences and a group of logical connectives, students will expand each sentence in at least four different ways, while maintaining logical sense.*

Teacher E   Have each student write a simple declarative sentence (e.g., The man laughed.) on their own paper. List logical connectives on board (such as and, but, because, although, therefore, whenever, if, since, then, so). Ask students to select any four connectives and rewrite their sentences using each of them. Check to see which connectives they choose and whether they position the connectives at the beginning as well as the end of their initial sentences (e.g., The man laughed, although he did not really think the joke was funny; *or* Although the man laughed, he did not really think the joke was funny).

Teacher F   Give students the following pretest to determine their understanding of logical connectives.

Here are two simple sentences:

The man laughed.
The dog barked.

Use the following words to combine these two sentences in as many ways as you can.

and	because	whenever
but	although	since
then	therefore	if

RESPONSE FORM III

1. What grade level are you planning for?

   _____

2. What questions will the teacher be able to answer about pupil knowledge and skills after using each of the diagnostic plans described above?

   Plan A. _____

   _____

   Plan B. _____

   _____

   Plan C. _____

   _____

   Plan D. _____

   _____

   Plan E. _____

   _____

   Plan F. _____

   _____

3. Select two alternative diagnostic procedures from among the teacher plans reported on the preceding pages. Which plans do you prefer?

   _____

   _____

4. Think of another possible procedure for diagnosing pupil attainment in relation to one of the following goals: *Pupils will expand a sentence in at least two ways; or, Given a set of simple sentences and a group of logical connectives, students will expand each sentence in at least four different ways, while maintaining logical sense.* Describe your procedure below.

   _____

   _____

   _____

   _____

   _____

   _____

   _____

5. Compare the three procedures you have chosen. How are they similar to each other?

_____

_____

_____

6. Check your answers to question 2 in the analysis that follows. There is also some additional information about diagnostic procedures.

Comparing Diagnostic Plans

The diagnostic plans presented earlier in relation to the two objectives, (1) *Pupils will expand a sentence in at least two ways*, and (2) *Given a set of simple sentences and a group of logical connectives, students will expand each sentence in at least four different ways*, are almost all alike in one respect. In every case but one, the teacher will go on to build the lesson around the ideas pupils express in this introductory segment. An alternative to this, of course, is to give a brief pretest at an earlier time and plan a lesson, or a set of lessons, around the information obtained in the pretest. This is the procedure used by Teacher F.

The teacher plans differ from each other in a number of other respects. For example, Plans A, B, E, and F all provide the teacher with a chance to study *individual* pupil attainment, while Plans C and D give the teacher a chance to determine what the class as a whole knows. In addition, Plans A, B, E, and F have the students *writing* words or sentences, while Plans C and D have them *talking about* sentences.

Another difference among these plans relates to the specific skill or knowledge being checked. Plan A checks whether pupils can *construct a complete sentence*. Plan B tests whether students can *add a word* at a designated spot to a sentence that has already been started. Plan E examines pupil ability to *construct an appropriate clause* to follow a given word. Plan F identifies pupil understanding of the various *ways of combining two sentences* through use of logical connectives. Plan C determines what *characteristics* students can identify when they compare two specific written sentences. Plan D alerts the teacher to pupil knowledge about the *characteristics* of sentences in general. Plans A, D, and E diagnose pupil knowledge about *simple* sentences, assuming that this is a prerequisite to the lesson on sentence expansion. Plans B, C, and F, on the other hand, look immediately at pupil understanding of *expanded* sentences.

Because of all this variation, each of the planned diagnostic procedures discussed here asks a basically different question about pupil attainment. These questions are:*

Plan A. Can each pupil construct a simple sentence?

Plan B. Can each pupil expand a simple sentence by adding a word in a designated spot?

* You can check your responses to question 2 on Response Form III by comparing them with this set of questions.

Plan C. Can the group as a whole identify the difference between a simple sentence and an expanded sentence?

Plan D. Can the group as a whole define the terms "sentence," "subject," and "predicate"?

Plan E. What logical connectives does each pupil use readily, and in what positions in the sentence does he or she use them when asked to construct new clauses?

Plan F. Can each pupil combine two sentences by using different logical connectives?

The plan that you invented to diagnose pupil attainment may ask a different question than any of these. You may find it useful to review your planned diagnostic procedure to identify the specific question it will answer for you as a teacher.

What Can Pupils Tell You?

Actually, all of the planned diagnostic procedures reported earlier are inadequate in some way. That is, none of them provides the teacher with complete information about pupil attainment in relation to the objective. This is probably unavoidable, for if a teacher were to attempt to get really complete diagnostic information for every skill or concept to be taught, there would be almost no time left for teaching or learning. What a skilled teacher attempts to do is to acquire the most useful and pertinent information in the most efficient way possible. Usually it is helpful to evaluate a planned diagnostic procedure beforehand by attempting to predict the types of responses pupils will make. Study the planned diagnostic procedure described below. Then, using Response Form IV, suggest three different ways that an individual pupil might respond.

The stated objective is: *Pupils will expand a simple sentence in at least two ways.* The diagnostic question to be answered is: How does each student expand a given sentence when the possibilities are left open? (That is, what ways to expand sentences do students already know about?)

The procedure is to write a simple sentence on the board, for example, "The bird flew." Each student is given a piece of paper and asked to think of a way to make the sentence bigger (or expand it, depending on the grade level). As each student writes an expanded sentence on paper, the teacher walks around and studies the responses.

RESPONSE FORM IV

1. Suppose that this procedure were used with a group of third graders. What are three different ways that these children might expand the sentence, "The bird flew"?

_____
_____
_____
_____
_____
_____

2. Suppose that this procedure were used with a group of eighth graders. What are three different ways that students might expand the sentence, "The bird flew"?

_____
_____
_____
_____
_____
_____

3. Compare the responses you anticipate with actual responses from third and eighth grade classes in the analysis that follows.

_____
_____
_____
_____
_____
_____

Responses of Pupils to Diagnostic Task

One third grade class using the procedure just described responded in the following ways. (These are representative sentences.)

1. The bird flew away.
2. The bird flew off.
3. The bird flew south.

4. The bird flew to her nest.
5. The bird flew off the nest.
6. The bird flew around the cage.
7. The bird flew over the car and dropped a feather.
8. The bird flew high in the sky and then went home.

Sentences 1, 2, and 3 are all examples of expanding by adding a single adverb. Sentences 4, 5, and 6 are expanded by the addition of an adverbial phrase. Sentences 7 and 8 are more complex constructions, including phrases and conjunctions. In all instances the sentence is expanded by adding to the predicate, and in all cases the additions are made at the *end* of the sentence.

The diagnostic information obtained from this class shows that the pupils differ in the complexity of the constructions they use to expand sentences, but they are similar in that none of them expand by inserting words into the middle of a sentence. Thus the teacher can quickly determine that it will be useful to the whole class to introduce an adjective expansion to them (for example, "The *yellow* bird flew"). Another expansion which could be introduced would be an adverbial expansion *before* the verb (for example, "The bird *often* flew") or before the subject (for example, "*Yesterday* the bird flew").

An eighth grade class using the procedure just described responded in the following ways. (Again, these are representative sentences.)

1. The bird flew into the coral reef.
2. The bird flew over the tree tops and under the clouds.
3. The bird flew to the market and dug worms out of the moon.
4. The bird and his mate flew across the sky.
5. The exotic bird gracefully flew around.
6. The bird flew for miles and miles until he came to a lake.

Sentences 1 and 2 are examples of adverbial phrase expansion. Sentence 3 expands by forming a compound predicate, while sentence 4 uses a compound subject. Sentence 5 uses an adjective expansion. (Note that both sentences 4 and 5 are expanded by *inserting* words in the original sentence, something that none of the third graders did.) Sentence 6 includes an adverbial clause. The only logical connectives used are "and" and "until." None of the sentences were expanded by adding a word at the beginning of the sentence.

This diagnostic information demonstrates to the teacher that the whole class can benefit from practice in expanding sentences through use of logical connectives other than "and."

Picking a Procedure

Every diagnostic procedure provides some kind of information to the teacher about pupil skills and knowledge, but none provides all the information that might be obtained and only one can be used at any given time. In selecting the diagnostic procedure to be used for a particular lesson, the teacher needs to consider: (1) whether individual or group diagnosis is needed, and (2) what specific question(s) the procedure will answer about pupil attainment. Keep these considerations in mind as you answer the questions on Response Form V.

RESPONSE FORM V

1. Select one of the three diagnostic procedures that you listed on Response Form III, and apply it to *one* of the following two objectives: *Pupils will expand a simple sentence in at least two ways*, or *Given a set of simple sentences and a group of logical connectives, students will expand each sentence in at least four different ways, while maintaining logical sense.* Write a brief description of the procedure below.

   _____

   _____

   _____

   What question will this procedure answer in terms of your chosen objective?

   _____

   _____

2. If possible, compare the procedure you have chosen to those chosen by your peers. Does the group tend to emphasize diagnosis of individual or group attainment?

   _____

   _____

   Is there much similarity among the group members regarding the specific questions to be answered by the chosen procedures?

   _____

   _____

3. Compare your reason for selecting a particular procedure with those given by your peers. What two reasons are the most different from each other?

   _____

   _____

   _____

   _____

4. Now that you have gathered more information on alternative diagnostic procedures, can you generate one additional procedure that might be used in relation to the objective under discussion? Describe it below.

   _____

   _____

   _____

   _____

5. What new ideas have you developed while working through the task on identifying alternative methods of diagnosing pupil attainment? List them below.

_____

_____

_____

_____

_____

6. What questions do you still have about pupil diagnosis?

_____

_____

_____

_____

More About Diagnosis

The purpose of any diagnosis is to answer a question about what pupils are already capable of doing and what they need to study further. In analyzing a diagnostic procedure, you will want to note the following important information.

1. Are pupils being diagnosed individually or as a group?
2. What is the specific knowledge that is being checked?
3. In what form are the diagnostic problems or questions presented (oral, written, visual, etc.)?
4. In what form are pupils asked to respond to the diagnostic questions (oral, written, etc.)?

This brief introduction to the process of diagnostic planning was designed to start you thinking about the alternatives and procedures that might be available to you. You will want to develop much more skill in diagnosis as you continue your training. You will find two other chapters helpful to you. These are the chapters on classroom observation and evaluation (Chapters 9 and 10). Each of them will touch on different aspects of diagnosis or collection of information about pupils. But now it is time to check your understanding of the concepts presented in this learning activity.

Mastery Test

OBJECTIVE 2

Given a set of alternative diagnostic procedures, to identify the diagnostic question being asked in each case.

For each diagnostic procedure given below, identify the question that is asked about pupil attainment by writing the appropriate question on the right.

Objectives and Diagnostic Procedures

Questions Asked

A. *Objective:* Given ten problems on addition of one-digit numerals, pupils will complete them with an accuracy of 80 percent or higher.

1. *Diagnostic Procedure:* Give all pupils a written pretest on the basic addition facts, all combinations of 1 through 9 (1 + 1, 2 + 1, 1 + 2, 3 + 1, etc.).

1. _____
   _____
   _____
   _____
   _____
   _____

2. *Diagnostic Procedure:* Divide class into preestablished math groups (established on basis of kindergarten teacher's recommendation). Work with each group separately, doing oral addition problems (combinations of 1 through 5) and using concrete objects (blocks, crayons, etc.) to illustrate each problem. Make written notes about the examples missed by each group.

2. _____
   _____
   _____
   _____
   _____

3. *Diagnostic Procedure:* Divide the class into pairs. Give each pair a set of flash cards of addition combinations (1 through 9). Have them test each other. Have each child circle combinations that he or she missed on their personal record sheet.

3. _____
   _____
   _____
   _____
   _____

B. *Objective:* Given articles from three different newspapers, all dealing with the same event, students will compare the articles to decide which newspaper provides the most objective account.

4. *Diagnostic Procedure:* Students will be given copies of three articles to read. Then the class will be divided into discussion

4. _____
   _____

Objectives and Diagnostic Procedures	*Questions Asked*

groups of five to seven students per group. Each discussion group is to decide which paper they would prefer to subscribe to, and why. Groups will report back to the class on their decision. Teacher will listen to discussion groups to note how frequently (or whether) the criterion of objectivity of the account is suggested.

5. *Diagnostic Procedure:* All pupils will be given a written pretest in which they are asked to identify the more objective sentence in each of several pairs of sentences.

5. _____

Check your answers (questions) in the Answer Key which follows.

ANSWER KEY

Mastery Test, Objective 2

Your questions may be worded somewhat differently from those given below. Exact wording does not matter, but check to see whether your question incorporates the same basic ideas (those italicized).

Question 1. What addition problems *(combinations of 1 through 9)* can *each pupil* already answer accurately when problems are presented *in written form* and *answers must be written down?*

Question 2. What addition problems *(combinations of 1 through 5)* can each *math group* already answer accurately when problems are presented *with concrete objects and answers are given orally?*

Question 3. What addition problems *(combinations of 1 through 9)* can *each child* already answer accurately when problems are presented *in written form and answers are given orally?*

Question 4. Which, if any, *discussion groups (or individuals within the groups)* are already aware of *objective reporting as a criterion* for selecting a newspaper and *what other criteria are mentioned* frequently?

Question 5. How accurately can *each pupil judge the objectivity of sentences* when they are *presented in pairs* rather than in the context of a story?

If you accurately identified the question being asked for four out of five of the diagnostic procedures, you have demonstrated understanding of the basic ideas in this section, and you are ready to proceed to objective 3.

If you accurately identified *less than four* of the questions being asked, you need to review the ideas presented in this section. You might find it helpful to "work backward," by taking the four questions that follow Response Form V (More About Diagnosis), choosing answers to them, and constructing a diagnostic procedure to fit those answers.

Objective 3

Given a set of instructional procedures, to identify in each case the skills practiced, the materials used, and the provisions for pupil ideas, individual differences, and evaluative feedback.

LEARNING ACTIVITY 3

Teachers write lesson plans in many different ways. Some plans are highly organized and detailed. Others are very sketchy. But one thing almost all written plans have in common is a list of steps or procedures that the lesson will follow. Almost all teachers find that notes on the sequence of lesson activities serve as useful reminders to them while they are actually teaching the lesson.

A fairly common format for writing a lesson plan is (1) to state the objective of the lesson, (2) to list the instructional materials to be used, and (3) to indicate the steps to be followed in the lesson. Many teachers add detail to this type of plan by designing a worksheet to use with children during a lesson. Others list specific questions to be asked at each step in the lesson; some even write in expected pupil responses to these questions. Teachers who plan to elicit and use pupil ideas as a major source of information in a lesson will frequently make notes about how they plan to write these ideas down on the chalkboard.

Lesson plans serve three basic functions for the teacher, and these should be kept in mind when choosing a format for writing plans. First, the act of writing down both the purpose and the planned procedures for a given lesson can help the teacher to clarify them in his or her own mind. Thus, a plan can be an *organizer of ideas*.

Second, a written lesson plan can function as a *record* of teacher ideas and classroom activities. Teachers must keep so many details in mind as they engage in their daily work with students that their memory banks sometimes become overloaded. Written notes can be referred to while a lesson is in progress to remind the teacher of the next step. The same notes can be used later to remind the teacher of what ideas or skills were actually covered in a given lesson. This can also be useful in planning later lessons.

Third, a lesson plan can be used as a guide for classroom observers. This function is probably more important for novice teachers than for experienced teachers, since the former are apt to be observed more frequently. However, all teachers are observed at times, and it is not always easy for the observer to tell what the teacher is trying to accomplish. A written lesson plan helps the observer to focus on the lesson being taught. Thus, a lesson plan can function to *direct the observation* of someone who is watching a lesson in progress.

Because the first function of a lesson plan (organizing teacher ideas) is the most important, teachers should make notes about instructional procedures they have planned in whatever way is useful for them. If a plan is also to serve the third function (directing observation), it should be written in a form that is useful or comprehensible to others as well. Many different formats can accomplish both these goals simultaneously. As you work through this learning task, one of your personal goals might be to discover the format that is most useful to you. Study the information on the following pages and then fill out Response Form VI, which follows.

PLANNED PROCEDURES FOR TEACHING SENTENCE EXPANSION

Do you recall the earlier section describing third and eighth graders' attempts to expand the sentence, "The bird flew"? The third graders' additions involved simple words and phrases and, occasionally, more complex constructions, but all the additions were made at the *end* of the sentence. They did not know how to expand a sentence by inserting words into the middle of it. The eighth graders' additions involved phrases and clauses, but there were no additions at the beginning of the sentence and no logical connectives other than "and" or "until" were used.

When elementary and secondary classroom teachers were faced with the task of planning lessons for groups of children like these, they outlined the following alternative procedures.

Plan A (Elementary)

1. Review what a sentence is.
2. Define *expand*; describe how and why sentences can be expanded.
3. Go over charts on adjectives, adverbs, and prepositional phrases.
4. Show them the process you want them to use in expanding sentences, for example:
   (a) The child laughs. (Subject and predicate)
   (b) The happy child laughs. (Add an adjective)
   (c) The happy child laughs loudly. (Add an adverb)
   (d) The happy child laughs loudly at the clown. (Add a prepositional phrase)
   (e) The happy child laughs loudly at the silly clown. (Add anything you like)
5. Pass out worksheets.
   Do the first exercise together, if necessary; then have children work by themselves. (See worksheet which follows.)

WORKSHEET FOR PLAN A

Name _____

Expanding Sentences

1. Subject and predicate.
2. Add an adjective.
3. Add an adverb.
4. Add a prepositional phrase.
5. Add anything you like to expand the sentence further.

1. The cat plays.

2. _____

3. _____

4. _____

   _____

5. _____

   _____

1. The boy walks.

2. _____

3. _____

4. _____

   _____

5. _____

   _____

1. The motorcycle races.

2. _____

3. _____

4. _____

   _____

5. _____

   _____

1. The birds fly.

2. _____

3. _____

4. _____

   _____

5. _____

   _____

Try some on your own:

1. _____

2. _____

3. _____

4. _____

   _____

5. _____
   _____

1. _____
2. _____
3. _____
4. _____
   _____
5. _____
   _____

Plan B (Elementary)

Any simple sentence can be expanded by adding phrases, clauses, or descriptive words.

Objective: Children learn they can expand a sentence by adding descriptive words or words that tell when or where something happened.
(The class has just completed "The Gulls," a story of the Mormons in their first year in Utah. Sentences using information from the story will be used.)

1. Discuss with class the meaning of *expand*.

2. Write on the board:

   The   corn   grew.

   Ask: What kinds of corn? (for example, in the garden)
   The sentence might look something like:

   $$\begin{bmatrix} \text{green} \\ \text{fresh} \\ \text{graceful} \end{bmatrix} \qquad \begin{bmatrix} \text{in the garden} \\ \text{in the field} \\ \text{in the summer (when)} \end{bmatrix}$$

   The   corn   grew

3. Ask volunteers to read the sentence using one or more of the additions.

4. Continue in the same manner with the following sentences:

   $$\begin{bmatrix} \text{Suddenly} \\ \text{All at once} \\ \text{All of a sudden} \end{bmatrix} \quad \begin{bmatrix} \text{blue} \\ \text{gray} \\ \text{cloudy} \end{bmatrix} \quad \begin{bmatrix} \text{white} \\ \text{graceful} \\ \text{large} \end{bmatrix}$$

   the   sky was filled with   gulls.

   The cornstalks were covered with insects.
   The gulls ate.

5. If children seem interested, have them copy the following sentence on paper:

   The   snow   covers   the   street.

Ask: Can you expand or change the sentence by
    (a) describing the snow?
    (b) describing the street?
    (c) telling where?
Encourage the students to read their sentences.

Plan C (Elementary)

Objective: Most of the children will be able to add words to a simple two-word sentence that will change the meaning of the original sentence in at least two ways.

Materials:
1. Wooden chart for sentence strips
2. Sample strips of two-word sentences with companion expanded sentences
3. Two-word sentence suggestions for the children in the group

Introduction:
Place a simple two-word sentence on the chart with the expanded sentence under it. Children will be asked to find *similarities* and *differences*.
Sample:
    Birds fly.
    The graceful birds fly swiftly in the sky.
(Have another sample ready if children seem to need it.)

Lesson for Children: Each child will be provided a two-word sentence to expand. (Option for children — to originate their own if sample doesn't "appeal.") Since these will be prepared in advance, reading levels and interests of the children will be considered.

David C.	Airplanes fly.
Mike D.	Firemen work.
Rebecca F.	Scientists experiment.
Keith E.	Dogs bark.
Chris E.	Cars race.
Larry G.	Planets rotate.
Judith H.	Flowers bloom.
Billy M.	Astronauts prepare.
Anne-Marie M.	Children play.
Guy McC.	Monsters hide.
Decio R.	Doctors help.
Jamie S.	Spring appears.

Summary:
Lead children to discuss which sentences "tell more" and to think about opportunities they have to use expanded sentences.

Plan D (Secondary)

Objective: Given a set of simple sentences and a group of logical connectives, students will expand a sentence in at least four different ways, while maintaining logical sense.

Materials: overhead projector
             chalkboard

Procedure:

1. Have each student write a simple sentence on his/her paper by completing the sentence frame, The _____ _____.

2. Have several students read their sentences aloud. Record these sentences on chalkboard.

3. On overhead projector, write "The helicopter landed *because* . . ." Have students suggest ways to end the sentence. Write these on transparency.

4. Ask pupils to expand their own simple sentences by adding "because" and an appropriate clause. Have several examples read aloud.

5. Proceed in same manner for "but," "therefore," "whenever," "since," "then," and "so."

6. On the overhead projector write "*Although* the helicopter landed, . . ." Have students suggest ways to end the sentence. Write a few on the transparency.

7. Ask students which of the logical connectives already discussed could be used at the beginning of their sentence. Have them write one or two and have some read aloud.

Evaluation:

Ask each pupil to take any three of the sentences written on the board at the beginning of the lesson and to expand each sentence in four different ways, using the logical connectives listed on the transparency.

Plan E (Secondary)

List the logical connectives on board. Divide the class into eight groups. Each group will be given one logical connective (because, but, etc.) and must expand the sentence "The man stumbled," using the connective they have been given. Members of the group will act out the sentence thus constructed, while the rest of the class tries to figure out what logical connective is being demonstrated and how the sentence ends. When each group has performed, list four simple sentences on board, and ask each pupil to expand each of the four sentences in four different ways, using the logical connectives.

RESPONSE FORM VI

1. What grade level are you planning for?

   _____

2. What specific skill in expanding sentences would you expect pupils to develop by participating in the activities described on the preceding pages?

   Plan A. Pupils would be able to . . . _____

   _____

   _____

Plan B. Pupils would be able to . . . _____

_____

_____

Plan C. Pupils would be able to . . . _____

_____

_____

Plan D. Pupils would be able to . . . _____

_____

_____

Plan E. Pupils would be able to . . . _____

_____

_____

3. Select two alternative instructional procedures from among the teacher plans reported here. Which plans do you prefer?

_____

4. Think of another possible procedure for helping students attain the objective of expanding a simple sentence in at least two ways, or the objective of using logical connectives to expand sentences in four different ways. Remember that you are planning for a group of children who can already add words and phrases on to the end of a sentence (elementary) or a group that can already use the logical connective word "and" (secondary). Describe the steps you would follow below.

_____

_____

_____

_____

_____

_____

_____

_____

_____

_____

_____

_____

_____

_____

_____

_____

_____

5. Compare the three alternative sets of instructional procedures that you have chosen. How are they similar to each other?

_____

_____

_____

How are they different from each other?

_____

_____

_____

Identifying Procedural Differences

One important consequence of different instructional procedures is that they involve children in different kinds of learning activities. The skills that are learned may vary according to the instructional procedure used. For example, in the five lesson plans presented earlier, all the teachers had a similar goal in mind — they were working with pupils who expanded sentences in limited ways, and they wanted to teach these pupils to expand a sentence in more extensive ways. Nevertheless, the activities that these teachers included in their lesson plans varied widely.

The skills actually practiced in each lesson are generally related to the learning outcome of the lesson. The lesson activities are described below. (Compare this presentation with your answer to question 2 on Response Form VI.)

Plan A. Pupils individually write several expanded sentences of different, specified types.

Plan B. Pupils as a group suggest words and phrases to be added at several specified points in a lesson. Pupils individually construct one expanded sentence, adding specified types of content.

Plan C. Pupils individually write one expanded sentence after seeing one example of an expanded sentence. The types of expansions used are specified.

Plan D. Pupils individually write a simple sentence, then expand it through the addition of several different logical connectives, both at the end and beginning of the sentence.

Plan E. Pupils as a group expand a simple sentence through use of a single, given, logical connective. Then they act out the sentence, while others try to guess it.

One procedural difference that probably affects learning outcomes involves *group versus individual activity*. In a group activity not every pupil may have an opportunity actively to practice the skill to be learned. Some teachers deal with this by trying to call on every student at some point in the group lesson. Other teachers use a group activity to demonstrate the skill and then have individual pupils practice the skill on their own.

Another difference that affects learning is the *amount of skill practice* given a child. The child who writes three or four expanded sentences will probably remember the concept longer than the child who only writes one. The child who writes twenty may become so weary of the process that he or she learns to *dislike* expanded sentences instead of learning to write them well.

A third procedural difference that can affect learning is the *specificity of the skill* being practiced. A child who writes three or four different types (adjective, adverb, phrase, clause) of expanded sentences probably develops a clearer concept of sentence expansion than the child who writes several unspecified types of expansions, all of which may turn out to duplicate one another.

In planning a lesson, these procedural differences should be kept in mind. A teacher must think carefully about the *skills being practiced*, whether they involve *group or individual practice*, the *amount of practice*, and the *specificity of the practice*. The teacher who can describe instructional procedures in these terms will be better equipped to predict the learning outcome of a given lesson.

The five planned procedures presented here can also be compared on a number of other interesting bases. They vary in the *instructional materials* to be used and in their provision for *independent pupil ideas, individual differences*, and *feedback on pupil learning*. It is important for a teacher to be alert to these types of differences in instructional procedure, as well as to differences in the type of skill practice provided pupils.

Reexamine the five plans, paying particular attention to these four types of variation, and compare the lessons, using Response Form VII.

RESPONSE FORM VII

1. Which plan(s) use the most typical or traditional instructional materials?

_____

_____

Which plan(s) use the least typical or traditional materials?

_____

_____

What additional alternative instructional materials might be used for a lesson?

_____

_____

_____

_____

2. Which plan(s) make the most provision for development of independent pupil ideas?

_____

_____

Which plan(s) make the least provision for development of independent pupil ideas?

_____

_____

What are some additional alternative procedures that might be used to encourage independent pupil ideas in a lesson?

_____

_____

_____

_____

3. Which plan(s) provide for individual differences of pupils?

_____

_____

Which plan(s) have no provision for individual differences of pupils?

_____

_____

What are some additional alternative procedures that might be used to provide for individual differences in a lesson?

_____

_____

_____

_____

4. Which plan(s) provide for written feedback to the teacher regarding what pupils learned?

_____

_____

Which plan(s) do not provide for written feedback to the teacher?

_____

_____

What are some additional alternative procedures that might be used to provide a teacher with feedback on pupil learning?

_____

_____

_____

_____

Comparison of Instructional Procedures

1. Most Typical Instructional Materials. Plans A and B.
Least typical instructional materials: Plans C and E.
(Plans A, B, and E all use the chalkboard as the basic medium for recording information. In Plan A this is supplemented with worksheets, while Plan E uses student demonstration as an additional source of information. Plan D uses an overhead projector, the chalkboard becoming supplemental. Plan C uses a chart and sentence strips to present examples of simple and expanded sentences and follows up with individual worksheets. This plan requires much more prelesson time for preparation of materials than do the others, because the sentence strips and worksheets must be made in advance.)
Additional alternative materials: Use word cubes (like dice) or word cards to form sentences; examples of students' own creative writing; etc.

2. Most Use of Independent Pupil Ideas. Plans A and E.
Least use of independent pupil ideas: Plans B and C.
(Plan A is probably the most open to pupil ideas, with its worksheet saying "Add anything you like" and "Try writing some sentences of your own." Plan E provides for another type of pupil independence by organizing small groups of pupils who must cooperate to expand and act out sentences. Plans B and C provide little opportunity for independent pupil thinking. In Plan B pupils merely generate words or phrases to fit in spaces the teacher specifies. In Plan C pupils are only given the option to write their own simple sentences if the ones they are given don't appeal to them. Plan D provides a moderate opportunity for independent thinking. Pupils generate their own individual simple sentences, make up their own clauses to follow the given connectives, and test to see which connectives can be used at the beginning of their sentences.)
Additional alternative provisions for independent pupil ideas: Ask pupils to design a game for expanding sentences, developing their own rules and point system; (and others).

3. Provision for Individual Differences. Plans A, C, and D.
Little or no provision for individual differences: Plans B and E.
(Plan A provides for individual differences by the worksheet section that says "Try writing some sentences of your own." Pupils can write sentences of varying complexity here. Thus, children with more advanced language skills can practice expanding with more complex sentences. Plan C provides for individual differences by giving indi-

vidually assigned sentences based on pupil interest. Plan D invites pupils to write their own simple sentences. The other two plans make no real provision for individual differences. They are geared to the group. None of the plans seem to make provision for differences in time individual pupils or groups may require to complete the task assigned. What will pupils do if they finish their work early?)

Additional alternative provisions for individual differences: Provide pupils with options, for example, write your own sentence or choose one of these, work with a partner or work alone; divide students into groups on the basis of early responses (or pretest) and use tasks of varying difficulty with the different groups; (and others).

4. Provision for Written Feedback to Teacher.   Plans A, B, C, D.
No provision for written feedback: Plan E.

(All but one of these five plans have made provision for written feedback to the teacher, so that he or she can examine pupils' papers at the end of the lesson to determine whether pupils were able to achieve the instructional goal. Plan E involves pupils physically acting out sentences, but they do not do any written work.)

Additional alternative provisions for feedback on pupil learning: Have each child give an oral example of an expanded sentence at end of lesson; have children identify examples of simple and expanded sentences (various types) read by teacher, by holding up small card of red (simple sentence) or blue (expanded sentence); (and others).

Advantages and Disadvantages

Each of the planned procedures presented here has some advantages and some disadvantages. Each one accomplishes some goals and fails to accomplish others. That is true of all lesson plans ever written or carried out by a teacher. Furthermore, the advantages of a given plan will vary according to the pupils with whom it will be used.

One aspect of the procedures that has not been discussed so far is the grade level for which they were planned. Think back over the plans. Which ones would you expect to be most effective with first or second graders? Which ones would you expect to be most effective with fifth or sixth graders, or with eighth or ninth graders? It is highly unlikely that you would pick the same plan for use with all age levels.

Designing appropriate procedures for instruction involves thinking about a number of aspects of the lesson. Only the most important have been discussed here. They are shown below.

Aspects of the Lesson
1. Skills to be practiced
2. Group vs. individual practice
3. Amount of practice
4. Specificity of practice
5. Materials to be used
6. Provision for independent pupil ideas
7. Provision for individual differences
8. Provision for feedback on pupil learning

Probably no single plan will ever be perfect with respect to all of these aspects. As we have seen in the five plans reviewed here, certain aspects will be emphasized in one lesson, while others take the fore in the next lesson. But a teacher needs to be aware of the decisions he or she is making with regard to instructional procedures.

As you plan lessons, you might find it helpful to ask yourself questions based on the preceding points, for example:

What skills will students practice in this lesson?

Will students receive group practice or individual practice?

How much practice will each individual student actually get?

How specific will the practice be?

What alternative instructional materials can be used?

What provisions can be made for development of independent pupil ideas?

What are some ways to provide for individual differences in pupils?

What kind of feedback can be obtained regarding what pupils learned?

The answers to these questions will differ from lesson to lesson, for there is no one best procedure that can achieve all objectives.

These are good questions to keep in mind as you work through Response Form VIII, which follows.

RESPONSE FORM VIII

1. Review the three instructional procedures you selected or invented on Response Form VI. Select *one* of these that you would like to try out. Indicate your reasons for selecting it below.

_____

_____

_____

_____

_____

_____

_____

2. If possible, compare the instructional plan you have chosen with those chosen by other students who are reading this chapter. Discuss your reasons for selection. What aspects of instruction does the group tend to emphasize?

_____

_____

_____

_____

Are there any aspects of instruction that the group tends to ignore?

_____

_____

_____

_____

3. After reading and hearing more about various instructional procedures, can you think of additional ways of teaching sentence expansion? If so, describe your new plan below.

_____

_____

_____

_____

_____

_____

_____

_____

4. While working through the task, what new ideas have you developed on identifying alternative procedures for achieving an instructional goal? List them below.

_____

_____

_____

_____

5. What questions do you still want to have answered about planning instructional procedures?

_____

_____

_____

_____

Your planning skills will grow as you learn more about alternative instructional strategies and work through the other chapters in this Handbook. The questions you raise now will help you focus your attention in studying later topics. It is time now to assess your understanding of the ideas presented in this section.

Mastery Test

OBJECTIVE 3 Given a set of instructional procedures, to identify in each case the skills practiced, the materials used, and the provisions for pupil ideas, individual differences, and evaluative feedback.

Read each of the following two lesson procedures and answer the questions which follow them.

PROCEDURE A

Objective: Students will identify similarities and differences in roles of family members.

1. Ask each student to list the tasks or jobs his or her mother performs.
2. Have students tell class the jobs they have listed. Write these on chalkboard.
3. Follow same procedure for tasks or jobs fathers do.
4. Compare lists for fathers and mothers. What tasks are on both? What tasks are only on one?
5. Discuss tasks that appear on both lists. Do *all* mothers and fathers perform these tasks?
6. Discuss tasks that appear on only one list. Are they unique to fathers or mothers? Do any fathers cook dinner, for example? Do any mothers wash the car? Are there big differences between what mothers do and fathers do?
7. Have each student study both lists and write down any tasks on the lists that he or she helps with at home. Collect the papers.

Questions

1. What skill is practiced in this lesson?

_____

_____

_____

2. Do students receive group or individual practice in use of this skill?

_____

_____

3. What instructional materials are used?

_____

_____

4. Is there any provision for pupil ideas? If so, what?

_____

_____

_____

5. Is there any provision for individual differences? If so, what?

_____

_____

_____

6. Is there provision for written feedback to the teacher on what pupils learned? If so, what?

_____

_____

_____

PROCEDURE B

Objective: Given a film that depicts a different culture ("The Hunters," a film about the Kalihari Bushmen), pupils will identify at least three differences from and two similarities to their own culture.

1. Explain the task to students. Tell them that as they view the film they are to take notes about events they see that are different from or similar to their own experiences.
2. Show the film.
3. Have each pupil use notes to list three differences and two similarities.
4. Discuss the differences and similarities noted. Ask students how they felt as they watched certain events, for example, boys shooting tiny arrows into cricket; a father kissing his baby; a hunter spearing a giraffe.
5. After a discussion, have the students draw a line under their initial lists and add as many items as possible to each list. Collect the papers.

Questions

1. What skill is practiced in this lesson?

_____

_____

2. Do students receive group or individual practice in use of this skill?

_____

_____

3. What instructional materials are used?

_____

_____

4. Is there any provision for pupil ideas? If so, what?

_____

_____

_____

5. Is there any provision for individual differences? If so, what?

_____

_____

_____

6. Is there provision for written feedback to the teacher on what pupils learned? If so, what?

_____

_____

_____

ANSWER KEY

Mastery Test, Objective 3

(Your written responses need not be worded in exactly the same way as the answers given below.)

Procedure A

1. The skill of comparing or noting similarities and differences.
2. Group practice.
3. Paper, pencil, chalkboard.
4. Yes. In discussion, pupils can form their own ideas about the norms of family tasks and share these with each other.
5. Some. In listing tasks and in discussion, students can identify facts of their individual home situations and note how these differ from other homes. (However, there is no provision noted for pupils who have no mother or father in the home.)
6. No. Student's final writing assignment does not relate to identifying similarities and differences. It gives the teacher information on students' home backgrounds, but not on what was learned in this lesson.

Procedure B

1. The skill of comparing or noting similarities and differences.

2. Individual practice, supplemented by group practice.
3. Film, paper, and pencil.
4. Yes. Pupil ideas about similarities and differences in cultures form the basis of the whole discussion.
5. Yes. Pupils are encouraged to talk about their individual emotional reactions to various events in the film.
6. Yes. The teacher gets written feedback concerning each student's initial identification of similarities and differences and also concerning the information that was picked up during the discussion (additions to lists).

If you answered eight or more of the twelve questions accurately, you have demonstrated understanding of the ideas presented in this section. Proceed to Learning Activity 4.

If you answered less than eight questions correctly, you need to review the ideas in this section. Reread one of the lesson procedures described at the beginning of Learning Activity 3 and try to answer the eight questions in the section called "Advantages and Disadvantages" preceding Response Form VIII. Then check your answers by rereading the sections following Response Forms VI and VII.

Objective 4

Given two alternative lesson plans for teaching the same content, to identify the differences and similarities in the two plans in terms of their: (a) specific objective, (b) diagnostic procedure, (c) instructional materials, (d) skills to be practiced, (e) group or individual skill practice, (f) provision for pupil ideas, (g) provision for individual differences, and (h) provision for written feedback.

LEARNING ACTIVITY 4

Planning and teaching two alternative lessons on the same topic is a procedure that has been used with both experienced teachers and teachers-in-training to introduce them to the process of self-evaluation. The teachers who have used this procedure have generally found it to be an interesting experience. They have noted that pupils respond differently to the alternative procedures and that they themselves act and feel differently.

For our purposes here, planning two alternative lessons serves to emphasize the importance of thinking of alternatives, and it also provides an opportunity to double the practice of the planning skills developed so far in this chapter.

Alternative lessons can vary in several different ways. They might utilize different instructional materials, ask pupils to engage in different types of activities (that is, practice different skills), or provide different roles for the teacher (as lecturer vs. discussion leader). They may even vary in all of these ways at once. But alternative lessons always have one basic similarity: They both deal with the same topic and expect pupils to learn the same general content.

An example of alternative lessons is given below. These two lessons were planned by an eighth grade teacher and taught to two different groups of eighth grade students. (Both groups of students attended a storefront school, were public school "dropouts," and had difficulty with both reading and mathematics.)

Subject matter: Mathematics

Topic: Introduction to Topology

Lesson objective: To have students develop a new awareness of lines and the various relationships they can have to each other in space and to indicate an interest in further study of the topic.

Materials: Chalkboard

Procedure for Lesson One	*Procedure for Lesson Two*
1. Write letters of the alphabet on the board in capitals.	1. Ask students if someone can write the alphabet on the board in capital letters.
2. Say: "Some of these letters are similar to other letters in certain ways. I have one kind of similarity in mind, and I want to see if you can figure out what my idea is. Here are some of the letters that I think belong together." Write on the board: Yes A, H, I	2. Say: "Some of the letters of the alphabet are like each other in certain ways. Can you find some letters that you think are alike?" (Students will raise hands.) "Okay, come up and write down the letters that you think belong together" (maybe E, F, L or B, D, P).

Procedure for Lesson One (cont'd)	Procedure for Lesson Two (cont'd)

3. Say: "A lot of the letters in the alphabet can't fit in my group. They don't have the characteristic I have in mind. Here are some letters that don't fit." Write on the board:

    No B, G, Z

4. Say: "Look at the letters that are left and pick some that you think might fit in my group. I'll tell you if you're right." As letters are suggested, write them down in the Yes or No group (that is, add M, O, T, U, V, W, X, Y to Yes group, all others to No).

5. When all letters are written in Yes or No group, ask: "Can anyone see the rule I'm using to tell what letters fit in my group? Can you see how all these letters are alike?" (They are all "mirror-letters" when divided on the vertical axis, e.g., A.)

6. Ask students to think of another grouping that could be made. Have each student write examples of letters that fit his/her group and also write down the common characteristics of the letters in the group. Collect the papers.

7. Ask who would like to try this again with some other kinds of shapes. Note the responses.

3. Say: "Great. Does anyone else have a group of letters that they think belong together because they are alike somehow?" (Another student comes to the board.)

4. Continue asking students to suggest groups until all letters are included in a group and/or all students have suggested a group.

5. Say: "We have a lot of groups now, so let's look back and decide why the letters in a group belong together. Let's give our groups names that tell how they are alike." (For example, E, F, L could be called "sidelines.")

6. Ask students to think of another way that letters could be grouped, different from the groupings on the board. Have each student write down his new group and give it a name. Collect the papers.

7. Ask who would like to try this again with some other kinds of shapes. Note the responses.

One way to compare these two alternative lessons is to review the aspects of planning that have been dealt with so far in this chapter. The following chart presents a comparison based on the types of characteristics that have been discussed.

	Lesson One	Lesson Two
Specific objective	To develop awareness and interest.	Same as One
Diagnostic procedures	None used. Plan assumes pupils know alphabet shapes.	Same as One
Skills to be practiced	Noting similarities and differences in shape. Discovering someone else's "rule" for grouping.	Noting similarities and differences in shape. Forming your own "rule" for grouping.
Type of skill practice	Group. Students help each other with their "guesses" and their discussion of possible reasons.	Individual. Each pupil can form his/her own group.
Materials	Chalkboard, letters of the alphabet.	Same as One
Provision for pupil ideas	Pupils hypothesize about basis for teacher's group and test their hypotheses by suggesting other letters to be added.	Pupils invent their own groupings and their own names for groups.

	Lesson One	Lesson Two
Provision for individual differences	Some pupils may guess the rule earlier than others. They can test their guess by adding new letters to group, while others are still trying to figure out the rule.	Pupils may perceive letters differently and focus on different characteristics.
Provision for feedback	Written check on whether pupils can get another fresh perspective on similarities in letters.	Same as One

The basic difference in these two alternative lessons is that the pupils' mental activity is different, that is, pupils have to think in different ways in the two lessons. But other variations could be easily developed. For example, open and closed shapes could be used rather than letters of the alphabet (alternative materials). Or pupils could be given a worksheet of logical problems to work on alone or in pairs, problems such as: If O, Q, and G belong together because they are alike in some way, which of the following letters would belong in the same group: J, C, T? (alternative with less provision for independent pupil ideas).

RESPONSE FORM IX

1. Decide on a subject matter area, topic, and grade level and plan two alternative lessons, using the form given below.

   Subject matter: _____

   Topic: _____

   Grade level: _____

   PLAN ONE

   Objective:

   Preliminary diagnostic procedure:

   Materials:

   Procedures:

PLAN TWO

Objective:

Preliminary diagnostic procedure:

Materials:

Procedures:

2. Compare your two plans by filling in the following form, noting where they are similar (write "S" in blank) and different (explain the differences you see).

	Plan One	Plan Two
Specific objective		
Diagnostic procedure		
Instructional materials		
Skills to be practiced		
Group or individual skill practice		
Provision for pupil ideas		
Provision for individual differences		
Provision for feedback		

	Plan one (cont'd)	Plan Two (cont'd)
Other (___ ___)		

3. Exchange both your plans and analysis forms with another student; study each other's papers to decide whether you agree on the similarities and differences between the two alternative plans. Check your agreements and disagreements below.

Partner's Name _____

	Agreed	Disagreed
Specific objective		
Diagnostic procedure		
Instructional materials		
Skills to be practiced		
Group or individual skill practice		
Provision for pupil ideas		
Provision for individual differences		
Provision for feedback		
Other		

Mastery Test

OBJECTIVE 4 Given two alternative lesson plans for teaching the same content, to identify the differences and similarities in the two plans in terms of their: (a) specific objective, (b) diagnostic procedure, (c) instructional materials, (d) skills to be practiced, (e) group or individual skill practice, (f) provision for pupil ideas, (g) provision for individual differences, and (h) provision for written feedback.

To determine whether you have understood the concepts presented in this section, review your record sheets for Response Form IX.

In response to question 3, were you and your partner able to agree on the similarities and differences between your plans in at least six of the eight basic areas listed for analysis? If so, you have demonstrated accuracy in your analysis of the two plans.

In response to question 2, were you able to note differences in your two plans in at least four of the eight basic areas? If so, you have demonstrated an ability to plan lessons that are really varied. You are beginning to develop the competencies that are the ultimate goals of this chapter.

Testing Alternatives

The real purpose of thinking in terms of alternatives when you plan lessons is that this enables you to vary your teaching and to learn more about what procedures work or don't work for you. The only real way to test the alternatives you have planned is to see how pupils react to them. The ultimate mastery test for Objective 4, and for the entire chapter, therefore, is a test that you must create for yourself. Here are the steps to follow.

1. Find two groups of students of about the same age level and ability and make arrangements to meet with each group for about half an hour to teach your lessons, one lesson to each group.

2. As you teach the lessons, have a fellow student observe the lessons or make an audiotape to listen to later. The lessons should be observed so that the differences in pupil responses can be noted (comments made, questions asked, interest displayed, amount learned).

3. When the lessons are over and you have the results of the observation, decide whether the two lessons were more or less different than you originally thought. Did you prefer one lesson over the other? Why? Can you think of additional alternative lessons for the same topic? What are they?

   (*An alternative:* If no elementary or secondary pupils are available to you, form a group of your fellow students who are studying this chapter and teach your two alternative lessons to them. When the lessons are over, you can ask them what differences they noted and whether they [as pupils] felt differently in the two lessons.)

The "ultimate mastery test" may take time for you to arrange, but you will find it to be of great value. For more rapid feedback on what you have learned from this chapter, take the written mastery test presented here.

Final Mastery Test

Directions: Study the two alternative lesson plans presented here. Then answer each of the questions which follow.

Subject matter: Social studies

Topic: Inventions

General goal: To introduce the topic of inventions and provide opportunity for creative thinking.

PLAN ONE

Objective: Given an everyday object, each pupil will invent at least one new use for it.

Diagnostic procedure: Ask each pupil to list at least three different things they might do with a deck of cards. Collect the papers. Identify the number of common uses (e.g., play card games, build a cardhouse, do a magic trick) and the number of uncommon uses (e.g., make a mobile) listed by each pupil.

Instructional materials: Chalkboard, a chain of paper clips, a newspaper, several decks of cards, general art supplies.

Procedures:
1. Introduce the topic of inventions. Ask pupils what inventions they have heard of. Explain that an invention can be something very new, but it can also be a new use for a familiar thing.
2. Show pupils a paper clip. Ask why it was invented — what it is used for. Ask if they can think of any other uses. Show them a chain of paper clips. Does that help them think of additional uses?
3. Show pupils a newspaper. Identify its normal use. Ask for inventive uses. List these on chalkboard. Note that changing the form of an object can help us think of other uses. Roll the newspaper up. Tear off a piece and crumple it up. What additional uses do these forms suggest?
4. Bring out a deck of cards. Ask pupils to think of a new way to use a deck of cards. They can work alone or with a partner. Tomorrow they will be asked to explain or show their invention to the rest of the class. Remind them that changing the form of the object can help them to be inventive. If they need any supplies like pens, scissors, paper, paste, etc., let them help themselves.

Evaluation: At the end of the "reporting" period next day, pupils will again be asked to list at least three different things they might do with a deck of cards. Compare each pupil's first and second lists. Are there more total items? Are there more uncommon uses?

PLAN TWO

Objective: Given an example of one humorous account of an early invention, pupils will write an imaginative explanation of how something else might have been first invented.

Diagnostic procedure: Ask each pupil to pick an invention that he or she is familiar with (e.g., has seen or used it) and in a brief paragraph tell how or why they think it was invented. Collect the papers. Note how many pupils pick machines to discuss. What other types of things are seen as inventions? How realistic or accurate are the explanations of how or why things were invented?

Instructional materials: Charles Lamb's essay on the origin of roast pork, chalkboard, paper and pencils for pupils, several common objects such as a cup, a bowl, a spoon.

Procedures:
1. Introduce the topic of inventions. Ask pupils what things they think of when the word "invention" is used. Ask why people invent things. Do inventions ever occur by accident?
2. Explain that almost everything we use today was once invented. Most things are so familiar that we don't think of them as having been invented. It can be fun to imagine how some of the earliest things were invented.

3. Read (or tell) Charles Lamb's account of the origin (invention) of roast pork. (This is a funny story about a Chinese boy who accidentally burns down his hut and discovers that a pig has been burned inside it. He burns his hand on the pig and licks his fingers. The burned pig tastes so good, he begins to burn down the hut regularly, in order to eat a roasted pig each time. The practice spreads until everyone in the village is burning down their house once a week.)

4. Ask pupils what other common things they can think of that were once invented. List their ideas on the board. Display common objects like a cup, a bowl, or a spoon if they need help to get started.

5. Pick one or two things from the list to discuss. What might this have been made from originally? How might people have gotten the idea? Why did they need something like this? Can they think of a funny explanation? Write ideas on the board.

6. Ask pupils to write an explanation of how or why something was invented. They can choose something from the list or think of something else. Papers will be read aloud to the class the next day.

Evaluation: Compare papers at the end of the lesson to those written before the lesson. Are more common objects or procedures (that are not machines) listed the second time? Are the explanations of how or why things were invented more humorous or imaginative the second time?

Questions

1. For each of the two stated objectives, identify its characteristics by circling one answer after *each* of the three specified areas.

   Plan One

   Content focus: operation   application   facts   process   other
   Expected actor: teacher   pupil   not specified
   Learning outcome: vague   specific   detailed

   Plan Two

   Content focus: operation   application   facts   process   other
   Expected actor: teacher   pupil   not specified
   Learning outcome: vague   specific   detailed

2. For each of the two diagnostic procedures described, write the question that is asked about pupil attainment on the lines provided below.

   Plan One _____

   _____

   _____

   Plan Two _____

   _____

   _____

3. For each of the two instructional procedures described, identify its characteristics by answering the questions below.

   (a) What skill is practiced in the lesson?

   Plan One _____

   _____

   Plan Two _____

   _____

(b) Do students receive individual or group practice in use of this skill?

Plan One _____

Plan Two _____

(c) What instructional materials are used?

Plan One _____

_____

Plan Two _____

_____

(d) Is there any provision for pupil ideas? If so, what?

Plan One _____

_____

_____

Plan Two _____

_____

_____

(e) Is there provision for individual differences? If so, what?

Plan One _____

_____

_____

Plan Two _____

_____

_____

(f) Is there provision for written feedback to the teacher on what pupils learned? If so, what?

Plan One _____

_____

_____

Plan Two _____

_____

_____

4. Compare the two lesson plans by noting whether they are basically similar or basically different in each of the following eight areas. (Circle "similar" or "different" for each area.)

Specific objective	Similar	Different
Diagnostic procedure	Similar	Different
Instructional materials	Similar	Different
Skills to be practiced	Similar	Different

Group or individual skill practice	Similar	Different
Provision for pupil ideas	Similar	Different
Provision for individual differences	Similar	Different
Provision for written feedback	Similar	Different

ANSWER KEY
Final Mastery Test

1. *Plan One*   Content focus: process
Expected actor: pupil
Learning outcome: specific

   Plan Two   Content focus: application
Expected actor: pupil
Learning outcome: specific

2. *Plan One*   How many uncommon uses for a common object can each pupil think of (when asked to list a minimum of three different uses)?

   Plan Two   How many pupils in the class think of familiar objects as inventions and/or provide imaginative explanations of how an invention occurred (when asked to choose an invention and tell how or why it was invented)?

3. (a) *Plan One*   The skill of generating new or uncommon uses for everyday objects.
   Plan Two   The skill of imagining possible explanations for how or why familiar things were first invented.

   (b) *Plan One*   Both group and individual practice.
   Plan Two   Both group and individual practice.

   (c) *Plan One*   Paper clips, newspaper, decks of cards, art supplies.
   Plan Two   Story by Charles Lamb, some common objects such as a cup or a spoon.

   (d) *Plan One*   Yes. In several instances pupils are asked their ideas (about new uses for objects), and these are listed on the board.
   Plan Two   Yes. Pupils are asked for their ideas (about how familiar objects might originally have been invented), and these are listed on the board.

   (e) *Plan One*   Yes. Pupils can opt to work alone or with a partner. They can select the kind of materials they want to work with in inventing a new use for cards.
   Plan Two   Some. Pupils can select the object they want to write about, but all of them are asked to write a paper. This may not be the best form of communication for all pupils.

   (f) *Plan One*   Yes. Each pupil's list of three different uses for cards can be compared to the original papers to inform the teacher if additional ideas have been developed. (In addition, there will be oral feedback as pupils report on their inventions.)
   Plan Two   Yes. Each pupil's final paper can be compared to the original paper to determine whether imaginative ideas were developed.

4. | | |
|---|---|
| Specific objective: | Different |
| Diagnostic procedure: | Different |
| Instructional materials: | Different |
| Skills to be practiced: | Different |
| Group or individual skill practice: | Similar |
| Provision for pupil ideas: | Similar |
| Provision for individual differences: | Different |
| Provision for written feedback: | Similar |

NOTES
1. Greta Morine and Elizabeth Vallance, *Teacher Planning*, Beginning Teacher Evaluation Studies Technical Report, Special Study C (San Francisco: Far West Laboratory, 1976). The research was conducted for the California Commission for Teacher Preparation and Licensing with funding from the National Institute of Education.

2. Barak Rosenshine and Norma Furst, "Research in Teacher Performance Criteria," in *Research in Teacher Education*, ed. B. Othanel Smith (Englewood Cliffs, New Jersey: Prentice-Hall, 1971).

ADDITIONAL READINGS
Jackson, Philip. *Life in Classrooms*. New York: Holt, Rinehart, and Winston, 1968.

Morine, Greta, and Ned A. Flanders. "Teacher Responsiveness — Pupil Initiative: Theme and Variations." *Social Education* 38 (May 1974): 432–439.

Norman Hurst, Stock, Boston.

TERRY TENBRINK

Writing Instructional Objectives

Objectives

1 To list the sources of instructional objectives and to describe the kind of objectives to be found for each source.

2 To select instructional objectives that will be useful to you and your students.

3 To rewrite poorly written objectives.

4 To write well-defined and useful objectives of your own.

You are probably well aware of the controversy that has continued for several years over the value of the instructional objectives. Before you begin to develop your skills in selecting, writing, and using instructional objectives, you should understand their value to you as a teacher. The first few pages of this chapter will be devoted to the value of instructional objectives; the remainder of the chapter will show you *how* to use them.

Think for a moment about what teachers do. Sit back and try to remember the *one* teacher who you felt had the most influence upon you. In the space provided below, write down the characteristics of that teacher as well as you can remember them.

Characteristics of a Favorite Teacher

_____

_____

_____

_____

_____

_____

Chances are that among the characteristics of your favorite teacher was the fact that the teacher knew you as an individual and knew what he or she wanted for you. This favorite teacher probably had a significant influence on your life, playing a part in the development of your attitudes, the formation of your habits, and the acquisition of information that was new and exciting to you. This teacher may have guided you subtly or may have directly "pushed" you toward these behavior changes. The teacher may have used a great many visual aids or none at all; or may have given multiple choice tests, essay tests, or no tests at all. What effective teachers have in common is *not* their techniques, their teaching styles, or the kinds of tests they use. It is *what* they accomplish, not how they accomplish it, that makes the difference.

If teachers are going to make a significant difference in the lives of their students, they must know precisely what they want their students to accomplish. Having formulated such precise goals, teachers can share them with their students so that the students will *also* know where they are going and what is expected of them.

There is considerable evidence[1] to support the contention that when teachers have clearly defined instructional objectives and have shared them with their students, a number of things happen:

1. Better instruction occurs.
2. More efficient learning results.
3. Better evaluation occurs.
4. The students become better self-evaluators.

Furthermore, it is important to note that the most successful instructional-design and systems-design approaches to education rely heavily upon well-defined objectives.

However, objections have been raised about the use of instructional objectives. The major objections are summarized as follows:

1. Writing good instructional objectives requires a lot of work and expertise.
2. Using instructional objectives hampers the process of individualizing and humanizing education.
3. The use of instructional objectives curtails spontaneity and decreases the teacher's flexibility.
4. Using instructional objectives leads to trivial learning outcomes.

If you examine each of these objections carefully, you will soon see that the objectives themselves are not at fault, but the way they are used. If a teacher becomes a slave to the writing and making use of instructional objectives instead of skillfully using them as an important teaching aid, then the above objections become valid. However, when objectives are viewed in proper perspective and used appropriately, there emerges a positive side to each of these objections. Let us briefly examine the positive counterparts to the above objections.

1. Writing Instructional Objectives Is Well Worth the Effort Involved.   There is no denying the fact that writing good instructional objectives can be time-consuming and difficult. However, the really important question is whether the effort is worth it. If, as some of the recent studies noted earlier seem to indicate, instructional objectives can improve instruction and produce more efficient learning, then surely the effort involved in writing and in using objectives is worth it.

One of the things that you should keep in mind is that writing instructional objectives is a task that need not be accomplished by a single teacher. Teachers can work together in teams, writing objectives for a common unit of study. Likewise, much time and effort can be saved by learning to rework objectives prepared by others.

Also keep in mind that teachers usually can develop their instructional materials over a period of time. It is not always possible to begin the year with a comprehensive list of objectives for each subject you are teaching. As you teach, you are continually updating and upgrading old objectives and writing appropriate new ones as needed. Thus, it is not only permissible, but valuable, to be working on objectives while the instructional process is in progress. This allows you to alter the objectives you discover are inappropriate for your students.

2. Instructional Objectives Can Be Helpful in Individualizing and Humanizing Education. In order to individualize instruction successfully, teachers need to know each individual student's abilities, strengths and weaknesses, and likes and dislikes. Furthermore, they need to be able to monitor each student's progress as he or she moves toward their individually assigned goals. The more clearly and precisely those goals are stated, the easier it will be to determine when an individual student reaches them.

Of course, not all students will reach the same educational goals at the same time. Therefore, well-defined subgoals, specified in observable terms, serve as important "landmarks" along the way. As a given student progresses toward a goal, these "landmarks" help in pinpointing exactly what the student has learned so far and what he or she needs to learn next. This kind of diagnostic information is invaluable in planning appropriate learning experiences for each student. Thus, teachers can take each student from a given level of achievement and move them through successive learning levels to their individually prescribed goals.

3. Instructional Objectives Help the Teacher To Be Flexible. There is a phenomenon in education which occurs regularly in most classrooms. The students call it "getting the teacher sidetracked." The teachers call it "capitalizing on the interests of the moment." In any dynamic classroom, unplanned but potentially powerful learning situations sometimes arise spontaneously from the classroom activities. Teachers who have clearly defined instructional objectives will be more able to capitalize on those spontaneous activities, seeing them as alternate ways to reach their objectives. If there are no well-defined objectives, these same spontaneous activities are likely to sidetrack instruction rather than move the class toward desired goals. In short, objectives can help teachers harness spontaneity instead of being derailed by it. Having clearly defined instructional objectives will not only help the teacher capitalize on spur-of-the-moment situations but will also help in planning a variety of activities specifically designed to help the students reach their objectives.

It is not uncommon to find teachers who depend on textbooks and other classroom materials for a definition of what their students should accomplish. In these situations the student or the teacher often finds the materials uninteresting or inappropriate, and the teacher may decide to switch to new materials. Furthermore, chances are that the newly acquired materials were *not* designed to help the students toward the same educational objectives as the materials they replaced. Consequently, switching materials often means switching goals, which can become frustrating and confusing to students. On the other hand, teachers who have clearly specified their *own* instructional objectives can be more flexible in the selection and use of instructional materials. Because they know precisely what they want their students to accomplish, they can select and use materials on the basis of their own objectives. In this situation, a midstream change of materials does not automatically produce a change of objectives.

4. Well-Written Instructional Objectives Help Produce Important Learning Outcomes. A common misuse of instructional objectives is to write trivial ones that emphasize the memorization of unimportant facts. The result is that the instructional objectives are blamed for trivia being taught in the schools. However, an examination of the classroom tests does reveal that much purely factual, trivial information is being taught. Whether or not teachers write instructional objectives, they are subject to the common error of emphasizing the memorization of trivia. However, if instructional objectives are drawn up *before* instruction begins, then they can be evaluated to see if there is a proper balance of memory versus the higher levels of learning. Once a good balance is achieved, the objectives can serve as a guide in lesson planning as well as in test construction. Well-written objectives, rather than causing the teaching of trivia, can help teachers avoid that error by reviewing their objectives to see if a proper balance of learning levels has been achieved prior to teaching.

Instructional objectives fulfill a number of useful functions. Primary among these are the following:

1. Instructional objectives are useful in lesson planning.
2. Instructional objectives are useful in the selection of learning aids such as textbooks, films, etc.
3. Instructional objectives are useful in determining appropriate assignments for individual students.
4. Instructional objectives are useful in selecting and/or constructing classroom tests.
5. Instructional objectives are useful in determining when to gather evaluative data.
6. Instructional objectives are useful in summarizing and reporting evaluation results.
7. Instructional objectives can help learners determine where they are and where they have to go as they strive toward becoming independent learners.

Objective 1

To list the sources of instructional objectives and to describe the kind of objectives to be found for each source.

LEARNING ACTIVITY 1.1

In developing a set of objectives for your own class, you may find it useful to begin with objectives that have already been written by others. Some of these objectives may be usable in their original form, whereas others may have to be rewritten to suit your needs and the needs of your students. Among the major sources of objectives available to you, these should be particularly useful:

1. Published learning materials
2. Course syllabi
3. Other teachers
4. Professional journals
5. Instructional objectives exchange

1. Published Learning Materials. One important source of instructional objectives is the material that you use in teaching your students. Textbooks, educational games, workbooks, slide-tape programs, films, and so on are all potential sources for instructional objectives. The objectives they contain will vary greatly according to how well they are written or produced. Some may be clearly stated in observable terms, while others may be vague and somewhat ambiguous. Some may state specific short-term objectives; others may include only long-term goals. Sometimes there may be no observable objectives stated at all. However, by carefully examining the content of the materials, you should perceive what the student is expected to learn and, consequently, have a valuable source of ideas for designing your own objectives.

The objectives (or goals) that accompany published materials are usually appropriate for the grade level specified by the materials themselves. However, make certain there is a "match" between the objectives and the lessons. Sometimes a publisher's claims about what students will accomplish when using the materials are unrealistic. Always examine educational materials carefully and ask yourself this important question:

> If the students use these materials as they were designed to be used, what will they likely be able to do that they couldn't do before using them?

If your answer to the above question resembles the publisher's claims, then those claims may indeed serve as realistic objectives for your students.

If published materials do not include learning objectives per se, then use the materials as a source of ideas when you construct your own set of objectives. Examine the following items in particular:

Sources of Ideas from Published Materials

1. General goals
2. Statements of purpose
3. Publisher's claims of success
4. Test items
5. Exercises and suggested assignments
6. Preface

2. Course Syllabi. Sometimes the objectives published by the local school district in a course syllabus are quite clear. When this is so, you can use them as written. However, the course syllabus objectives are often vague and represent long-term goals rather than the specific, short-term goals that make good instructional objectives. These long-term goals are normally accompanied by outlines of the content to be covered and a list of recommended and/or mandated textbooks to be used. Furthermore, a course syllabus usually reflects the philosophy of the school or department for which the syllabus was designed. This statement of philosophy, along with the rationale for the course, is an excellent source for affective objectives (objectives that deal with developing a positive attitude toward the course subject matter).

There are a couple of very important advantages to using objectives found in a course syllabus. First, the objectives are usually a part of a larger set of goals (e.g., objectives for a ninth grade English class are part of the objectives for the total English curriculum in the school). Seeing your instructional objectives as part of a much larger set may help you better understand what to expect of your students when they enter your class and when they leave it. This kind of information should help you determine which objectives are most important for future success and which ones are less important. You will want to be certain that your students master the objectives that are prerequisite to the work they will be asked to do after they leave your class.

A second advantage of objectives found in course syllabi is that they are not usually tied to particular instructional materials. Thus, you can exercise your academic freedom, possibly using a variety of materials, to help your students attain the goals set by your school.

3. Other Teachers. Teachers teaching the same subject matter and/or grade level can be a great deal of help to each other. Often what one will not think of, another will; so, when writing objectives for a given course, it is helpful for the teachers of that course to work as a team. This procedure not only will lighten the load on individual teachers but will also broaden their perspective and probably ensure a more appropriate set of objectives.

Since many teachers have not been trained to specify their instructional goals clearly, don't be surprised if some of those you borrow are poorly conceived and written. Instead of being critical, accept whatever statements of expected outcomes you can get. If the intent of the borrowed objectives seems appropriate, you can always rewrite them so that they will be more useful to you and your students. Later in this chapter you will learn how to do this.

4. Professional Journals. Professional journals frequently carry articles describing successful units of instruction or helpful approaches to teaching certain topics. Sometimes, these articles will include a list of objectives the authors used to measure the learning outcomes of their students. Although these objectives are frequently well written and at an appropriate level, they are usually highly specific, related to one small aspect of a given course or tied to a particular instructional methodology. Do not expect to find a well-balanced set of objectives for an entire course in a single journal article. If the specific objectives detailed in a given article fit well into your overall objectives, then use them accordingly.

5. Instructional Objectives Exchange. A particularly valuable source of instructional objectives is the behavioral objective exchange directed by W. James Popham. By contributing instructional objectives to the exchange, you become eligible to withdraw objectives which may suit your own needs. The exchange has objectives available for virtually all subject matter areas at many different grade levels.

The objectives received from this exchange have been checked for clarity and are likely to be well written and stated in observable terms. You can read more about this instructional objective exchange in an article which appeared in the *Phi Delta Kappan* in 1970.[2]

LEARNING ACTIVITY 1.2

Most colleges and universities and many public school systems have a library of classroom materials including textbooks, learning kits, films, recordings, educational games, etc. Go to one of these libraries near you and browse through the offerings of the various publishers. Check for learning objectives accompanying the materials. What similarities and differences do you find from one publisher to the next? Does the kind and quality of the learning objectives vary from textbooks to other kinds of materials from the same publisher? Do the tests accompanying the materials reflect the goals or objectives of those materials?

Mastery Test

OBJECTIVE 1

To list the sources of instructional objectives and to describe the kind of objectives to be found for each source.

There are five major sources of instructional objectives. List each source and briefly describe the kind of objective you would likely find there.

_____

_____

_____

_____

_____

_____

_____

_____

_____

_____

ANSWER KEY
Mastery Test, Objective 1

1. *Published materials.* A variety of objectives will be found here. They will usually be appropriate for the grade level specified, but they might not be very clearly written. Besides objectives per se, published materials will often contain general goals, statements of purpose, claims of success, test items, exercises and assignments, and a preface, all of which may help you formulate your own objectives.

2. *Course syllabi.* Here one can find general goals and objectives appropriate for the grade level specified and related to a larger set of goals for the total curriculum. These objectives will not usually be tied to a particular set of instructional materials.

3. *Other teachers.* Objectives from other teachers will vary in quality but will probably be appropriate for the grade level specified. Those obtained from a single teacher may be narrow in scope, reflecting the interests and skills of that teacher only.

4. *Professional journals.* Here one can find highly specific objectives related to a small aspect of a given course or to a particular instructional methodology. They will usually be quite well written.

5. *Instructional objectives exchange.* This source will provide you with the widest variety of objectives. They will include cognitive, affective, and psychomotor objectives for virtually all subject matter areas and grade levels. They will be well written and observable.

Objective 2

To select instructional objectives that will be useful to you and your students.

LEARNING ACTIVITY 2.1

Instructional objectives that are useful in the classroom must meet certain criteria. We have outlined these criteria* below. Look them over carefully, and then we will discuss each of them in turn.

A Useful Instructional Objective Must Be:

1. Student-oriented
2. Descriptive of a learning *outcome*
3. Clear and understandable
4. Observable

1. Good Instructional Objectives Are Student-Oriented. An instructional objective which is student-oriented places the emphasis upon what the *student* is expected to do, not upon what the teacher will do. Look at the following examples; notice that they all describe student behavior and not teacher behavior.

Examples of Student-Oriented Objectives

1. Students should be able to solve long-division problems using at least two different methods.

* List taken from *Evaluation: A Practical Guide for Teachers*, by T. D. TenBrink. Copyright © 1974 by McGraw-Hill Book Company. Used with permission.

2. Students should be able to list the five punctuation rules discussed in the textbook.
3. Students should be able to write down their observations of a simple experiment, stating what was done and what happened.
4. The student should be able to identify and label the major parts of a business letter.
5. When given the description of a form of government, the student should be able to classify that form of government and list its probable strengths and weaknesses.

Sometimes teachers use instructional goals which emphasize what they are expected to do rather than what they expect of their students. Such teacher-oriented objectives only have value to the extent that they direct the teacher to do something which ultimately leads to student learning. A teacher attempting to help his or her students attain the goal of solving long-division problems may work out some of the problems on the blackboard, explaining each of the steps involved. A teacher-oriented objective associated with this behavior might read something like: "To explain the steps in long division on the blackboard." Notice that this might be a helpful teacher activity, but it is only *one* of many possible activities that could help the students reach the goal of solving long division.

Your Turn

SELECT STUDENT-ORIENTED OBJECTIVES

The following exercise will give you practice in distinguishing between student-oriented and teacher-oriented objectives. Place an *S* before each student-oriented and a *T* before each teacher-oriented objective.

_____ 1. To read at least 250 words per minute with no less than 80 percent comprehension.

_____ 2. To show students proper eye movements for scanning material.

_____ 3. To outline my lecture on the board before class begins.

_____ 4. When given the description of a complex machine, to identify the simple machines contained within it.

_____ 5. To help the students appreciate classical music.

_____ 6. To lecture on the basic steps in the scientific method.

_____ 7. To carry out an investigation using the scientific method.

_____ 8. To maintain discipline in my class.

_____ 9. To write a unified paragraph on a single topic.

_____ 10. To evaluate a poem on the basis of the criteria for good poetry as discussed in class.

Now check your answers with the Answer Key. If you missed more than three, you may wish to reread this section before going on.

ANSWER KEY

Your Turn: Select Student-Oriented Objectives

1. *S.* A desirable learning outcome.
2. *T.* Students will need to learn proper eye movements, but it is likely that the teacher will have to demonstrate them to the students.
3. *T.* Probably helpful to students, but not an expected student outcome.
4. *S.* A student who can do this has learned well.
5. *T.* How would a teacher do this?
6. *T.* Lecturing is only important if it helps the students reach a desirable learning outcome.
7. *S.* A learning outcome requiring several prerequisite skills.
8. *T.* Of course, maintaining good self-discipline may be an important student-oriented objective.
9. *S.* A goal most English teachers hope their students will eventually attain.
10. *S.* A student-oriented objective. However, the teacher might work through such an evaluation with his or her students as one activity designed to help them reach this goal.

2. Good Instructional Objectives Describe Learning Outcomes. The important thing to keep in mind here is that we are interested in what the students will learn to do. In other words, it is the learning *outcome* that is important, not the learning activities that should lead to that outcome. To say that students will practice long-division problems using two different methods is not to specify a learning outcome. It specifies an activity designed to help the students reach some outcome. As such, it is a student-oriented activity, *not* an outcome.

It may be valuable for you as a teacher to determine what kind of learning activities you may want your students to carry out. However, determining which learning experiences and activities are most appropriate for your students can only be made *after* you have decided what it is you want your students to accomplish. Once learning outcomes are identified and described, then activities which are appropriate for attaining those outcomes can be determined. In the table that follows you will find a number of learning outcomes listed in the left-hand column and the corresponding learning activities in the right-hand column. Look these examples over carefully, noting how each learning outcome dictates the kind of learning activity which might help the students reach it. Note, too, that many learning activities may be needed for students to successfully reach a single learning outcome.[3]

RELATIONSHIP BETWEEN LEARNING OUTCOMES AND LEARNING ACTIVITIES

Learning Outcomes	Learning Activities
1. To label the parts of a flower.	(a) Read pp. 17–22 in your science book.
	(b) Study the diagram of a flower in your book.
	(c) Use the unlabeled diagrams on the study table. Practice filling in the blanks. Check your labels with those in the book.

Learning Outcomes (cont'd)	Learning Activities (cont'd)
2. To identify the four main parts of speech in simple and complex sentences.	(a) Complete Workbook pp. 75–78. (b) Listen to the teacher's explanation of nouns, verbs, adjectives, and adverbs. (c) Play the grammar game (part 5) with some of your classmates. (d) Pick a paragraph from your reading book. List the nouns and verbs. Have your teacher check your work.
3. To reduce fractions to the lowest common denominator.	(a) Watch the teacher reduce fractions. (b) Practice at the blackboard with the teacher's help.
4. To compute the area of a circle.	Read p. 78 and do Exercise 15.
5. To choose to listen to classical music during free time.	Listen to classical music and to the teacher's explanation of it.
6. To make a correct introduction of a friend to your teacher.	Listen to the record, "Introducing Friends."

Your Turn

SELECT OUTCOMES, NOT ACTIVITIES

Now it's your turn to practice distinguishing learning activities from learning outcomes. For each statement below, mark an *A* next to each learning activity and an *O* next to each outcome. *Remember:* Activities are necessary for the attainment of outcomes, but outcomes specify what students should ultimately be able to do.

_____ 1. To review the notes taken during yesterday's lecture.

_____ 2. To explain the function of the carburetor.

_____ 3. To practice multiplication with flash cards.

_____ 4. To read Chapters 17 and 18.

_____ 5. To distinguish between learning outcomes and learning activities.

_____ 6. To identify the parts of speech in a prose passage.

_____ 7. To identify correctly the types of trees found in this part of the country.

_____ 8. To locate on a topographical map the most likely place for the development of a large metropolitan area.

_____ 9. To study the diagram of the structure of an atom.

_____ 10. To listen to the "Nutcracker Suite."

_____ 11. To identify the instruments being played in the "Nutcracker Suite."

_____ 12. To identify the instruments being featured in a particular musical performance.

_____ 13. To practice hearing the difference between a French horn and a trombone.

_____ 14. To watch the film "How Your Brain Works."

_____ 15. To describe briefly the two-party system, listing its strengths and weaknesses.

Now compare your answers with those given in the Answer Key that follows. It is possible that you may have misinterpreted one or two statements. If this happened, don't worry about a couple of "wrong" answers. However, if you missed many of the items in this exercise, you may have read this section too rapidly. Go back and reread it, thinking carefully about what is being said. As you read, try to think of further examples taken from your own school experiences.

ANSWER KEY

Your Turn: Select Outcomes, Not Activities

1. *A*   2. *O*   3. *A*   4. *A*   5. *O*   6. *O*   7. *O*   8. *O*
9. *A*   10. *A*   11. *O (although this could be a practice exercise for the outcome specified in 12)* 12. *O*
13. *A*   14. *A*   15. *O.*
   Note: Some of the above outcomes (such as 5, 6, 7, and 8) might best be learned by trying to do them and then getting feedback on how successful you were. This kind of practice, using a learning outcome as a learning activity, can be highly successful if (1) the student has reached a high enough level of understanding of the task and (2) good feedback is provided.

3. Instructional Objectives Are Clear and Understandable. The first prerequisite for a clear and understandable objective is explicitness. It should contain a clearly stated verb that describes a definite action or behavior and, in most cases, should refer to an object of that action. Examine the examples below. In each case the verb and its object have been italicized. As you read these examples, try to see if there is more than one possible meaning for any of them. If they are well stated and explicit, only one meaning should be possible.

Examples of Clearly Stated Objectives

1. The student should be able to *label* the *parts of the heart* correctly on a diagram of the heart similar to the one on p. 27 of the text.

2. When given words from the list in the back of the spelling book, the student should be able to *identify words that are incorrectly spelled* and make any necessary corrections.

3. The pupils should be able to use a yardstick to *measure* the *length, width, and height* of any piece of furniture in the room. The measurements should be accurate to within half an inch.

4. To be able to *identify* correctly the *ingredients in a mixture of chemicals prepared in advance* by the teacher.

5. When given a *contemporary poem*, the student should be able to *evaluate* it according to the criteria discussed in class.

6. To *list* the *major parts of a friendly letter*, briefly *describing* the *function of each part.*

7. Given several occasions to listen to different types of music, the student will *select* at least *three different types of music* that he or she likes.

8. To *read out loud* a *prose passage of approximately 300 words*, making no more than three errors. The reading level of the passage will be at the 5.5 grade level.

Notice that in each of the above examples, not only are there a clearly defined verb and its accompanying object, but there is only one possible meaning for each of the statements. Furthermore, it is important to note that most people observing someone engaged in the behaviors described above, or observing the products of those behaviors, would agree in their judgments about whether the behavior had occurred as stated. In other words, the above objectives are not only explicitly stated but are also observable. This characteristic (observability) will be described in the next section.

A Word of Caution

Let me digress from the present discussion to caution you against something which occurs frequently when teachers are first learning to write instructional objectives. It is very easy to confuse the notion that an objective must be explicit with the idea that it must be highly specific. Objectives should be explicit, that is, unambiguous and understandable. However, being explicit does not mean they have to be highly specific, written down to the very minutest of details and the lowest level of a given behavior. Below is an example* of an instructional objective that has been written in very general terms and then rewritten several times, each time becoming a bit more specific.[4]

1. Students should be able to read with understanding.

2. When given a story to read, the student should be able to answer questions about the content of the story.

3. When given a short story, the student should be able to identify the passages which identify the traits of the main characters.

4. Students should be able to identify the passages which identify the personality traits of the main characters in *Catcher in the Rye.*

5. Students should be able to identify at least five passages from *Catcher in the Rye* that illustrate Holden's confidence in himself.

6. Students should be able to recognize five passages cited in Handout 3 which illustrate Holden's lack of confidence in himself.[5]

Notice that the most useful instructional objectives in the above examples are those which fall somewhere in the middle of the continuum from very general to very specific. When instructional objectives become too specific, they lose much of their value as a guide to study and become little more than test questions to be answered. Instructional objectives that are too specific might very well encourage poor study habits. Students may tend to learn just enough to meet the specific objectives but not enough to meet the more general end-of-the-course objectives. The value of getting students to identify the passages from *Catcher in the Rye* which illustrate descriptions of personality traits is that this ability will transfer to other short stories as well. Transferability makes the objective more valuable than one which asks the student to recognize those passages from *Catcher in the Rye* which had previously been discussed and identified (like objective 6).

Your Turn

SELECT CLEAR AND UNAMBIGUOUS OBJECTIVES

For each of the following objectives, determine whether it has a single meaning (mark it with a "1") or two or more meanings (mark it with a "2"). The first three items have been done for you. The first is ambiguous. In fact it could be interpreted to mean the same thing as items 2 and 3. The problem with item 1, of course, is the fact that the verb is not explicit. Using a more explicit verb (as in item 2 or item 3) clears up the ambiguity.

__2__   1. To know the Presidents of the United States.

__1__   2. To list in writing the Presidents of the United States.

__1__   3. To recognize and call by name each President of the United States upon seeing his picture.

_____   4. To see the connection between well-written sentences and good short stories.

_____   5. To identify the vanishing points in a three-point perspective drawing.

_____   6. To establish eye contact with at least five different persons during a three-minute persuasive speech.

_____   7. To develop a roll of 35-mm black-and-white film.

_____   8. To run a 10-minute mile.

_____   9. To appreciate good music.

_____   10. To mold a lump of clay into the shape of an animal which can be recognized and correctly named by the rest of the class.

_____   11. Not to show favoritism to any given child in the preschool.

_____   12. To understand the workings of an atomic energy plant.

_____   13. To plant a miniature garden according to the criteria for such a garden as described in the article "Apartment Gardening."

_____   14. To enlarge your concept of realism.

4. Good Instructional Objectives Are Observable. The evaluation of learning outcomes hinges on the observability of those outcomes. The key to an observable objective is an observable verb. Consequently, when selecting instructional objectives for use in your teaching, *watch the verbs!* As discussed earlier, a good objective contains an explicit verb and (usually) a well-defined object of the verb. Both these requirements help make an objective clear and unambiguous. Now we add another requirement: the verb must describe an observable action or an action that results in an observable product.

The verbs in the box* are vague and unobservable. Avoid them.

<table>
<tr><td colspan="2">Vague, unobservable verbs that should be avoided</td></tr>
<tr><td>to know</td><td>to enjoy</td></tr>
<tr><td>to understand</td><td>to familiarize</td></tr>
<tr><td>to comprehend</td><td>to value</td></tr>
<tr><td>to grasp</td><td>to realize</td></tr>
<tr><td>to believe</td><td>to like</td></tr>
<tr><td>to appreciate</td><td>to cope with</td></tr>
<tr><td>to think</td><td>to love</td></tr>
</table>

If you do select an objective which contains a verb like those in the list, be certain to rewrite the objective, substituting a verb that describes a more observable action.

The kind of verb you hope to find in instructional objectives is also exemplified below. When you write objectives, use these kinds of verbs.

<table>
<tr><td colspan="2">Verbs describing observable actions or actions which yield observable products*</td></tr>
<tr><td>to identify</td><td>to analyze</td></tr>
<tr><td>to speak</td><td>to predict</td></tr>
<tr><td>to list</td><td>to locate</td></tr>
<tr><td>to select</td><td>to explain</td></tr>
<tr><td>to choose</td><td>to isolate</td></tr>
<tr><td>to compute</td><td>to divide</td></tr>
<tr><td>to add</td><td>to separate</td></tr>
<tr><td>to draw</td><td>to infer</td></tr>
</table>

* For a more complete list of these kinds of verbs see Appendix 3 in N. E. Gronlund's *Stating Behavioral Objectives* (London: Collier-Macmillan Ltd., 1970).

* The verbs in the boxed material on this page were taken from *Evaluation: A Practical Guide for Teachers,* by T. D. TenBrink. Copyright © 1974, by McGraw-Hill Book Company. Used with permission.

There are many processes and skills which cannot be directly observed but which produce observable products. It is not possible for us to observe the thinking process of a student as he strives to solve an algebraic equation. However, we can examine the solution he arrives at and decide whether or not it is correct. Furthermore, we may be able to look at each of the steps he takes to arrive at that solution if he writes them down for us (displaying his thinking as a product). On the other hand, a well-written prose paragraph, a poem, and an oil painting can all be observed and analyzed. These end products and others like them can serve as "observables," which may help to indicate whether or not an expected learning outcome has occurred.

When selecting or writing instructional objectives, it is important to distinguish between those that specify observable behaviors and those that specify end products of behaviors.

The use of strong, active verbs, such as those in the second box, will yield objectives which are either observable or whose end products are observable. However, if the object of any of these verbs does not describe an observable end product, the resulting objective would be vague and nonobservable. For example, examine the following objective: "To explain the Middle East Crisis."

What is supposed to be explained? The *causes* of the Middle East Crisis? The *positions taken by each side* in the Middle East Crisis? The *political ideologies* involved in the Middle East Crisis? All of these, and more, are possible explanations. The problem is not in the verb, but in the object of the verb. Make certain that both the verb and its object are clearly defined, pointing to observable actions or observable end products.

Your Turn

SELECT OBSERVABLE OBJECTIVES

Mark each observable objective with an *O* and each nonobservable objective with an *N*. Keep in mind that to be an observable objective, either the action *or* the end product of that action must be visible, audible, touchable, etc.

_____ 1. To reduce fractions to their lowest denominator.

_____ 2. To locate the fulcrum on a balance beam weighted in a variety of ways.

_____ 3. To grasp the significance of the Monroe Doctrine.

_____ 4. To separate the incomplete sentences from the complete ones in a list containing both types.

_____ 5. To familiarize oneself with the rules of basketball before beginning to play the game.

_____ 6. When given a limited amount of time, to learn the Morse code.

_____ 7. To translate a passage from Plato's *Republic*.

LEARNING ACTIVITY 2.2

Obtain copies of teacher's manuals for a subject matter area of interest to you. Find the statements of objectives listed in these manuals and evaluate them. Are they well written, meeting the criteria for good objectives specified earlier in this chapter? If not, what is wrong with them? You may wish to keep a tally of the type of error you find most frequently.

Type of Error (if any)	*Tally*
1. No errors; well defined	_____
2. Not student-oriented	_____
3. Not descriptive of a learning outcome	_____
4. Not clear and understandable	_____
5. Not observable	_____

Mastery Test

OBJECTIVE 2   To select instructional objectives that will be useful to you and your students.

For each of the following pairs, check the objective which best meets the requirements for useful objectives.

1. _____(a)   To be able to develop a roll of black-and-white film.

   _____(b)   To understand how a developing agent works.

2. _____(a)   To select useful objectives.

   _____(b)   To know what makes an objective useful.

3. _____(a)   To select from alternative definitions the one which best defines the terms provided on Handout 10.

   _____(b)   To know the meaning of the terms on Handout 10.

4. _____(a)   To solve math problems requiring an understanding of the place holder.

   _____(b)   To understand problem-solving techniques.

5. _____(a)   To recognize the pictures of men in the news.

   _____(b)   To match the names of men in the news with their pictures.

6. _____(a) To select the good poems from good and bad examples.

   _____(b) To evaluate a set of poems.

7. _____(a) To remember the life cycle of the butterfly.

   _____(b) To label, from memory, a diagram of the life cycle of a butterfly.

8. _____(a) To hear clearly short and long vowel sounds.

   _____(b) To distinguish between short and long vowel sounds.

9. _____(a) To know the phonetic rules and their application in reading.

   _____(b) To sound out nonsense words.

10. _____(a) To punctuate a prose paragraph correctly.

    _____(b) To list the punctuation rules.

In the space provided, list four criteria for judging the quality of an instructional objective.

11. _____

12. _____

13. _____

14. _____

For each of the following objectives, determine the primary fault:

15. To grasp the meaning of conservation.
    (a) affectively oriented
    (b) teacher-oriented
    (c) vague and unobservable

16. To demonstrate to the students the need for cleanliness.
    (a) teacher-oriented
    (b) unobservable
    (c) student-oriented

17. To paint.
    (a) poorly defined product
    (b) vague
    (c) teacher-oriented

18. To do workbook, pp. 18–20.
    (a) vague
    (b) poorly defined product
    (c) a learning activity

19. To listen to the guest speaker from the narcotics division.
    (a) teacher-oriented
    (b) a learning activity
    (c) vague

Objective 3

To rewrite poorly written objectives.

LEARNING ACTIVITY 3.1

In order to correct poorly written objectives, you must first know what is wrong — what it is about the objective that makes it unacceptable. That shouldn't be too difficult if you remember what makes an objective acceptable. Review the criteria for well-written objectives in the list that follows.

A Well-Written Objective:

1. Is student-oriented.
2. Defines a learning outcome.
3. Is clear and explicit.
4. Describes an observable performance (or end product).

To say that an objective should be student-oriented means that the focus is on what the student does, *not* on what the teacher does. Consequently, objectives which describe teacher activities are unacceptable as instructional objectives. However, an objective can be student-oriented and still be unacceptable. If an objective specifies a learning activity rather than a learning outcome, it is unacceptable. Notice that both the teacher-oriented *and* the student-oriented learning activities are designed to help the student arrive at some learning outcome. Consequently, whenever an objective fails to meet either of the first two criteria stated above, the major problem is that learning activities (teacher-oriented or student-oriented) have been emphasized instead of the learning outcomes they serve.

The third and fourth criteria require that an objective be clear, explicit, and observable. As stated earlier, when an objective fails to meet these criteria, it is either because the student's performance was poorly described *(Watch the verbs!)* or the end product of that performance was not well defined *(Good direct objects are needed!)*.

There are three major problems with poorly written objectives:

The Major Problems of Poorly Written Objectives

1. An emphasis on learning activities.
2. A vague description of student performance.
3. Poorly defined products of student performance.

Each of these problems is discussed in turn and practice is provided for correcting each.

Correcting Problem 1

An Emphasis on Learning Activities. A common problem with instructional objectives is that they are stated in terms of learning activities, not in terms of learning outcomes. Sometimes objectives are stated as the teacher's objectives. For example, "Discuss with the student the relationship between good writing and the use of active rather than passive verbs." Notice that this describes what the teacher will do in guiding learning but does not describe the outcome expected of the students.

Another kind of error frequently made is one where the objective is stated in terms of a student activity. For example, "The students will work in groups, finding the passive verbs in a passage supplied by the teacher. Then they will change the passive verbs to active wherever possible." This may be a very worthwhile activity for the students and may lead them to some outcome, but it is not the outcome itself and, therefore, it is not useful as an instructional objective. What is really needed to guide both the students and teacher is a student-oriented learning outcome such as the following: "When given a passage containing passive verbs, the student should be able to improve that passage by changing those verbs to appropriate active verbs." This objective is stated so that it is clear what the students should be able to do *after* they have learned.

Once you realize that there is a close connection between any learning activity and its corresponding learning outcome, it becomes easier to correct this first problem of instructional objectives. Any learning activity, whether teacher-oriented or student-oriented, is designed to help the student reach some learning outcome. Consequently, whenever you have an objective stated as a learning activity instead of a learning outcome, you can convert it into an acceptable objective simply by answering the following question:

What will this learning activity help the student be able to do?

Take some examples of objectives specified in terms of activities instead of outcomes and try to answer the above question about each activity. In each case, the answer to the question should yield a learning outcome that will be usable as an instructional objective.

Suppose, for example, the teacher's manual accompanying a reading text suggests that the teacher place the new sight words on the blackboard, read them to the pupils, and offer assistance in saying them aloud. What will this series of teacher activities help the pupils to be able to do? It is fairly obvious that the idea behind the activities is to get the students to the point where they can recognize and pronounce each of the new sight vocabulary words. We might state this as a learning outcome as follows: "Upon seeing any one of the new sight vocabulary words found in the teacher's manual, the student should be able to pronounce the word correctly."

As another example, a seventh grade social studies teacher has students bring in news items which illustrate conflicts among nations. As the items are brought in, the students discuss them and attempt to identify the source of each conflict. Although several possible learning outcomes might result from this set of activities, a likely one would be: "When given enough information about a conflict among nations, students should be able to identify the source of that conflict." It is interesting to note that successfully reaching this learning outcome might enable students to apply that knowledge or skill to their own lives. The teacher might have long-range goals related to the students' ability to understand and deal with the sources of the conflicts within their own lives.

Suppose a teacher's lesson plan includes the following teacher-oriented objectives: "Show the students how rectangles and squares can be divided into two equal triangles. Review the rules for finding the area of a rectangle. Introduce the formula for computing the area of a triangle." What will the students be able to do because of the above teacher-oriented objectives? If the students listen carefully and understand the teacher's explanations, they should be able to explain the relationship between triangles and rectangles and probably should be able to apply the formula for computing the area of a triangle successfully. It is also true that other learning activities, such as practice problems, might be needed. The students might also draw two equal triangles within a rectangle, measure them, compute the area of the rectangle, and divide by 2 in order to obtain the area of the triangle. Such activities, in combination with the teacher-oriented objectives, should help the students reach the same objective.

In another case, suppose that a high school speech teacher decides to have the students listen to the Gettysburg Address. What will the student-oriented learning activity help the students be able to do? What learning outcome does this teacher have in mind? High school students could learn something about the type of sentence structure utilized by President Lincoln, or they might try to remember the major points being made in the address. Because it is a speech class, the teacher probably would not want them to be able to recall from memory the content of the Gettysburg Address. However, it is possible that the speech teacher would want the students to be able to pick out the point at which the introduction to the address stops and the main body of the address begins. That would lead them one step closer to the longer-range objective of being able to identify the transition points in a given speech.

Many good learning activities (lectures, assignments, projects, etc.) are *potentially* useful for helping students reach any one of a number of learning outcomes. Consequently, you should specify precisely what it is you want *your* students to learn from any given activity. If you do not do this, your students might approach the learning tasks inappropriately, looking for the wrong kinds of things and coming away with the wrong information or with incomplete skills. All too frequently students are asked to read material, listen to tapes, watch films, etc., but are never told *why* they are to do these things and precisely what is expected of them upon completion. Learning outcomes are tied to learning focus (selective perception), which, in turn, is tied to specified goals and objectives.

Your Turn

CORRECTING PROBLEM 1

Listed below are a number of teacher- and student-oriented learning activities. For each activity listed, answer the question, "What will this activity help the students be able to do?" Write your answer in the form of a clearly stated learning outcome. When you have completed this exercise, check your answers with the Answer Key that follows.

1. A class discussion about the effect of inflation on the economy.

_____

_____

_____

_____

2. The students will work out long-division problems on the blackboard. Their answers will be checked by the teacher and discussed with the class.

_____

_____

_____

_____

3. The students will watch a film on the use of the reference section in the library.

_____

_____

_____

_____

4. A spelling workbook includes the following instructions for the students: "Fill in the blanks in the following sentences. Use the words found in this week's review list."

_____

_____

_____

5. The students will try to write down the learning outcomes associated with given learning activities. They will check their answers with those of the instructor.

_____

_____

_____

ANSWER KEY
Your Turn: Correcting Problem 1

As you know, any given learning activity can be used to help the students attain a number of possible outcomes. Compare your answers with those given below and also with those written by your peers.

1. (a)   To be able to describe in two to three pages the effect of inflation on the economy.
   (b)   To be able to predict economic trends, given information about the rate of inflation.
   (c)   To be able to define *inflation*.
   (d)   To be able to cite examples (from news stories) of inflation's effect upon our economy.

2. (a)   To be able to solve long-division problems.
   (b)   To be able to identify errors made in an attempted solution to a long-division problem.

3. (a)   To be able to locate specified reference works in the library.
   (b)   To list the major types of reference works found in the library.
   (c)   When given the reference works discussed in the film, to be able to describe the kind of information each one contains.

4. (a)   To be able to spell review words correctly, when using those words in a sentence.
   (b)   To be able to spell words correctly long after they were first learned in spelling class.

5.   When given a learning activity, to be able to identify correctly what learning outcomes the activity would be likely to serve.

Correcting Problem 2

A Vague Description of Student Performance. Whenever the performance expected of the students is not clearly stated, the problem lies in the verb selected to describe that performance. The solution to this problem is relatively simple: Replace any vague, ambiguous verbs with strong, active verbs that describe observable actions. The objective "To know the multiplication tables" is obviously not clearly stated. Teachers undoubtedly want their students to be able to do more than simply recognize the multiplication tables, but how much more — to recite them, to write them, or both?

Examine the following objective: "To know how to shift a manual transmission." Does this objective mean that the student has "head-knowledge" or that the student has actually learned a skill? The verb used will make the difference. Suppose we replace the verb phrase "to know how to shift" with the phrase "to list the steps to take when shifting." The objective, as originally written, calls for "head-knowledge." But, if we delete the words "to know" and simply say "to shift a manual transmission," we are then specifying the skill of actually doing the shifting.

Suppose a teacher decides that it is important for his or her students "to comprehend what they read." Does this mean *recalling* the facts, or does it mean listing the main points made by the author? Perhaps it means having students explain what they read to someone else, using their own words. Then it would read, "To explain to someone else, in your own words, what you have read."

Now let's try correcting an affective objective, one that deals primarily with emotion and feeling. Suppose a teacher thinks it is important for his or her students "to enjoy science projects." It is difficult to decide what any given teacher might accept as evidence of enjoyment. This objective becomes much clearer when better verbs are selected. Any one of the following alterations could be made, each changing what enjoyment means slightly:

> To choose to work on a science project when given other possible choices.
>
> To smile while working on a science project.
>
> To ask for extra science projects to do.
>
> To check out books from the library explaining various science projects.

Now study the following examples, noting how changing the verb clarifies the description of the expected performance.

> ***Examples:*** *How to Correct Vague Descriptions of Student Performance*

Vague: To understand long division.
Clarified: To solve long-division problems.

Vague: To grasp the importance of good gestures.
Clarified: To use good gestures in each speech given.

Vague: To be familiar with recent research findings on the effects of smoking pot.
Clarified: To recall from memory the findings of recent research on the effects of smoking pot.

Vague: To realize the importance of warming up properly before each session.
Clarified: To warm up properly before each session.

Vague: To understand the weather.
Clarified: To predict the weather.

Vague: To follow a map.
Clarified: To use a map to find a designated place.

Notice that in some of the preceding examples it was necessary not only to change the verb but also to clarify the object of that verb (the whole verb phrase needed changing). You will get some practice doing that in the next section.

Your Turn

CORRECTING PROBLEM 2

Before you begin this exercise you may wish to look over the list of verbs found on p. 90. These are the kinds of verbs you will need to use in order to clarify the descriptions of student performances found in this exercise.

Correct each of the following objectives by changing the vague verbs (or verb phrases) to more observable ones.

1. To know the causes of the Civil War.

_____

_____

_____

2. To learn this week's French vocabulary words.

_____

_____

_____

3. To *really* know Chapter 3 in your chemistry book.

_____

_____

_____

4. To understand the difference between hard and soft woods.

_____

_____

_____

5. To know the rules for correct punctuation.

_____

_____

_____

ANSWER KEY

Your Turn: Correcting Problem 2

Suggested corrections are given below. Other corrections are possible. What is important is to use verbs that describe observable action (or end products of that action).

1. (a) To list the causes of the Civil War in writing.
   (b) To arrange the events causing (leading up to the beginning of) the Civil War in sequential order.

2. (a) To write the English equivalent of each French word in this week's vocabulary.
   (b) To use correctly each word in this week's French vocabulary in a conversation with the teacher.
   (c) To spell correctly each of the words in this week's French vocabulary.

3. (a) To recall the major facts in Chapter 3 and list them from memory.
   (b) To explain the contents of Chapter 3 to the teacher, using your own words.

4. (a) To sort a pile of wood into hard woods and soft woods.
   (b) To explain the difference between hard and soft woods in one page or less.
   (c) To list the names of the hard woods and the soft woods.

5. (a) To list the rules for correct punctuation.
   (b) To punctuate a paragraph correctly.
   (c) To correct the improper punctuation in a given paragraph.
   (d) To explain each punctuation rule and write a sentence illustrating the proper application of each rule.

Correcting Problem 3

Poorly Defined Products of Student Performance. To use a strong, active verb is to produce an observable objective — most of the time. However, there are times when more is needed. If the objective specifies an end product, something the student is expected to produce, then that product must also be clearly defined. Take, for example, the following objective: "To be able to solve problems in math." There is nothing wrong with the verb, "to solve." However, the object of that verb, "problems in math," is not well defined. What kind of problems? Addition? Subtraction? Multiplication? Division? Straight computation? Story problems?

Sometimes a good verb alone is not enough to produce a good objective. Study the following examples. Note, in each case, how a vague objective was clarified by specifying the object of the verb more precisely (thus more clearly defining the *product* of student performance).

Examples: How to Correct Poorly Defined Products of Student Performance

Poorly defined: To write well.
Specified: To write a paragraph containing a topic sentence and several supporting sentences.

or

To write all your letters with proper shape and form.

Poorly defined: To calculate area.
Specified: To calculate the area of any geometric plane which is defined by straight lines.

	Poorly defined:	To make introductions.
	Specified:	To introduce a person to another person (or group of persons).
		To write an introductory paragraph to an expository theme.

Your Turn

CORRECTING PROBLEM 3

In the following, mark well-defined products of student performance with a "+" and poorly defined products with a "−".

_____ 1. poetry

_____ 2. poems written in iambic pentameter

_____ 3. multiplication tables through 12 × 12

_____ 4. arithmetic facts

_____ 5. concepts listed in the summary of p. 17

_____ 6. major concepts of psychology

_____ 7. drawings

_____ 8. line drawings in two-point perspective

Correct the following objectives by specifying the products of student performance.

9. To recall the important history dates.

_____

_____

10. To explain ecology.

_____

_____

11. To interpret literature.

_____

_____

12. To describe democracy.

_____

_____

ANSWER KEY
Your Turn: Correcting Problem 3

1.− 2.+ 3.+ 4.− 5.+ 6.+ 7.− 8.+

9. To recall the dates of the events listed on Handout 2.

10. To explain how nature maintains a proper balance and how man can disrupt that balance.

11. To interpret a short story by describing the author's purpose and illustrating how he or she accomplishes that purpose.

12. To describe the primary characteristics of a democratic form of government.

LEARNING ACTIVITY 3.2

Get together with a small group of your peers. Each person in the group should write four to five objectives. At least three of those should be poorly written to illustrate the three problems discussed in this chapter. Exchange objectives and correct each other's poorly written objectives. Discuss the results.

Were any problem objectives "undiscovered"?

Were any improperly corrected?

Were any correct objectives made worse by attempts to correct them?

Was the original intent of the author left intact when a given objective was corrected?

What do you need to know about well-written objectives before you can purposely write one with a specific kind of error "built in"?

Mastery Test

OBJECTIVE 3   To rewrite poorly written objectives.

Each of the following objectives is poorly written. Identify the major problem and rewrite the objective to correct that problem.

1. To listen to the lecture carefully.

Problem _____

_____

Correction _____

_____

2. To see the value of learning how to compute percentage.

Problem _____

_____

Correction _____

_____

3. To show the class how to clean and oil a sewing machine.

Problem _____

_____

Correction _____

_____

4. To be organized.

Problem _____

_____

Correction _____

_____

5. To understand the problems of small, struggling nations.

Problem _____

_____

Correction _____

_____

6. To capture the students' interest.

Problem _____

_____

Correction _____

_____

7. To grasp the significance of Watergate.

Problem _____

_____

Correction _____

_____

8. To collect newspaper clippings about détente.

Problem _____

_____

Correction _____

_____

ANSWER KEY

Mastery Test, Objective 3

1. *Problem:*   Learning *activity* rather than outcome.
   Correction: To recall the major points being made in the lecture or to explain in your own words the major concepts presented in the lecture.

2. *Problem:*   Vague verb.
   Correction: To list actual situations in which it is necessary to be able to compute percentage.

3. *Problem:*   Teacher-oriented learning activity.
   Correction: To be able to clean and oil one of the sewing machines in class.

4. *Problem:*   Vague; no product of student performance.
   Correction: To organize your desk so that everything has its place and can be easily located; to organize a class project, assigning jobs in an equitable way; or . . . .

5. *Problem:*   Vague; unobservable.
   Correction: To describe the problems a small, struggling nation is likely to encounter; to present the pros and cons of solutions to the typical problems of small, struggling nations; or . . . .

6. *Problem:*   Teacher-oriented; vague.
   Correction: During a given lecture, students will ask many questions, take accurate notes, and contribute information they might have to the discussion.

7. *Problem:*   Vague; unobservable.
   Correction: To be able to predict future trends in American government which are likely to occur as a result of Watergate or to speculate about the future of America (economically, politically, etc.) if Watergate had gone unnoticed.

8. *Problem:*   Learning *activity* rather than outcome.
   Correction: To list the major political agreements coming out of the détente with the Soviet Union.

Objective 4

To write well-defined and useful objectives of your own.

LEARNING ACTIVITY 4.1

There are four simple steps* for writing good instructional objectives. Although these steps should normally follow the given order, you may occasionally wish to go back and rework a step before moving on. This constant monitoring of your own work, always checking against the criteria for well-defined objectives, will help you produce a clear list of objectives for your own use. The four steps are shown below. Each step will be discussed in turn.

* From *Evaluation: A Practical Guide for Teachers*, by T. D. TenBrink. Copyright © 1974 by McGraw-Hill Book Company. Used with permission.

Four Steps for Writing Instructional Objectives

1. Describe the subject matter content.
2. Specify the general goals.
3. Break down the general goals into more specific, observable objectives.
4. Check objectives for clarity and appropriateness.

Although these four steps can be applied to course planning as well as lesson planning, it is important to remember that you will not be able to write a set of objectives for an entire course in a short time. You will find it useful, therefore, to work on small units of instruction, one at a time. Eventually, you will have a set of objectives that will cover the full course you are teaching. However, your unit objectives and daily objectives should fit into the overall plan for your course. Consequently, the first two steps listed above should be fairly well completed before you begin working on the objectives for specific units of instruction or for daily lesson plans.

So that you will be able to see the interrelationship of all four steps, we will now proceed to develop a set of objectives for a complete course. We will develop objectives for a high school psychology course, because this is a subject area that all teachers should be familiar with. Examples from other subject matter areas at various grade levels will also be used as each step is explained. The four steps discussed here can be used for the development of objectives for any course at any grade level.

Step 1

Describe the Subject Matter Content.   Many things have to be considered when describing the content of a given course or unit of instruction. There are the major concepts to be covered, the relationship the material has to a broader base of knowledge, and the value of the content for the student. Perhaps the easiest way to get a good description of the content of a course is to answer the following questions:

In general, what is the course about?
How does this course fit into the total curriculum?
What would be included in an outline of the course?
What value does this course have for the student?

What is the course all about? The answer should be very general. All you need to do is describe the kinds of things the course will cover in a paragraph or two. Suppose you were writing a friend about what you will be teaching. This friend would probably not be interested in a long, detailed discourse of the subject matter; a general description of the kinds of concepts to be covered in the course would be sufficient. Such a summary could serve as the basis for a more detailed course outline. The summary, along with the main topics included in a course outline, will provide the basis for the selection of a textbook and other learning materials.

A summary for a high school psychology course is shown in Exhibit A. Read it carefully. Later you will see how the summary leads to a course outline and to the general goals of the course.

EXHIBIT A Subject Matter Content of High School Psychology Course

This introductory psychology course is designed to acquaint students with psychology as a science and as a potential area for further study, leading to a specialized career in psychology. Psychology will be discussed both as a research-oriented science, which is in the process of theory building, and as a science of practical application. The content of the course will center on the study of human behavior, seeking answers to such questions as "Why does man act the way he does, and what causes him to be the kind of being he is?" and "How does he function as an individual and as a group member?"

The aspects of human behavior that are most important to high school students will be stressed, such as problems dealing with the psychological, physical, and social development of man; personality; learning; motivation; mental health; and social psychology. The emphasis throughout the course will be on major psychological research findings and how these findings have been, and can be, applied to the solution of everyday problems.

If you had been asked to write a summary like the one in Exhibit A, what would you have included? Does a summary statement like this one help you to begin thinking about what the students might learn from such a course?

How does this course fit into the total curriculum? Once the general content of the course has been described, the next task is to write a short statement describing how the course fits into the total curriculum. In order to do this, you must know something about what else is being taught in the school system. You should know what kinds of courses your students have had and are likely to have after they finish your own course. Likewise, you will want to know what the other teachers of your course expect of their students.

Obviously, what is expected of students at various levels of a curriculum will vary considerably in terms of both skills and attitudes.

Suppose the high school psychology course is the first course of this type the students will be exposed to. It will lead some of them into more advanced courses in college and eventually to degrees in that field. For others, it will be the only course in psychology they will ever take. Think about what this means to the development of such a course. A "statement of fit" for this course is presented in Exhibit B. Read it carefully. How does it differ from one you might have written? Would such a statement differ considerably from one school system to the next?

EXHIBIT B Statement of Fit into Curriculum

This course is to be taught at the senior level and has no prerequisites. The only other area where students might encounter similar information is in home economics or one of the family-living courses. While most senior-level courses culminate a series of courses, this one really begins a sequence that will fit into the college curriculum. It is felt, however, that this course not only must serve the needs of students who will continue their studies in psychology but must also serve the needs of students about to go out into the working world. A greater understanding of what man is like, how he developed, how he thinks, what his emotional reactions are like, how he learns, and how he works with other men may be useful information for maintaining mental health and in learning to live with a variety of personalities.

What instructional goals came to mind as you read Exhibit B? Are there any goals that will not be appropriate because of limitations suggested by the statement in Exhibit B?

What would be included in an outline of the course? This third question involves specifying the major topics to be covered in the course in more detail. It should also determine a logical and defensible sequence for teaching those topics. Given a relatively complete course outline, one should be able to work on the development of instructional objectives for one part of the outline at a time. This will help make the task of writing objectives a manageable one. The outline for the high school psychology course is presented in Exhibit C.

EXHIBIT C   Suggested Course Outline

UNIT I. Psychology as a Science
    A. History of psychology
    B. Psychological theory
    C. Methodology of psychological research
    D. Applicability of psychological concepts and principles

UNIT II. How Humans Develop
    A. General theory
    B. Physical development
    C. Intellectual and emotional development
    D. Social development

UNIT III. Personality
    A. Theory of personality
    B. Measuring personality
    C. Individual differences in personality characteristics

UNIT IV. The Learning Process
    A. Learning theory
    B. Kinds of learning
    C. Measurement of performance
    D. Intelligence
    E. Learning to learn

UNIT V. Motivation
    A. Theories of motivation
    B. Extrinsic motivation
    C. Intrinsic motivation
    D. Motivating yourself and others

UNIT VI. Mental Health
    A. Indicators of mental health
    B. Factors accounting for mental health
    C. Neuroses and psychoses
    D. Maintaining mental health and preventing mental illness
    E. Physiological causes of mental illness

UNIT VII. Social Psychology
    A. Theories of social psychology
    B. Cultures and subcultures
    C. Nationalism
    D. The influence of the group

What value does this course have for the student? Notice that the topics in Exhibit C reflect the general content of the course as summarized in Exhibit A. What is *not* reflected in this course outline are the affective components of the course. Affective objectives are more likely to arise from a statement of the value of the course to the students. Such a statement for the high school psychology course is made in Exhibit D.

EXHIBIT D   List of the Values of this Course to the Students

1. Introduces the students to a new subject matter area.

2. Indicates to the students how psychology is a science which is important in all walks of life — in industry, in education, in business, in politics, in war, etc.

3. Helps the students to see the relationship between scientific research and the application of research findings to practical situations.

4. Gives the students information useful in helping them maintain their mental health.

5. Gives the students the basic tools with which to understand the behavior of people around them.

6. May help the students to understand the motives of others as well as their own motives.

7. Gives information about how we learn, which may be helpful in the improvement of their own learning strategies.

8. May make students more aware of the needs of others around them.

9. May help students understand the social pressures that operate within a society such as ours.

Most teachers hope to develop positive attitudes among their students toward the subject matter they are teaching. That is why the question "What value does this course have for the student?" is so important. A good way to answer this question is to imagine yourself having to defend your course to the students who must take it, to the parents of those students, and to the administrative staff of your school. Pretend, for a moment, that your course has just been introduced into the curriculum and you have been asked to write a defense of it for the school newspaper. Students, parents, and other people in the community are all interested in finding out why this course should be taught. The better you are able to tell them, the better base you will have for formulating the affective goals which you hope your students will accomplish.

The list of values found in Exhibit D not only suggests affective goals such as "becoming more aware of the needs of others" but also suggests cognitive ones such as "to understand the social pressures which operate within our society." These goals, you can see, could be readily translated into clear, observable objectives.

Your Turn

DESCRIBE THE SUBJECT MATTER CONTENT

Suppose you were asked to describe the subject matter content of a psychology course similar to the one described in Exhibits A through D. However, this time the students would be seventh and eighth graders.

1. How would the general course description differ from the one in Exhibit A?

2. How would the course outline differ from the one in Exhibit C?

3. Would the value of such a beginning psychology course be different for seventh and eighth graders than for high school seniors? How? Why?

4. Would there be differences that would not show up in a course description like the one found in Exhibits A through D? Where would these differences be made apparent?

Compare your own answers to these questions with the Answer Key that follows.

ANSWER KEY

Your Turn: Describe the Subject Matter Content

1. There would probably be very little difference. The general topics to be covered could remain the same. The level of understanding expected might be different for seventh and eighth graders, but that would not show up in a general description of course content. Because the course will not serve as a precursor to a college-level course in this case, less emphasis might be placed on research and more on how-to-do-it techniques.

2. Seventh and eighth graders might take a little longer to learn the concepts involved in these topics, so one might shorten the outline slightly. Also, one could replace some of the terms with more common-usage words which would appeal more to seventh and eighth graders.

3. Probably not.

4. Yes, the primary differences would probably be in the level of understanding expected and the kinds of learning activities that would be assigned. These differences would only show up in the specific, behavioral objectives at the unit level and in the assignments designed to help the students reach those objectives.

Step 2

Specify the General Goals.   In this step you will be determining in a general way what you would expect the students to be able to do. It is usually best to carry out this step in two parts. First, write down the general goals for the entire course. These will be most helpful (along with the course outline) when selecting textbooks, films, and other instructional materials. Second, specify general goals for each unit of instruction. These are intermediate goals and, therefore, should be somewhat more specific.

Look at the general end-of-course goals found in Exhibit E. These are some of the possible goals for the high school psychology course. Compare these goals to the summary of course content (Exhibit A) and the course outline (Exhibit C). The goals represent the first step in defining what the students should be able to do with the subject matter specified. Notice that the goals are not yet very observable. At this point that's not too serious. What's important is getting the general goals down on paper so that they can be rewritten according to our criteria.

EXHIBIT E   General Goals for High School Psychology Course

I. Terminal Goals

1. Students should understand what it means when we say that psychology is a science.

2. Students should know the major facts about the way in which men develop.

3. Students should know, in general, how man interacts with his environment, including his interaction with other humans.

4. Students will be aware of the various theories of personality, motivation, learning and mental health, and social psychology.

5. Students should be aware of the major research findings in the area of psychology.

6. Students should be able to apply major findings of psychology to the solutions of specific problems of human behavior and interaction.

7. Students should be more aware of their own typical behavior and the reasons for that behavior.

Your Turn

SPECIFYING GENERAL GOALS — PARTS 1 AND 2

Now try writing some general end-of-course goals for the psychology course. Do not duplicate those found in Exhibit E. You should be able to write at least five more general goals for this course. Examples of such additional goals are found in the Answer Key for Part 1. Compare what you have written with those examples.

Once the end-of-course goals have been determined, intermediate goals can be written for each unit of instruction. Again, do not worry about whether or not they are initially observable. First get them down in a general way, and then they can be rewritten.[6]

EXHIBIT F

II. The General Intermediate Goals for Unit I: Psychology as a Science

A. The Cognitive Goals

1. Students should know the major dates in the history of psychology.

2. Students should know the major avocations which have made psychology an important applied science.

3. Students should know the steps that are taken from the development of a theory to the research and testing of that theory to the final application of the research findings to practical situations.

B. Affective Goals

1. The student should appreciate the value of the science of psychology to a civilized country.

2. The student should show appreciation for the usefulness of various psychological theories.
3. The students should be sensitive to the problems of doing psychological research.

Exhibit F presents some possible goals for Unit I: Psychology as a Science. Three cognitive and three affective goals have been written. Read them carefully and then try writing some yourself. *Remember:* Unit-level goals should reflect the broader, end-of-course goals. Compare your work with the further examples of Unit I goals presented in the Answer Key for Part 2.

ANSWER KEY

Your Turn: Specifying General Goals

PART 1

Here are further general goals for a high school psychology course. Your goals may not be identical to these, but there should be some similarity between these and the ones you have written. If there is not, have your instructor check your work.

1. Students should be aware of their major personality traits, usual learning strategies, the intrinsic and extrinsic motivating factors that influence their decisions and behavior, and the ways in which they respond under social pressure.
2. Students should have an appreciation for the value of psychological research.
3. Students should have an understanding of the importance of specialists in the area of psychology.
4. Students should have an appreciation for the intricacies of personality development.
5. Students should have developed better study habits based on the principles of learning.
6. Students should have a better understanding of why people act the way they do.
7. Students should have developed attitudes of concern and understanding toward the mentally ill.

8. Students should have developed an attitude toward mental illness that is positive.

PART 2

Here are some further goals for Unit 1: Psychology as a Science. Many other goals could be written. They need not be written in observable terms, but they should be compatible with the end-of-course goals that have been specified.

Cognitive Goals

1. Students should know the major founders of psychological theory and the important points within their theories.
2. Students should be able to describe those aspects of psychology which make it a science.
3. The student should be able to list the methodological steps in psychological research.
4. The student should be able to define the major concepts and terms found in psychological science and research.

Affective Goals

1. The student should be able to accept differences that exist among the ideas of famous psychologists.
2. Students should enjoy doing simple psychological research.
3. Students should become interested in finding out more about specific aspects of psychology.

Step 3

Break Down the General Goals into More Specific, Observable Objectives.   In this step each general goal is broken down into its two major parts: the subject matter content and the expected student response to that content. Look at one of the general goals from Unit I of the psychology course:

> Students should know the major founders of psychological theory and the important concepts within their theories.

First of all, notice that the subject matter content is divided into: (1) the major founders of psychological theories and (2) the important concepts from each of these theories. When we finalize our list of objectives, these two areas should be kept separate, each serving as the basis for at least one objective. It is usually best to deal with only one area of the subject matter in a given objective.

Now we will take these descriptions of subject matter content and answer the following questions about each:

1. Is the subject matter content clearly defined and specific enough?
2. Precisely what response(s) do I want the students to make to that subject matter content?

In the above goal the subject matter content (the founders of psychological theory and concepts important to each theory) is fairly well defined. However, this goal could be made more specific by listing the major founders of theory. The most important concepts for each theory might also be listed.

Of course, the real problem with the above goal lies in the use of the vague, unobservable verb "to know." What observable student response could be accepted as evidence that a student "knows"? Would "to list in writing" be acceptable?

The following three objectives were derived from the above general goal. The subject matter content of that goal was clarified, and the expected student response to that content was more precisely specified.

1. Students should be able to list in writing all the founders of psychological theory discussed in the textbook.
2. Students should be able to match each important concept to the theory with which it is associated. (This goal is limited to the theories found in Unit I in the text.)
3. When given the name of an early psychological theorist, students should be able to identify the concept(s) which were central to the theory.

Try breaking down an affective goal:

> Students should become interested in finding out more about the specific aspects of human behavior which have been studied by psychologists.

Sometimes teachers fail to plan for the teaching of affective goals because these goals seem difficult to define in observable terms. However, it is relatively easy if you clearly define the subject matter content and then specify the *behavior(s)* that are likely to accompany the desired attitude toward that content. The following objective was derived from the above goal in just that way.

> In an open discussion about the value of psychology, students should ask questions that would help them discover what aspects of human behavior psychologists have studied.

In this objective the content is "questions" that would help them discover what aspects of human behavior psychologists have studied. The behavior expected is "to ask." Notice, however, that something else has been added: "In an open discussion about the value of psychology." This phrase suggests a condition or type of situation under which we expect the desired student behavior to occur.

Although not necessary to the formation of a good objective, a statement describing the *condition* under which we expect the student to respond is often helpful. Here is another such objective, derived from the above goal (the condition is italicized):

> *When given the task of formulating questions to be sent to famous living psychologists*, the students will include questions like: "What aspects of human behavior have psychologists studied?"

Besides a statement specifying the condition under which the student response is expected to occur, there is one other useful (though not necessary) addition which can be made to most objectives. There are times when it may be useful to specify the *level of performance* expected of the students. For example, we might derive the following objective from the above goal:

> When books and pamphlets describing the aspects of human behavior studied by psychologists are placed in the class library, the students will sign out *two or more* of these resources.

This objective has the criterion for success built in: two or more resources signed out.

Not only is it possible to set a standard (level of performance expected) for each student, but this can also be done for the class as a whole. By determining the level of performance of each student, each student's performance on that objective can be evaluated. By determining how well the class as a whole should learn, you assess your performance as a teacher. Suppose, for example, the above objective is written so it reads as follows:

> When books and pamphlets describing the aspects of human behavior studied by psychologists are placed in the class library, *at least 75 percent of the students* will sign out two or more of these resources.

Then, if less than 75 percent of the students reach the expected level of performance, the goal has not been reached (even though some of our students may have signed out two or more resources).

<hr>

*A Review: Breaking down general goals
into specific, observable objectives*

1. Break the goal into two parts: (1) subject matter content and (2) student response to that content.
2. Clarify the subject matter content and, where necessary, make it more specific.
3. Determine the expected student response(s) to each statement of subject matter content.
4. As needed, identify the conditions under which the student response is expected to occur and/or any useful criteria for judging the level of performance expected.

<hr>

Your Turn

BREAKING DOWN A GENERAL GOAL INTO SPECIFIC, OBSERVABLE OBJECTIVES

Write observable objectives for the following goal. Make certain you:

1. Identify the subject matter content and decide whether or not it is clearly enough defined. If not, describe what is needed to clarify it.
2. For each aspect of subject matter content identified above, describe at least one *observable* response the students might be expected to make to it.
3. If appropriate, specify the conditions under which the student response is expected to occur and specify a level of performance which would be acceptable.

   The students should understand the major concepts, terms, and principles used in psychological research.

_____

_____

_____

_____

_____

_____

_____

_____

_____

_____

_____

ANSWER KEY

Your Turn: Breaking Down a General Goal into Specific, Observable Objectives

Below are three objectives that could have been derived from the goal you were given. Compare your objectives to these. Do your objectives contain the necessary elements to make them understandable and observable? Also, compare your objectives with those written by your classmates.

1. When given a major concept or term used in psychological research, the student should be able to select from among a number of alternatives the one definition or example that best illustrates that concept or term.

2. When asked to write a short paper explaining the methodologies of psychological research, the student should be able to use correctly 10 out of 15 major concepts that were presented in class lecture.

3. When given a description of psychological research problems, the student should be able to select from among a number of alternatives the principle(s) that would be most appropriate to the solution of the problem.

Step 4

Check Objectives for Clarity and Appropriateness.   To some extent this last step may be unnecessary. If you do a good job in the first three steps, your objectives should be ready to use. However, a final check on your work may save you the embarrassment of trying to explain to your students what it was that you "really meant to say."

A good way to check for the clarity of your objectives is to have a friend (preferably one teaching the subject matter under consideration) review them. If your friend will tell you in his/her own words what each objective means, you can usually tell whether or not the objective is understandable. If it isn't, it probably needs clarification.

Not only must an objective be clearly stated in observable terms, but it must also be appropriate for your students. Use the following checklist to help you determine whether or not an objective is appropriate:

Criteria for Appropriate Objectives

_____   1. Attainable by the students within a reasonable time limit.

_____   2. In proper sequence with other objectives (not to be accomplished prior to a prerequisite objective).

_____   3. In harmony with the overall goals of the course (and curriculum).

_____   4. In harmony with the goals and values of the institution.

If your objectives are clearly stated in observable terms and meet the above criteria, they should be useful to both you and your students. Now take the Mastery Test for this objective. However, if you feel you would like more practice developing objectives, try the suggested additional learning activities or work through the exercises found in the Workbook that accompanies this Handbook.

The following additional learning activities can be done individually or in small groups. In either case, the results should be shared with the other class members.

LEARNING ACTIVITY 4.2

Select a unit of study from the psychology course outline found in Exhibit C. Develop a list of instructional objectives for one or more of the topics in the unit you selected. You will probably want to write general goals first and then break them down into more observable objectives.

LEARNING ACTIVITY 4.3

Exchange your set of objectives (from the activity above) for a set that was developed by a classmate (or group of classmates). Analyze the set you received in the exchange. For each objective in the set, identify the following parts:

1. The subject matter content. (Is there only one? Is it clearly defined?)
2. The expected response to that content. (Is it observable? Is it reasonable to expect the students will reach it?)
3. Where appropriate, the conditions under which the response is expected and/or the level of performance expected.

Mastery Test

OBJECTIVE 4   To write well-defined and useful objectives of your own.

List the four steps involved in writing instructional objectives.

1. _____

2. _____

3. _____

4. _____

5. General, end-of-course goals do not need to be written in observable terms. (true or false)

Write at least two observable objectives for each of the following three goals.

6. Students should understand how people learn.

(a) _____

_____

(b) _____

_____

7. Students should know what motivates people to act.

(a) _____

_____

(b) _____

_____

8. Students should understand the value of the metric system.

(a) _____

_____

(b) _____

_____

9. What are the two parts needed in a well-written instructional objective?

(a) _____

_____

(b) _____

_____

10. What are the two useful (although not always needed) parts of a well-written objective?

(a) _____

_____

(b) _____

_____

ANSWER KEY

Mastery Test, Objective 4

1. Describe the subject matter content.
2. Specify the general goals.
3. Break down the general goals into more specific, observable objectives.
4. Check these objectives for clarity and appropriateness.
5. True. When broken down into more specific objectives, the end-of-course goals should be observable. However, the general goals are just a step along the way toward the development of usable, observable objectives.

Below are suggested answers for items 6–8. Other possibilities exist. Make certain each objective written specifies a clearly defined subject matter content, an observable response to that content, and, where necessary, a statement describing the conditions under which the response is expected to occur and/or the level of performance expected in the response.

6. (a) Given a description of a learning task, students should be able to describe the process utilized by the learner to accomplish that task.
   (b) Describe the major variables affecting the learning process — tell what makes a learning task easier and what makes it more difficult.

7. (a) Given several possible "motivators" and a description of a particular human behavior, students should be able to select the "motivator(s)" which would most likely stimulate that behavior.
   (b) To list the major motivators of human behavior.

8. (a) To list the advantages and disadvantages of the metric system.
   (b) When given the choice between using the metric system or some other system for solving a given problem, the student should be able to explain why the use of the metric system would be more appropriate.

9. (a) A description of subject matter content.
   (b) An observable, expected response to that content.

10. (a) The conditions under which the student response is expected to occur.
    (b) Level of performance expected or level of performance that would be acceptable as evidence that the objective was met satisfactorily.

NOTES

1. See the Additional Readings at the end of this chapter.

2. A discussion on how to rework poorly written objectives follows later on in this chapter.

3. W. J. Popham, "The Instructional Objectives Exchange: New Support for Criterion Referenced Instruction," *Phi Delta Kappan* 52, 3 (1970): 174–175.

4. For further examples see Chapter 4 in T. D. TenBrink, *Evaluation: A Practical Guide for Teachers* (New York: McGraw-Hill Book Company, 1974).

5. This list was adapted from T. D. TenBrink, *Evaluation: A Practical Guide for Teachers* (New York: McGraw-Hill Book Company, 1974), p. 102.

6. Follow the suggestions for rewriting poorly written items when you rewrite your own objectives. These were discussed in objective 3 of this chapter.

ADDITIONAL READINGS

Burns, R. W. *New Approaches to Behavioral Objectives*. Dubuque, Iowa: Wm. G. Brown Company Publishers, 1972.

Gronlund, Norman E. *Stating Behavioral Objectives for Classroom Instruction*. Toronto: Macmillan Co., 1970.

Kibler, R. J., L. L. Barker, and D. T. Miles. *Behavioral Objectives and Instruction*. Boston: Allyn and Bacon, Inc., 1970.

Mager, Robert F. *Preparing Instructional Objectives*. Palo Alto, Calif.: Fearon, 1962.

Popham, W. James. "Probing the Validity Arguments Against Behavioral Goals." In R. C. Anderson, G. W. Faust, M. C. Roderick, D. J. Cunningham, and Thomas Andre, eds. *Current Research on Instruction*. Englewood Cliffs, New Jersey: Prentice-Hall, 1969.

Elizabeth Hamlin, Dietz/Hamlin.

ROBERT SHOSTAK

Lesson Presentation Skills

Objectives

1 To define set induction, explain its purposes, and give examples of when it is used as a lesson presentation skill.

2 To identify the unique characteristics of three basic sets and name the appropriate set to use when given a hypothetical series of classroom presentations.

3 To define stimulus variation and explain its purposes as a lesson presentation skill.

4 To describe the characteristics of five stimulus variation techniques and identify the different situations in which they are used in lesson presentation.

5 To define closure, explain its purposes, and give examples of when it is used as a lesson presentation skill.

6 To identify the unique characteristics of three basic types of closure and name the appropriate closure to use when given a hypothetical series of classroom presentations.

It's been a rough day and you still have a lot to do. But you need a break. Anyway, it's just about time for your weekly weakness on the tube — whether it's a detective, doctor, lawyer, or family show — so you turn on the set, sit back, wait for the screen to light up, and relax. If you are lucky, you missed the last commercial spot before the program begins. Now, in brilliant color, with the musical theme throbbing through a quick series of tension-producing, emotion-grabbing, "teaser" scenes, the world of your favorite hero or heroine begins. You settle down for the drama of the next fifty minutes or so.

Even the occasional television viewer is familiar with this opening format. Every successful TV series uses it. Actually there is really nothing new each week. The plot follows a familiar pattern — one which you could block out with little effort. What keeps you turning it on each week is, in large part, the stimulation you experience in viewing the latest in chase scenes, shootouts, or lifesaving medical techniques. Once the show satisfies the viewer's appetite for thrills, excitement, or pathos, the story winds down, the heros and heroines relax, the loose ends are all neatly tied together, and you can breathe easily once more, knowing that next week it will be back again.

It is no accident that TV uses this formula. Radio used it before TV, and before that dramatists practiced the art of teasing their audiences through a long list of weekly and monthly publications. Producers of popular television series meticulously plan, prepare, and direct their shows using audiovisual techniques designed *to get viewers "into" the show, to keep them glued to their sets, and to satisfy their needs for having participated in a complete experience.*

Learning theorists as well as practitioners interested in teacher training have known for some time how effective these techniques can be when skillfully employed by teachers in a classroom setting. Educators have developed elaborate schemes for classifying and analyzing the techniques and their underlying concepts. Although recent research[1] has identified 25 lesson presentation skills that are considered part of the classroom recitation process, the most frequently researched ones were found to be (1) introducing the lesson, or *set induction*;[2] (2) retaining student attention throughout the lesson, or *stimulus variation*;[3] and (3) providing reinforcement through planned summarizing procedures, or *closure*.[4]

Gage and Berliner, in their research, describe the most common teaching method as a combination of lecture, discussion, and individual instruction.[5] This combination method requires that teachers do a considerable amount of verbal structuring and directing of the lesson. Other research on teachers' verbal classroom behavior gives additional support to the fact that teachers do tend to do most of the talking in their classrooms. Flanders states that almost 70 percent of the talk that goes on in the average classroom is teacher talk.[6]

This does not mean that teachers should always talk more than students. It simply emphasizes the fact that in many situations teachers must assume the important role of presenter. Regardless of the grade level one teaches, the necessity of exposing students to new facts, concepts, and principles, of explaining difficult procedures, of clarifying conflicting issues, and of exploring complicated relationships more frequently than not places the teacher in the position of having to do a great deal of presenting. Consequently, any prospective teacher ought to be interested in mastering those skills needed to become an effective presenter.

Think back for a moment to our opening description of the formula for the successful TV show. The technique used to gain the attention of viewers and to prepare them for the action which follows can be compared to that used by Aubertine in his teacher training experiments.[7] Aubertine, using what he called the process of *set induction*, found that instructional "sets" (special kinds of activities which precondition the learner) can have a significant positive effect on learning.

You can probably recall from your own experience many examples of how prior instructions ("sets") have influenced your responses in a new situation. If you have been told that a particular person you are going to meet is a "jerk," a "brain," "aggressive," or "sneaky," you prepare yourself to behave in a certain way when you come face to face with that person. Your entire behavior pattern, both verbal and nonverbal, is influenced by your prior information or "set."

Similarly, you can compare the kinds of techniques used to maintain a high level of audience attention in a TV production with teachers' efforts at varying their physical or verbal behavior during a classroom presentation. Gage and Berliner cite numerous studies to show that when teachers skillfully vary their verbal and physical behavior in the classroom, there is a strong positive effect on student learning.[8] Again, your own experience undoubtedly confirms that the lecturer who drones on and on in the same monotonous tone inevitably has a dulling effect on most listeners. Your mind tends to wander, your attention is easily diverted, or your eyelids grow too heavy to hold open.

Last, consider the satisfaction of TV viewers when their hour of escape comes to a tidy end. There is a feeling of completeness, a sense that all is right with an orderly, regulated world. Similarly, learning theorists and teacher trainers have strong data to support the notion that skillful closing of a classroom presentation does enhance learning.

At the Stanford Center for Research and Development in Teaching, Margaret Bierly and others reported on the basis of survey research that most teachers are genuinely concerned with motivating and reinforcing their students.[9] In other words, they are interested in acquiring skills that will enable them both to initiate learning and to see that it is retained. Mastery of the three lesson presentation skills which follow is aimed at assisting you toward the same goal.[10]

Objective 1

To define set induction, explain its purposes, and give examples of when it is used as a lesson presentation skill.

LEARNING ACTIVITY 1.1

SET INDUCTION

Set induction refers to those actions and statements by the teacher that are designed to relate the experiences of the students to the objectives of the lesson.[11] Effective teachers use set induction to put students in a receptive frame of mind that will facilitate learning — be it physical, mental, or emotional.

A story is told about a traveler who came upon an old man beating his donkey in an effort to make the animal rise. The animal sat placidly in the middle of the road refusing to get up, and the old man continued to whip the animal until a stranger stepped up and stopped his hand. "Why don't you tell the donkey to rise?" asked the stranger. "I will," replied the old man, "but first I have to get his attention."

Set induction has this as its first purpose — *to focus student attention on the lesson.* DeCecco, after reviewing the relevant theory and research on motivation, says that the first motivational function of the teacher is "to engage the student in learning."[12] Gagné and Briggs, in describing the events of instruction, echo the same notion.[13]

As its second purpose, set induction attempts *to create an organizing framework for the ideas, principles, or information which is to follow.* Gage and Berliner, in discussing the importance of lecture introductions, speak of *advance organizers* — "telling students in advance about the way in which a lecture is organized is likely to improve their comprehension and ability to recall and apply what they hear."[14] DeCecco calls attention to what he terms the expectancy function of teachers. He bases this notion on research which has shown that teachers can best shape student behavior when students have been told in advance what is expected of them.[15]

A very dramatic and certainly controversial study which demonstrates the power of set induction was reported by Robert Rosenthal and Lenore Jacobson in their book, *Pygmalion in the Classroom.* The authors conducted an experiment in which they tested all of the pupils from kindergarten through grade six in a particular school. Teachers were told that the test ". . . will allow us to predict which youngsters are most likely to show an academic spurt."[16] In September following this testing period, each teacher was given a list of students and was told that the students on their lists were the ones most likely to show a marked improvement in their school performance. Actually, the student names had been chosen at random.

However, after three successive testing periods the researchers claim that the test performance of these randomly identified students actually began to rise to meet the erroneous expectations of their teachers. In other words, the teachers, being told that their students were likely to do well academically, worked with the children in such a way that these expectations became a reality. By passing their expectations on to their students, the teachers were actually practicing a form of set induction, which, in this case, had a positive effect on learning.

A third purpose of set induction is *to extend the understanding and the application of abstract ideas through the use of example or analogy.* An idea or principle that is abstractly stated can be difficult for many students to comprehend. Moreover, many students who do understand an idea or principle have difficulty in applying their knowledge to new situations. The clever use of examples and analogies can do much to overcome such limitations. Novelists, dramatists, and poets are particularly good at using analogies to create expanded meaning in their works.

For example, read the following short poem:

A Patch of Old Snow

There's a patch of old snow in a corner
   That I should have guessed
Was a blow-away paper the rain
   Had brought to rest.

It is speckled with grime as if
   Small print overspread it,
The news of a day I've forgotten —
   If I ever read it.

— Robert Frost[17]

Literally speaking, the poet is describing a patch of old snow which resembles an old newspaper. However, by use of metaphor (analogy) the poet creates a literary experience which enables the reader to extend his or her understanding far beyond the simple comparison of a patch of old snow to a discarded newspaper. At one level, the metaphor suggests that the snow, once fallen and now melted, has very little meaning in the grand scheme of things. Then, perhaps with tongue in cheek, Frost seems to suggest that what is recorded in the newspaper — today or yesterday — may not really be much more important than the remains of an old snowfall.

The fourth and last purpose of set induction is *to stimulate student interest and involvement in the lesson.* A great deal of research has been carried on over the years on student motivation and the need to increase the student's interest in learning. Maria Montessori observes how strong involvement in play activities can keep a young child motivated and interested in a single game over an extended period of time. The point here is that active involvement at the beginning of a lesson can increase curiosity and stimulate student interest in the lesson.[18] A good example is the teacher who wishes to teach the concept of categorizing and brings a collection of baseball player cards, record jackets, or even a basket of leaves to class. Then the students, divided into groups, are asked to categorize their collections and explain how and why they did what they did.

LEARNING ACTIVITY 1.2

Now that set induction has been defined and its purposes explained, you are ready to focus on when teachers generally use set induction in the course of a lesson. To understand set usage better, think of a classroom lesson as a game. Bellack, in his research on the language used by teachers to direct classroom lessons, talks about "structuring moves [which] *set the context* for the entire classroom *game.*" [19] Furthermore, he views the lesson as containing several "subgames," each of which is identified primarily by the type of activity taking place during a given period of play.

For example, the teacher plans during the course of a lesson to carry on several different activities such as reading, writing, and discussion, each dealing with different subject matter. Each new activity can be seen as a subgame within the context of a larger game, the entire day's lessons. The teacher, then, must structure each situation so that students can participate (play) effectively in the lesson (game).

The kinds of classroom situations (subgames) for which it is necessary to employ a set are innumerable. To assist you in learning when to employ set induction in your own lessons, study carefully the list which follows.

Examples of When to Use Set Induction

To begin a long unit of work in which the class might be studying plants, rockets, or local government.

To introduce a new concept or principle.

To initiate a discussion.

To begin a skill-building activity such as reading comprehension or visual discrimination.

To introduce a film, TV program, record, or tape.

To initiate a question-and-answer session.

To prepare for a field trip.

To present a guest speaker.

To introduce a homework assignment.

To begin a laboratory exercise.

To redirect a presentation when you see that students do not understand the content.

Mastery Test

OBJECTIVE 1
To define set induction, explain its purposes, and give examples of when it is used as a lesson presentation skill.

Questions 1 and 2 are designed to determine your knowledge and comprehension level. Successful completion of these questions meets the objective of the learning activity. Question 3 is designed to test a more advanced level of learning — analysis and application. It is a "bonus" and tests your ability to identify and analyze a set when it is being used in a teaching situation.

1. Define set induction as a teaching skill and explain three specific purposes it serves in lesson presentations.

   _____

   _____

   _____

   _____

   _____

   _____

   _____

   _____

2. Describe briefly three different situations in which you would use set induction in making a classroom presentation.

   _____

   _____

   _____

   _____

   _____

3. Identify and explain how set induction has been employed in the presentation of this chapter.

   _____

   _____

   _____

   _____

   _____

ANSWER KEY
Mastery Test, Objective 1

1. *General definition:* Should include the idea that a set is something a teacher does or says in order to relate the experiences of students to the objectives of the lesson.

   Any three of the following purposes could be listed: (1) to focus student attention on lesson, (2) to create an organizing framework for the information to be learned, (3) to extend the understanding and applications of the lesson content, and (4) to stimulate student interest in the lesson.

2. You may use any of the situations described in the examples or include situations of your own creation.

3. The author used previous TV viewing experiences of the reader and drew an extended analogy of what the TV director does in the presentation of a drama to what the teacher must do in the presentation of a classroom lesson.

Objective 2

To identify the unique characteristics of three basic sets and name the appropriate set to use when given a hypothetical series of classroom presentations.

LEARNING ACTIVITY 2

Now that you know what set induction is and the general purposes for which it is used, you are ready to learn the distinguishing characteristics of three basic types of set and the appropriate application of each during the lesson presentation.

Three Basic Sets
1. Orientation
2. Transition
3. Evaluation

In the material which follows you should familiarize yourself with the general characteristics of the set first and then examine carefully the set model and application analysis which follow. The analysis is keyed directly to the general characteristics which precede each set model.

1. ORIENTATION SET

Characteristics

(a) Used primarily to focus the student's attention on the presentation the teacher is about to make.
(b) Employs an activity, event, object, or person which the teacher knows students have interest in or experience with.
(c) Provides a structure or framework which enables the student to visualize the content or activities of the presentation.
(d) Aids in clarifying the goals of the lesson presentation.

Set Model

The teacher has planned to get into the topic of percent and is aware of students' interest in local baseball fortunes. The teacher decides to introduce the unit with a brief discussion of the previous day's game. Talk is directed to batting averages, and the teacher demonstrates how they are calculated. Students are permitted to work out one or two of the averages for favorite players.

Application Analysis

This set is most appropriately used for introducing a unit on percent or the concept of percent itself. Referring to the general characteristics for the orientation set listed above, you should note the following:

(a) The orientation set focuses students' attention on the concept of percent, which is the unit or topic being initiated by the teacher in this lesson.
(b) It uses an event (like yesterday's baseball game) and an activity that are familiar to the students and in which they have considerable interest.
(c) It provides a ready frame of reference (batting averages) for application of the percent concept to other situations.
(d) Through teacher comment, the concept of batting averages and percent can be easily connected to help clarify the goals of the new unit or topic.

2. TRANSITION SET

Characteristics

(a) Used primarily to provide a smooth transition from known or already covered material to new or unknown material.
(b) Relies heavily on the use of examples (either verbal or nonverbal), analogies, and student activities the teacher knows students have interest in or experience with.

Set Model

The students working in a science unit have already demonstrated in the first part of their lesson some basic understanding of mixtures. The teacher has planned to conduct an experiment to demonstrate visually the concept of mixtures. He or she brings to class several bottles of different kinds of popular salad dressings. The students are directed to experiment with the various bottles and observe differences in their appearance before and after they are vigorously mixed.

Application Analysis

This set is most appropriately used to begin a laboratory exercise. Referring to the general characteristics for the transition set listed above, you should note the following:

(a) It is used specifically to provide a smooth transition from what the students already know (knowledge of mixtures) to the new material to be covered in the lesson.
(b) It relies on the use of an activity (experiment) which is familiar to all the students.

3. EVALUATION SET

Characteristics

(a) Used primarily to evaluate previously learned material before moving on to new material or skill-building activities.

(b) Relies heavily on student-centered activities or student-developed examples and analogies that demonstrate understanding of previously learned content.

Set Model

Students have been reading short stories and examining the techniques authors use to create a mood through the setting. The teacher begins the lesson by providing the class with a list of words which suggest different moods. Each student is asked to select one word and tell how he or she, as an author, might create a setting appropriate to the suggested mood.

Application Analysis

This set is most appropriately used to initiate a discussion or question-and-answer session. Referring to the general characteristics for the evaluation set listed above, you should note the following:

(a) It is being used to determine how well students understand the relationship of setting to mood.

(b) It relies on student-developed examples which demonstrate their understanding of the relationship of setting to mood.

Mastery Test

OBJECTIVE 2

To identify the unique characteristics of three basic sets and name the appropriate set to use when given a hypothetical series of classroom presentations.

1. Below is a list of the characteristics of the three basic sets. Following the last characteristic in the list, you will find each of the three basic sets appropriately numbered. In the space provided next to each set, place the letters of the characteristics which apply to that set.

(a) Used primarily to provide a smooth transition from known or already covered material to new or unknown material.

(b) Employs an activity, event, object, or person which the teacher knows the students have interest in or experience with.

(c) Aids in clarifying the goals of the lesson.

(d) Relies heavily on student-centered activities or student-developed examples and analogies which demonstrate understanding of previously learned content.

(e) Used primarily to focus students' attention on the presentation which the teacher is about to make.

(f) Provides a structure or framework which enables the student to visualize the content or activities of the presentation.

(g) Used primarily to evaluate previously learned material before moving on to new material or skill-building activities.

(h) Relies heavily on the use of examples (either verbal or nonverbal), analogies, and student activities the teacher knows students have interest in or experience with.

(1) Orientation _____

(2) Transition   _____

(3) Evaluation   _____

2. Read carefully each of the following classroom situations. Then, for each situation, suggest which type of set is most appropriate and give a reason for the choice you make.

Situation 1.   The class has been working on a unit in government. During the first part of the period the students have been viewing a short filmstrip on the three branches of government. The filmstrip is not an in-depth experience but gives a good overview. The teacher wishes to use the remainder of the period to promote a more thorough understanding of the role or function of each branch of the government with a different kind of activity.
   Indicate which type of set is most appropriate at this point and defend your answer in terms of its unique characteristics.

_____

_____

_____

_____

_____

Situation 2.   You are introducing the study of pollution and the environment to your class. It is important that you "get off on the right foot."
   Indicate which type of set is most appropriate at this point and defend your answer in terms of its unique characteristics.

_____

_____

_____

_____

_____

Situation 3.   You are exploring the world of work with your class and have an excellent film you wish to show.
   Indicate which type of set is most appropriate at this point and defend your answer in terms of its unique characteristics.

_____

_____

_____

_____

_____

Situation 4.   Your class has been studying the letters of the alphabet. You wish to use part of the day to take up this subject matter again and determine how far your students have come in being able to place the letters in order.
   Indicate which type of set is most appropriate at this point and defend your answer in terms of its unique characteristics.

_____

_____

_____

_____

_____

Situation 5.   Your class has been working on different techniques to put life into their writing. In this lesson you wish to present the idea of using descriptive words to paint verbal pictures.

Indicate which type of set is most appropriate at this point and defend your answer in terms of its unique characteristics.

_____

_____

_____

_____

_____

ANSWER KEY

Mastery Test, Objective 2

1. (1) Orientation   b, c, e, f
   (2) Transition   a, h
   (3) Evaluation   d, g

2. Your answers could be different from the ones suggested here. If your reasons are sound and you defend your choice of answer well, they should be acceptable.

   Situation 1: Evaluation set   *Reason:* The evaluation set would be used to determine how well the students understand the filmstrip or could apply what they learned in the new activity.

   Situation 2: Orientation set   *Reason:* The orientation set would be used to focus student attention on importance or significance of pollution and the environment.

   Situation 3: Orientation set   *Reason:* The orientation set would focus attention on the important concepts or ideas in the film.

   Situation 4: Evaluation set   *Reason:* The evaluation set would be used to see how well students learned the alphabet through a new activity.

   Situation 5: Transition set   *Reason:* The transition set moves the students from knowledge of previously learned writing techniques to new ones.

STIMULUS VARIATION

Think of yourself, for a moment, talking with a small group of friends at your usual outdoor meeting spot on campus. The conversation is animated, everyone is deeply involved, when suddenly there is a loud BANG! You all jump. The conversation stops almost instantly and all heads turn, as if one, in the direction of the sound. Similar thoughts are probably rushing through everyone's mind — car backfire? gun shot? bomb explosion? Well, whatever, you have just experienced stimulus variation.

A few moments later you are sitting in class. The professor is at the front of the room and has been talking now for about fifteen minutes. He has not moved from the spot where he first sat down on the edge of his desk when class began. His voice drones on and on. As time passes you may feel your eyes growing heavy. You are experiencing a lack of stimulus variation.

Objective 3

To define stimulus variation and explain its purposes as a lesson presentation skill.

LEARNING ACTIVITY 3

Stimulus variation refers to those teacher actions, sometimes planned and sometimes spontaneous, that are designed to develop and maintain a high level of student attention during the course of a lesson by varying the presentation. The effective teacher not only is knowledgeable regarding stimulus variation techniques but also knows how and when to employ them at critical times in a lesson presentation.

In its simplest form stimulus variation represents movements, sounds, or visual impressions which change or vary over time. You can watch or listen to the same sight or sound only so long before you want a change. TV directors, as noted in the introduction to this chapter, understand this problem very well. Once they have gained the audience's attention, they must hold it. So they shift the pace of their show using a number of stimulus variation techniques. They shift from dialogue to action, use fade-ins and fade-outs, shift from one locale to another, and use numerous other audio and visual techniques to make certain the audience stays with the show.

Music provides another good example of how stimulus variation works. Classical symphonic pieces usually begin with an opening movement in a fast tempo, followed by a contrasting slower movement. The third movement is usually dancelike in nature, and the final or fourth movement is again rapid in nature. Popular music, as well, is written and performed in different tempos with the express purpose of influencing one's mood or feeling.

Gagné says that learning takes place when three elements are present — the learner, the stimulus, and the response.[20] The stimulus, of course, may take many forms, the most familiar being textbooks, films, recordings, lectures, and discussions. Thus, as learning theorists have traditionally used the term, stimulus variation refers to the medium and materials employed in a learning situation.

In our use of the term, the focus will be directly on the teacher, who is both a source of and a conscious manipulator of stimuli. Strong support for this notion is given by Gage and Berliner, who cite and discuss the most recent research depicting the teacher as both a stimulus and a manipulator of stimuli.[21] You will understand this dual role of the teacher better once the purposes of stimulus variation are explained.

An easy way to understand the purposes of stimulus variation is to view it as part of a basic communications model. In any communications model there is a sender and a receiver. In Figure 4.1 the teacher and student(s) alternate in the role of sender and receiver. Under ideal conditions, the channel or medium through which messages are sent and received would be free of interference or what is sometimes referred to as "noise"; consequently, the chances for accurate reception and valid responses would be extremely good. Unfortunately, the classroom does not offer ideal communication conditions. However, by skillfully applying stimulus variation techniques, teachers can reduce the level of interference and thereby improve the communication system.

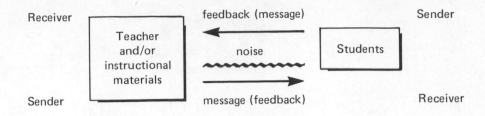

FIGURE 4.1 A basic communications model.

Consider, for a moment, the kinds of interference or "noise" that the teacher must overcome in the average classroom situation. The following list, although incomplete, will give you some idea of what you are up against:

1. Excessive talk
2. Tuning out
3. Physically uncomfortable surroundings
4. Semantic confusion

1. *Excessive talk,* whether from students or teachers, sets up interference in the communication channel in two different ways. Have you ever tried to communicate anything when more than one person at a time was talking? On the other hand, what happened when you were confronted with a teacher who talked and talked and talked? In all probability it resulted in a loss of attention to the presentation. Both conditions produce "noise" in the communication channel.

2. *Tuning out,* regardless of its cause, represents another kind of interference or "noise" in the communication channel. Lack of interest in the subject matter, learning disabilities, deep concern over personal problems, and daydreaming are but a few of the many forms of "tune out" present in all classrooms. Each of these conditions can be a strong deterrent to successful communications.

3. *Physically uncomfortable surroundings* are another difficult kind of interference to overcome. Overheated rooms during the cold winter months or unairconditioned rooms in extremely warm climates take a terrible toll on student attention and motivation. Many of the open classroom schools built in the early 70s have modified their open, barnlike architecture. Excessive noise levels in the open rooms made it extremely difficult for teachers to conduct lessons. Some research has even shown that aesthetically unpleasant classrooms may have a detrimental effect on the student's ability to learn.

4. *Semantic confusion* is another frequent reality in the communication process. The teacher, relying on previous learning or experience, may begin the verbal flow of his presentation on the assumption that students have a similar learning set. Unfortunately, this assumption (similarity of experience or a clear understanding of previously learned material) is often incorrect. Many students are simply unable to comprehend the teacher's language. The message keeps coming, but students are unable to decode it; the resulting semantic confusion destroys the communication process.

The skillful teacher realizes the existence of these communications problems and attempts to avoid or overcome them by using stimulus variation. The skillful use of these techniques will enable the teacher to (1) focus and maintain student attention on the lesson, (2) provide special emphasis to key points in the presentation, and (3) change the pace of the lesson.

Mastery Test

OBJECTIVE 3 To define stimulus variation and explain its purposes as a lesson presentation skill.

1. Define stimulus variation as a teaching skill and explain its purposes in lesson presentations. You must include the following points in your answer:
   (a) A general description of stimulus variation.
   (b) Three specific purposes of stimulus variation.

_____

_____

_____

_____

_____

_____

_____

_____

_____

ANSWER KEY

Mastery Test, Objective 3

1. (a) *General definition:* Should include the concept that stimulus variation refers to those teacher actions, planned or spontaneous, that are designed to develop and maintain a high level of student attention during a lesson by varying the presentation.

   (b) 1. Focus and maintain attention on lesson.
   2. Provide emphasis to key points in a presentation.
   3. Change the pace of a lesson.

Objective 4

To describe the characteristics of five stimulus variation techniques and identify the different situations in which they are used in lesson presentation.

LEARNING ACTIVITY 4

Now that you know what stimulus variation is and the general purposes for which it is used, you are ready to examine the distinguishing characteristics of various techniques.

Stimulus Variation Techniques

1. Kinesic variation
2. Focusing
3. Shifting interaction
4. Pausing (silence)
5. Shifting senses

1. Kinesic Variation

Kinesic variation, simply stated, is a teacher's physical ability to move from one location to another in the classroom for the express purpose of improving communication. The technique is not difficult and can be accomplished through any combination of the following actions:

(a) Move freely from right to left and then from left to right in front of the classroom.
(b) Move freely from front to back and then from back to front.
(c) Move freely among and/or behind students.

Such simple teacher movements can have an important effect on student behavior. The physical shift from one part of the room to the other causes the students' attention to be focused directly on the teacher during the presentation. The important thing to remember in using this technique is not to distract the student by your actions. Rapid, jerky, or nervous movements can irritate students, interrupting rather than enhancing communication.

2. Focusing

The term *focusing* will be used here in a very special sense that relates to the intention of the teacher. Focusing is the teacher's way of intentionally controlling the *direction* of student attention. This control is accomplished either through verbal statements, through specific gestural behaviors, or by some combination of the two.

The use of focusing to enhance communication is well documented. In recent years the use of nonverbal communication has been elevated to a high art by such well-known performers as Marcel Marceau, the world renowned mime.

A number of years ago a university professor who wished to demonstrate the use of positive reinforcement to encourage verbal student responses conducted a simple experiment. Without telling the class beforehand, he asked a question of one of the students sitting in the front of the room. When the student began her response, the professor gave her his undivided attention using direct eye contact only. As the student continued to speak, the professor nodded, smiled, and threw in a verbal "aha" every once in a while. The student responded with more talk. The professor continued to nod and smile, and the student kept right on talking.

Although the question had been answered long ago, the professor's simple gestures, acting as reinforcers, served to encourage additional commentary. This activity lasted about seven or eight minutes. After that time the class, almost as if on cue, burst out laughing. Everyone, by then, knew what was going on. This true story indicates just how effective gestures can be not only as psychological reinforcers but as a highly effective means of controlling the direction of student attention.

Some examples of focusing will make clearer this concept of controlling the direction of student attention.

Examples of Different Types of Focusing

Verbal

"*Look* at that diagram!"
"*Listen* closely to this!"
"Here's something *really* important!"
"*Watch* what happens when I connect these two points!"
"*Follow* the flowchart carefully!"
"*Observe* the difference in the colors!"
"*See* the picture?"

Gestural

Using a pointer to indicate an object.
Turning the body in the direction of an object.
Nodding the head.
Using the hands expressively.
Motioning with the arms.
Tapping or clapping the hands.
Raising the eyebrows.
Smiling.
Frowning.

Verbal–Gestural

(Teacher points to diagram.) "Look at that diagram!"
(Teacher nods in direction from which sound is to come.) "Listen closely to this!"
(Teacher taps on blackboard where student has just completed an arithmetic example.) "Here's something *really* important!"
(Teacher uses visual pointer on the opaque projector.) "Follow the flowchart carefully!"
(Teacher lifts hand above head, fingers extended, and brings arm down slowly, simulating gentle rain with fluttering fingers.) "The rain fell *gently* on the ground!"

3. Shifting Interaction

Gagné and Briggs describe in detail the "events of instruction" which are designed to move the learner "from 'where he is' at the beginning of a lesson to the achievement of some capability identified in the lesson's objective."[22] One important element in planning these "events of instruction" is the *interaction style* the teacher chooses to use. In this chapter three basic interaction styles — teacher–group, teacher–student, student–student — will be emphasized.

Teacher–group interaction is a teacher-centered instructional style where the teacher is usually lecturing or demonstrating to the class as a whole. Although questions may be asked, they are directed to the group as a whole rather than to a specific individual.

Example

In this situation the teacher might be showing students alternate problem-solving techniques for a problem in mathematics; presenting in a social studies class important historical background information related to a political problem not available in a text; or demonstrating the use of a power tool to students in a woodworking class.

Teacher–student interaction is a teacher-directed rather than teacher-centered instructional style. In this situation the teacher directs student recitation and/or discussion. Questions are used to engage specific students in the lesson.

Example

This type of interaction is used frequently when students have been assigned to read something in or out of class and the teacher has prepared a series of questions based on the material contained in the reading. The questions usually range in difficulty from simple recall to interpretation, and the teacher directs these questions to particular students in the class or may ask for volunteers.

Student–student interaction is a student-centered instructional style where the teacher's role consists of redirecting student questions to other students for comment or clarification. The teacher may also ask one student to explain something to another student, thus encouraging student–student interaction.

Example

In classroom discussions of any kind, students will frequently initiate their own questions or comment on something the teacher has said. The teacher, rather than responding, attempts to withdraw from the discussion by redirecting the question or comment to other students with statements like "What do *you* think Joseph meant by that remark, Nancy?" or "How would you answer Rand's question, Elena?"

The deliberate patterning of these interaction styles — using first one then another, as the events of the lesson dictate — can provide the stimulus variation necessary to maintain a high level of student attention and involvement in the lesson.

4. Pausing (silence)

Recent research has attempted to evaluate the effect that pausing has upon the communication process. Although speech and theater people have long known the power of the "pregnant pause," scholars have only recently begun studying such matters as the frequency, duration, and uses of planned silence or pausing.

Unfortunately, too many teachers lack the ability to use pauses effectively in the classroom. Experience shows that many beginning teachers are, in fact, afraid of silence. They seem to fear what might happen if the sound of the teacher's voice stopped for even a moment. As a result of this fear of silence many teachers come to use teacher talk not as a means of effective communication but as a defense mechanism to maintain classroom control.

As a stimulus variation technique, the effective use of pausing or silence can enhance your teaching in numerous ways:

1. It can break informational segments into smaller pieces for better understanding. Reading oral problems or dictating material for transcription requires careful attention to the effective use of pausing.
2. It can capture attention by contrasting sound with silence (alternating two distinctly different stimuli). Remember that attention is maintained at a high level when stimuli are varied, not when you increase the intensity of a single stimulus.
3. It can be a signal for students to prepare for the next teacher action.
4. It can be used to emphasize or underscore an important point.
5. It can provide time for thinking about a question or formulating an answer.
6. It can prevent teachers from unconsciously dominating discussion.
7. It encourages teachers to listen to individual student responses. (Remember, you do not listen well when you are talking.)
8. It can create suspense or expectation. The effective reader of all types of literature uses the pause to stir the emotions and heighten the anticipation of the listener.
9. It can help provide a model of listening behavior for other students.
10. It can be used to show disapproval of undesired student behavior.

5. Shifting Senses

During a classroom presentation students can normally process information on five different "channels." You know them better as the five senses — seeing, touching, smelling, tasting, and hearing. Media experts within the field of education now have research evidence to support their long-standing claim that the student's ability to absorb and process information can be significantly increased by appealing to their senses of sight and sound alternately.[23]

Unfortunately, as stated earlier in this chapter, research of another kind indicates that what actually goes on in classrooms is an overwhelming amount (70%) of teacher talk.[24] Experience supports Flanders's claim that most of what is communicated in elementary and secondary school classrooms is done through verbal stimuli, either spoken or written. Yet, when a group of teachers were asked what they felt was the most important language skill to teach, only 16% thought listening was the most important.

Consider for a moment the media background of today's students. They watch the most television, buy the most records and audiocassettes, and watch the most movies of any student population in history. How can classroom teachers who talk most of the time appeal to students brought up on such a rich diet of sensory stimuli? They cannot!

Teachers must take advantage of the fact that students possess five senses and plan to appeal to all five sensory channels in their presentations. Specifically, stimulus variation can be accomplished through any combination of sensory shifts. Some effective shifts might be:

(a) Listen → See → Listen
(b) See → Listen → See
(c) Listen → Smell → Listen
(d) Smell → Listen → Smell
(e) Listen → Touch → Listen
(f) Touch → Listen → Touch
(g) Listen → Taste → Listen
(h) Taste → Listen → Taste

To help you understand how each of these shifts might come about, a brief example of each follows:

(a) *Listen → See → Listen*

Teacher explains verbally → points to prepared chart → continues with further verbal clarification.

(b) *See → Listen → See*

Teacher flashes slide on screen → turns projector off and follows with verbal commentary → flashes slide once more.

(c) *Listen → Smell → Listen*

Teacher verbally explains chemical change → allows students to smell fumes → continues with further verbal clarification.

(d) *Smell → Listen → Smell*

Teacher permits students to smell an Indian spice → follows with verbal explanation → permits students to smell spice again.

(e) *Listen → Touch → Listen*

Teacher explains verbally the concept of texture → permits students to feel various fabrics → follows with additional verbal clarification.

(f) *Touch → Listen → Touch*

Teacher allows students to run soil samples through their fingers → follows with verbal explanation → permits further student examination of soil.

(g) *Listen → Taste → Listen*

Teacher verbalizes about Dutch cheeses → permits each student to taste cheeses → follows with additional verbal commentary.

(h) *Taste → Listen → Taste*

Students sample foods to discover textures → teacher discusses results of tasting → students are permitted to retaste foods.

Mastery Test

OBJECTIVE 4 To describe the characteristics of five stimulus variation techniques and identify the different situations in which they are used in lesson presentation.

1. Five techniques a teacher may use to employ stimulus variation as a lesson presentation skill are:

_____

_____

_____

_____

_____

2. Give one example of how each stimulus variation technique might be used to focus or maintain student attention on the lesson presentation.

_____

_____

_____

_____

_____

_____

3. Identify, in the space provided below, the type of stimulus variation being described.

_____ (a) The teacher points to spot on globe as she begins her talk on Western bloc countries.

_____ (b) After a brief lecture the teacher throws a broad question out to the class.

_____   (c) The teacher moves from his desk toward the window as he notes how weather can affect one's mood.

_____   (d) The teacher uses the blackboard to illustrate a concept which he has been explaining verbally.

_____   (e) The teacher asks the class a question, gets no immediate response, and waits until she sees a hand raised tentatively in the rear of the room before she says anything.

_____   (f) "There are two (the teacher raises two fingers high in the air) critical issues facing underdeveloped countries."

_____   (g) "We have discussed the difference in tone-color of the main instruments in the concert band. Now let's listen to a brief demonstration of how each one sounds."

_____   (h) "I've told you what I liked best about the story. Now let's hear what you liked best."

_____   (i) As the teacher reaches the climax of the story he is reading to class, he stops and looks up slowly, eyes opened wide.

_____   (j) As she talks, the teacher moves to the side of the room where a student appears to be daydreaming.

ANSWER KEY

Mastery Test, Objective 4

1. Stimulus variation techniques
   (1) Kinesic variation
   (2) Focusing
   (3) Shifting interaction
   (4) Pausing (silence)
   (5) Shifting senses

2. Examples
   (1) In order to focus attention on herself/himself, the teacher would move slowly across the room as she/he continues to explain.
   (2) Teacher points to the eye while saying the Spanish word for eye.
   (3) Teacher starts by working with large group and then breaks the class into small committees.

   (4) Teacher remains silent to gain attention of noisy class before beginning to read directions.
   (5) Teacher lectures and uses overhead projector.

3. Type of stimulus variation described:
   (a) Focusing (verbal)
   (b) Shifting interaction
   (c) Kinesic variation
   (d) Shifting senses
   (e) Pausing
   (f) Focusing (verbal/gesture)
   (g) Shifting senses
   (h) Shifting interaction
   (i) Focusing (gesture/pausing)
   (j) Kinesic variation

CLOSURE   In the introduction to this chapter the concept of closure was likened to the practice of TV directors who faithfully bring their weekly shows to a comfortable close. Think how uncomfortable the TV viewer would be not knowing what punishment the wrongdoer was to receive or how the detective actually solved the crime. Is there any reason that classroom learners should feel any differently regarding information being presented within a classroom context? With this in mind, let us proceed to our final lesson presentation skill, that of closure.

Objective 5

To define closure, explain its purposes, and give examples ..... .ien it is used as a lesson presentation skill.

LEARNING ACTIVITY 5.1

Closure refers to those actions or statements by teachers that are designed to bring a lesson presentation to an appropriate conclusion. Teachers use closure to help students bring things together in their own minds, to make sense out of what has been going on during the course of the presentation.

A good way to think about closure is to consider it the complement of set induction. If set induction is an initiating activity of the teacher, then closure is a culminating activity. Research into the psychology of learning indicates that learning increases when teachers make a conscious effort to help students organize the information presented to them and to perceive relationships based on that information.

Another good way to view closure is to compare it to the paper-and-pencil process of lesson planning. A good lesson plan will usually indicate where the students will be going, how they will get there, and how they will know when they have arrived. Making certain that students know *when they have arrived* is the result of the skillful teacher's use of closure. Gage and Berliner suggest that although research has not given us "assurances about the causal effectiveness (for learning) of these kinds of teacher behavior" (i.e., closure techniques), nevertheless, the most effective teachers seem to practice closure consistently.[25]

Closure, then, has as its first purpose *to draw attention to the end of a lesson or lesson segment.* Unfortunately, many teachers have neglected the development of this important skill.

Your own experience will tell you that typical closure procedure goes something like this:

Teacher A: "Okay. There's the bell! Get going — you'll be late for your next class!"

Teacher B: "Enough of this! Let's close our books and line up for recess."

Teacher C: "The bell? All right, we'll stop here and pick up at the same point tomorrow."

Teacher D: "Any questions? No? Good. Let's move on to the next chapter."

Certainly the students are aware that something has concluded in each case, but that is about all. These unsophisticated forms of closure completely ignore the fact that effective learning depends on the effective sequencing of lesson presentations. And one of the most important events in effective sequencing is providing opportunity for feedback and review.

The teacher who uses closure effectively understands the importance of cueing students in to the fact that they have reached an important point in the presentation and that the time has come to wrap things up. This activity must be planned just as carefully as its counterpart, set induction, and timing is critical. The teacher must be aware of the clock and must begin to initiate closure proceedings well before the activity is due to end.

Consequently, a second major purpose of closure is *to help organize student learning.* Simply calling attention to the lesson's conclusion is not enough. A great deal of information and a great many activities may have been covered, and it is the teacher's responsibility to tie it all together into a meaningful whole. The learner, just like the TV viewer, should not be left with a feeling of incompleteness and frustration. Like the TV detective who explains to the audience how the various pieces of the puzzle finally formed a coherent picture, so the skillful teacher should recapitulate the various bits and pieces of his or her lesson and make them into a coherent picture for the learner.

Finally, closure has as its third purpose *to consolidate or reinforce the major points to be learned.* Having signaled the end of the lesson and made an effort to organize what has occurred, the teacher should briefly refocus on the key ideas or processes presented in the lesson. The ultimate objective here is to help the student retain the important information presented in the lesson and thus increase the probability that he or she will be able to recall and use the information at a later time.

Gagné and Briggs, in discussing information storage and retrieval, have this to say: "When information or knowledge is to be recalled, . . . the *network of relationships* in which the newly learned material has been embedded provides a number of different possibilities as cues for its retrieval."[26]

Closure, then, is the skill of reviewing the key points of a lesson, of tying them together into a coherent whole, and finally, of ensuring their use by anchoring them in the student's larger conceptual network.

LEARNING ACTIVITY 5.2

Now that closure has been defined and its purposes explained, you are ready to focus specifically on when the teacher uses closure in the course of the lesson. You should be able to understand more easily when closure is used if you completed the section on set induction. In that section a lesson was compared to a game containing several "subgames." In the classroom situation such "subgames" might involve a lesson introducing some new concept or skills or an activity with some combination of reading, writing, viewing, or discussing. Each of these activities can be viewed as a "subgame" within the context of a larger game — an entire class period for a particular subject or an entire day of nondepartmentalized instruction.

The role of the teacher is to structure each situation (subgame) so that it begins and ends in such a way as to promote student learning. This is the function of both set induction and closure technique. To assist you in learning when to use closure in a lesson presentation, study carefully the following list of situations:

Examples of When to Use Closure

To end a long unit of work in which the class might be studying animals, or the family, or a country.

To consolidate learning of a new concept or principle.

To close a discussion.

To end a skill-building activity such as locating words in the dictionary or practicing basic functions in arithmetic.

To follow up a film, TV program, record, or tape.

To close a question-and-answer session.

To consolidate learning experiences on a field trip.

To reinforce the presentation of a guest speaker.

To follow up a homework assignment reviewed in class.

To end a laboratory exercise.

To organize thinking around a new concept or principle (e.g., all languages are not written, or different cultures reflect different values).

Mastery Test

OBJECTIVE 5   To define closure, explain its purposes, and give examples of when it is used as a lesson presentation skill.

1. Define closure as a teaching skill and explain three specific purposes it serves in lesson presentations.

_____

_____

_____

_____

_____

2. Try responding to the following statements by placing the letter *T* next to those which are true and the letter *F* next to those which are false.

_____ (a) Closure as a lesson presentation skill is a natural complement to set induction.

_____ (b) Closure is less important than set induction, because students can tell by the clock when the class period ends.

_____ (c) Closure helps students know when they have achieved lesson objectives.

_____ (d) One of the purposes of closure is to draw attention to the end of a presentation.

_____ (e) Good closure opens the opportunity for students to review what they are supposed to have learned.

_____ (f) Closure is a natural phenomenon and does not require planning.

_____ (g) One of the purposes of closure is to help organize student learning.

_____ (h) Timing is critical in using closure.

_____ (i) Closure helps to get your lesson off on the right foot.

_____ (j) One of the purposes of closure is to consolidate or reinforce the major points to be learned in a presentation.

3. Describe briefly ten different situations in which you could use closure in your lesson presentations.

_____

_____

_____

_____

_____

_____

_____

_____

_____

_____

ANSWER KEY

Mastery Test, Objective 5

1. *General definition:* Should include the idea that closure is something a teacher says or does which brings a presentation to an appropriate close.

   Purposes:
   (1) To draw attention to the end of a lesson.
   (2) To help organize student learning.
   (3) To consolidate or reinforce major points to be learned.

2. (a) T. Whereas set induction *initiates* instruction, closure *terminates* it.
   (b) F. Clocks tell time, but only teachers can close a lesson.
   (c) T. Appropriate use of closure enables students to evaluate their own understanding of a lesson.
   (d) T. Closure signals the natural conclusion of a presentation sequence.

   (e) T. One purpose of closure is to recapitulate the important points in a lesson presentation.
   (f) F. Effective closure does not occur naturally but requires conscious control by the teacher.
   (g) T. Closure helps provide a coherence to learning through review.
   (h) T. Since closure is a part of a planned sequence of instructional events, it requires careful timing.
   (i) F. Closure *terminates* a lesson, whereas set induction *initiates* it.
   (j) T. Through review and evolution closure helps students organize and retain learning.

3. You may use any of the situations described in the examples or include situations of your own creation.

Objective 6

To identify the unique characteristics of three basic types of closure and name the appropriate closure to use when given a hypothetical series of classroom presentations.

LEARNING ACTIVITY 6

Now that you know what closure is and the general purposes for which it is used, you are ready to learn the distinguishing characteristics of three basic types of closure and the appropriate application of each during the lesson presentation.

Three Basic Closures

1. Review
2. Transfer
3. Serendipity

Closure relies heavily on two widely used general teaching procedures, overview and practice. Overview provides the student with an opportunity to organize and place in proper perspective key concepts or processes set forth in the presentation. Practice, generally speaking, gives the student an opportunity to apply learned material in familiar situations. The effectiveness of these general procedures is well documented in both verbal and skill learning.[27]

In the material on the next few pages you should familiarize yourself with the general characteristics of the closure and then examine carefully the closure model and application analysis which follow. The analysis is keyed directly to the general characteristics that precede each closure model. In reviewing each of the models, it is important to note *first* that each closure does not necessarily need to reflect all the characteristics attributed to it, and *second* that frequently a teacher will combine one or more types of closure, depending on the nature of the presentation being made.

1. REVIEW CLOSURE

Characteristics

(a) Attempts to draw students' attention to a closing point in the lesson.
(b) Reviews major points of teacher-centered presentation.
(c) Reviews sequence used in learning material during the presentation.
(d) Provides summary of important student-oriented discussion.
(e) Relates lesson to original organizing principle or concept.

Closure Model A

The lesson is in geography, and the teacher has planned to introduce two basic concepts: (1) man as the active shaper of his environment, and (2) environment as a limiting context within which man must operate. The teacher has reached the critical point in the lesson where he or she wishes to call students' attention to the fact that the presentation of the first concept is ready for closure.

Teacher closure: "Before moving to the next important idea, the restrictions which environment places on man, let's review the main points I've already covered on how man can play a critical role in shaping the environment." The teacher then proceeds to review the major points of the presentation, using either a prepared outline or one developed on the chalkboard during the lesson.

Application Analysis

This closure is appropriate to use when you wish to help students organize their thinking around a new concept before moving on to a new idea. Referring to the general characteristics listed above for this closure, you should note the following:

(a) It draws attention to end of lesson with verbal cue, "before moving to the next important idea."
(b) It reviews important points of the teacher's presentation.
(c) It helps organize student thinking around the first concept presented by utilizing an outline on the chalkboard.

Closure Model B

The lesson is in language arts, social studies, science, etc., and the teacher is conducting a discussion around some specific issue which is important in the lesson plan for that particular day. The time has come to bring the discussion to a close.

Teacher closure: Teacher calls on specific student and says, "Elena, would you please summarize what has been said thus far and point out what you felt were the major points covered?"

Application Analysis

This closure is appropriate to use when you wish to bring a classroom discussion to a close. Referring to the general characteristics listed above for this closure, you should note the following:

(a) It draws attention to the fact that teacher is calling for a temporary end to discussion by requesting a student summary.
(b) It summarizes what students have been discussing.
(c) It helps students to organize or rearrange their own ideas by specifically asking for students to point out major points made in the discussion.

2. TRANSFER CLOSURE

Characteristics

(a) Attempts to draw students' attention to a closing point in the lesson.
(b) Asks students to extend or develop new knowledge from previously learned concepts.
(c) Permits students to practice what they have learned.

Closure Model A

The lesson is in American history. The class has been given the homework assignment of recording the reaction in 1939–1941 of private citizens, the President, members of Congress, and the press to the idea of going to war. After reading student responses to that assignment, the teacher senses that the students seem to have the idea and wishes to close.

> *Teacher closure:* "Your responses to this homework assignment have been very good. Now let's turn to the present day and compare the responses of private citizens, the President, members of Congress, and the press to the current situation. How are they alike and how do they differ?"

Application Analysis

This closure technique is appropriate to use when following up on a homework assignment being reviewed in class before moving on to application of ideas newly learned. Referring to the general characteristics for this closure listed above, you should note the following:

(a) It draws attention to the close of the assignment through teacher's comment or approval, "Your responses to this homework assignment have been very good!"

(b) It reviews material covered in the assignment by having students extend their knowledge of what they have already learned about the past to what is happening in the present.

Closure Model B

The lesson is in mathematics and the teacher is presenting a general reading skills approach to problem solving: (1) preview, (2) identify details or relationships, (3) restate problem in own words, (4) list computational steps to be taken. The time has come to see how well the students have understood the use of the new procedure.

> *Teacher closure:* "Before you try to use this new approach to problem solving by yourselves, let's list the steps on the chalkboard and try to apply them to the first problem in your textbooks on page 27. When you finish, I will ask some of you to share with the class your experience using this new technique."

Application Analysis

This closure technique is a good one to use when ending a skill-building activity and you wish to help students consolidate what they have learned. You will have to refer to the characteristics above for *both review and transfer* in the analysis which follows:

(a) It draws attention to close of the presentation by teacher's verbal signal, "Before you try to use this approach . . . let's list the steps . . ."

(b) It reviews the sequence used in learning new reading skills during the presentation.

(c) It permits students to practice immediately what they have learned.

Closure Model C

The lesson is in science and the teacher is conducting an experiment involving the process of photosynthesis. Students were introduced to the concept earlier in the lesson. The time has come to bring the demonstration to a close.

> *Teacher closure:* "Before writing your conclusions to this experiment on your laboratory exercise sheets, let's review by listing the steps in the photosynthesis process."

Application Analysis

This closure technique is a good one to use when bringing a laboratory exercise to a close. It allows you to review the observations before students write their conclusions. You will have to refer to the characteristics above for *both review and transfer* in the analysis which follows:

(a) It draws students' attention to the completion of the exercise by causing them to pause for reflection before writing their conclusions.

(b) It reviews the new concept of photosynthesis by relating it to the laboratory experiment just conducted.

(c) It helps students to organize their thinking and extend their knowledge about a concept through its application in a laboratory setting.

3. SERENDIPITY CLOSURE

Characteristics

(a) Teacher looks for "unsuspected" closure. Frequently during a lesson a unique situation will arise that will provide the teacher with an excellent (but unplanned) opportunity to close on a key idea. Or the teacher will perceive something in a way never seen before and can use this new perception to develop material into a new pattern or structure.

Closure Model

The lesson could be taking place at any grade level or in any subject matter area. The class has been studying effective study habits and has been spending a brief part of each lesson discussing them. Today, the class discussion was focused on how interruptions break our concentration. Just before the discussion begins to reach a closure point, a voice on the intercom interrupts with a brief message (a situation which happens often and at the most inopportune times).

> *Teacher closure:* "There it goes again! Would you believe it? How many of you can tell me how what just happened is related to what we have just been discussing?"

Application Analysis

This closure technique can be used only when the situation happens to present itself and the teacher is sharp enough to pick it up. You will have to refer to the characteristics above for *both serendipity and transfer* in the analysis which follows:

    (a) It uses an unplanned event to provide a natural closure to a discussion.

    (b) It asks students to extend their knowledge about the material just covered to a new situation.

Mastery Test

OBJECTIVE 6   To identify the unique characteristics of three basic types of closure and name the appropriate closure to use when given a hypothetical series of classroom presentations.

1. Below is a list of the characteristics of the three basic closure techniques. Following the last item in the list you will find each of the three basic closure techniques appropriately numbered. In the space provided next to each closure technique, place the letter(s) of the characteristic(s) which apply to that set.

    (a) Asks students to extend or develop new knowledge from previously learned concepts.
    (b) Reviews major points of presentation.
    (c) Situation just happens to present itself for an effective close.
    (d) Relates lesson to original organizing principle or concept.
    (e) Reviews sequence used in learning material during the presentation.
    (f) Permits students to practice what they have learned.
    (g) Provides summary of important discussion.

        (1) Review   _____

        (2) Transfer   _____

        (3) Serendipity   _____

2. For each of the examples below, in the spaces provided, you are to name a closure technique which appropriately fits the situation and state specifically the characteristic function of the technique. You must use each of the three basic techniques at least once.

    (a) You have just completed a presentation on the steps one takes in preparing a green salad.

        Closure technique: _____
        Characteristic:

    _____

    _____

    (b) You have just completed a demonstration of parallel bar exercise and have asked students to try the exercise.

        Closure technique: _____
        Characteristic:

    _____

    _____

(c) You have reached a point in a class discussion at which it would be appropriate to close.

Closure technique: _____
Characteristic:

_____

_____

(d) The teacher begins a lesson on theme in literature by comparing it to the threads running through a colorful tapestry.

Closure technique: _____
Characteristic:

_____

_____

(e) At an unexpected juncture in the lesson, a student makes an important discovery which lends itself to a really effective close.

Closure technique: _____
Characteristic:

_____

_____

(f) You are ready to close a history lesson covering the major events leading to World War II.

Closure technique: _____
Characteristic:

_____

_____

(g) You have presented an important concept to the class and asked them how the idea might be used in other situations.

Closure technique: _____
Characteristic:

_____

_____

ANSWER KEY
Mastery Test, Objective 6

1. (1) Review   b, d, e, g
   (2) Transfer   a, f
   (3) Serendipity   c

2. (a) *Closure technique:* Review
      Characteristic: Review sequence learned in presentation

   (b) *Closure technique:* Transfer
      Characteristic: Students are permitted to practice what is taught

   (c) *Closure technique:* Review
      Characteristic: Summarize main ideas

   (d) *Closure technique:* Review
      Characteristic: Relates lesson to original organizing principle (i.e., analogy of threads in tapestry)

   (e) *Closure technique:* Serendipity
      Characteristic: Unsuspected closure

   (f) *Closure technique:* Review
      Characteristic: Review of major points

   (g) *Closure technique:* Transfer
      Characteristic: Allows students to apply something learned in different circumstances

NOTES

1. Margaret Bierly et al., "Cataloguing Teacher Training Materials in a Computerized Retrieval System: Separating the Baby from the Bath Water" (Paper presented to the American Educational Research Association, Chicago, April 1974), p. 6.

2. H. E. Aubertine, "An Experiment in the Set Induction Process and Its Application in Training" (Ph.D. diss., Stanford University, 1964).

3. "Stimulus variation" as a lesson presentation skill was originally developed for use in a teacher training setting by Dr. D. C. Berliner for the Stanford Center for Research and Development in Teaching, Stanford University, Stanford, California.

4. "Closure" as a lesson presentation skill was originally developed for use in a teacher training setting by Dr. W. D. Johnson for the School of Education, Stanford University, Stanford, California.

5. N. L. Gage and David C. Berliner, *Educational Psychology* (Chicago: Rand McNally & Company, 1975), p. 482.

6. Ned A. Flanders, *Teacher Influence, Pupil Attitudes, and Achievement*, U.S. Department of Health, Education, and Welfare, Office of Education, Cooperative Research Monograph no. 12 (Washington, D.C.: U.S. Government Printing Office, 1965), p. 1.

7. Aubertine, *op. cit.*

8. Gage and Berliner, *op. cit.*, p. 516.

9. Margaret Bierly et al., *Teacher Training Products: The State of the Field*, Research and Development Memorandum no. 116 (Stanford University, California, Stanford Center for Research and Development in Teaching, January 1974), p. 22.

10. The prototype modules for these lesson presentation skills were developed and field tested by Dr. Francis T. Sobol for the School of Education at Florida International University, Miami, Florida, in 1972–1973.

11. "Set induction" as a lesson presentation skill was developed for use in teacher training by Dr. J. C. Fortune and Dr. V. B. Rosenshine for the School of Education, Stanford University, Stanford, California.

12. John P. DeCecco, *The Psychology of Learning and Instruction: Educational Psychology* (Englewood Cliffs, New Jersey: Prentice-Hall, 1968), p. 159.

13. Robert M. Gagné and Leslie J. Briggs, *Principles of Instructional Design* (New York: Holt, Rinehart & Winston, 1974), p. 123.

14. Gage and Berliner, *op. cit.*, p. 496.

15. DeCecco, *op. cit.*, p. 162.

16. Robert Rosenthal and Lenore Jacobson, *Pygmalion in the Classroom* (New York: Holt, Rinehart & Winston, 1968), p. 7.

17. Robert Frost, *You Come Too* (New York: Holt, Rinehart & Winston, 1959), p. 23.

18. Maria Montessori, *The Montessori Method* (New York: Schocken Books, 1964), p. 170.

19. Arno A. Bellack et al., *The Language of the Classroom* (New York: Teachers College Press, Columbia University, 1966), p. 134.

20. Robert M. Gagné, *Conditions of Learning* (New York: Holt, Rinehart & Winston, 1959), p. 32.

21. Gage and Berliner, *op. cit.*, p. 516.

22. Gagné and Briggs, *op. cit.*, p. 123.

23. Gerald M. Goldhober, "PAUSAL: A Computer Program to Identify and Measure Pauses," *Western Speech* 37 (Winter 1973): 23–26.

24. Flanders, *op. cit.*, p. 1.

25. Gage and Berliner, *op. cit.*, p. 524.

26. Gagné and Briggs, *op. cit.*, p. 132.

27. Robert M. W. Travers, *Essentials of Learning: An Overview for Students of Education* (New York: Macmillan Co., 1967), p. 201.

ADDITIONAL READINGS

Aubertine, H. E. "An Experiment in the Set Induction Process and Its Application in Training." Ph.D. dissertation, Stanford University, 1964.

Bellack, Arno A., et al. *The Language of the Classroom.* New York: Teachers College Press, Columbia University, 1966.

Bierly, Margaret, et al. "Cataloguing Teacher Training Materials in a Computerized Retrieval System: Separating the Baby from the Bath Water." Paper read at the American Educational Research Association, Chicago, April 1974.

Bierly, Margaret, et al. *Teacher Training Products: The State of the Field.* Research and Development Memorandum no. 116. Stanford Center for Research and Development in Teaching, Stanford University, Stanford, California, 1974.

DeCecco, John P. *The Psychology of Learning and Instruction: Educational Psychology.* Englewood Cliffs, New Jersey: Prentice-Hall, Inc., 1968.

Flanders, Ned A. *Teacher Influence, Pupil Attitudes, and Achievement.* U.S. Department of Health, Education, and Welfare, Office of Education, Cooperative Research Monograph no. 12. Washington, D.C.: U.S. Government Printing Office, 1965.

Gage, N. L., and David C. Berliner. *Educational Psychology.* Chicago: Rand McNally & Company, 1975.

Gagné, Robert M. *Conditions of Learning.* New York: Holt, Rinehart & Winston, 1959.

Gagné, Robert M., and Leslie J. Briggs. *Principles of Instructional Design.* New York: Holt, Rinehart & Winston, 1974.

Goldhober, Gerald M. "PAUSAL: A Computer Program to Identify and Measure Pauses." *Western Speech* 37 (Winter 1973): 23–26.

Montessori, Maria. *The Montessori Method.* New York: Schocken Books, 1964.

Rosenthal, Robert, and Lenore Jacobson. *Pygmalion in the Classroom.* New York: Holt, Rinehart & Winston, 1968.

Travers, Robert M. W. *Essentials of Learning: An Overview for Students of Education.* New York: Macmillan Co., 1967.

MYRA SADKER AND DAVID SADKER

Questioning Skills

Objectives

1 To classify classroom questions according to Bloom's *Taxonomy of Educational Objectives: Cognitive Domain.*

2 To construct classroom questions on all six levels of Bloom's *Taxonomy of Educational Objectives.*

3 To describe the nature and dynamics of (a) wait time, (b) reinforcement, and (c) probing questions in increasing the quantity and quality of student response.

The student teacher was attractive and composed. She quickly dispatched with the administrative details of classroom organization — attendance records and homework assignments. The classroom chatter about the Saturday night dance and the upcoming football game subsided as the tenth grade students settled into their seats. The students liked this teacher, for she had the knack of mixing businesslike attention to academic content with a genuine interest in her students. As the principal of Madison High walked by her room, he paused to watch the students settle into a discussion about *Hamlet.* Classroom operation appeared to be running smoothly, and he made a mental note to offer Ms. Ames a contract when her eight weeks of student teaching were over.

Had he stayed a little longer to hear the discussion, and had he been somewhat sophisticated in the quality of verbal interaction, he would not have been so satisfied.

Ms. Ames: I would like to discuss your reading assignment with you. As the scene begins, two clowns are on stage. What are they doing? Cheryl?

Cheryl: They are digging a grave.

Ms. Ames: Right. Who is about to be buried? Jim?

Jim: Ophelia.

Ms. Ames: Yes. One of the grave diggers uncovers the skull of Yorick. What occupation did Yorick once have? Donna?

Donna: He was the king's jester.

Ms. Ames: Good. A scuffle occurs by Ophelia's graveside. Who is fighting? Bill?

Bill: Laertes and Hamlet.

Ms. Ames: That's right. In what act and scene does Ophelia's burial occur? Tom?

Tom: Act V, Scene 1.

Throughout the forty-five minute English class, Ms. Ames asked a series of factual questions, received a series of one- and two-word replies

— and Shakespeare's play was transformed into a bad caricature of a television quiz show.

It is extremely important that teachers avoid ineffective questioning patterns such as the one above, for the questioning process has always been crucial to classroom instruction. The crucial role that questions play in the educational process has been stated by a number of educators.

> To question well is to teach well. In the skillful use of the question more than anything else lies the fine art of teaching; for in it we have the guide to clear and vivid ideas, and the quick spur to imagination, the stimulus to thought, the incentive to action.[1]

> What's in a question, you ask? Everything. It is the way of evoking stimulating response or stultifying inquiry. It is, in essence, the very core of teaching.[2]

> The art of questioning is . . . the art of guiding learning.[3]

It was John Dewey who pointed out that thinking itself is questioning. Unfortunately, research indicates that most student teachers, as well as experienced teachers, do not use effective questioning techniques. Think back to your own days in elementary and secondary school. You probably read your text and your class notes, studied (or, more accurately, memorized), and then waited in class for the teacher to call on you with a quick question, usually requiring only a brief reply. It did not seem to matter much whether the subject was language arts or social studies or science; questions revealed whether or not you remembered the material. But questions need not be used this way, and the appropriate use of questions can create an effective and powerful learning environment. Consider the following description of Mark Van Doren's use of questions:

> Mark would come into the room, and, without any fuss, would start talking about whatever was to be talked about. Most of the time he asked questions. His questions were very good, and if you tried to answer them intelligently, you found yourself saying excellent things that you did not know you knew, and that you had not, in fact, known before. He had "educed" them from you by his questions. His classes were literally "education" — they brought things out of you, they made your mind produce its own explicit ideas . . . . What he did have was the gift of communicating to them something of his own vital interest in things, something of his manner of approach; but the results were sometimes quite unexpected — and by that I mean good in a way that he had not anticipated, casting lights that he had not himself foreseen.[4]

It is all too easy to describe Van Doren as a gifted teacher and to dismiss his technique of questioning as an art to which most teachers can never aspire. It is our very strong belief that the teacher's effective use of questions is far too important to dismiss in this way. Unfortunately, research concerning the use of questions in the classroom suggests that most teachers do *not* use effective questioning techniques. If one were to review the research on questioning, the results would reveal both the importance of questioning in school and the need for teachers to improve their questioning technique. For example, did you know about any of the following facts or research that had been done about questioning techniques?

1. The first major study of classroom behavior was performed way back in 1912. The findings showed that 80 percent of classroom talk was devoted to asking, answering, or reacting to questions. Most of these questions were strictly memory, calling for only a superficial understanding of the material.[5]

2. Since 1912, the United States has seen several world wars, a depression, a dozen Presidents, the cure for several major diseases, the conquest of space, and tremendous social, economic, and political upheavals; but the state of questioning techniques in the classroom has remained basically unchanged. Studies into the 1970s show that most teachers still use questions as a major tool of learning, but the vast majority of these questions depend only on rote memory for a correct response.[6]

3. Teachers ask a tremendous number of questions. One study reveals that primary school teachers ask $3\frac{1}{2}$ to $6\frac{1}{2}$ questions per minute! Elementary school teachers average 348 questions a day. A recent study of student teachers found them asking 70 to 90 questions in several twenty-minute science lessons. Both at the elementary and secondary levels, there are an enormous number of questions asked by the typical teacher.[7]

4. Although teachers ask an incredible number of questions, they generally show little tolerance in waiting for student replies. Typically, only *one second* passes between the end of a question and the next verbal interaction! After the answer is given, only $\frac{9}{10}$ second passes before the teacher reacts to the answer. The tremendous number of questions asked and the brief amount of time provided before an answer is expected reinforce the finding that most questions do not require any substantive thought. Classroom questions simply call for the rapid recall of information.[8]

5. Although the research on the effect of questions on student achievement has accumulated slowly and at times is contradictory, tentative findings do suggest that higher order questions, questions which require thought rather than memory, increase student achievement. In classes where higher order, thought-provoking questions are asked, students perform better on achievement tests.[9]

6. Studies also reveal that the quality and quantity of student answers increase when teachers provide students with time to think. If teachers can increase the one second of silence which usually follows a question to three seconds or more, student answers will reflect more thought, and more students will actively participate in the classroom.[10]

7. Although learning is designed to help students receive answers for their questions, become independent citizens, and understand their world, little provision is made in schools for student questions. The typical student asks approximately one question per month.[11]

The significant number of research findings related to classroom questions indicates that questions play a crucial role in the classroom and that teachers need to improve their questioning strategies. Other studies reveal that programs designed to improve this crucial skill have been effective.[12] A variety of self-instructional booklets have been published with the purpose of providing teachers with questioning skills. One that we have found to be particularly helpful as we developed this chapter was *Minicourse 9: Higher Cognitive Questioning* by Gall, Dunning, and Weathersby.[13] The activities in this chapter are designed to increase your mastery of questioning skills.

Objective 1

To classify classroom questions according to Bloom's *Taxonomy of Educational Objectives: Cognitive Domain.*[14]

LEARNING ACTIVITY 1.1

As the research in the introductory section reveals, questioning plays an important role in the classroom. Ever since Socrates, teaching and questioning have been viewed as integrally related activities. In order to be an effective teacher, one must be an effective questioner. The first step in effective questioning is to recognize that questions have distinct characteristics, serve various functions, and create different levels of thinking. Some questions require only factual recall; others cause students to go beyond memory and to use other thought processes in forming an answer. Both kinds of questions are useful, but the heavy reliance teachers place on the factual type of question does not provide the most effective learning environment. Learning the different kinds of questions and the different functions they serve is a crucial step in being able to use all types of questions effectively.

There are many terms and classifications for describing the different kinds of questions. Most of these classification systems are useful in that they provide a conceptual framework, a way of looking at questions. However, we have selected only one system, in order to simplify the process and eliminate repetitive terms. Bloom's *Taxonomy* is probably the best known system for classifying educational objectives as well as classroom questions. There are six levels of Bloom's *Taxonomy*, and questions at each level require the person responding to use a different kind of thought process. Teachers should be able to formulate questions on each of these six levels in order to encourage their students to engage in a variety of cognitive processes. Before teachers are able to formulate questions on each of these levels, they first must understand the definitions of the six categories, and they must be able to recognize questions written on each of these six levels. The six levels are:

1. Knowledge
2. Comprehension
3. Application
4. Analysis
5. Synthesis
6. Evaluation

The following definitions, examples, and exercises are designed to help you recognize and classify questions on the six cognitive levels of Bloom's *Taxonomy*. (By the way, taxonomy is another word for classification.)

Level 1. Knowledge

The first level of the *Taxonomy*, knowledge, requires the student to recognize or recall information. The student is not asked to manipulate information, but merely to remember it just as it was learned. To answer a question on the knowledge level, the student must simply remember facts, observations, and definitions that have been learned previously.

Examples of Knowledge Questions

What is the capital of Maine?

What color did the solution become when we added the second chemical?

Who is the secretary of state?

Who wrote *Hamlet*?

Recently, it has become fashionable to scoff at questions which ask the student to rely only on memory. For example, a common complaint about some college exams is that they ask students to "spit back" the information they have memorized from their text and class notes. However, memorization of material is important for several reasons. The knowledge, or memory, category is critical to all other levels of thinking. We cannot ask students to think at higher levels if they lack fundamental information. Some memorization of information is also required in order to perform a variety of tasks in our society, ranging from being an effective citizen to being a good parent. Our society expects that a good many things be memorized.

Although important, the knowledge category does have severe drawbacks, the main one being that teachers tend to overuse it. Most questions which teachers ask both in class discussions and on tests would be classified in the knowledge category. Another drawback to questions on this level is that much of what is memorized is rapidly forgotten. And a third drawback to memory questions is that they assess only a superficial and shallow understanding of an area. Parroting someone else's thoughts does not, in itself, demonstrate any real understanding.

Some words frequently found in knowledge questions are listed in the box that follows:

Words often found in knowledge questions	
define	who?
recall	what?
recognize	where?
remember	when?

Your Turn

KNOWLEDGE

The following questions will test your understanding of knowledge level questions and your ability to classify questions at the knowledge level of Bloom's *Taxonomy* correctly. Your answers will also provide you with a useful study guide when preparing for the Mastery Test.

In questions 1–5, mark a "T" for true and an "F" for false statements.

_____ 1. The first level of Bloom's *Taxonomy* requires higher order thinking.

_____ 2. Most classroom and test questions teachers ask are memory questions.

_____ 3. A drawback to knowledge, or memory, questions is that they are unimportant.

_____ 4. Knowledge, or memory, questions are important because they are necessary steps on the way to more complex, higher order questions.

_____ 5. All the questions asked so far in this activity (questions 1–4) are on the first level of the *Taxonomy* — Knowledge and Memory.

Mark a "K" in the space in front of those questions that are at the knowledge level and a "—" for those that are not.

_____ 6. Who discovered a cure for yellow fever?

_____ 7. Can you analyze the causes of World War I?

_____ 8. Where does the United States get most of its tin from?

_____ 9. What does this poem mean to you?

_____ 10. Who was the eighth President of the United States?

_____ 11. Define *antediluvian*. (The class has previously been given the definition of this word.)

_____ 12. Can you think of a title for this poem?

_____ 13. What do you predict would happen to teachers if this recession were to continue over the next several years?

_____ 14. When did the Spanish–American War end?

Check your answers with the answers and comments included in the Answer Key that follows. If you answered all correctly — terrific! One wrong is pretty good also. Two wrong suggests that you should check your answers again. If you got three or more wrong, perhaps you should reread this section to make sure that you understand it before you proceed to the next level.

ANSWER KEY

Your Turn: Knowledge

1. F. Knowledge, or memory, requires recall, a lower level activity.
2. T. Unfortunately.
3. F. Memory, or knowledge, questions are important. Learners must have mastery of a wide variety of information. Other levels of thought are not possible without such a base.
4. T.
5. T.
6. K.
7. —. Unless the student has just learned this material, and is remembering it, this is *not* a knowledge level question. It calls for analysis, a higher level thought process.
8. K.
9. —. Calls for higher order thinking.
10. K.
11. K.
12. —. Calls for a more creative thought process than recall or recognition.
13. —. Unless the student has been told what will happen if the recession continues, he or she must use a thought process at a higher level than memory to answer this question.
14. K.

Level 2. Comprehension

Questions on the second level, comprehension, require the student to demonstrate that he or she has sufficient understanding to organize and arrange material mentally. The student must select those facts that are pertinent to answering the question. In order to answer a comprehension level question, the student must go beyond recall of information. The student must demonstrate a personal grasp of the material by being able to rephrase it, to give a description in his or her own words, and to use it in making comparisons.

For example, suppose a teacher asks, "What is the famous quote of Hamlet's that we memorized yesterday, the quotation in which he puzzles over the meaning and worth of existence?" By asking students to recall information, in this case a quotation, the teacher is asking a question on the knowledge level. However, if the teacher had asked instead, "What do you think Hamlet means when he asks, 'To be or not to be: that is the question'?", the teacher's question would have been on the comprehension level. With the second question, the student is required to rephrase information in his or her own words.

Frequently, comprehension questions ask students to interpret and translate material that is presented on charts, graphs, tables, and cartoons. For example, the following are comprehension questions:

Examples of Comprehension Questions

What is the main idea that this chart presents?
Describe in your own words what Herblock is saying in this cartoon.

This use of the comprehension question requires the student to translate ideas from one medium to another.

It is important to remember that *the information necessary to answer comprehension questions should have been provided to the student.* For example, if a student has previously read or listened to material that discusses the causes of the Revolutionary War and then the student is asked to explain these causes in his own words, the student is being asked a comprehension question. However, if the student has *not* been given material explaining the causes of the

Revolutionary War and is asked to explain why the war started, he or she is *not* being asked a comprehension question, but, rather, a question on a different level of the *Taxonomy*.

> *Words often found in comprehension questions*
>
> describe   rephrase
> compare   put in your own words
> contrast   explain the main idea

Your Turn

COMPREHENSION

In questions 1–4, mark a "T" for true and an "F" for false statements.

_____ 1. A comprehension question may require the student to use new information not previously provided.

_____ 2. Comprehension questions may require students to rephrase information.

_____ 3. It is possible to remember a definition without being able to put the definition in your own words.

_____ 4. A comprehension question asks students to recall information exactly as they have learned it.

Some of the following questions are at the knowledge level and others are at the comprehension level. Write a "C" next to those questions on the comprehension level and a "K" next to those questions on the knowledge level.

_____ 5. When did the American Revolution begin?

_____ 6. Compare socialism and capitalism.

_____ 7. How do whales differ from sharks?

_____ 8. What is the meaning of this cartoon?

_____ 9. Who is the author of "Stopping by Woods on a Snowy Evening"?

_____ 10. What is the main idea of this poem?

_____ 11. Describe what we saw on our visit to the planetarium.

_____ 12. Compare Hemingway's style with that of Steinbeck.

_____ 13. Where was the Declaration of Independence signed?

_____ 14. Explain in your own words what the author suggests were the main reasons for the Civil War.

Check your answers with those in the Answer Key that follows. If you missed two or more, you had better reread the description of comprehension questions before going on to the next section.

Level 3. Application

It is not enough for students to be able to memorize information or even to rephrase and interpret what they have memorized. Students must also be able to apply information. A question that asks a student to apply previously learned information in order to reach an answer to a problem is at the application level of the *Taxonomy*.

Application questions require students to apply a rule or process to a problem and thereby determine the single right answer to that problem. In mathematics, application questions are quite common. For example,

$$\text{If} \quad X = 2 \text{ and } y = 5,$$
$$\text{then} \quad X^2 + 2y = ?$$

But application questions are important in other subject areas as well. For example, in social studies, a teacher can provide the definitions of latitude and longitude and ask the student to repeat these definitions (knowledge). The teacher can then ask the student to compare the definitions of latitude and longitude (comprehension). At the application level, the teacher would ask the student to locate a point on a map by applying the definitions of latitude and longitude.

To ask a question at the application level in language arts, the following procedure might be used. After providing students with the definition of a haiku (a type of poem), a teacher would hand out a sheet with several different types of poems, then ask the students to select the poem which is a haiku, that is, the one which fits the definition of a haiku poem. To do this, the students must apply the definition to the various poems and select the poem which fits the definition.

In all the examples given, the student must apply knowledge in order to determine the single correct answer. Here are some other examples of questions at the application level.

Examples of Application Questions

In each of the following cases, which of Newton's laws is being demonstrated?

According to our definition of socialism, which of the following nations would be considered socialist?

Write an example of the rule we have just discussed.

According to our criteria, which answer is correct?

If John works three hours to mow the lawn, and it takes Alice only two hours, how many hours would it take for them to mow the lawn together?

What is the rule that is appropriate in case 2?

Words often found in application questions	
apply	write an example
classify	solve
use	how many?
choose	which?
employ	what is?

Your Turn

APPLICATION

Indicate the level of the *Taxonomy* that each of the following questions represents. Use a "K" for those at the knowledge level, "C" for those at the comprehension level, and "Ap" for those at the application level.

_____ 1. What did I say we would do today?

_____ 2. What does "freedom" mean to you?

_____ 3. Using the rules we discussed, solve the following problems.

_____ 4. How are these two solutions similar?

_____ 5. Using the scientific method, solve this problem.

_____ 6. Who was the author of *The Great Gatsby*?

_____ 7. If these figures are correct, will the manager make a profit or suffer a loss?

_____ 8. Applying the rules of supply and demand, solve the following problem.

_____ 9. Classify the following plants according to the ten categories we reviewed.

Check your answers with those provided in the Answer Key that follows. If you missed two or more, reread this section and do the additional questions provided below. If you would like extra practice, the additional questions will provide you with that opportunity. When you feel ready, go on to the next level of the *Taxonomy*. At this point, you're half way through with the first learning activity.

Additional Questions

_____ 10. We have learned the definition of a noun. What are three examples of nouns?

_____ 11. Rephrase the definition of a noun in your own words.

_____ 12. Which of the following sentences has an error in punctuation?

_____ 13. State the three steps we have learned which must be followed before starting on a hike in the forest.

_____ 14. Solve this problem by using the procedure we discussed for quadratic equations.

_____ 15. According to our definition of a mammal, which of the five animals listed would be considered a mammal?

Check your answers in the Answer Key. If you still need help, you may want to check with your instructor, with some other students who are getting the exercises correct, or with the references listed at the end of the chapter. If you understand the application level, move on to the analysis level.

ANSWER KEY
Your Turn: Application

1. K. Calls for recall of teacher's words.
2. C. Interpret in your own words.
3. Ap. Learner must apply the rules to solve a problem.
4. C. Calls for a comparison.
5. Ap. Learner must apply the scientific method to solve the problem.
6. K. Recall of a name is needed.
7. Ap. Must apply information about profit and loss to determine if there will be a profit or a loss.
8. Ap. In this case, the rules of supply and demand must be applied. The verb "apply" is a giveaway.

9. Ap. To classify the plants, the definitions of the categories must be applied to each case.

Additional Questions

10. Ap. To write examples of the definition, the rules of the definition must be applied.
11. C. "In your own words" is the clue.
12. Ap. Applying the rules of punctuation to a specific example.
13. K. Recalling previous information.
14. Ap. To solve the problem, a certain procedure must be applied.
15. Ap. To choose the correct answer, the rules of the definition must be applied.

Level 4. Analysis

Analysis questions are a higher order of questions that require students to think critically and in depth. Analysis questions ask students to engage in three kinds of cognitive processes.

1. To identify the motives, reasons, and/or causes for a specific occurrence.
2. To consider and analyze available information in order to reach a conclusion, an inference, or a generalization based on this information.
3. To analyze a conclusion, inference, or generalization to find evidence to support or refute it.

Following are examples of the three kinds of analysis questions:
1. To identify the motives, reasons, and/or causes for a specific occurrence.

What factors influenced the writings of Robert Frost?

Why did Senator Robert F. Kennedy decide to run for the Presidency?

Why was Israel selected as the site for the Jewish nation?

Why does our economy suffer from economic upswings and downturns?

In all these questions students are asked to discover the causes or reasons for certain events through analysis.

2. To consider and analyze available information in order to reach a conclusion, an inference, or a generalization based on this information.

After reading this textbook, how would you characterize the author's background, attitudes, and point of view?

Look at the diagram of this new invention. What do you think the purpose of this new invention is?

After studying the French, American, and Russian Revolutions, what can you conclude about the causes of revolution?

Now that your experiments are completed, what is your conclusion as to the name of the gas in the sample test tube?

This type of analysis question calls upon the learner to draw a conclusion, inference, or generalization based on evidence.

3. To analyze a conclusion, inference, or generalization to find evidence to support or refute it.

What information could you use to support the proposition that President Nixon was not a successful President?

What evidence can you cite to support the statement that Emily Dickinson was a more effective poet than Robert Frost?

Now that we have finished playing the simulation game, what did you experience that supports the idea of peaceful coexistence among nations?

These questions require students to analyze information to support a particular conclusion, inference, or generalization.

If you tried to answer any of these questions, you probably realized that several answers are possible. Furthermore, because it takes time to think and analyze, these questions cannot be answered quickly or without careful thought. The fact that several answers are possible and that sufficient time is needed to answer them is an indication that analysis questions are higher order ones. Unfortunately, teachers too often avoid higher order questions in favor of lower order ones, especially memory questions. But analysis questions are important because they foster critical thinking in students. Analysis questions not only help students learn what happened but also help them search for the reasons behind what happened.

A student cannot answer an analysis question by repeating information or by reorganizing material to put it into his or her own words. Students cannot rely directly on instructional materials when answering an analysis question.

Once again, analysis questions require students to analyze information in order to identify causes, to reach conclusions, or to find supporting evidence.

> *Words frequently found in analysis questions*
> identify motives or causes
> draw conclusions
> determine evidence
> support
> analyze
>
> why?

Review of the First Four Levels

1. *Knowledge* Requires memory only, repeating information exactly as memorized (define, recall, recognize, remember, who, what, where, when).

2. *Comprehension* Requires rephrasing and comparing information (describe, compare, contrast, rephrase, put in your own words, explain the main idea).

3. *Application* Requires application of knowledge to determine a single correct answer (apply, classify, use, choose, employ, write an example, solve, how many, which, what is).

4. *Analysis* Requires student to go beyond direct reliance on instructional materials to analyze a problem or situation.
   1. Identify motives or causes
   2. Draw conclusions
   3. Determine evidence (support, analyze, conclude, why)

Your Turn

ANALYSIS

_____ 1. Analysis questions call for higher order thinking. (true or false)

_____ 2. Which of the following processes is *not* required by analysis questions? (a) identifying evidence to support a statement (b) making a statement based on evidence (c) explaining motives or causes (d) making evaluations.

_____ 3. "Why" questions are often on the analysis level. (true or false)

_____ 4. Analysis questions require students only to rephrase information, to state it in their own words. (true or false)

_____ 5. Analysis questions require students to use or locate evidence in formulating their answers. (true or false)

Identify the levels of the following questions. (K = knowledge, C = comprehension, Ap = application, An = analysis)

_____ 6. Why didn't Hamlet act when he first learned of the treachery? (The student has not previously been given these reasons.)

_____ 7. What did Hamlet say?

_____ 8. What evidence can you find to support your statement that Hamlet was a coward? (The student has not previously been given this evidence.)

_____ 9. What was Hamlet's position or title in Denmark?

_____ 10. In your own words, how did we characterize Hamlet in yesterday's discussion?

_____ 11. After reading *Hamlet*, *Macbeth*, and *King Lear*, what can you conclude about Shakespeare's writing style? (These conclusions have not been given in previous reading or discussion.)

_____ 12. Using the definition of "climax," what part of *Hamlet* would you consider to be the climax?

Check your answers with the Answer Key that follows. Two or more wrong answers suggest you should review this section and answer the additional questions. If you made fewer than two errors, you may wish to solidify your expertise by answering the additional questions, anyway. If not, move on to the fifth level of the *Taxonomy*, Synthesis.

Additional Questions

_____ 13. When did Robert Kennedy campaign for the Democratic nomination for Presidency?

_____ 14. Why did R. F. Kennedy lose the Oregon primary? (The causes have not been given previously in reading or discussion.)

_____ 15. What can you conclude about the narrow victory for R. F. Kennedy over Eugene McCarthy in California? (The conclusions have not been given previously in reading or discussion.)

_____ 16. Can you analyze Kennedy's campaign strategy?

_____ 17. What evidence can you cite to support the contention that had Robert Kennedy lived, he would have won the Presidency?

_____ 18. How would you describe Kennedy's campaign style?

The answers are in the Answer Key. If you missed more than one of these additional questions, find out why. If the reading and examples aren't working for you, check with the references at the end of the chapter, with another student, or with your teacher. It is important that you understand the analysis level before you move on to the last two levels.

ANSWER KEY
Your Turn: Analysis

1. True.
2. (d) Making evaluations belongs at another level of the *Taxonomy*.
3. True. "Why" questions usually require the analysis of data to locate evidence or to determine causes, reasons, or motives.
4. False. Rephrasing information is required when a student answers a comprehension question.
5. True.
6. An. The student must analyze Hamlet's actions to identify a motivation.
7. K. Memory only is required.
8. An. Evidence to support a statement is sought.
9. K. Only memory is required.
10. C. Rephrasing a previous discussion.
11. An. A conclusion is called for.
12. Ap. Applying a definition to *Hamlet* to determine an answer.

Level 5. Synthesis

Synthesis questions are higher order questions that ask students to perform original and creative thinking. These kinds of questions require students (1) to produce original communications, (2) to make predictions, or (3) to solve problems. Although application questions also require students to solve problems, synthesis questions differ in that they do not require a single correct answer but, instead, allow a variety of creative answers. Here are some examples of the different kinds of synthesis questions:

1. To produce original communications.

   Construct a collage of pictures and words that represent your values and feelings.

   What's a good name for this machine?

   Write a letter to the editor on a social issue of concern to you.

2. To make predictions.

   What would the United States be like if the South had won the Civil War?

   How would life be different if school were not mandatory?

   How would life be different if the courts did not exist?

3. To solve problems.

   How can we measure the height of a building without being able to go into it?

   How can we raise money for our ecology project?

Teachers can use synthesis questions to help develop the creative abilities of students. Unfortunately, as in the case of analysis questions, teachers too often avoid synthesis questions in favor of lower order questions, particularly knowledge questions. Synthesis questions rely on a thorough understanding of material. Students should not take wild guesses in order to answer synthesis questions. For example, one synthesis question that we suggested, "What would the United States be like if the South had won the Civil War?" requires the student to have a firm grasp of information before being able to offer a sound prediction.

To review, synthesis questions require predictions, original communications, or problem solving in which a number of answers are possible.

> *Words often found in synthesis questions*
>
> | | |
> |---|---|
> | predict | construct |
> | produce | how can we improve? |
> | write | what would happen if? |
> | design | can you devise? |
> | develop | how can we solve? |
> | synthesize | |

Your Turn

SYNTHESIS

In questions 1–10, identify the level of the questions by using the code provided (K = knowledge, C = comprehension, Ap = application, An = analysis, and S = synthesis).

_____ 1. What is the state capital?

_____ 2. Where is it located?

_____ 3. Point it out on the map.

_____ 4. If you could decide on a location for a new state capital, what location would you choose?

_____ 5. Why?

_____ 6. What would happen if we had two state capitals?

_____ 7. Draw a simple blueprint of your ideal state capital.

_____ 8. Quote what your textbook says about the primary function of a state capital.

_____ 9. Describe this primary function.

_____ 10. Given the categories of different kinds of state capitols, how would you classify the capitol of Maine?

_____ 11. Synthesis questions require students to do all the following *except*
(a) make predictions
(b) solve problems
(c) rely primarily on memory
(d) construct original communication

_____ 12. Synthesis questions require original and creative thought from students. (true or false)

The Answer Key that follows will provide you with feedback on your progress in this section. If you want additional practice, then tackle these questions.

Additional Questions

_____ 13. How would you describe your school?

_____ 14. What would your ideal school be like?

_____ 15. Write a letter describing your ideal school.

_____ 16. What name would you give to this school?

_____ 17. Why?

ANSWER KEY
Your Turn: Synthesis

1. K.
2. K, C, or Ap. Depending on the student response, it could be at any of these levels. Pure repetition would be the knowledge level. Rephrasing the description of the location would place the answer at the comprehension level. Actually going to a map to point it out would place the response on the application level.
3. Ap. Calls for the student to demonstrate or apply the information.
4. S. Calls for problem solving with more than one answer possible.
5. An. Calls for evidence to support decision.
6. S. Calls for a prediction.
7. S. Original communication required.
8. K. Memorization of author's comments.
9. C. Rephrasing and description needed.
10. Ap. The student needs to apply rules in order to solve a problem.
11. (c). Synthesis is a higher order activity that calls for much more than memorizing.
12. True.

Additional Questions
13. C. Description is all that is necessary to answer this question. However, if the student responds to this question with a creative essay, it could be considered synthesis.
14. S. Response to this question calls for prediction, an original statement, and some problem solving.
15. S. Original communication.
16. S. Problem solving. Whenever an original name or title or main idea is called for, we are at the synthesis level.
17. An. Supporting evidence needed to explain the reason(s) for the name that was selected. To explain "why."

Level 6. Evaluation

The last level of the *Taxonomy* is evaluation. Evaluation, like synthesis and analysis, is a higher order mental process. Evaluation questions do not have a single correct answer. They require the student to judge the merit of an idea, a solution to a problem, or an aesthetic work. They may also ask the student to offer an opinion on an issue. Following are some examples of different kinds of evaluation questions:

Examples of Evaluation Questions

Do you think schools are too hard?

Should young children be allowed to read any book they want, no matter what it is about?

Which picture do you like best?

Which song do you prefer?

Is busing an appropriate remedy for desegregating schools?

Which approach offers the best method for attacking this problem?

Do you think that the statement "Americans never had it so good" is true?

Which U.S. Senator is the most effective?

In order to express your opinion on an issue or to make a judgment on the merit of an idea, solution, or aesthetic work, you must use some criteria. You must use either objective standards or a personal set of values to make an evaluation. For example, if you answer the last question above using a personal set of values, you might decide that the senator whose voting record is most congruent with your own political philosophy is the most effective senator. If you are strongly against defense spending or strongly in favor of civil rights legislation, these personal values would be reflected in your evaluation of the most effective senator.

Another way of evaluating senators would be through the use of objective criteria. Such criteria might include attendance records, campaign financing practices, influence on other senators, the number of sponsored bills that became law, etc. By comparing each senator to these criteria, a judgment can be made in relation to "the most effective senator."

Of course, many individuals use a combination of objective criteria and personal values when making an evaluation. The important thing to remember about evaluation questions is that some standard must be used. Differing standards are quite acceptable, and they naturally result in different answers. Evaluation questions are higher order questions, and different answers are expected.

Words often used in evaluation questions	
judge	give your opinion
argue	which is the better picture,
decide	solution, etc.?
evaluate	do you agree?
assess	would it be better?

Review of the Taxonomy

1. *Knowledge*   Requires memory only, repeating information exactly as memorized (define, recall, recognize, remember, who, what, where, when).

2. *Comprehension*   Requires rephrasing, rewording, and comparing information (describe, compare, contrast, rephrase, put in your own words, explain the main idea).

3. *Application*   Requires application of knowledge to determine a single correct answer (apply, classify, choose, employ, write an example, solve, how many, which, what is).

4. *Analysis*
   1. identify motives or causes
   2. draw conclusions
   3. determine evidence
   (support, analyze, conclude, why)

5. *Synthesis*
   1. make predictions
   2. produce original communications
   3. solve problems (more than one possible answer)

(predict, produce, write, design, develop, synthesize, construct, how can we improve?, what happens if?, how can we solve?, can you devise?)

6. *Evaluation*
1. make judgments
2. offer opinions
(judge, argue, decide, evaluate, assess, give your opinion, which is better?, do you agree?, would it be better?)

Your Turn

EVALUATION

Using all levels of the *Taxonomy*, classify the following questions (K = knowledge, C = comprehension, Ap = application, An = analysis, S = synthesis, and E = evaluation).

_____ 1. Who was the founder of the school of abstract art?

_____ 2. Describe the first attempts of the pioneers of abstract art.

_____ 3. What were some of the factors which motivated Picasso to join this new school?

_____ 4. We have read about the techniques of Picasso and Miro. Compare and contrast Picasso's techniques to those of Miro.

_____ 5. Which artist do you prefer, Miro or Picasso?

_____ 6. Paint your own abstract piece.

_____ 7. We have learned about the principle of balance. How is it used in this work?

_____ 8. Considering the different kinds of abstract paintings we have studied, what generalizations can you make about abstract art?

_____ 9. What do you predict is the future of abstract art?

_____ 10. What is your opinion of abstract art?

ANSWER KEY
Your Turn: Evaluation

1. K. Recall required.
2. C. Description in one's own words needed.
3. K or An. Knowledge if the material was already learned. Analysis if the causes must be thought out.
4. C. Calls for comparison.
5. E. Calls for a judgment.

6. S. Original communication.
7. Ap. Calls for the application of a principle or rule to a given work.
8. An. Asks student to consider evidence and make a generalization.
9. S. Prediction called for.
10. E. Calls for a judgment.

At this point, we have reviewed all levels of the *Taxonomy*, and you should have a good idea of whether or not you are ready for the Mastery Test. In the Mastery Test you will be asked to identify the levels of a number of questions; all six levels of the *Taxonomy* will be represented. If, before taking the Mastery Test, you would like to have some more practice and also to compare your responses with those of another student, you might want to try Learning Activity 1.2, "The Question Master Game." You will find it in the perforated section at the back of the book. Two to six people can play at a time. The game should provide you with more practice in understanding the *Taxonomy* and in classifying questions. As a side benefit, you might enjoy it and, undoubtedly, you will be victorious over siblings, friends, relatives, and strangers who probably will not be able to use the *Taxonomy* with your facile abandon.

LEARNING ACTIVITY 1.2

THE QUESTION MASTER GAME

The Question Master Game is designed to help you achieve competence in the first objective: "To classify questions on all six levels of Bloom's *Taxonomy*." In addition, we hope that you will enjoy playing the game.

To play the Question Master Game, you must be able to recall specific information about the characteristics of questions on the different levels of the *Taxonomy*; you must be able to classify questions on the various levels of the *Taxonomy*; and you should try to maintain your sense of humor. Having read Learning Activity 1.1 should help you to achieve the first two requirements. (Turn to Appendix A at back of the book to play.)

Mastery Test

OBJECTIVE 1

To classify classroom questions according to Bloom's *Taxonomy of Educational Objectives: Cognitive Domain.*

Read the paragraph below and then classify the following questions according to their appropriate level on Bloom's *Taxonomy*. Use the following abbreviations: (K = knowledge, C = comprehension, Ap = application, An = analysis, S = synthesis, and E = evaluation).

To pass the Mastery Test, you should classify 10 out of the 11 questions accurately. Good luck!

School reading texts were also studied. It was found that the major reading series used in almost all public and private schools across the country teach that being a girl means being inferior. In these texts, boys are portrayed as being able to do so many things: they play with bats and balls, they work with chemistry sets, they do magic tricks that amaze their sisters, and they show initiative and independence as they go on trips by themselves and get part-time jobs. Girls do things too: they help with the housework, bake cookies and sit and watch their brothers — that is assuming they are present. In 144 texts studied, there were 881 stories in which the main characters are boys and only 344 in which a girl is the central figure.

Nancy Frazier and Myra Sadker, *Sexism in School and Society*, New York: Harper and Row, 1973, pp. 103–104.

_____ 1. In your own words, compare the portrayal of males and females in school texts.

_____ 2. Why do you think feminists are concerned with the passive way in which girls are portrayed in textbooks?

_____ 3. What do boys do in the school reading texts that were studied?

_____ 4. What is the main idea of this paragraph?

_____ 5. Considering the category descriptions that we have studied of sexist and nonsexist books, how would you classify *Miracles on Maple Hill*?

_____ 6. What would your ideal nonsexist book be like?

_____ 7. How many texts were analyzed for sexism?

_____ 8. If all books became nonsexist during the next five years, what do you predict would be the effects on children?

_____ 9. Why do you think that girls have been portrayed in such a stereotyped manner in school texts?

_____ 10. What is your opinion on the issue of sexism in books?

_____ 11. Do you think that sexist books should be banned from children's libraries?

ANSWER KEY

Mastery Test, Objective 1

1. C   2. An   3. K   4. C   5. Ap   6. S   7. K   8. S   9. An   10. E   11. E

Objective 2

To construct classroom questions on all six levels of Bloom's *Taxonomy of Educational Objectives*.

LEARNING ACTIVITY 2.1

The first, and perhaps the most difficult, step in learning to ask effective classroom questions is that of gaining a thorough understanding of Bloom's *Taxonomy*. Now that you have demonstrated your ability to classify questions, you are ready to begin constructing them. Effective classroom questions make provision for student thinking on all levels of the *Taxonomy*. Although during a short period of time only one or two levels of the *Taxonomy* may be reflected in a teacher's questions, over the course of an entire semester students should have ample opportunity to answer questions phrased at all levels. The sample questions and the information in Learning Activity 1.1 provide you with useful information for constructing questions. The following review should provide you with a ready reference as you construct questions on the various levels of the *Taxonomy*.

SUGGESTIONS FOR CONSTRUCTING QUESTIONS

In the next few pages, we will review the nature of the cognitive processes and the verbs and key phrases that are frequently associated with specific levels of the *Taxonomy*. However, as you go over this review, remember that it is important to analyze each question you write, because inclusion of key phrases is not an unconditional guarantee of the taxonomic level of a particular question. After the brief review, you will get a chance to practice constructing questions that pertain to a specific reading selection.

1. *Knowledge:*   recall   who?
define   what?
recognize   where?
identify   when?

A knowledge question requires students to recall or recognize information.

2. *Comprehension:*   describe   in your own words compare
compare   pare similarities and differences
illustrate   differences
interpret   derive main idea
rephrase
reorder
contrast
differentiate
explain

To answer a comprehension level question, the student must be able to organize previously learned material so that he or she can rephrase it, describe it in his or her own words, and use it for making comparisons.

3. *Application:*   apply   select
solve (one answer only   use
is correct)   employ
classify
choose

An application question asks students to use previously learned information in order to solve a problem.

4. *Analysis:*   analyze   why?
identify motive,   determine the evidence
cause, or reason   determine a conclusion
conclude
infer
distinguish
deduce
detect

Analysis questions ask students (1) to identify reasons, causes, and motives; (2) to consider available evidence in order to reach a conclusion, inference, or generalization; and (3) to analyze a conclusion, inference, or generalization to find supporting evidence.

5. *Synthesis:*   solve (more than one answer correct)
predict
write

draw
construct
produce
originate
propose
plan
design
synthesize
combine
develop

Synthesis questions require students (1) to produce original communications, (2) to make predictions, or (3) to solve problems.

6. *Evaluation:*   judge   what is your opinion?
                    argue   do you agree?
                    decide   which is better?
                    appraise
                    evaluate

Evaluation questions ask students to judge the merit of an idea, a solution to a problem, or an aesthetic work.

Before proceeding into the exercises in this learning activity, you may find it helpful to keep in mind the following general comments about question construction.

It is important to phrase your questions carefully. You have probably been a student in more than one class where the teacher's questions were so cumbersome or so wordy that you lost the meaning of the question. In fact, one study indicates that 40 percent of teacher questions are ambiguous and poorly phrased. You should be explicit enough to ensure understanding of your questions, but, at the same time, you should avoid using too many words. When a question is too wordy, students become confused and unable to respond; frequently, the result is that the question has to be rephrased.

Now you are ready to construct questions at each of the six levels of Bloom's *Taxonomy*. Read the paragraph in the test that follows. Then construct at least 12 questions relating to it. When you are done, you should have two questions on each of the six levels of the *Taxonomy*. As you construct your questions, keep the following in mind. What facts are in the paragraph that you might want students to recognize or recall (knowledge level)? What are the main points in the reading selection that you would want students to comprehend and be able to rephrase in their own words (comprehension level)? What information is there in the paragraph that students could apply to solving problems, to classifying, or to giving examples (application level)? What questions can you ask about the reading selection that require students to consider reasons and motives, to examine the validity of a conclusion, or to seek evidence to support a conclusion (analysis level)? Using this paragraph as a springboard, how can you stimulate original student thought — creative problem solving, the making of predictions, and the production of original communication — in writing, music, dance, art, etc. (synthesis level)? Finally, what issues can you raise from the material in this paragraph that will cause students to judge the merit of an idea, the solution to a problem, or an aesthetic work (evaluation level)? As you develop your questions, it may be helpful to review the information in Learning Activities 1.1, 1.2, and 2.1.

After you have finished writing your questions, compare them with the sample questions in the Answer Key that follows. Obviously, a wide variety of questions could be written pertaining to this particular selection. The sample questions are simply meant to give you a basis for comparison and to indicate the kinds of questions that can be asked on each of the six levels of the *Taxonomy*.

Compare your questions with the information and examples in Learning Activities 1.1 and 2.1. Discuss the questions you develop with your instructor and with other members of your class. If 11 or 12 of your questions accurately reflect the appropriate level of the *Taxonomy*, you are doing very well. If you miss two or three, you will probably want to review the information in Learning Activity 2.1 and to study the sample questions very carefully, particularly those on the levels where you did not construct the questions accurately. If you miss more than three, a careful review of the Learning Activity 1.1 and additional practice in constructing questions may be necessary before you take the Mastery Test.

Your Turn

CONSTRUCTING QUESTIONS ON THE SIX LEVELS OF BLOOM'S TAXONOMY

In Des Moines, Iowa, two high school students and a junior high student, in defiance of a ban by school authorities, wore black armbands to class as a protest against the Vietnam War. As a result, they were suspended from school. But the U.S. Supreme Court later ruled the suspensions were illegal, holding that the first amendment to the Constitution protects the rights of public school children to express their political and social views during school hours.

.   .   .

This case illustrates a significant new trend in American life. Young people, particularly those under 21, are demanding that they be granted rights long denied them as a matter of course. And, with increasing frequency, they are winning those rights.

Michael Dorman, *Under 21* (New York: Delacorte, 1970) pp. 3 and 5.

1. Knowledge level questions

_____

_____

_____

_____

2. Comprehension level questions

_____

_____

_____

_____

3. Application level questions

_____

_____

_____

_____

4. Analysis level questions

_____

_____

_____

_____

_____

5. Synthesis level questions

_____

_____

_____

_____

_____

6. Evaluation level questions

_____

_____

_____

_____

_____

_____

ANSWER KEY

Your Turn: Constructing Questions on the Six Levels of Bloom's *Taxonomy*

Here are some questions on the six levels of the *Taxonomy* that you might have asked about the paragraphs. They are not the *only* questions that could have been asked but are simply meant to provide examples.

1. *Knowledge level questions*
   1. What action did the three students in Des Moines, Iowa, take that caused their suspension?

2. What was the ruling of the Supreme Court on their case?
3. What part of the Constitution did the Supreme Court refer to as a basis for its decision?

2. *Comprehension level questions*
   1. What is the main idea in this paragraph?
   2. In your own words, explain why the Supreme Court declared the suspensions illegal.

3. *Application level questions*
   1. Considering the ruling in the Des Moines case, what would the legal ruling be on a student who, despite a ban by school authorities, wore a yellow cloth star sewn on her jacket as a protest against the United Nations policy toward Israel?
   2. Considering the Supreme Court ruling in the Des Moines case, what do you think the legal ruling would be on a group of students who blockaded the entrance to a classroom as a protest against race discrimination?

4. *Analysis level questions*
   1. Why did the Supreme Court support the rights of students to express their political and social beliefs during school hours?
   2. What evidence, other than the specific case described in this paragraph, can you cite to support the conclusion that young people are now gaining long denied rights?

5. *Synthesis level questions*
   1. Develop a short story that portrays a young person seeking to attain a legal right denied to those under 21.
   2. If children gained the full legal rights enjoyed by adults in America, what implications would it have for family life?

6. *Evaluation level questions*
   1. What is your opinion on the issue of minors enjoying the full legal rights of adults?
   2. If you had been a judge on the Court in the case of the Des Moines students who protested the Vietnam War with black armbands despite a school ban, how would you have ruled?

LEARNING ACTIVITY 2.2

If you feel that you need further practice in constructing questions or if you would like to improve your question construction skills, Learning Activity 2.2 provides that opportunity. This learning activity involves another way of playing the Question Master Game. All you need do is make one rule change. Instead of using the "Classification Cards" that have already been developed, you must construct a question of your own whenever you land on a square marked with a "C." The question must be at the same level of the *Taxonomy* as the number of spaces you move. Avoid using the same question more than once, and try to vary your question stems.

Example

The die (or cards or spinner) indicates "6," and you move your piece six spaces. If you land on a "C" space, you must construct a question at level six of the *Taxonomy* (Evaluation). If you fail to do this, you must go back three spaces from your original space. If you are successful, you can remain on that space until your next turn.

The "C" spaces now represent *Construct* a question rather than *Classify* a question. All other rules remain the same. Any missed questions result in going backward three spaces.

If the die shows:	Question must be at:
1	Knowledge
2	Comprehension
3	Application

4	Analysis
5	Synthesis
6	Evaluation

Any disputes that cannot be resolved by referring to the explanations and examples in Learning Activity 1.1 will have to be arbitrated by your instructor.

Good luck!

Mastery Test

OBJECTIVE 2   To construct classroom questions on all six levels of Bloom's *Taxonomy of Educational Objectives*.

Read the following paragraphs and then construct twelve questions based on this reading selection. Two of your questions must be at the knowledge level, two at the comprehension level, two at the application level, two at the analysis level, two at the synthesis level, and two at the evaluation level. To pass this Mastery Test successfully, 9 of the 12 questions should accurately reflect the level of the *Taxonomy* at which they are constructed.

Death may be an unwelcome terrifying enemy, a skeleton with an evil grin who clutches an ugly scythe in his bony hand. Or death may be a long awaited friend who waits quietly, invisibly, beside the bed of a dying patient to ease his pain, his loneliness, his weariness, his hopelessness.

Man alone among the things that live knows that death will come. Mice and trees and microbes do not. And man, knowing that he has to die, fears death, the great unknown, as a child fears the dark. "We fear to be we know not what, we know not where," said John Dryden. But what man dreads more is the dying, the relentless process in which he passes into extinction alone and helpless and despairing. So he puts death and dying out of his mind, denying that they exist, refusing to discuss them openly, trying desperately to control them. He coins phrases like "never say die," and somehow, when he says something is "good for life," he means forever. Unable to bear the thought of ceasing to be, he comforts himself with thoughts of a pleasant afterlife in which he is rewarded for his trials on earth, or he builds monuments to himself to perpetuate at least his memory if not his body.

John Langone, *Death Is A Noun* (Boston: Little-Brown, 1972) pp. 3–4.

Now that you have read the paragraphs, construct 12 questions in the appropriate spaces below. When you write the application level questions, you may find it helpful to consider that the following information has previously been given to the class: (1) definitions of various literary images including metaphor, simile, and personification; (2) a list of terms and definitions that characterize various psychological states; and (3) several novels that portray death as a central or minor theme.

Knowledge questions

1. _____

_____

2. _____

_____

Comprehension questions

1. _____

_____

2. _____

_____

Application questions

1. _____

_____

2. _____

_____

Analysis questions

1. _____

_____

2. _____

_____

Synthesis questions

1. _____

_____

2. _____

_____

Evaluation questions

1. _____

_____

2. _____

_____

ANSWER KEY

Mastery Test, Objective 2

In order to pass the Mastery Test for objective 2, you must have constructed 12 questions relating to the given reading selection. There should be two questions on each level of the *Taxonomy*; at least 9 of the 12 questions you develop should be well constructed and should accurately reflect the appropriate taxonomic level.

Obviously there is a wide variety of questions that could be constructed on the given paragraphs. Below are three sample questions for each of the six levels of the *Taxonomy*.

Knowledge questions

1. What are two somewhat contradictory images that man holds of death?
2. Who alone, among all things that live, realizes the eventual coming of death?
3. Who was the author who said, "We fear to be we know not what, we know not where"?

Comprehension questions

1. In your own words, what did Dryden mean by his sentence "We fear to be we know not what, we know not where"?
2. People often hold different images of death. Compare two different conceptions of death that people hold.
3. What is the main idea of the second paragraph?

Application questions

1. Considering our previous study of metaphor and simile, which of these two literary devices applies to the statement in the first paragraph: "Death may be an unwelcome, terrifying enemy, a skeleton with an evil grin who clutches an ugly scythe in his bony hand"?
2. You have previously been given a list of terms and definitions that characterize various psychological states. Which of these terms best applies to people's tendency to push the reality of death and dying out of their minds?
3. Give an example of a character from one of the novels we have read this semester who clearly exhibits this tendency to deny the reality of death.

Analysis questions

1. Why do you think that people push the reality of death and dying out of their minds?
2. The author suggests that people are unable to face the notion of death. What evidence can you find to support this contention?
3. Considering the information you have in these paragraphs, how do you think the author feels people should react to death?

Synthesis questions

1. Write a poem or a short story in which the main character must face his own or another's impending death.
2. What do you predict life would be like if there were no death?
3. What ideas can you propose to help people become more accepting of their own mortality?

Evaluation questions

1. Do you think it would be better for people to ignore death, as many do now, or to be more aware and accepting of death in their daily living patterns?
2. What do you judge to be the finest literary or artistic expression which has the inevitability of death as its central theme?
3. In your opinion, is it a good idea for children to read books about death?

Objective 3

To describe the nature and dynamics of (a) wait time, (b) reinforcement, and (c) probing questions in increasing the quantity and quality of student response.

LEARNING ACTIVITY 3

This learning activity is composed of three brief sections, each of which discusses a teaching technique that can increase the quantity and quality of student response in your classroom.

Wait Time[15]

If we were to stop and listen outside a classroom door, we might hear classroom interaction similar to this:

Teacher: Who wrote the poem "Stopping by Woods on a Snowy Evening"? Tom?

Tom: Robert Frost.

Teacher: Good. What action takes place in the poem? Sally?

Sally: A man stops his sleigh to watch the woods get filled with snow.

Teacher: Yes. Emma, what thoughts go through the man's mind?

Emma: He thinks how beautiful the woods are . . . . (She pauses for a second)

Teacher: What else does he think about? Joe?

Joe: He thinks how he would like to stay and watch. (Pauses for a second)

Teacher: Yes — and what else? Rita? (Waits half a second) Come on, Rita, you can get the answer to this. (Waits half a second) Well, why does he feel he can't stay there indefinitely and watch the woods and the snow?

Rita: He knows he's too busy. He's got too many things to do to stay there for so long.

Teacher: Good. In the poem's last line, the man says that he has miles to go before he sleeps. What might sleep be a symbol for? Sarah?

Sarah: Well, I think it might be — (Pauses a second)

Teacher: Think, Sarah. (Teacher waits for half a second) All right then — Mike? (She waits again for half a second) John? (Waits half a second) What's the matter with everyone today? Didn't you do the reading?

There are a number of comments we could make about this slice of classroom interaction. We could note the teacher's development from primarily lower order questions to those of a somewhat higher order nature. We could comment on the inability of the students to answer her later questions and on the teacher's increasing frustration. But, perhaps the most devastating thing we could say about this interaction segment is that it lasts for less than a single minute.

In less than one minute of dialogue this teacher manages to construct and ask six questions, some of them, at least, requiring a fairly high cognitive level of response. As discussed earlier, a very rapid questioning rate is not at all atypical of many classrooms across the country. The mean number of questions a teacher asks averages between two and three per minute, and it is not unusual to find as many as seven to ten questions asked by a teacher during a single minute of classroom instruction.

The effect of this incredibly rapid "bombing rate" is that students have very little time to think. In fact, research shows that the mean amount of time a teacher waits after asking a question is approximately *one second*! If the students are not able to think quickly enough to come up with a response at this split second pace, the teacher repeats the question, rephrases it, asks a different question, or calls on another student. Moreover, if a student manages to get a response in, the teacher reacts or asks another question within an average time of nine-tenths of a second. It is little wonder that high rates of teacher questioning tend to be associated with low rates of student questions and student declarations. In classrooms where questions are asked at this "bombing rate," students have little time to think, little time to express themselves, and often little desire to express themselves in an atmosphere so charged with a sense of verbal evaluation and testing.

When teachers break out of the "bombing rate" pattern and learn to increase their wait time from one second to three to five seconds after asking a question, many significant changes occur in their classrooms. For example:

1. Students give longer answers.
2. Students volunteer more appropriate answers, and failures to respond are less frequent.
3. Student comments on the analysis and synthesis levels increase. They make more evidence–inference responses and more speculative responses.
4. Students ask more questions.
5. Students exhibit more confidence in their comments, and those students whom teachers rate as relatively slow learners offer more questions and more responses.

Simply by increasing his or her ability to wait longer after asking a question, a teacher can effect some striking changes in the quantity and the quality of student response. It is not as easy as you might think to learn to wait three to five seconds after asking a question. If teachers do not get an immediate response to a question, the natural reaction seems to be one of panic — an assumption that the question is not a good one and that the students do not know the answers. Indeed, teachers who have experimented with trying to increase their wait time find that they become frustrated at about the second or third week of practice. They go through a period of indecision, uncertain as to exactly how long they should wait after asking a question. However, if they receive encouragement during this difficult time, most teachers are able to increase wait time from one second to three to five seconds. Some teachers have found that the following suggestions are helpful to them as they try to increase their wait time.

1. Avoid repeating portions of student response to a question (teacher echo).
2. Avoid the command "think" without giving the student clues to aid his thinking or sufficient time in which to get his thoughts together.
3. Avoid frequent evaluative comments such as "fine," "good," and "okay."
4. Avoid the "yes . . . but" reaction to a student response. This construction signals teacher rejection of the student's idea.

Currently, too many classrooms are characterized by an incredibly rapid rate of interaction as teachers fire one question after another at students without giving them sufficient time to think, to formulate their answers, and to respond. If teachers can master the skill of increasing wait time from one second to three to five seconds, particularly after questions at a higher cognitive level, they will probably find some very positive changes in both the quantity and quality of student response.

Reinforcement

Reinforcement, or the rewarding of desired student performance, has been a long recognized and much used teaching skill. Typical teacher reinforcers such as "Good answer!" and "Excellent!" ring through the classrooms and corridors of schools throughout the nation. Yet, recent studies indicate that educators do not fully understand the effects of reinforcement and that, under certain circumstances, reinforcement can actually detract from the learning process and decrease the quality of student response.

Reinforcement techniques fall into two broad categories: verbal and nonverbal. Probably the most common verbal reinforcers are the one-word or brief-phrase responses: "Okay," "Good," "Nice job," "That's right," "Excellent," and the like. But there are a number of other verbal reinforcers that are not used as extensively, yet can provide students with other powerful rewards. An important type of verbal reinforcement, but one used far less than 10 percent of the time, occurs when teachers use student ideas in developing their lessons. Applying, comparing, and building on the contributions of students are important reinforcement techniques and research shows us that they provide students with a voice in directing their own learning. Moreover, in classes where such reinforcement techniques are applied, students have more positive attitudes and higher achievement than in classrooms where student ideas are not incorporated into the development of the lessons. Such verbal reinforcement can be an important motive for increasing the student's desire to participate.

Nonverbal reinforcement may, in fact, be even more powerful than verbal reinforcement. Nonverbal reinforcement refers to the physical messages sent by teachers through cues such as eye contact, facial expression, and body position. Does the teacher smile, frown, or remain impassive as a student comments in class? Is the teacher looking at or away from the student? Where is the teacher standing? Does the instructor appear relaxed or tense? All these physical messages indicate to the student whether the teacher is interested or bored, involved or passive, pleased or displeased with a student's comment. In various, subtle ways, nonverbal reinforcement can be used to encourage student participation or to inhibit it.

Several interesting studies comparing the relative effect of nonverbal and verbal reinforcement on students have been undertaken. One study actually had teachers send out conflicting reinforcement messages to determine which message students accepted as the more powerful. In one group, the teacher displayed positive nonverbal reinforcement (smiled, maintained eye contact, indicated positive attitude to student answers with facial and body cues) but, at the same time, sent out negative verbal reinforcement through negative comments. In the second case, the process was reversed, and negative nonverbal reinforcement was coupled with positive verbal reinforcement (frowns, poor eye contact, etc., coupled with "good," "nice job," etc.).

Although no evidence was accumulated as to whether the teacher was perceived as schizophrenic, the results of the study were nonetheless interesting. In both cases, the nonverbal reinforcement was accepted as the primary message by the majority of students. Whether the nonverbal message was positive or negative, most students responded to the nonverbal rather than the verbal reinforcement. This study provides fascinating support to the notion of a "silent language," or of "body language," and it emphasizes the importance of teachers' attending to what they do *not* say as well as to what they do say as they reinforce student participation.

For many years educators have assumed that reinforcement, verbal and nonverbal, was a positive tool in promoting student learning and, certainly, this is frequently the case. But reinforcement is not always an effective teaching skill. In some cases reinforcement is ineffectual and, on occasion, it is actually detrimental to learning.

When a teacher relies totally on one or two favorite types of reinforcement and uses these reinforcers repeatedly, the eventual result may be that the reinforcement becomes ineffectual. The teacher, for example, who continually says "Okay" after each student response is not reinforcing, but simply verbalizing a comment that has lost its power to reward. Overusing a word or phrase is a pattern many teachers, both new and experienced, fall into. Continual repetition of a word like "okay" or "good" seems only to ease teacher anxiety and to provide the teacher with a second or two to conceptualize his or her next comment or question.

In other cases reinforcement can actually detract from educational objectives and student learning. Reinforcement given too quickly and too frequently may interfere with or block the complete development of student ideas and interactions. When students are engaged in problem-solving activities, continual reinforcement can be an interruption to their thought processes and may actually terminate the problem solving altogether. Reinforcement can also interfere with pupil-to-pupil interactions. Teachers who react to each student comment refocus the discussion on themselves and stop the possibility of student-to-student interactions.

Another inhibitor of student-to-student interactions is the strict use of direct eye contact. This nonverbal reinforcer also tends to refocus attention on the teacher, and strong eye contact bolts the student's eyes to the teacher's eyes, thus reducing the opportunity for student-to-student exchanges. In classrooms where teachers want to increase student interaction, problem-solving activity, and higher order thinking, the use of reinforcement must be moderated; otherwise, it may hamper rather than encourage student growth in these areas.

Another misuse of reinforcement is exemplified by those teachers who are unable to differentiate the student's comment from the student's ego and, as a result, praise virtually every student response, regardless of its appropriateness. To these teachers, fearful of alienating or discouraging students, every student comment is automatically rewarded, and critical thinking and accuracy are sacrificed for the sake of goodwill. It is possible, however, for teachers to reward student participation ("thanks for that answer") and still indicate that the student response is not appropriate. ("Remember now, we are focusing on American civilization before the introduction of the railroad. Can someone tackle the question again, keeping this in mind?") In other words, it is possible to separate a student's ego from the answer. Rewarding all answers indiscriminately is an example of a poor use of reinforcement, but rewarding the student's participation is possible even when the answer itself may be incorrect.

Finally, it should be pointed out that different individuals respond to different kinds of reinforcement. Teachers should learn to recognize that while some students find intensive eye contact rewarding, others find it uncomfortable; that some students respond favorably to a teacher referring to their contributions by name, but others find it embarrassing. Although it is unrealistic to expect that a teacher will be able to learn the various rewards to which each and every student responds, it is possible for teachers to try, in general, to be sensitive to the effects of different rewards on students.

In summary, reinforcement is a traditional and often used teaching skill that consists of both verbal and nonverbal behaviors. Although reinforcement is a positive prod for learning and can increase student participation, it is frequently misused and can result in decreasing student participation and learning. Reinforcement can interrupt student thinking, discourage interactions among students, or, if overused, become weak and ineffectual. The use of reinforcement should be planned with care, so that such rewards encourage, rather than inhibit, the quantity and the quality of student response.

Probing Questions

Reinforcement and increased wait time are two means whereby teachers can increase student participation in classroom discussion. A third technique designed to increase the quantity and particularly the quality of student participation is the probing question.

Probing questions follow student responses and attempt to stimulate students to think through their answers more thoroughly. They cause students to develop the quality of their answers and to expand on their initial responses. Probing questions require students to provide more support, to be clearer or more accurate, and to offer greater specificity or originality.

Probing questions may be used to prompt student thinking on any level of the *Taxonomy*, but they are probably most effective at the analysis, synthesis, and evaluation levels. Here are some examples of probing questions as they might appear in a classroom discussion.

Teacher: How is a President elected?
Student: By the people.
Teacher: How? Be more specific. (probe)
Student: They vote.
Teacher: Explain how the votes determine who is President. (probe)
Student: I think that an electoral college — state representatives — actually do the voting. The people's votes decide which representatives will be chosen. The representatives actually choose the President.
Teacher: How are the people certain that these representatives, these electors, wouldn't vote for somebody else? (probe)
Student: They give their word. They promise to vote for a certain candidate.
Teacher: Was there ever a case when an elector did not keep this promise? (probe)
Student: Yes. I remember that one elector in the 1960 election decided not to vote for Kennedy even though most of the people in his state voted for Kennedy. I think he voted for Senator Byrd, who wasn't even running.

In this brief dialogue, the teacher asks a series of probing questions at various levels of the *Taxonomy*. The teacher does not accept the student's initial response, "By the people," but probes for more specificity as to how the electoral system works and eventually moves the student to a higher cognitive response. Without probing the student's initial answer, the teacher would have been left with a superficial answer, and the student would not have had the opportunity to consider his response more carefully. Probing questions increase the level of student thinking as well as the quality of student response.

Here is another sample classroom dialogue, with some more examples of probing questions.

> *Teacher:* How can we convince auto manufacturers to build smaller cars, cars which burn less gasoline?
> *Student:* Pass a law.
> *Teacher:* Can you be more specific? (probe)
> *Student:* Sure. Put a limit on the size of cars.
> *Teacher:* Why do you think that would work? (probe)
> *Student:* Well, smaller cars burn less gas. If you just ask them to make smaller cars, they wouldn't do it. So pass a law requiring it.
> *Teacher:* Wouldn't car manufacturers rebel at being forced to make smaller cars? (probe)
> *Student:* I guess. But they would do it.
> *Teacher:* What effect might such a law have on businessmen in other industries? How would they perceive such a law? (probe)

The three techniques discussed in this section — wait time, reinforcement, and probing questions — provide teachers with classroom strategies designed to make the student a more active participant in the learning process. When you feel that you understand these skills, go directly to the Mastery Test. In order to pass the Mastery Test, you need to demonstrate a knowledge and comprehension level understanding of the major points contained in the preceding three sections.

Mastery Test

OBJECTIVE 3
To describe the nature and dynamics of (a) wait time, (b) reinforcement, and (c) probing questions in increasing the quantity and quality of student response.

Discuss how wait time, reinforcement, and probing questions can increase the quantity and/or quality of student response in the classroom. You should include the following in your discussion:

(a) A description of the "bombing rate" and the amount of "wait time" characteristic of most classrooms today.
(b) A description of four positive effects that increased "wait time" has on student participation.
(c) A description of how reinforcement can promote, as well as how it may, if used ineffectively, inhibit student response.
(d) A description of how probing questions can increase the quantity and quality of student response.

ANSWER KEY
Mastery Test, Objective 3

(a) *Bombing rate:* Teachers ask questions at an extremely rapid rate, on the average of two or three per minute. It is not unusual to find as many as seven to ten questions asked during a single minute of classroom instruction.
Wait time: The mean amount of time a teacher waits after asking a question is only one second.

(b) Increased "wait time" has these positive effects on student participation (you may have chosen any four):
1. Students give longer answers.
2. They volunteer more appropriate answers.
3. Failures to respond are less frequent.
4. Student comments on the analysis and synthesis levels increase.
5. Students ask more questions.
6. Slower students offer more questions and responses.
7. Students exhibit more confidence in their comments.

(c) Reinforcement could promote student participation by rewarding students for their comments, thus encouraging further participation. This reward may be verbal or nonverbal in nature.

Reinforcement can hinder student participation when (1) teacher comments interfere with student thinking, (2) teacher eye contact is so strong that it detracts from student-to-student interaction, (3) a particular verbal reinforcer is overused and loses its power, (4) reinforcement is given too frequently or too quickly, without a thorough analysis of the quality of student response.

(d) Probing questions increase the quantity and quality of student participation by requiring the student to go beyond the initial answer and extend his or her thinking.

NOTES

1. Charles DeGarmo, *Interest and Education* (New York: Macmillan Co., 1902), p. 179.

2. John Dewey, *How We Think*, rev. ed. (Boston: D. C. Heath, 1933), p. 266.

3. Joseph Green, "Editor's Note," *Clearing House* 40 (1966): 397.

4. Thomas Merton, *The Seven Storey Mountain* (New York: Doubleday Co., 1948), p. 139.

5. Romiett Stevens, "The Question as a Measure of Classroom Practice," *Teachers College Contributions to Education*, no. 48 (New York: Teachers College Press, Columbia University, 1912).

6. O. L. Davis and Drew Tinsley, "Cognitive Objectives Revealed by Classroom Questions Asked by Social Studies Teachers and Their Pupils," *Peabody Journal of Education* 44 (July 1967): 21–26. Also see O. L. Davis and Francis P. Hunkins, "Textbook Questions: What Thinking Processes Do They Foster?," *Peabody Journal of Education* 43 (March 1966): 285–292.

7. Stevens, *op. cit.* See also E. Dale and L. Raths, "Discussion in the Secondary School," *Educational Research Bulletin* 24 (1945): 1–6; Davis and Hunkins, *op. cit.*; W. D. Floyd, "An Analysis of the Oral Questioning Activity in Selected Colorado Primary Classrooms" (Ph.D. diss., Colorado State College, 1960); and Roger T. Cunningham, "A Descriptive Study Determining the Effects of a Method of Instruction Designed to Improve the Question-Phrasing Practices of Prospective Elementary Teachers" (Ph.D. diss., Indiana University, 1968), p. 156.

8. Mary Budd Rowe, "Wait-Time and Rewards as Instructional Variables: Their Influence on Language, Logic and Fate Control" (Paper presented at the National Association for Research in Science Teaching, Chicago, April 1972).

9. Hilda Taba, Samuel Levine, and Freeman Elzey, *Thinking in Elementary School Children*, Cooperative Research Project No. 1574, San Francisco State College, San Francisco, California, April 1964, p. 177; see also Francis P. Hunkins, *Questioning Strategies and Techniques* (Boston: Allyn and Bacon, 1972).

10. Rowe, *op. cit.*

11. G. L. Fahey, "The Questioning Activity of Children," *Journal of Genetic Psychology* 60 (1942): 337–357. See also V. M. Houston, "Improving the Quality of Classroom Questions and Questioning," *Educational Administration and Supervision* 24 (1938): 17–28; and W. D. Floyd, *op. cit.*

12. Virginia Rogers, "Varying the Cognitive Levels of Classroom Questions in Elementary Social Studies: An Analysis of the Use of Questions by Student Teachers" (Ph.D. diss., University of Texas at Austin, 1968). See also Hilda Taba, *Teaching Strategies and Cognitive Functioning in Elementary School Children*, Cooperative Research Project No. 2404 (Washington D.C.: U.S. Office of Education, 1966).

13. Meredith D. Gall, Barbara Dunning, and Rita Weathersby, *Minicourse 9: Higher Cognitive Questioning, Teacher's Handbook*, Far West Laboratory for Educational Research and Development, Beverly Hills: Macmillan Educational Services, 1971.

14. Benjamin Bloom, ed., *Taxonomy of Educational Objectives, Handbook I: Cognitive Domain* (New York: David McKay, 1956).

15. The findings in this section are based on work by Mary Budd Rowe, *op. cit.*

ADDITIONAL READINGS

Bloom, Benjamin, ed. *Taxonomy of Educational Objectives, Handbook I: Cognitive Domain*. New York: David McKay, 1956.

Cunningham, Roger T. "Developing Question-Asking Skills." In *Developing Teacher Competencies*. Edited by James Wiegand. Englewood Cliffs, New Jersey: Prentice-Hall, 1971.

Gall, Meredith, Barbara Dunning, and Rita Weathersby. *Minicourse 9: Higher Cognitive Questioning, Teacher's Handbook*. Far West Regional Laboratory for Educational Research and Development. Beverly Hills: Macmillan Educational Services, 1971.

Gillin, Caroline, Marcella Kysilka, Virginia Rogers, and Lewis Smith. *Questioneze: Individual or Group Game Involvement for Developing Questioning Skills*. Columbus, Ohio: Charles E. Merrill, 1972.

Sanders, Norris. *Classroom Questions: What Kinds*. New York: Harper and Row, 1966.

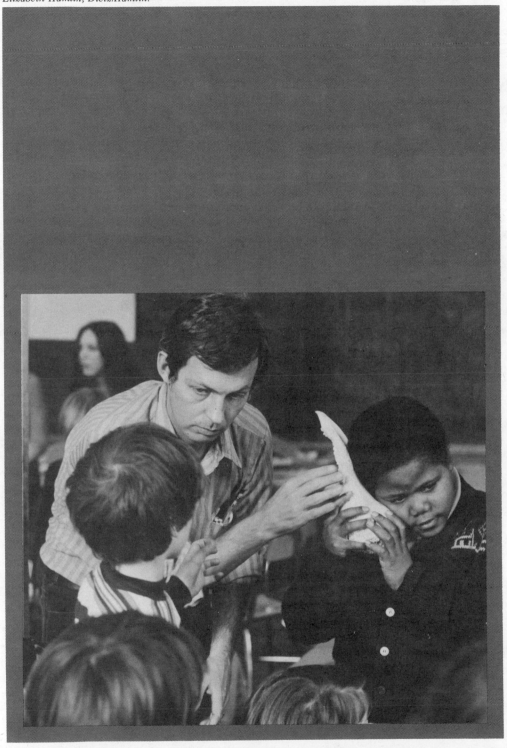

PETER H. MARTORELLA

Teaching Concepts

Objectives

1 (a) To identify five different ways in which the term "concept" is used in educational literature; (b) to identify the basic characteristics of concepts; and (c) to distinguish between essential and nonessential characteristics of a concept.

2 (a) To classify concepts according to types, using four classification systems; (b) to identify developmental differences that occur among students in concept learning; and (c) to distinguish concepts from other intellectual phenomena according to criteria.

3 (a) To distinguish between the private and public dimensions of concept learning; and (b) to identify and briefly describe the three stages of preparation for the teaching of concepts.

4 (a) To identify five dimensions of concept learning that can be measured and to arrange them according to their level of complexity; and (b) to identify and briefly describe three procedures for measuring the private dimensions of students' concepts.

It began like any other day. Ginny Peters awoke at approximately 7 o'clock, stretched, and rolled out of bed. She put on her clothes, neatly folded on the chair where she had placed them the night before, rolled her pajamas into a ball, and stuffed them under her pillow. Unaware of what was happening downstairs, she brushed her hair the usual 100 times and then washed her face and hands and brushed her teeth.

As she descended the stairs, she greeted her dog Missy and bounded into the kitchen. "Mornin', mom, dad," she said with her usual good cheer. The worried looks on her parents' faces called her up short, and signaled to her that something was amiss. "Sh-h, we're trying to hear the latest report," her mother said gently.

The radio on the kitchen table continued blaring out a news bulletin in excited tones. "Last night while most of Dublin City slept, an unprecedented robbery took place. Striking swiftly and quietly, the thieves moved with unusual efficiency. Informed sources report that law enforcement officials are completely baffled by the case. No clues have been uncovered nor have any eye witnesses come forth. A night watchman working in the 1700 block of Highland Avenue, however, reported that a speeding blue car was observed at approximately 3:00 A.M. No one in Dublin City recalls such a theft occurring where . . . ." Ginny's patience gave out, "What's going on? What happened?" she interrupted.

Her father switched off the radio. Glancing nervously at his wife, he said in solemn tones, "I guess we better tell her, Martha. She's sure to find out about it from someone else, if we don't." Martha began with slow and measured phrases, "Ginny, I don't want you to be upset by what I am about to tell you. Things may be difficult at first, but you — we all — will learn to adjust to it. After a while, our lives will go on just as before."

"Mother, please tell me *what* has happened. I can't stand the suspense," Ginny implored.

Her father leaned across the table and picked up the conversation. Ginny thought she saw a tear in his eye. "Ginny, someone has stolen *happiness*. From now on, no one will ever be able to know about, feel, or share happiness." Just then Ginny awoke with a start. "Wow," she shuddered, "that was a terrible dream."

Fortunately for all of us, as well as our hypothetical Ginny, we still have the concept of happiness among us. The above melodrama was contrived to draw attention to the importance of concepts. The loss of even one of our most precious concepts would be a significant personal, as well as a social, loss.

We build our world on concepts. They come in all types, and some are much more significant than others. Throughout any day, hundreds, perhaps thousands of them, will be pressed into service. Ginny's concepts of "tooth brushing," "politeness," "news," "radio," and "sadness" — to name just a few — were employed in her brief dream. Countless other concepts were at work also, just as they are for each of us every conscious moment of our lives. As we learn and experience new things, we both draw upon and increase our conceptual banks. We constantly put old concepts to use and, in the process, frequently extend them and acquire new, related ones.

Where does it all end? The chain of concept acquisition, usage, enlargement, and revision is continuous for as long as we are able to think. For some of us, the conceptual juices flow faster or slower depending upon such factors as our current and past experiences and the formal instruction we receive.

Everyone learns concepts, whether they like to or not. Most of us enjoy learning them — at least, some of the time. Concepts enrich, as well as extend and order, our psychological worlds. Many concepts, such as *chair*, are acquired because they have functional value; they are useful for something we need or want to do. Others, such as *cowboy*, are learned just because they are fun or because they make our lives more interesting and pleasant. Still others, such as *square root, balance of trade, verb*, and the like, are learned on a "good faith" basis. They are not immediately functional nor are they much fun, so we must simply take it on faith that some day they will be useful or entertaining. Much of our concept learning in schools is on such a good faith basis. When a teacher appears to tax or violate our good faith, we may balk at learning. We begin to suspect that we are "being had."

In addition to their ability to entertain us and to help satisfy our immediate needs, concepts serve us in three additional ways.

1. They simplify our learning tasks.
2. They expedite communication.
3. They help us distinguish between reality and imagery.

Our intellectual world is comprised of millions of bits and pieces of knowledge. If each of these items required a separate category in our knowledge network, information retrieval would be extremely unwieldy. Concepts allow us to organize and store similar pieces of information efficiently. Once formed, they eliminate our need to treat each new piece of knowledge as a separate category. In a sense, concepts are *hooks* on which we can hang new experiences. When we confront a sufficiently novel situation for which we have no hooks, we either force the information onto an incompatible hook or else we create a new one. In short, concepts organize our knowledge structure and keep it from becoming unwieldy and dysfunctional.

Perhaps the most useful aspect of concepts lies in their ability to speed up and simplify communication among people. Because you and I share similar concepts, we can easily communicate without any need on my part to explain in great detail every idea, event, or object. Each new concept builds upon preceding ones; their cumulative pattern and sequencing make extended descriptions of each one unnecessary. When communication between two people breaks down, it is often because one member has not learned concepts that are basic to the conversation. Frequently, this problem occurs in textbooks when the author incorrectly assumes knowledge of certain concepts on the part of the readers. On the other hand, communication proceeds very efficiently between individuals who are at a similar stage of conceptual learning. We frequently refer to such people as "being on the same wavelength." However, for communication to proceed at all, mutual knowledge of some concepts is essential.

One of the more subtle functions of concepts is their ability to help us distinguish between illusion and reality. One who has acquired the concept of cow has no trouble distinguishing between a picture or a three-dimensional model of a cow and a real Holstein. Similarly, knowledge of other concepts allows one, without much conscious analysis, to recognize that various pictures and models are only representations. Confusion between real examples of concepts and their secondhand representation can occasionally be detected in children, as with a little girl who believed that chickens were an inch and a half high.

What is the nature of concepts? How are they different from one another? How are they learned? The remainder of this chapter revolves about these three fundamental questions.

Your Turn

WHAT DO YOU KNOW ABOUT CONCEPTS?

Let's see what you already know about concepts. Mark a "T" for true and an "F" for false statements.

_____ 1. This page is filled with concepts.

_____ 2. Down deep, all concepts are alike.

_____ 3. Every subject matter area is built around concepts.

_____ 4. It is the subject matter area from which a concept is drawn that makes it easy or difficult to learn.

_____ 5. Another name for a concept is "generalization."

_____ 6. No matter what your age, concept learning occurs in the same way.

_____ 7. Learning a concept occurs in the same way that everything else does.

_____ 8. The more information we have about a concept, the easier it is to learn.

_____ 9. You teach for concept learning in the same way that you teach for other objectives.

_____ 10. Unless you can tell what a concept is in your own words, you have not really learned it.

Compare your answers to these questions with the Answer Key that follows.

ANSWER KEY

Your Turn: What Do You Know About Concepts?

1. T	6. F
2. F	7. F
3. T	8. F
4. F	9. F
5. F	10. F

Objective 1

(a) To identify five different ways in which the term "concept" is used in educational literature; (b) to identify the basic characteristics of concepts; and (c) to distinguish between essential and nonessential characteristics of a concept.

LEARNING ACTIVITY 1

THE NATURE OF CONCEPTS

People's concepts of a concept vary considerably. Some use the term concept synonymously with *idea:* "That's my concept of how a house should be designed." Others use the term to mean a *theme* or *topic:* "These are the concepts we will study in history: 'the Great Depression,' 'the New Deal,' . . . ." A third way to use "concept" is to express a *general, all-encompassing statement:* "All men are mortal." And a fourth way is to refer to the most fundamental *elements* or *structures of disciplines,* such as in the sciences and social sciences: "The concept of culture underlies all of anthropology."

In psychology and specifically in areas where different types of learning outcomes are being considered, concepts have a distinct fifth meaning with which the remainder of this chapter will be concerned. Concepts in this last sense refer to the *categories* into which we group our knowledge and experiences. Once formed, these categories act as intellectual magnets that attract and order related thoughts and experiences. The categories we create generally have single or multiword *labels* or *names* that serve to identify them, such as *tree* or *balance of trade.* As we experience objects or events, we sort them into the various categories we have created; once sorted, we begin relating them to other items in the same category. This relating process may be very brief and simple, or it may evolve into an extended analysis of multiconcept interrelationships.

Thus, we may simultaneously speak of concepts as being (1) *categories* into which our experiences are organized and (2) *the larger network of intellectual relationships brought about through categorization.* We do not merely sort out and label the objects and events we encounter; we actively reflect upon them to greater or lesser degrees. As we are faced with new or old phenomena, we must relate them, sometimes very quickly, to what we already know in order to make much sense of them. Thus, our concepts not only organize our experience but also affect *how* we attend to or reflect upon that experience. Suppose that each day we pass a hole in the ground partially filled with dirt and water. We may label it a "hazardous mud hole," thereby ensuring that we carefully avoid it. On the other hand, a passing biologist, using a different set of conceptual glasses, might experience the hole as a scientific gold mine filled with interesting organisms. His or her conceptual glasses, developed through specialized training, produce a different set of categories that, in turn, lead to different reflections concerning the same object.

Conceptual categories and related reflections may be limited or extensive, simplistic or complex, depending on one's interests and experiences. Occasionally, concepts may lack labels or precise referents. When this is so, communication with others may be difficult. We say things such as "I can't exactly describe it; you sort of have to *feel* it." "I don't know what you call it, but all of these paintings have it." "They don't have any names. I just call them 'squiggles' because they are sort of squiggly."

Objects or events are sorted into concept categories through a check of their basic characteristics or *criterial attributes*. If an item of information meets the criteria for a concept category we hold, we attach the concept name to the item and begin to relate it to other information we have. A check of criterial attributes alone, however, does not produce efficient categorization. The criterial attributes must be present in a particular sequence, relationship, or pattern to qualify for category placement. This specific ordering of attributes is known as the concept definition or *rule*.

Let's examine why the rule, as well as the identification of the criterial attributes, is necessary for accurate categorization. Suppose we fly over a small area and observe the following environmental characteristics: *land, water*, and a *surrounding* body. Into what conceptual category do we place our observation? Without the *rule* or way in which each of the three observed criterial attributes are related, we cannot be sure whether the correct answer is *island* or *lake*. The rule tells us that "land surrounded by water" is an island, whereas "water surrounded by land" is a *lake*.

Essentially then, concepts consist of (1) names such as "island," (2) criterial attributes such as "body of land," and (3) rules such as "body of land surrounded by water." Cases or illustrations of a concept are referred to as *examples; nonexamples* of a concept are any cases or illustrations that lack one or more of the criterial attributes of the concept or else have a different rule. Each concept is a nonexample for every other one; for instance, island is a nonexample of the concept of isthmus. The closer the "resemblance" of the concepts (i.e., their sets of related criterial attributes), the greater the difficulty in discriminating among them. In Figure 6.1 there is some potential confusion since

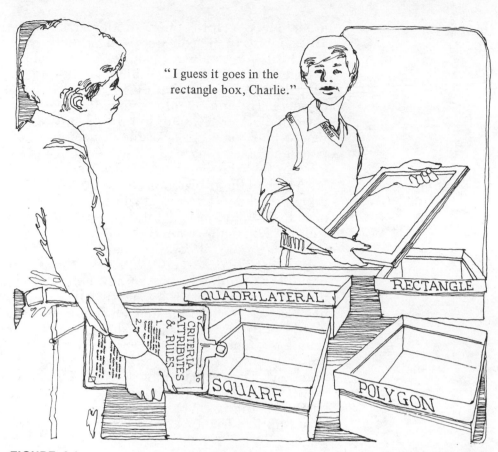

FIGURE 6.1

the three nonexamples of the concept "rectangle" are very similar to the concept "rectangle."

As with examples and nonexamples, criterial attributes also have a negative counterpart — *noncriterial attributes*. These are features that frequently are present in concept illustrations, though they are *not* an essential part of the concept. They are analogous to accessories on a car. Almost always, some accessories come with an automobile though they are unnecessary for the vehicle to function. Noncriterial attributes are present under many forms as seen in the following table. They may appear as *length* in examples of the concept "sentence"; as *color* when dealing with the concept "chair"; as *size* in examples of "triangle" or "island"; and so on.

Concept	Noncriterial Attribute
sentence	length
chair	color
triangle	size
island	size

The list of possibilities for noncriterial attributes is endless.

When we attend too closely to noncriterial attributes and begin to treat them as criterial ones, we often create *stereotypes* and *overgeneralizations*. For example, on the basis of three dates with three different Italian men, a girl might conclude that all Italian men are great lovers. A child being introduced to geometric shapes notes that in all examples of the concept *triangle* there are two equal sides and that the third side is always parallel to the plane of the floor. He or she overgeneralizes these conditions as essential for all triangles. A high school boy observes that every poem he has ever heard or read has rhymed. He mistakenly concludes that verse must rhyme to be classified as poetry. Children in a family grow up in a neighborhood where most of the blacks they encounter are physically aggressive, poor, and boisterous. From these limited and isolated cases, they begin to form their concepts of all blacks.

Much of the instruction we give and receive inadvertently confuses noncriterial and criterial attributes. To correct this error and sharpen our discrimination capabilities, we must periodically be called up short and be made to analyze carefully the similarities and differences in diverse cases of concept examples and nonexamples.

Almost never, except perhaps with certain abstract concepts, are examples completely free of any noncriterial distractors. Inevitably, there are some details in nearly all illustrations that may serve to mislead us concerning the concept's essential properties. For one whose grasp of a concept is shaky, noncriterial properties may be a source of great perplexity. On the other hand, for one who has a clear understanding of the concept, noncriterial features often provide enrichment. They enhance our already formed concept and enlarge our range of examples. Having already learned to sort out cases on the basis of defining characteristics, we can appreciate and even seek out new, subtle variations on old themes.

Mastery Test

OBJECTIVE 1   (a) To identify five different ways in which the term "concept" is used in educational literature; (b) to identify the basic characteristics of concepts; and (c) to distinguish between essential and nonessential characteristics of a concept.

1. In brief, what are five different ways in which the term "concept" is used in educational literature?

_____

_____

_____

_____

_____

2. List below the basic characteristics of concepts.

_____

_____

3. Take a moment to examine the list of concepts in the left-hand column. What are some of the more common noncriterial attributes that might be present in examples of these concepts? (Record your answers in the right-hand column.)

Concepts	*Typical Noncriterial Attributes*
mammal	
tree	
river	
winter	
prime number	
mountain	
state	
death	
cloud	
comb	

Now compare your answers with those that follow in the Answer Key.

ANSWER KEY

Mastery Test, Objective 1

1. (a) to mean the same thing as an "idea"; (b) to mean a "theme" or "topic"; (c) as a general, all-encompassing, or broad statement; (d) to mean the basic structure or elements of a discipline; (e) as categories into which we group our knowledge and experience.
2. Names, criterial attributes, rules.

3. There are a number of possible noncriterial attributes that you might have listed. Consider the following ones for comparisons:
mammal — color; tree — size; river — length; winter — temperature; prime number — size; mountain — location; state — size; death — age; cloud — shape; comb — color.

Objective 2

(a) To classify concepts according to types, using four classification systems; (b) to identify developmental differences that occur among students in concept learning; and (c) to distinguish concepts from other intellectual phenomena according to criteria.

LEARNING ACTIVITY 2

TYPES OF CONCEPTS AND OTHER FORMS OF KNOWLEDGE

What makes a concept easy or hard to learn? Let's try an experiment to find out. Detach (along the dotted lines) the various cards shown at the back of the book in Appendix B; sort them into two piles. Place those you consider *easy* to learn into the first pile and those you consider *hard* into the second. Arrange these two piles into nine new piles, ranging from easiest to hardest. You may sort as many cards as you wish into each pile, but each pile must have *at least one* card in it. When you finish your sorting, take some time to compare your results and the rationale you used with someone else.

What were the similarities and differences in the two sets of piles and in the two rationales? When your discussion is completed, record the names of the concepts from the nine piles in the appropriate boxes on the continuum in Figure 6.2.

Below the listing, note the criteria you used in judging the con-

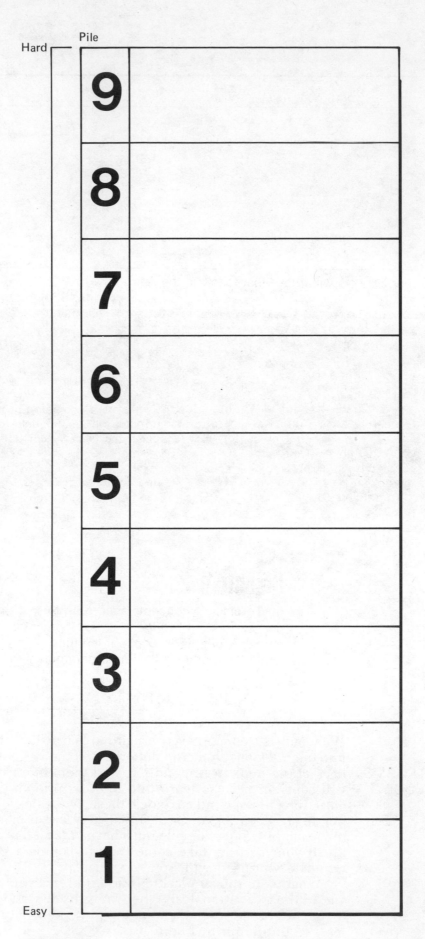

FIGURE 6.2

cept's level of difficulty. After reading the remainder of the section you may wish to refer back to your conclusions.

Types of Concepts

There are many different bases by which to classify concepts as easier or harder to learn. A frequently cited criterion of difficulty is the extent to which concepts are perceived to be *concrete* or *abstract*. For purposes of simplification, let us use the rough definition that concreteness refers to what we can perceive directly through one of the five senses: taste, smell, touch, sound, sight. In contrast, abstractness refers to what we acquire only indirectly through the senses or cannot perceive directly through the senses. There are some problems with these distinctions in practice, but they will suffice to illustrate one type of classification system. Clearly, in this system, chair, tree, glass, and similar objects are concrete concepts and presumably easier to learn. Similarly, beauty, freedom, justice, empathy, and similar terms are abstract and presumably harder to learn. In between are a wide range of concepts that defy simple classification in this system.

Another way to view concepts is to examine whether they are most frequently learned in *formal* or *informal* contexts. Many of the concepts we acquire come through informal channels of experience (car, house, television, fire), while others come through systematic channels of instruction such as schools, job-training programs, or parents (legislature, hydrogen, preposition, square). Not all abstract concepts are acquired formally, however. Beauty and truth, for example, result from a complex blend of formal and informal instruction. It would be difficult to assess which type of instruction is generally dominant for such concepts.

A third perspective on concept types divides them into three classes: *conjunctive, disjunctive*, and *relational*. According to this frame of reference, a *conjunctive* concept is less difficult to learn because it has only a *single* set of qualities or characteristics that one has to learn. A little girl might say to herself, "If it has this and that and those things, it must be a whatchamacallit." *Chair* is a conjunctive concept, as the dictionary definition testifies: "A piece of furniture consisting of a seat, legs and back, and often arms, designed for one person." There *are* many kinds or examples of chairs, but the *easy* part of learning the concept is that the basic set of defining characteristics always are essentially the same.

A *disjunctive* concept is slightly more complicated. In order to learn this type of concept, one must learn two or more sets of alternative conditions under which the concept appears. *Citizen* is such a concept. The dictionary states that a citizen is "a native *or* naturalized member of a state or nation who owes allegiance to its government and who is entitled to its protection." Either being born in a country or fulfilling some test of citizenship can lead to the status of *citizen*. In short, disjunctive concepts can have more than one set of criterial attributes.

The most complex type of concept to learn is a *relational* one. Waste, resource, pollution, a little, a lot, parallel, and symmetry are all relational concepts. Their meaning stems from a comparison or a relationship between objects or events. A line segment or an object cannot be assessed "parallel" unless something specific about its relationship to another line or object is known. Similarly, one cannot tell if something is "a lot" unless it is compared to something else — another item, an average or norm of some kind, or the whole of which it is a part.

So it is with all relational concepts; they describe *relationships* between items. A line segment that is parallel on some occasions can be perpendicular on other occasions. Only its particular relationship to *another* line segment makes it perpendicular or parallel. Five apples are a lot of apples for a small child's snack; but they are only a little for a troop of boy scouts. Learners of relational concepts must focus on the characteristics of the items being compared and also on the basis being used for comparison. In observing a line segment, for example, a student also must note another line segment, as well as the relationship between the two.

Figure 6.3 summarizes the characteristics and the relationships among conjunctive, disjunctive, and relational concepts. Determining whether a concept is one of the three preceding types allows a teacher to anticipate learning difficulties and to prepare corresponding instruction. One investigator discovered, for example, that preschoolers have a tendency to treat relational concepts as if they were conjunctive ones.

> When the four-year-old first learns the concept dark, he regards it as descriptive of an absolute class of color — black and related dark hues. The phrase "dark yellow" makes no sense to him, for dark signifies dark colors, not relative darkness.[1]

Older students who have misconceptions of *resource* and *waste* reflect similar problems when they fail to understand that oil, water, wood, and the like may be examples of resources and waste simultaneously.

A fourth system for classifying concepts has a developmental basis. It concentrates on the dominant medium through which our concepts are represented as we develop chronologically. According to Jerome Bruner, three representational media for acquiring concepts exist:

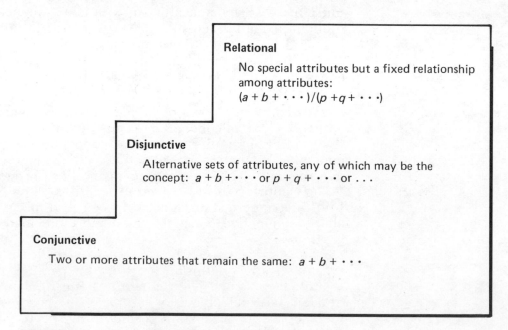

Relational

No special attributes but a fixed relationship among attributes:
$(a + b + \cdots)/(p + q + \cdots)$

Disjunctive

Alternative sets of attributes, any of which may be the concept: $a + b + \cdots$ or $p + q + \cdots$ or . . .

Conjunctive

Two or more attributes that remain the same: $a + b + \cdots$

FIGURE 6.3 Levels of concept difficulty.

enactive — "knowing something through doing it"; iconic — "through a picture or image of it"; and symbolic — "through symbols such as language."[2] Thus one might learn the concept of swimming through doing it (enactive); through viewing a filmstrip on swimming techniques (iconic); or through reading a book on the topic (symbolic). Bruner also notes of these three representational forms: "Their appearance in the life of the child is in that order, each depending upon the previous one for its development, yet all of them remaining more or less intact throughout life — barring such early accidents as blindness or deafness or cortical injury."[3] Enactive representation is dominant during infancy and early childhood; iconic representation becomes the norm through preadolescence; thereafter, symbolic representation dominates.

From a teacher's perspective, this system of classifying concepts has two basic applications. Concepts may be analyzed with respect to which one of the three representational forms — enactive, iconic, or symbolic — seems most appropriate for teaching that concept. Another application is to match the developmental level of the children with the mode of representation. A rule-of-thumb approximation for such planning might be

Up to 7 years:	Enactive forms
Up to 11 years:	Enactive moving to iconic forms
11 years and beyond:	Iconic moving to symbolic forms

As noted earlier, the process of examining and categorizing concepts may take many forms. The four perspectives, summarized in Figure 6.4, suggest only some of the possibilities. From an instructional viewpoint, the important issue is that we, as teachers, try to: (1) determine which concepts are most likely to present learning difficulties, (2) identify what the potential problems are likely to be, and (3) use such data to build systematic assistance into learning activities. All concepts are not alike with respect to how they are learned and, to the extent that our instruction reflects this fact, it will be more or less effective.

CLASSIFICATION SYSTEM FOR CONCEPTS

Basis for Classification	Types of Concepts
Degrees of concreteness	1. concrete (chair, lake) 2. abstract (lonely, hot)
Context in which learned	1. formal (school, training program) 2. informal (socializing, casual observation)
Nature of criterial attributes	1. conjunctive (chair) 2. disjunctive (citizen) 3. relational (dark)
Form or manner in which learned	1. enactive (play tennis) 2. iconic (watch tennis match on TV) 3. symbolic (read book on tennis)

FIGURE 6.4 Concept types.

Other Forms of Knowledge

If the various types of concepts are the basic organizers of our knowledge, providing a foundation from which we can build elaborate intellectual structures, what other elements comprise the rest of the structure? An adequate discussion of this complex topic is well beyond the scope of this chapter, but we can, at least, outline four other types of knowledge that psychologists and other social scientists have distinguished from concepts. They are (1) percepts, (2) facts, (3) conclusions, and (4) generalizations.

Percepts are the raw impressions that are immediately filtered through any of our five senses. They are the basic initiators of all thought. Not many of these perceptions result in thoughtful activities, for there are far too many stimuli in our daily activities for us to respond to all of them. Walk through the public marketplace of any major city and your senses of smelling, hearing, feeling, seeing, and even tasting will be so bombarded that some form of filtering mechanism is essential before reflection can take place. Concepts act as our filtering device, regulating which percepts are accepted into or rejected from our consciousness. Our conceptual categories tell us what we are encountering and how it should be interpreted.

Facts are defined in several ways. Perhaps the most common way is in reference to any well-grounded, clearly established piece of information. "Men from the earth have landed on the moon" is an example of a fact. *Conclusions* are pieces of information that follow logically from an investigation, formal or informal, and which are presented in the form of a statement. "It's going to rain today." "The field is infested with Japanese beetles." "Beaker *A* contains hydrochloric acid, while *B* has traces of hydrofluoric." When a conclusion has been submitted to the best test of evidence and has been definitively verified, it is regarded as a fact. For example, you may conclude that you have learned nothing from this book. Further investigations by you or your instructor may or may not verify the conclusion as a fact. Many conclusions never qualify as facts, and many more are never even tested as potential facts.

Generalizations, like facts, are a special class of conclusions. They summarize a collection of wide-ranging, carefully tested facts. As such, they apply to a wide range of cases and have predictive power. Generalizations, then (1) are true or have been verified by the best tests of evidence available (i.e., are facts); (2) predict things in the sense of making "if . . . , then . . . ." statements; (3) apply to all relevant cases without exception; and (4) express significant relationships among concepts.

Consider these generalizations: "All circles have 360°." "Bears hibernate in the winter." "Every sentence has a verb, stated or understood." All of them tell us something that we can be certain of if we encounter a circle, bear, or sentence.

Facts, conclusions, and generalizations all employ concepts to tell their story. Without the conceptual referents embedded in them, facts, conclusions, and generalizations would be meaningless. We must have learned what a circle and degrees are before we can appreciate and understand the above generalization. Our concepts make our facts, conclusions, and generalizations possible, and these latter elements, in turn, help produce new concepts and concept relationships.

Similarly, each concept may organize a host of facts, conclusions, and generalizations. This is what we mean when we say of someone that he or she could "write a book about that." A realtor's concept of *house* is laced with interrelated structures of facts, conclusions, and generalizations. Teachers must look to the prerequisite concept knowledge of students as they plan instruction. Similarly, they must consider *alternative* instructional models for concept learning. We will take up this latter point in some detail later in the chapter.

Mastery Test

OBJECTIVE 2   (a) To classify concepts according to types, using four classification systems; (b) to identify developmental differences that occur among students in concept learning; and (c) to distinguish concepts from other intellectual phenomena according to criteria.

1. Give a brief definition of the following types of concepts, each of which was used in one of the concept classification systems.

   (a) concrete _____

   _____

   (b) abstract _____

   _____

   (c) formal _____

   _____

   (d) informal _____

   _____

   (e) conjunctive _____

   _____

   (f) disjunctive _____

   _____

   (g) relational _____

   _____

   (h) enactive _____

   _____

   (i) iconic _____

   _____

   (j) symbolic _____

   _____

2. Which of the concept types you have just defined are most closely related to developmental differences among children?

_____

_____

_____

_____

_____

_____

3. Give a brief definition of the following forms of knowledge that psychologists and other social scientists have distinguished from concepts.

(a) percepts   _____

_____

(b) facts   _____

_____

(c) conclusions   _____

_____

(d) generalizations   _____

_____

Now compare your conclusions with those in the Answer Key that follows.

ANSWER KEY

Mastery Test, Objective 2

1. Answers should be similar to the following definitions:
   (a) *Concrete.* Those concepts we can perceive directly through one of the five senses.
   (b) *Abstract.* Those which cannot be directly perceived through one of the senses.
   (c) *Formal.* Concepts acquired through systematic channels of instruction.
   (d) *Informal.* Concepts acquired through undirected and unorganized means.
   (e) *Conjunctive.* Concepts defined by a single set of qualities or characteristics.
   (f) *Disjunctive.* Concepts defined by two or more alternative sets of qualities or characteristics.
   (g) *Relational.* Concepts defined by the relationships among objects or events.
   (h) *Enactive.* Concepts acquired through doing or acting.

   (i) *Iconic.* Concepts acquired through imagery or pictures.
   (j) *Symbolic.* Concepts acquired through verbal or symbolic forms (such as reading or speaking).

2. Enactive, iconic, and symbolic; concrete and abstract.

3. Answers should be similar to the following definitions:
   (a) *Percepts.* Raw impressions filtered through any of the five senses.
   (b) *Facts.* Well-grounded, clearly established pieces of information.
   (c) *Conclusions.* Any pieces of information that follow logically from an investigation, formal or informal.
   (d) *Generalizations.* Facts that express significant relationships among concepts, are predictive statements, and apply to all relevant cases.

Objective 3

(a) To distinguish between the private and public dimensions of concept learning; and (b) to identify and briefly describe the three stages of preparation for the teaching of concepts.

LEARNING ACTIVITY 3

LEARNING AND TEACHING CONCEPTS

No matter what the subject area or the particular concept, each of us has a unique personal history that influences how we use concepts. My concepts of *primate, rhombus,* or *whiskers* are slightly different from anyone else's, the unique product of specific percepts being processed through my total conceptual network. Compared to the biologist, mathematician, and dermatologist, I may appear to be a conceptual dunce if the conversation deals solely with primates, rhombi, or whiskers. Still we can communicate at a very basic level since we share a minimal level of concept learning.

Personal and Public Dimensions of Concepts

We may label the unique, personalized side of concepts their *personal dimension.* This idiosyncratic aspect is not really teachable, although traces may sometimes be acquired through formal instruction. For concepts to function as shared experiences, they must also possess a *public dimension* that each of us holds in common. These are the shared attributes or properties that serve as the basis of communication and which must be understood by anyone claiming to have learned the concept. When we move beyond that basic public level of understanding, we generally need to explain in some detail our *personal* associations with the concept. Two individuals who find they "have a lot in common" often mean they have discovered their personal associations with concepts are surprisingly similar.

Try an experiment to discover your own personal associations with a concept that you share with most other people in our culture. Refer to the object shown in Figure 6.5. Give it a name and write that name in

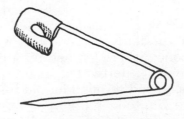

FIGURE 6.5

the circle at the center of the diagram in Figure 6.6 Next jot down your immediate associations following the first set of arrows in the spaces marked 1. Now consider what the words in these spaces remind you of and record these new associations in the spaces marked 2. Repeat the process for the spaces marked 3.

Take no more than two minutes to complete the diagram. Compare your results with those of others. First examine the names used to categorize the object, then the associations found in the spaces marked

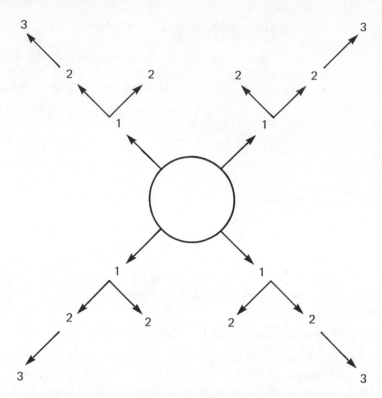

FIGURE 6.6   An illustration of a conceptual network.

1, 2, and 3. In what ways were all of the associations similar? In what ways did they differ? At what points, if any, did some of the concepts' criterial attributes get listed? At what points were noncriterial attributes listed? What did you learn about your own personal concept from Figure 6.6?

Whatever the character of the personal network each of us generates, it would seem that the *criterial* attributes are the common or *public* aspects of concepts that provide the basis of communication. While formal instruction, such as that occurring in classrooms, always makes some contribution to the personal dimensions of concept learning, its primary focus initially should be on the *public* dimensions. Such basic, culturally shared elements of concepts generally can be derived from dictionaries, encyclopedias, scholarly works, tradition, authoritative experience, or the mass media. While the vast majority of concepts are learned informally, with highly personal and public elements intertwined, many are so specialized that they can only be acquired through formal instruction. Also, a person's lifestyle may be so limited or different from the lifestyles of others that he or she requires assistance in learning the public elements of concepts.

What's It Like To Learn a Concept?

Everyone learns hundreds of new concepts without ever giving much thought to the matter. Trial-and-error, question-and-answer, and chance observations bring us a wealth of concepts that we are not even aware we are learning. As time passes and we mature, many of these concepts are reinforced, refined, and amplified. This process continues naturally throughout our lives.

Let us try to capture the sensation of someone who is trying to learn a new concept. What strategies are employed? What feelings do we have? What successes and failures do we encounter and what led to them?

Your Turn

COMPARE FOUR CONCEPT EXAMPLES

Shown below are some materials taken from the elementary science study unit of *Teacher's Guide for Attribute Games and Problems.*[4] We can treat each of the four sets of figures as a concept to be learned. Examine the first two rows of each set, looking for the criterial attributes (defining properties) of that concept, then select the examples of that concept from the third row. Below each of the four sets, write as specifically and clearly as possible what you consider to be the definition or criterial attributes of the concepts. Compare your conclusions with others who have examined the four sets. If your choices and definitions differ, consider whose results seem most accurate and why. Then turn to the Answer Key that follows.

FIGURE 6.7

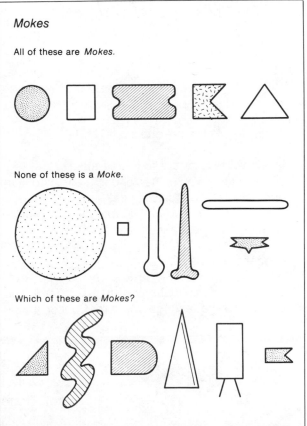

FIGURE 6.8

Figures 6.7, 6.8, 6.9, and 6.10 were originally published in *Teacher's Guide for Attribute Games and Problems* (New York: McGraw-Hill, 1968), pp. 75 and 77. They are reprinted here by permission of the Elementary Science Study of Education Development Center, Inc.

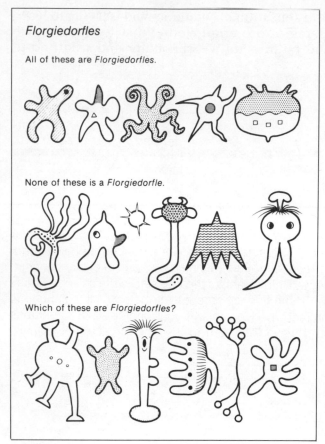

FIGURE 6.9

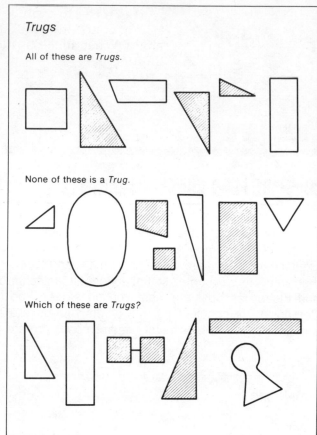

FIGURE 6.10

Consider the following questions:

1. In what ways are the four sets alike?
2. What makes some of the concepts easier to learn than others? (In other words, what is the meaning of the term "easier" in these cases?)
3. If you or anyone else was unable to identify or define one or more of the concepts correctly, what were the problems you encountered?
4. In what ways is the learning of these artificial concepts similar to the learning of other reality-based new concepts?
5. Were any of you able to *identify* concept examples correctly but not *define* them accurately? If so, what are the implications of this fact for school learning?
6. What were the feelings you experienced in the various stages of trying to learn the concepts?

ANSWER KEY

Your Turn: Compare Four Concept Examples

These four examples should have sensitized you to what it's like to confront a concept for the first time. In order to qualify as a Mellinark, examples must have spots, a black dot, and a tail. Moke examples have only one defining attribute, the fact that they are of the same height. The criterial attributes of Florgiedorfles are their height and number of arms, while Trugs may be *either* shaded triangles *or* unshaded quadrilaterals.

A final learning demonstration may suggest yet a few more potential obstacles for learners. You will need three sheets of paper, one large enough to cover this page. Follow the instructions carefully, and at the conclusion of the sequence you will be given a short test.

Place one sheet at the top of the page on which Figure 6.11 appears and the second sheet directly following Figure 6.11. Use the third sheet for making any notes that you wish. Once you have finished examining a figure, cover it with the top sheet and move the bottom sheet until the next figure has been uncovered and so on. DO NOT UNCOVER A FIGURE ONCE IT HAS BEEN EXAMINED.

Figure 6.11 shows an example of the concept you are to learn; the concept name is "Squip."

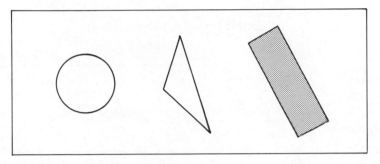

FIGURE 6.11 This *is* a Squip.

Figure 6.12 is also a Squip.

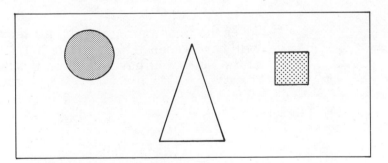

FIGURE 6.12 This *is* a Squip.

Figure 6.13, however, is *not* a Squip.

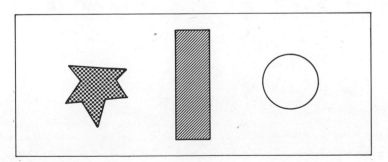

FIGURE 6.13 This is *not* a Squip.

Figure 6.14 also is *not* a Squip.

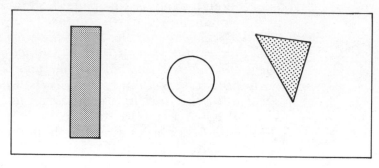

FIGURE 6.14 This is *not* a Squip.

But Figure 6.15 is a Squip.

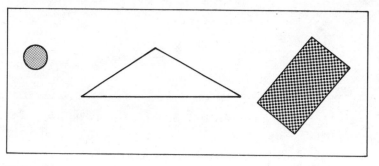

FIGURE 6.15 This *is* a Squip.

Cover the final figure, and do *not* reexamine any of the materials (you will have a chance to do so later). Take the test below, referring to any of the notes you have taken on the third sheet.

Your Turn

INSTANCES OF SQUIP

Examine each of the four sets of figures below and identify any instances of a Squip. (Each set of figures is to be read across from left to right.)

1.

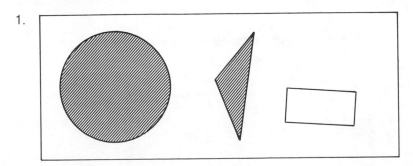

FIGURE 6.16 Is this a Squip?

2.

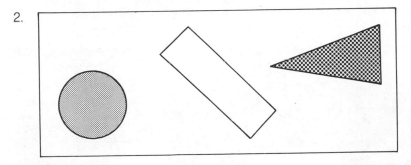

FIGURE 6.17 Is this a Squip?

3.

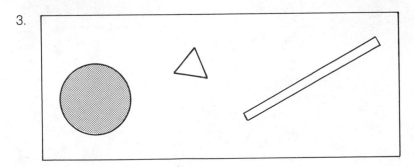

FIGURE 6.18 Is this a Squip?

4.

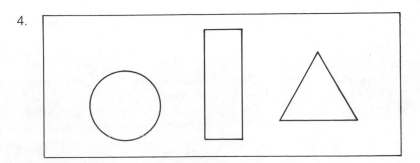

FIGURE 6.19 Is this a Squip?

If this test was taken with a group, check to see how many selected 1, 2, 3, or 4 as squips. If there are no disagreements, go on to the next test.

But, if you took the test alone or if there were disagreements within the group, evaluate your answers by the following procedure. *Remove* and *discard* the sheets covering Figures 6.11–6.15 and reexamine each of them. Compare similarities and differences in each of the figures. What is your individual or the group's new collective conclusion about which figures are Squips? If some doubts or disagreements still exist, we will deal with them after you have completed the following test.

Your Turn

CONCEPT OF SQUIP

Write below, as precisely as possible, a definition of a Squip.

_____

_____

Compare your definition with those of others and determine which one appears to be the most accurate. Then consult the Answer Key that follows.

ANSWER KEY

Your Turn: Concept of Squip

Suppose I were to examine the results of all who participated in the preceding demonstration and discover that 25 percent of the participants did *not* learn from my instruction.[5] That is, 25 percent of them did not select 1 and 3 as examples of a Squip, and 25 percent did not write a definition essentially similar to this one: *A Squip is a circle, triangle, and rectangle arranged in that order* (the correct answers).

Which of the following evaluations seems warranted to you?
1. Twenty-five percent of the participants were slow learners.
2. Twenty-five percent of the participants were cul-turally deprived: that is, they lacked appropriate readiness experiences with Squips.
3. Twenty-five percent of the participants probably had lower IQs than the rest.
4. Since 75 percent of the group got the correct answers, the 25 percent are the normal number of failures to be expected.

If none of these explanations appeal to you, offer one that focuses on the deficiencies of the *instructional sequence*, not of the learner. What, in the instruction provided, led some learners astray? Talk to those who failed the tests and analyze why they answered as they did. Then proceed with the reading of the chapter.

You are likely to find that those who answered incorrectly have a consistent and logical basis for their answers. For demonstration purposes, several pitfalls that invariably mislead some learners were built into the instruction. Although the design follows a sound instructional plan based upon principles to be discussed later in the chapter, it cannot take into account the learning differences of all individuals. Some will focus on particular characteristics such as size or color, while others will concentrate on all the characteristics of one particular element in the total array. In trying to learn the concept of Squip, these tendencies to focus on irrelevant characteristics work to the learner's disadvantage and cause him or her to draw incorrect conclusions. The readers who followed this path paralleled the learning experiences of children who incorrectly infer that the "White House" is a necessary part of the concept "President" or that "dark hair" and "dark skin" are necessarily characteristic of "Italians."

The phenomenon of confusing noncriterial attributes with criterial properties, while deliberately introduced into this demonstration, occurs naturally in the learning of academic concepts. On these occasions, unless a teacher is willing to reexamine his or her instruction rather than fault the learner's capabilities, little progress toward the learning of concepts will occur. An instructor must *resist* the easy defensive position, "Most of the class got the correct answer when I explained the concept. If you didn't, then I guess you are just not trying hard enough!"

Let's reflect a moment on some of the instructional assistance given you relative to the preceding five concepts, Mellinarks, Mokes, Florgiedorfles, Trugs, and Squips. Most of the conditions provided for your instruction are not available in a typical concept learning situation.

Condition 1. Very little irrelevant material was included in your instruction — material that might have diverted your attention from the essential characteristics of the concept.

Condition 2. All the cases you needed, examples and nonexamples, were put before you *simultaneously.* This allowed you to recheck conclusions and to compare cases easily.

Condition 3. The characteristics of the concepts were relatively simple ones. Mellinarks and Squips were *conjunctive* concepts, the least difficult type to learn (see Figure 6.3), while the fourth concept, Trugs, was *disjunctive* and the second and third, Mokes and Florgiedorfles, were *relational.*

Condition 4. All five concepts had concise graphic referents that required little or no verbal ability to understand.

Those readers who experienced difficulty with the pronunciation of concept names or who could not now correctly spell some of them should be able to empathize with students' linguistic burden. Similarly, some readers may have discovered it is possible to identify *instances* of a concept correctly without being able to explain accurately or define the concept in one's own words. Students frequently exhibit this phenomenon, and it often leads to a misinterpretation of their learning level. Persons who can consistently discriminate examples of a concept from nonexamples may be said to have "learned" that concept, whether or not they can articulate a definition of it.

What's It Like To Teach a Concept?

To initiate the teaching process, you need to ask yourself several sets of questions. The first set pertains to whether the concept is appropriate to *teach,* and the second relates to prerequisite instructional planning.

Concept Appropriateness Inventory

1. Is the concept considered to be significant? That is, do educators and subject matter specialists seem to suggest that the concept is an important one for students to acquire?

2. Is the concept one that should be taught formally? That is, should a student receive systematic instruction in the concept or is it more appropriately acquired through informal means?

3. Is there sufficient agreement on the criterial attributes and the concept rule to have a basis for designing instruction? That is, can clear and specific guidelines concerning the essential characteristics of the concept be inferred from readings and reference sources?

Assuming the answers are "yes" to these three questions, you are ready to move on to the next set that actually starts the instructional planning.

Prerequisite Planning Inventory

1. What name is most commonly applied to the concept? (*Example:* lake)

2. What is the concept's rule or definition (i.e., the arrangement of its criterial attributes)? (*Example:* body of water surrounded by land)

3. What are the essential characteristics or *criterial attributes* of the concept, based upon your readings and reference sources? (*Example:* land, water, surrounding)

4. What are some *noncriterial attributes* typically associated with the concept? (*Example:* size, location, depth)

5. What are some interesting and learner-relevant *examples* or cases of the concept which you can use in its explanation? (*Example:* local lakes, mountain lakes, desert lakes)

6. What are some contrasting *nonexamples* of the concept that will help clarify and illustrate the concept? (*Example:* ocean, stream, bay)

7. What are some *cues, questions,* or *directions* that you can employ to call attention to criterial attributes and noncriterial attributes in the concept examples? (*Example:* "Look at all the points where the water meets the land.")

8. What is the most efficient, interesting, and thought-provoking *medium* (or media) by which to present examples and nonexamples? (*Example:* slides, air photos)

9. What level of *concept mastery* do you expect of students and how will you measure it? (*Example:* Be able to define "lake" and state the similarities and differences this body of water has with other major bodies of water through a project.)

With the answers to these inventories in hand, you are prepared to begin instruction. As noted earlier, there are many types of concepts, and the process of learning them differs from that used for other kinds of knowledge such as generalizations. Among concept types there are also differences that require alternative methods of instruction. Detailed discussions of these variations exist elsewhere.[6] In this chapter we shall limit ourselves to a single basic model for organizing concept learning instruction. It emphasizes essential phases of instruction underlying the approach to all types of concepts.

Basic Model for Concept Instruction

1. Complete the Concept Appropriateness Inventory and the Prerequisite Planning Inventory.
2. Develop an introduction to the instructional sequence. The introduction should orient the learner to the task and arouse his or her curiosity. It might be a short story, anecdote, relating of experiences, or brief sequence of questions that focus attention on the topic.
3. Present the series of varied examples and nonexamples of the concept that you have developed in some logical order. (There are no hard and fast rules on "how many." Consider a minimum of seven examples as a rule of thumb.)
4. If possible, present all the examples and nonexamples simultaneously or in close succession, so that the learner can compare all of the cases.
5. Interject the cues, directions, and questions throughout the materials as necessary to draw attention to criterial and noncriterial attributes and to similarities and differences in examples and nonexamples. Correspondingly, encourage learner questions. In written material, cues may be arrows, marginal notes, underlining, and the like.
6. Assess concept mastery at a minimal level, namely, whether students can correctly discriminate among *new* examples and nonexamples.
7. Assess concept mastery at more advanced levels, as consistent with the developmental capabilities of the students and with your own objectives.

The psychologist Robert Gagné offers a brief example of how such a basic model may be employed and, in addition, how *two* related concepts may be taught together — the examples for one serving as the nonexamples for the other.

1. Show the child a glass containing water and a glass containing a rock. Say "This is a solid" and "This is a liquid."
2. Using a different container, show the child some powdered substance in a pile in a container and some milk in another container. Say "This is a solid; this is a liquid."
3. Provide still a third example of solid and liquid, using different materials and containers.
4. Show the child a number of examples of liquids and solids which he has not seen before. Ask him to distinguish the liquids and the solids. (In this example, I assume the child has previously learned to repeat the words "liquid" and "solid" readily when he hears them; they are familiar in sound.)[7]

The organization of instructional materials for concept learning may take many forms. Several years ago, an engaging 16-mm film entitled *Model Man*[8] developed the concept of *model*, defined as a disjunctive concept. Blending examples and nonexamples in a humorous story, the film communicated clearly the criterial attributes of the concept in less than 20 minutes. Slides and pictures, though a more static medium, can be used in the same way, and the focus of learning can be controlled more easily.

Suppose we wish to teach the concept of *island* to a class of third graders. We have completed the Concept Appropriateness Inventory and have concluded that the concept is considered by social studies educators to be an important one for children to learn, that it should be taught formally, and that its essential characteristics can be spelled out. The Prerequisite Planning Inventory then is completed. The concept rule is "a body of water surrounded by land," and the criterial attributes are "land," "water," and "surrounding" (all-aroundness). After a brief introduction and a short question-and-answer session, the students are shown a series of slides as characterized below, accompanied by related questions and commentary.

Slide 1:	Example	Shot of large uninhabited island with vegetation.
Slide 2:	Example	Shot of small uninhabited island with no vegetation. Arrows on slide are pointing to the surrounding water.
Slide 3:	Nonexample	Shot of peninsula.
Slide 4:	Example	Shot of large island with buildings, etc.
Slide 5:	Example	Shot of small island with inhabitants.
Slide 6:	Nonexample	Shot of bay with inhabitants adjacent.
Slide 7:	Example	Shot of uninhabited island with unusual shape.
Slide 8:	Nonexample	Shot of an isthmus.
Slide 9:	Example	Shot of an island with a lake within.
Slide 10:	Nonexample	Shot of a lake with arrows pointing to the land all around.
Slide 11:	Example	Shot of an uninhabited island with mountains.
Slide 12:	Example	Shot of an inhabited island with mountains.
Slide 13:	Example	Shot of an island with an unusual shape.

After the slide presentation, a series of simple charts with hand-drawn and/or pasted pictures may be used to measure learning in conjunction with the following basic set of questions.

Chart 1:	Which of these pictures is a picture of an island?
Chart 2:	Which of these pictures is not a picture of an island?
Chart 3:	Which of these pictures shows something that all islands have? (illustrates one attribute)
Chart 4:	Which of these pictures shows something that all islands have? (illustrates another attribute)

Let us now consider an older group of students about to learn the concept of *nonverbal communication*. We might follow a similar format, using pictures and/or role-played episodes as examples and nonexamples. Both scenes from printed advertisements, as well as commercially made photographs and pictures, could be used.

Three-dimensional models also can be employed effectively as examples and nonexamples, particularly in the areas of science and mathematics, for demonstrating concepts like molecules and sets. Three-dimensional models have the additional advantage of providing "hands on" experience with the concept. Simple hand-prepared charts and posters are another medium that lends itself to all subject matter areas. In mathematics, for example, the concept of *mode* can be cleanly and quickly illustrated through a series of charts or through a single one, as shown here.

Examples of Mode
5, 6, 7, *8, 8,* 9, 10
9, 10, *12,* 13, 10, *12,* 8, *12, 12,* 6
97, 94, 32, *97,* 75, 63, 29, 85, *97*
1, 13, *22, 22,* 12, 14, 27, 83, 15, *22*
72, 72, 72, 72, 72, 72
65, 64, *65,* 63, 71, 62, 63, *65*
1, 0, 9, 6, 5, 7, 7, 8, *1,* 3, *1, 1*

An alternate format for the instruction would be to use the chalkboard or the overhead projector. A simple mastery test could consist of a series of new number examples and nonexamples for correct identification, or else a sequence of open-ended questions such as: "What do all the examples have in common?" "How would you define a *mode* in your own words?"

Materials for concept learning also may be designed as self-instructional units. A basic self-instructional sequence or *minitext* designed to teach the concept of *organization* is shown on the next few pages.[9]

ORGANIZATION

In this booklet, you are going to learn some things about an organization. Please be sure to read *all* the material on *all* the pages.

This booklet is short and will not take very long to complete.

After you have finished reading the material, you will be asked some questions about what you have just learned.

PLEASE DO *NOT* WRITE IN THE BOOKLET.

PLEASE TURN TO THE NEXT PAGE.

ORGANIZATION

Tia is a member of the Girl Scouts. James is a member of the Boy Scouts. The Girl Scouts and Boy Scouts *are* organizations. Girl Scouts and Boy Scouts agree to follow certain rules. They enjoy playing games and going on trips together.

All of the boys in one third grade class started a Pirate Club. It *was* an organization. The boys were interested in the same things — pirate stories and ships. So, when they made up a set of rules for the club, one rule was that they would meet once a month to hear pirate stories.

The people in the stands at a baseball game are *not* an organization. They are all interested in baseball, but they did *not* join a group and did not agree to rules in order to see the baseball game. All the fans in the stands at the game do not form an organization. But each of the baseball teams the fans are watching *is* an organization. All nine team members wish to play baseball, and they must obey the rules. Unless they agree to the rules of the team, they are not allowed to belong to it. During the year the team members practice and play together.

Susan and her parents belong to the temple near their house. Thomas and his parents belong to the church two miles from their house. Both the temple and the church *are* organizations. Their members come together to learn about God. Their members all agree to follow certain customs of the temple and the church. They all agree to believe certain things.

Mr. Morton owns a small bread company. He is the only member of the company. He bakes the bread himself and delivers it himself. His company is *not* an organization. Mr. Morton is very interested in his company, and he has set up rules to follow for himself. But since the company has only one member, it is *not* an organization.

All the neighbors in a block have a problem they want to solve. There is too much trash in the neighborhood. They form a Neighborhood Council. It *is* an organization. The members of the Neighborhood Council agree to report all cases of trash in the streets. They also agree to spend two hours a week picking up trash. Once every two weeks, the members call each other to report on the trash pickup.

The Senate of the United States *is* an organization. Senators must follow certain rules to become members of the Senate. There may only be 100 Senators. One of their main interests is to make laws for the country. In order to help pass a law, the Senators must come together in the Senate and vote.

Ten people are shipwrecked on an island. They are all interested in saving their lives. However, they do *not* belong to an organization. No one is able to make a set of rules that all ten can agree to.

Do you think you know now what an *organization* is?

If the answer is *yes,* return this booklet to the person who gave it to you.

If the answer is *no,* read over the material in the booklet again. Then, return the booklet.

When you are ready, you will be asked some questions about what you have just read.

Following completion of the minitext, students take a mastery test. The sample measure shown here also includes a simple evaluation of the minitext itself.

1. Which of these is an organization?
   (a) children playing in the street
   (b) the President of the United States
   (c) people at a concert
   (d) the Boy Scouts

2. Which of these is *not* an organization?
   (a) the football team in your neighborhood
   (b) the children on swings at the playground
   (c) the City Council
   (d) Girl Scouts

3. The Hot Rod Club is
   (a) a meeting
   (b) a council
   (c) an organization
   (d) a government

4. Which is true about *all* organizations?
   (a) They have rules and common interests.
   (b) They must have at least 10 members.
   (c) The members must pay dues.
   (d) The oldest member is always the leader.

5. Which is true about *all* organizations?
   (a) There must be at least two members.
   (b) Only adults may belong.
   (c) Members must meet every week.
   (d) They are always interested in governmental matters.

6. Which is *not always* true about an organization?
   (a) The members of an organization are all the same age.
   (b) There is more than one member.
   (c) All the members have the same problem or interests.
   (d) All the members agree to certain rules.

7. An organization is:
   (a) A gathering of people in the same place.
   (b) A group of people who vote for the same man.
   (c) A group of people who are used to doing many things in the same way every time that they get together.
   (d) A group of people with accepted rules who do things together because they have the same interests or problems.

8. An organization is a kind of
   (a) government
   (b) person
   (c) group
   (d) meeting

9. Look at the pictures below. Which face best describes how *you feel* about organizations. Write the letter of the face on your answer sheet.

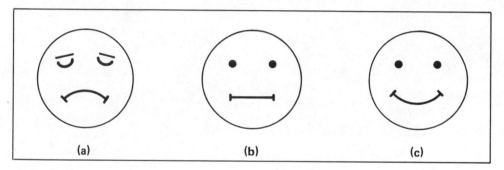

(a)   (b)   (c)

FIGURE 6.20

10. Which of the answers below tells best how *you feel* about the booklet on organization?
    (a) I feel very happy about it.
    (b) I feel sort of happy about it.
    (c) It was okay.
    (d) I did not like it.
    (e) I really did not like it at all.

11. Would you tell a friend that he or she ought to read this booklet if he or she asked you about it?
    (a) Yes, all of it.
    (b) Yes, parts of it.
    (c) No.
    (d) I am not sure.

Note: If you are done, please return these questions and your answer sheet to the person who gave them to you.

Several dimensions of concept mastery are measured in this test, as well as some characteristics of the instructional materials.

Item 1 measures whether, given the name of a concept, the student can select an example of the concept.

Item 2 measures whether, given the name of a concept, the student can select a nonexample of the concept.

Item 3 measures whether, given an example of a concept, the student can identify its name.

Items 4 and 5 measure whether, given the name of the concept, the student can select the names of relevant attributes of the concept.

Item 6 measures whether, given the name of the concept, the student can select the names of irrelevant attributes of the concept.

Item 7 measures whether, given the name of the concept, the student can select the correct definition of the concept.

Item 8 measures whether, given the name of a concept, the student can select a broader concept to which it is closely related.

Items 9, 10, and 11 measure the student's affective reaction to the instruction he or she has just received.

Audio recordings also are a useful medium for concept instruction, particularly for the areas of language arts, foreign language, and music. Playing contrasting examples and nonexamples of concepts such as *polyphony* and *counterpoint,* for example, offers learners concrete and structured experiences with the concept. Similarly, certain concepts from other subject matter areas, such as *soliloquy, feedback,* and *idiomatic expression,* are effectively presented through audio formats.

Case studies are a general vehicle for concept instruction. They may be drawn from commercially prepared materials, constructed by a teacher, or adapted from a variety of sources, including commercial materials. Such materials contain carefully structured vignettes with as much noncriterial material as possible removed and with focusing instructions and questions included. Where case studies are used in conjunction with teacher directions, the questions and focusing may occur in the context of general discussion. Case studies are suitable for all areas of the curriculum, especially social studies, science, language arts, music, and health education.

A concept learning activity that can take many forms and which can be used at all grade levels and for a variety of subject matter areas involves students in the construction of *concept folders.* Older students can use 8½ × 11 folders, and young children boxes, to store data on particular concepts. A concept is identified, and after its attributes and rule have been identified and clarified and some examples provided, students are asked to collect data — pictures and/or cases, etc. — over a period of time that are examples of the concept. When the projects are completed, the various folders may be exchanged and shared. Where required, students may be asked to explain the meaning and content of their collections. Several different concepts may be assigned simultaneously.

Mastery Test

OBJECTIVE 3　　(a) To distinguish between the private and public dimensions of concept learning; and (b) to identify and briefly describe the three stages of preparation for the teaching of concepts.

1. What is meant by the "public" and "private" dimensions of concepts?

　　_____

　　_____

　　_____

　　_____

　　_____

2. Identify and briefly describe the three stages of preparation for the teaching of concepts.

　　_____

　　_____

　　_____

　　_____

　　_____

ANSWER KEY

Mastery Test, Objective 3

1. The "private" dimensions of concepts are all of the personal, noncriterial associations, correct or incorrect, that a given individual identifies with the concept name. The "public" dimensions of concepts are the essential or criterial properties that are agreed upon and shared by those who can correctly identify examples and nonexamples of the concept.

2. Basically, the three-stage process should proceed as follows: Initially, the teacher determines whether the concept is an appropriate one to *teach* (Concept Appropriateness Inventory). If the concept is appropriate for teaching, then the concept is analyzed and some instructional planning considerations are outlined (Prerequisite Planning Inventory). Finally, a detailed set of procedures for teaching the concept are developed (Basic Model for Concept Instruction).

Objective 4

(a) To identify five dimensions of concept learning that can be measured and to arrange them according to their level of complexity; and (b) to identify and briefly describe three procedures for measuring the private dimensions of students' concepts.

LEARNING ACTIVITY 4

MEASURING CONCEPT LEARNING

Several approaches to measuring concept learning already have been suggested through the illustrations in the preceding section. A basic measure of whether a concept has been learned involves the ability to discriminate new examples of the concept from nonexamples correctly. Unless a student can perform satisfactorily on this fundamental test, learning may not be inferred. Ability to verbalize the concept rule is another *more complex* dimension of concept learning. Young children particularly have great difficulty with this task, even though they perform satisfactorily on discrimination tasks.

Essentially, measurement of concept learning may be viewed as dealing with the following increasingly more complex dimensions:

1. Identification of criterial attributes and nonattributes
2. Discrimination of examples from nonexamples
3. Identification of the concept rule
4. Ability to relate the concept to other concepts
5. Use of the concept in a novel way

Depending upon the significance of the concept and a teacher's objectives, mastery may be assessed over one or all of these dimensions. For many simple instructional activities, identification of criterial attributes can be presumed and a discrimination test will suffice. Other situations will call for measurement of all five dimensions.

Often a teacher wishes to tap the *personal dimensions* of concept learning, either prior to or following related instruction. Such assessment can proceed informally through open-ended discussions, through simple paper-and-pencil questionnaires, or through inventories. Figure 6.5 is one such approach. Two alternative diagnostic activities are outlined here. The first is borrowed from the studies of Michael Wallach and Nathan Kogan on thinking in young children; the second is based upon research into thinking strategies conducted by Hilda Taba.

The Wallach and Kogan activity, although developed for young children, is applicable to all grade levels and subject areas. We will call it the *Like-Things Game*. Concepts from any curricular area may be substituted for the ones used in the example here. Instructions similar to those provided here are used with the students. The instructions may be modified as necessary for different age levels or concepts.

"In this game I am going to name two objects, and I will want you to think of all the ways that these two objects are alike. I might name any two objects — like door and chair. But whatever I say, it will be your job to think of all the ways that the two objects are alike. For example, tell me all the ways that an apple and an orange are alike." (The child then responds.) "That's very good. You've already said a lot of the things I was thinking of. I guess you could also say that they are both round, and they are both sweet, they both have seeds, they both are fruits, they both have skins, they both grow on trees — things like that. Yours were fine, too."[10]

Sets of similar objects, events, or people along the lines of the following might be used with some basic instructions.

1. Tell me all the ways in which squares and quadrilaterals are alike.
2. Tell me all the ways in which sharps and flats are alike.
3. Tell me all the ways in which a lithograph and a print are alike.
4. Tell me all the ways in which a river and a stream are alike.
5. Tell me all the ways in which rockets and planes are alike.
6. Tell me all the ways in which love and hate are alike.
7. Tell me all the ways in which density and cubic feet are alike.
8. Tell me all the ways in which wind and water currents are alike.
9. Tell me all the ways in which churches and banks are alike.
10. Tell me all the ways in which architects and engineers are alike.

Assume you are dealing with a high school government class. You might wish to use the gamelike activity to compare the students' concepts of

electoral college and legislature

primary and election

city and state

norm and law

executive privilege and judicial review

The list of concepts can be as long or as short as desired.

Several years ago, Hilda Taba developed, and later her associates refined, a systematic strategy that allows a teacher to diagnose student concept states easily. Her strategy consists of three key steps to be carried out in exactly the sequence indicated, with as much time spent at each point as is required. The three basic steps are as follows:

1. Enumerate and list students' responses to an opening question.
2. Have the students group the responses.
3. Have the students label the groups.

Within each of these three key activities, there is a structured role that the teacher must play. The Northwest Regional Educational Laboratory has developed some appropriate questions and statements for a teacher to use in carrying out this role. The following sequence is drawn and adapted from their analysis of the teacher's role.[11]

1. *Enumeration and Listing*

   Opening question.   Raise an open-ended question that calls for remembered information concerning the concept to be analyzed and expanded.

"What comes to mind when you hear the word *heredity*?"
"What do you know about triangles?"
"What do you think of when you hear the word *poetry*?"

Refocusing statement.   When the responses indicate that students have begun to stray from the topic, call attention to the opening question.

"Let me repeat the original question."

Clarifying question.   Frequently students use a term that is unclear or that has many meanings. Ask for clarification.

"What sort of modern paintings?"
"Can you give me an example of a 'way out' person?"
"Can you help me out? I'm not sure I understand what you mean by getting snookered."

Summarizing question.   Frequently a student will respond to your opening question with a paragraph or two. Request that he or she abstract the main idea.

"How could we put that on the board?"
"How could we write that in one sentence?"
"Can you help me out? How could we state that to get it in this little space on the board?"

Mapping-the-field question.   Try to get as much information as possible.

"Are there any areas that we have missed?"
"Can you think of any other things?"

2. *Grouping the Responses*

Grouping questions.   The initial question in the grouping process requests students to group their responses in any fashion they wish.

"Let's look over our list. Can you find any items that could be grouped together?"
"Are there any items on the board that could be grouped together?"

Grouping rationale question.   A key element in the grouping process is focusing attention on the rationale used to categorize items. When students do not provide it automatically, request a reason.

"Why did you put _____, _____, and _____ together?"

3. *Labeling the Groups*

Labeling question.   The basic question for the labeling process asks the students to analyze a group of items and state a name or label for the grouping.

"Let's look at the first group. What title could we give to this list?"

Unlike the preceding models, Taba's schema should be followed in *exactly* the order specified. It is also crucial that the teacher accept *all* student responses without judging them as correct or incorrect. While, to be sure, students are likely to offer factually incorrect statements or offer apparently illogical groupings and labels, the teacher's role in this model is *not* to challenge or correct, but to accept and list all responses. Keep in mind that the objective is to analyze and expand conceptual associations. In this vein, when students disagree on classmates' groupings, *they have to be reminded that each individual's conceptual organization is unique, and that the rules of discussion in this case require the freedom of self-expression.*

Mastery Test

OBJECTIVE 4   (a) To identify five dimensions of concept learning that can be measured and to arrange them according to their level of complexity; and (b) to identify and briefly describe three procedures for measuring the private dimensions of students' concepts.

1. List five different dimensions of concept learning that may be measured and arrange them in order of decreasing complexity by starting with the most complex process and working down to the least complex process.

_____

_____

_____

_____

_____

2. Identify and briefly describe three procedures for assessing the "private" dimensions of students' concepts.

_____

_____

_____

_____

_____

_____

_____

_____

Compare your answers with those found in the Answer Key that follows.

1. The correct arrangement of the items in order of decreasing complexity is

   Use of the concept in a novel way

   Ability to relate the concept to other concepts

   Identification of the concept rule

   Discrimination of examples from nonexamples

   Identification of criterial attributes and nonattributes

2. One approach is the *Like-Things Game.* It calls for students to describe how sets of objects, events, or people are similar by answering a series of open-ended questions. A second approach is a three-step strategy devised by Hilda Taba to assess what associations a group of students attach to a particular concept. The steps involve enumerating and listing associations, grouping them, and finally labeling them. Still a third approach involves each student completing a simple conceptual network diagram similar to Figure 6.5.

Final Mastery Test

At the outset, you were asked to assess what you knew about concepts through a basic true–false test. Reexamine your responses in that first test to determine how much information you have mastered in this chapter.

To test your mastery of various objectives established for the chapter, see how many of the following questions you can answer.

1. What are at least four different ways in which the term "concept" is used in educational literature?

2. What basic information is required to teach a concept?

3. How do criterial and noncriterial attributes differ?

4. Identify at least two basic reasons why concepts are important.

5. Identify at least three different systems for classifying concepts and explain their meaning.

_____

_____

_____

6. Which concept classification system takes into account developmental differences? In what way?

_____

_____

7. How do concepts, facts, conclusions, and generalizations differ?

_____

_____

_____

_____

8. How do the "private" and "public" dimensions of concepts differ?

_____

_____

9. Summarize the seven steps in the Basic Instructional Model.

_____

_____

_____

_____

_____

_____

_____

_____

10. What are three different levels of concept learning that may be measured?

_____

_____

_____

ANSWER KEY

Final Mastery Test

Your answers should be along the following lines:

1. As ideas; as themes or topics; as a general, all-encompassing statement; as elements or structures of a discipline; or as categories into which we organize and relate our knowledge and experiences.
2. Name, criterial attributes, noncriterial attributes, rule, examples, and nonexamples.
3. Criterial attributes are the essential, defining characteristics of concepts. Noncriterial attributes are those which frequently are present in concept examples but are not essential.
4. Concepts simplify our environment; they simplify our learning task; they make communication easier; they help us distinguish between reality and imagery; they enrich our lives.
5. Concrete and abstract; conjunctive, disjunctive, and relational; formal and informal; enactive, iconic, and symbolic. (Check pages 203–205 for the meanings.)
6. Enactive, iconic, and symbolic. (See page 205 for the meanings.)
7. Concepts are categories of knowledge, plus related associations; facts are well-grounded, clearly established bits of information; conclusions are any results that follow logically from investigations and which are presented in the form of a statement; generalizations are true statements, predict things, apply to cases without exception, and express significant relationships among concepts.
8. Private dimensions are the personal associations that each of us has with concepts; public dimensions are the basic or criterial characteristics of concepts that people share in common.

9. (a) Complete the Concept Appropriateness Inventory and the Prerequisite Planning Inventory.
   (b) Develop an introduction to the instruction sequence. The introduction should orient the learner to the task and arouse his or her curiosity.
   (c) Present the series of varied examples and nonexamples of the concept that you have developed in some logical order. (There are no hard and fast rules on "how many." Consider a minimum of seven examples as a rule of thumb.)
   (d) If possible, present all the examples and nonexamples simultaneously or in close succession, so that the learner can compare all the cases.
   (e) Interject the cues, directions, and questions throughout the materials as necessary in order to draw attention to criterial and noncriterial attributes and to similarities and differences in examples and nonexamples. Correspondingly, encourage learner questions. In written material, cues may be arrows, marginal notes, underlining, and the like.
   (f) Assess concept mastery at a minimal level, namely, whether students can correctly discriminate among *new* examples and nonexamples.
   (g) Assess concept mastery at more advanced levels, as consistent with the developmental capabilities of the students and with your objectives.
10. Identification of criterial attributes and nonattributes; discrimination of examples from nonexamples; identification of the concept rule; ability to relate the concept to other concepts; use of the concept in a novel way.

NOTES

1. Jerome Kagan, "Preschool Enrichment and Learning," *Interchange* II (1971): 17.

2. Jerome S. Bruner, *Beyond the Information Given: Studies in the Psychology of Knowing* (New York: W. W. Norton, 1973), p. 316.

3. *Ibid.*, pp. 327–328.

4. *Teacher's Guide for Attribute Games and Problems* (New York: McGraw-Hill, 1968), pp. 74–77.

5. The discussion in this section is adapted from Peter H. Martorella, *Elementary Social Studies as a Learning System* (New York: Harper & Row, 1976), pp. 88–97.

6. For additional models dealing with different types of concepts, see Martorella, *op. cit.*, Chapter 5.

7. Robert M. Gagné, "The Learning of Concepts," in M. David Merrill, ed., *Instructional Design: Readings* (Englewood Cliffs, New Jersey: Prentice-Hall, 1971), p. 299.

8. Produced by *Project Econ 12* at San Jose State University, California.

9. Peter H. Martorella, "Instructional Products for Concept Learning," Temple University, Philadelphia, Pennsylvania, 1973.

10. Michael Wallach and Nathan Kogan, *Modes of Thinking in Young Children* (New York: Holt, Rinehart & Winston, 1965), p. 32.

11. John A. McCollum and Rose Marie Davis, *Trainer's Manual: Development of Higher Level Thinking Abilities*, rev. ed. (Portland, Oregon: Northwest Regional Educational Laboratory, 1969), pp. 160–161.

ADDITIONAL READINGS   Brown, Roger. *Words and Things.* New York: Free Press, 1968.

Bruner, Jerome S., et al. *A Study of Thinking.* New York: John Wiley & Sons, 1956.

Carroll, John B. "Words, Meanings and Concepts." *Harvard Educational Review* XXIV (Spring 1964): 178–202.

Gagné, Robert M. *The Conditions of Learning.* 2nd ed. New York: Holt, Rinehart & Winston, 1970.

Glaser, Robert. "Concept Learning and Concept Teaching," in I. E. Sigel and F. H. Hooper, eds. *Learning Research and School Subjects.* New York: Holt, Rinehart & Winston, 1963.

Klausmeier, Herbert J., and Frank H. Hooper. "Conceptual Development and Instruction," in F. N. Kerlinger and J. B. Carroll, eds. *Review of Research in Education, 2.* Itasca, Illinois: F. T. Peacock, 1974.

Martorella, Peter H. *Concept Learning: Designs for Instruction.* New York: International Textbook, 1972.

Taba, Hilda. *Teaching Strategies and Cognitive Functioning in Elementary School Children.* Cooperative Research Project no. 2404. Washington, D.C.: U.S. Office of Education, 1966.

Vygotsky, L. S. *Thought and Language.* Ed. and trans. by Eugenia Hanfmann and Gertrude Vakar. Cambridge, Massachusetts: M.I.T. Press, 1962.

Elizabeth Hamlin, Dietz/Hamlin.

SANDRA SOKOLOVE, MYRA SADKER, AND DAVID SADKER

Interpersonal Communication Skills

Objectives

1 To describe the characteristics of effective attending behavior.

2 To differentiate between the intellectual and the emotional content of messages (active listening).

3 To differentiate among the three types of reflecting — word messages, behaviors, inferences.

4 Given written classroom dialogues, to construct the three types of reflection (word messages, behaviors, and inferences).

5 To differentiate among inventory questions that (1) describe responses, (2) identify response patterns, and (3) identify the consequences of responses.

6 Given written classroom dialogues, to construct inventory questions that (1) describe responses, (2) identify response patterns, and (3) identify consequences.

Mrs. Carroll glanced around the classroom, making a mental note of the students' activities. Everyone certainly seemed excited about the play. The room buzzed with enthusiasm. As her eyes surveyed the back of the room, she noticed Judy standing erect in front of a full-length mirror. She was trying to balance a crown on top of her head while bowing to an imaginary crowd. Mrs. Carroll moved quietly toward the mirror and thought to herself how beautifully and almost majestically Judy held her body. A faint smile crossed her face as she said, "Good morning, Queen Elizabeth. I trust you had a pleasant evening."

Judy turned toward the mirror, dropped her eyes, and gracefully nodded her head. She looked back to Mrs. Carroll and seemed to be pleased with her stately response. "I wish I knew a real queen," she said, "so I could talk to her and find out what it really felt like."

"Well, Judy, how do you imagine she felt?"

"I bet it was a lot of work, and not everyone liked her . . . that probably made her feel sad . . . and I bet she couldn't even show it."

"What do you mean?"

"Well sometimes when we feel sad, we don't want to show it, 'cause it makes other people sad too . . . we kinda keep it inside."

"It's like having private thoughts and feelings inside of us. Some we can share; others we may choose to hold inside."

Judy thought for a moment and said, "Yeah, when I'm good inside, I act good outside." She then turned back to the mirror, straightened her shoulders, lifted her head, and said, "I wish I could be special like a queen."

Quite spontaneously, Mrs. Carroll said, "But you are special, Judy."

Judy's eyes opened wide and, with a look of surprise, she asked, "What makes me special?"

Momentarily caught off guard, the teacher thought for a moment and said, "Because of the way you think and the way you feel about things and . . . and even the way you act. When you put them all together, you're just special."

The teacher's responses were also quite "special," for she was able to perceive her student as a whole entity, composed of thoughts, feelings, and behaviors. Furthermore, through this brief dialogue, she was able to help her student gain some awareness of her own thoughts and feelings and their relationships to her behavior.

As unique and idiosyncratic as each person's thoughts and feelings may be, the capacity to experience and transmit such thoughts and feelings is a shared human characteristic.

One branch of psychology, known as humanistic psychology, focuses on the thoughts and feelings people have regarding themselves. It proposes that what people think and feel about themselves helps influence or motivate their behavior. Humanistic psychologists have a positive regard for the nature of human beings. They perceive people as free and unique creatures, who, when given a choice, will intuitively choose effective paths of action. They see them as self-directed, capable of setting goals, making choices, and initiating action. They also view them as capable of judging the consequences and effectiveness of their own actions. Humanistic psychologists also believe that, in order to function in the most effective manner and to maximize individual potential, people must first become aware of their internal thoughts and feelings regarding both themselves (self-perceptions) and the world at large. By consciously describing these thoughts (cognition) and feelings (affect), people may gain an awareness of how such states influence their behavior. Such an awareness can help them to control their own behavior.

Weinstein and Fantini (1970)[1] propose that often the thoughts and feelings people have about themselves focus around three broad areas of concern which they have termed: identity, connectedness, and power. For example, they state that most persons have deep concerns (thoughts and feelings) about themselves and their sense of *identity*. They ask such questions as, "Who am I? Where am I going? What do I want out of life?" Most people are also concerned about their relationships with others. They may ask: "How do I fit or *connect* with other people? Do people like me? Do they want to be with me?" Still further, all people need to define their own limits, to develop a sense of *power* that will enable them to take some measure of control over their lives.

Although a variety of psychologists have defined other areas of concern [McClelland (1961), achievement, affiliation, power; Schutz (1967), inclusion, control, and affection; Glasser (1965), relatedness, respect; Horney (1942), sense of competence and approval], most of them can be included in the Weinstein and Fantini model. Regardless of the labels presented, humanistic psychologists stress that healthy development depends on people's conscious ability to define behavior. They further state that a critical part of the learning process is the ability to judge whether or not one's thoughts and feelings are productive or unproductive and then to make whatever modifications or adjustments seem necessary. The ultimate goal of this search for self-knowledge is greater self-control and more productive living.

Alschuler et. al (1975) present the following working definition of self-knowledge: "A verbal description of one's characteristics or habitual internal and external responses, (thoughts, feelings, and actions) to a set of similar stimuli and the consequences of those specified responses."[2] Further, they state that self-knowledge "increases one's options for going beyond unsatisfying habitual responses."[3] In other words, once human beings gain an increased awareness of how they respond to various situations and what the consequences of these responses are, they can then proceed to choose more satisfying options — options that can lead to more directed, purposeful, and productive lives.

The process of gaining self-knowledge is a continuous and complicated one that is dependent on people's interactions with one another. "How we interact, relate and transact with others, and the reciprocal impact of this phenomenon form the single most important aspect of our existence. Only through interaction with others can we become aware of our own identity."[4]

Within the context of public education, teachers are an integral part of this interactive process. They are the ones who can create a classroom environment that will stimulate and reinforce personal inquiry and help students gain insight into their own identities. Current research (Purkey, 1970; Combs, 1965) has shown that students' attitudes (feelings) about themselves are often influenced by how they imagine their teachers perceive them. When teachers project a positive regard for their students, students in return often begin to see themselves and their abilities in more positive ways. Still further, students' attitudes and values are often greatly influenced by their perceptions of their teachers' behaviors (Sokolove, 1975). Students consciously and unconsciously imitate their teachers' styles of behavior and often accept the attitudes and values projected by their teachers as their own.

Therefore, if teachers are to create an environment that is conducive to personal growth, they must first explore their own feelings, attitudes, and values about themselves and their students. Next they must consider the effects these emotions and values have on their actions and, finally, they must deliberately model a set of interpersonal communication skills that facilitate teacher–student interaction.

Interpersonal communication skills may be defined as a series of specific verbal and nonverbal behaviors that stimulate personal inquiry between two or more persons — inquiry that leads to greater self-knowledge. By employing these behavioral skills, a teacher can help students express and clarify their thoughts and feelings and understand how these internal states affect their behavior. The modeling of such behaviors by the teacher helps initiate this interactive process and provides guidance to students as they too learn to employ these skills.

Before providing a brief overview of these skills, let's look at the dynamics of effective interpersonal communications. As previously mentioned, the personal growth process is interactive in nature. That is, the assistance of other trusted persons is needed before interpersonal sharing can begin. Speakers must be willing to receive both verbal and nonverbal feedback from listeners, and listeners must feel secure enough to provide such feedback.

The following diagram, called the "Johari Window," will help to clarify how self-knowledge is gained through the process of interpersonal communication.

JOHARI WINDOW*

	(A) Known to Self	(B) Not known to Self
(C) Known to others	Area I (A,C) Public Self (common knowledge)	Area III (B,C) Blind Area
(D) Not known to others	Area II (A,D) Private Self (secrets, private thoughts)	Area IV (B,D) Unconscious Self (undeveloped potential)

* Joseph Luft and Harry Ingham, "The Johari Window, a graphic model of interpersonal awareness," in *Proceedings of the Western Training Laboratory in Group Development* (Los Angeles: University of California Extension Office, August 1955). For a more complete exposition of the Johari model see *Of Human Interaction* by Joseph Luft (Palo Alto, Calif.: Mayfield Publishing Co., 1969).

There is specific information that is known both to yourself and to others (Area I, Public Self). It may be information received from visual cues such as "You are wearing a red dress today," or it may be information that you are willing to disclose to others, such as a fear of snakes or a vote you cast for a particular candidate in the last election. The content may be thoughts (cognitive) or emotions (affective) and/or behaviors.

At the same time, you may have personal concerns such as "I need money," "I am afraid of speaking in front of others," or "I'm confused" that you may not wish to share with others. This represents the Private Self sector (Area II).

Still other information may be known to others but unknown to you: your face gets red when you are angry, you cut off speakers in the middle of their sentences, or your body is fidgeting when you speak. This information is known as the Blind Area (Area III).

Finally, there exists an area of information that is unknown both to yourself and to others: the Unconscious Self (Area IV). The goal of the personal growth process is to continue gaining more information about yourself (self-knowledge) and, ultimately, to open up areas of unknown potential (Area IV). Consider the following dynamics: As you develop a helping relationship with others and begin *disclosing* information about yourself, Area I (the Public Self) gradually becomes larger, and Area II (the Private Self) becomes smaller. Remember, this is a reciprocal process. Your disclosures prompt *feedback* from others concerning their perceptions of you. Consequently, Area I becomes still larger, while Area III (the Blind Area) becomes smaller. Through the combined interaction of disclosure and feedback, you can also begin opening up Area IV (the Unconscious Self), an area of unexplored thoughts, feelings, and behavior.

This disclosure and feedback process does not denote "telling everything to everybody." Rather, it involves the sharing of information that is relevant to a helping relationship. For example, you may have feelings of shyness or incompetence that can affect your ability to perform well in social situations. By sharing those feelings and receiving feedback from a sympathetic listener, you can gain an awareness of how another person sees you and the effects of your actions on that person. You and your friend have not only shared valuable information and clarified possible misperceptions, but the entire process, if honest and sincere, may have built a more satisfying relationship. The process of verbalizing internal thoughts and feelings also helps you to "hear" yourself and to determine if the messages you are sending really reflect what you are feeling inside, that is, if you are sending congruent messages.

Interpersonal communication skills include such behaviors as *attending behavior, active listening, reflection, inventory questioning,* and *encouraging alternative behaviors.* These skills, when practiced effectively, will encourage students: (1) to express their thoughts and feelings; (2) to analyze and clarify their thoughts, feelings, and behaviors; (3) to note potential discrepancies between their actual response patterns and their desired response patterns; and (4) to choose, from among alternatives, new behaviors more in keeping with their desired behavior pattern.

These interpersonal communication skills are hierarchical in nature, with each successive skill including elements of the preceding ones. Together they comprise a taxonomy, with the skills on the lower levels requiring mastery before the skills on the higher levels can be attained.

By gaining proficiency in each of the skills of this taxonomy, a teacher can aid students in the process of gaining greater self-knowledge. Such knowledge will help sensitize students to any discrepancies that might exist between their actual and desired behaviors and, thereby, set the stage for eliminating these discrepancies. Ineffective behavior need not remain static; it can be changed. Once teachers and students become aware of their actions, once they realize that not only do they have other choices, but they can also make such changes occur, they are in control.

The following table gives a further explanation of the interpersonal communication skills taxonomy.

TAXONOMY OF INTERPERSONAL COMMUNICATION SKILLS*

Student Process	Teaching Skill	
Cluster III		
Encouraging alternative behaviors	practicing alternative behaviors	
Cluster II		
Clarifying students' expressions of feelings	reflection	inventory questioning
Cluster I		
Eliciting students' expressions of feelings	attending behavior	active listening

* Adapted from Sadker and Sadker, *Interpersonal Skills of Teaching* (University of Wisconsin-Parkside, 1972).

Cluster I. Eliciting Students' Expressions of Feelings. The two skills or behaviors which initiate teacher–student interaction and provide the foundation of this taxonomy are (a) attending behavior and (b) active listening behaviors. They may be perceived as climate setting behaviors that stimulate personal disclosure on the part of both teachers and students. Students will not risk sharing their feelings and attitudes if they feel threatened or manipulated. Consequently, an environment that is conducive to sharing is supportive rather than antagonistic, questioning rather than judgmental, flexible and somewhat permissive rather than highly structured and controlled. Students need to feel that their personal disclosures are being listened to seriously and will not lead to ridicule and rejection.

(a) *Attending.* Through various nonverbal and verbal cues such as eye contact, facial and body gestures, and brief verbal acknowledgments, teachers can demonstrate that they are listening with care and empathy to what is being said. Consequently, they can encourage students to share their thoughts and feelings and know that they are being heard.

(b) *Active listening.* One of the key steps in active listening is being able to differentiate between intellectual content and emotional content. All messages contain both types of content, and teachers must be able to detect and differentiate them if they are to help their students gain awareness of their own internal thoughts and feelings and how these affect behavior. Active listening helps the listener to make inferences privately about these two types of content by attending to the speaker's verbal and nonverbal cues.

Cluster II. Clarifying Students' Expressions of Feelings. Once students feel comfortable enough to disclose information about themselves, teachers can then help them clarify that information. To do this teachers must be skilled at (a) reflecting and (b) inventory questioning.

(a) *Reflecting.* The skill of reflecting, in essence, involves holding a mirror up to the student. Teachers can give students direct feedback about the way their verbal and nonverbal messages are being received. They may choose to reflect verbal communication, nonverbal communication, or even to make some inferences regarding the feelings that underlie these verbal and nonverbal messages. Carl Rogers says: "The students, seeing his own attitudes, confusions, ambivalences, feelings and perceptions accurately expressed by another, but stripped of the complication of emotion with which he himself invests them, paves the way for acceptance into the self of all those elements which are now clearly perceived."[5]

(b) *Inventory questions.** By asking inventory questions teachers can help students describe their thoughts, feelings, and manifested actions. Questions like these help students to identify specific patterns of behavior or ways in which they characteristically respond to specific events. From that point, students can begin to assess the effectiveness of their behavior patterns. If this assessment shows a discrepancy between their actual and desired behavior, they may begin to look at other behaviors that are more congruent with their personal goals.

* Adapted from the Trumpet Model of Weinstein and Fantini. In *Towards Humanistic Education: A Curriculum of Affect* (New York: Praeger, 1970).

Cluster III. Encouraging Alternative Behaviors.* The final level of the taxonomy involves the exploration of alternative behaviors. This process includes (a) generating alternative behaviors, (b) practicing them and sensing how they feel, (c) receiving feedback from others regarding their effectiveness, (d) predicting their short-term and long-term consequences, and (e) choosing which pattern of behavior seems most congruent with personal needs.

Only the first two sets of skills, eliciting and clarifying, will be presented in this chapter. Once you have mastered the skills of attending, active listening, reflecting, and inventory questioning, the transition to the third cluster — Encouraging Alternative Behaviors — will be a natural one.

It is not enough for teachers to model these skills verbally, since their actions, especially with young students, often speak louder than their words. Behind their actions there must be a sincere concern for the personal growth of their students and an earnest commitment to the interpersonal communication process. Although effective interpersonal communication skills are to some extent intuitive, they can also be learned, practiced, and increasingly mastered. Their mastery is critical if you are fully committed to the growth and actualization of your students' potentialities.

Objective 1

To describe the characteristics of effective attending behavior.

LEARNING ACTIVITY 1

One of the factors that makes interpersonal communications so complicated is that both participants (the speaker and the listener) are sending and receiving messages simultaneously. For example, when you are involved in a conversation with another person, what cues are you looking at, reacting to, or being affected by? What nonverbal messages are being conveyed through the speaker's body language? What verbal message is the speaker conveying through his/her words? What environmental stimuli distract your attention? In order to create an environment that is conducive to disclosure and inquiry, you must first identify and then seek to control any stimuli that influence the interpersonal communication process. Among the more important stimuli are those labeled "attending behaviors."

We are all aware of what *nonattending* behavior looks like and the frustration that occurs when the listener is occupied with his/her clothes or hair or suddenly interjects, "I know exactly what you mean. Let me tell what happened to me . . . ." Such nonattending behaviors detract measurably from effective interpersonal communication. Conversely, attending behaviors are those that put the speaker at ease. The speaker is not interrupted; rather, he or she receives brief verbal or nonverbal acknowledgments during the conversation.

Since communication is both verbal and nonverbal, people's ac-

---

* Adapted from the Trumpet Model of Weinstein and Fantini. In *Towards Humanistic Education: A Curriculum of Affect* (New York: Praeger, 1970).

tions often speak louder than their words. In fact, through his research Mehrabian (1966)[6] determined that over 90 percent of the messages teachers send to their students are nonverbal. Teachers can often say more with the wink of an eye than they can with several sentences. Listed below are several suggestions for developing your own attending behavior. They have been divided into both verbal and nonverbal components.

Nonverbal Cues

1. Eye Contact.   Focus your eyes directly on the speaker but be sensitive to the effect such direct eye-to-eye contact may have. Many people feel uncomfortable with direct eye contact and tend to shy away from it. Readjust your focus accordingly.

2. Facial Expressions.   Your expressions (or lack of them) provide feedback to the speaker, thereby prompting him or her to say more, to slow down, to clarify. More important, let your face tell the speaker that you empathize with him or her. Smiles, frowns, expressions of surprise or disappointment don't cost very much. In fact, they are priceless, so share them! A word of caution though: too much expression, particularly negative expression, can be very distracting. Be aware of your own facial expressions and the effect that they have on the speaker, and adjust your reactions accordingly.

3. Body Posture.   You can help the speaker relax by relaxing your own body. Body gestures also communicate meaning. Think how you feel when a listener points a finger at you or stands straight and rigid with arms folded across the chest. What nonverbal message does that body position communicate to you? Does it stimulate you to say more? Probably not. In fact, Mehrabian (1969)[7] noted that an arms akimbo position most often occurs in conversation with a disliked person. In contrast, when the listener leans toward or touches the speaker, a high level of interest and involvement is communicated.

4. Physical Space.   Edward T. Hall (1966)[8] states that the distance people create between themselves has an inherent communication value. He describes an 18-inch distance between speakers as "intimate space," the 18-inch to 4-foot distance as "personal space," the 4-foot to 12-foot distance as "social distance," and beyond 12 feet as "public distance." Each of these distances communicates distinct nonverbal messages — from those of intimacy or emotional closeness where physical touching is possible to the space where physical touch is impossible and fine verbal and nonverbal details are imperceptible. Find a comfortable space between you and your students, one that communicates the message, "I want to make closer contact with you." If you are standing far away, walk across the room toward the student. Don't place physical as well as psychological obstacles in your path.

Verbal Cues

1. Silence.   When used appropriately, silence can, indeed "be golden." It can give both parties a chance to stop and reflect on what has been said. It may also encourage the speaker to say more if he or she doesn't have to anticipate an instant response. Too often listeners feel compelled to make an immediate response and, consequently, they begin searching for a reply before the speaker has concluded. Wait a few seconds to be sure that the speaker has completed his/her thoughts.

2. Brief Verbal Acknowledgments. On the other hand, nothing is more deadly than a "void silence," so you will do well to occasionally interject brief verbal acknowledgments, such as: "I see"; "Wow"; "Oh"; "That's too bad." The goal is to express interest and concern without interrupting or interjecting personal comments. Keep the reactions brief and quickly refocus on the speaker.

3. Subsummaries. When appropriate, summarize the essence of what the speaker has said in a sentence or two. By feeding back to the speaker the gist of his or her message, you validate the communication, and this often inspires further conversation.

Summary of effective attending behavior

Nonverbal cues
1. Eye contact.
2. Facial expressions that reflect empathy.
3. Relaxed body posture and body gestures that reflect empathy.
4. Close spatial proximity.

Verbal Cues
1. Effective use of silence.
2. Minimal verbal acknowledgments.
3. Brief subsummaries.

Mastery Test

OBJECTIVE 1   To describe the characteristics of effective attending behavior.

Study the pictures and read the accompanying dialogues. Then complete the following questions. You must answer both questions correctly in order to pass this assessment.

Student: "So after I bought the book, I realized that he didn't give me enough change . . . . (pause) So then I got back on the bus . . . (pause) but then I didn't have enough money to pay the fare."

Teacher: (wearing the scarf) sits quietly and waits until the student finishes, and then says: "Oh no."

1. Describe the two characteristics of effective attending (verbal cues) present in the above example.

_____

_____

Student: "Mrs. G. I felt like the kid in the story. It was pretty tough, but you feel great in the end."

Teacher: Walks over to the student, bends down, and says: "I'd feel good too."

2. Describe the two characteristics of effective attending (nonverbal cues) present in the above example.

_____

_____

Objective 2

To differentiate between the intellectual and the emotional content of messages (active listening).

LEARNING ACTIVITY 2

Unlike the reflecting and inventory questioning skills which follow, active listening is difficult to assess through overtly demonstrated behaviors. It is an internal state that can only be known to the listener. Although the listener can demonstrate, nonverbally, most of the characteristics of attending, he or she may still not be listening to the speaker. People's eyes can be focused on someone and they can be relaxed, while their minds are somewhere else.

As with all of the skills described in this chapter, active listening behavior cannot be developed unless specific motivation is present. What motivates you to be engaged in conversation — necessity or choice? Do you feel obligated to listen or do you have a genuine concern for the speaker? Are you listening to the *person*, his or her thoughts and feelings? Or, are you listening to the words in order to act as a judge, a problem solver, an analyzer, or a critic? Still further, are you entering into the conversation with preconceived expectations of what the speaker is feeling and/or thinking? Do you have any bias or prejudice toward the speaker that may turn you off or distort what you hear?

Charles Kelley (1974)[9] has divided listening into two categories: "deliberate listening" and "empathetic listening." The former describes the ability to "deliberately" hear the intellectual *content* or the information of the message with an intent to analyze it, to recall it at some later point, or to draw conclusions from it. Empathetic listening refers to the listener's ability to participate in the spirit or feeling of the message being expressed. The intent of the empathetic listener is to attend to the speaker's *affective* or emotional needs first. Kelley notes that such empathic listening does not denote that the listener is always uncritical of or always in agreement with the speaker's thoughts, feelings, attitudes, ideas, and values. Rather, the primary concern of the empathetic listener is to be involved fully and accurately with what is being said and felt, both verbally and nonverbally, by the speaker. Once empathetic listeners have heard a message, they can then begin to use their own critical thinking skills — skills that allow them to summarize, describe, infer, and interpret the information.

The skills of deliberate and empathetic listening are not mutually exclusive, for they both aim at a common goal: to understand oral communication accurately. However, such understanding is arrived at through different routes. There is a difference in timing and motivation. The empathetic listener is motivated by his/her need to "hear" the speaker's *feelings*. He/she will analyze the content after the dialogue is complete.

Kelley makes an interesting point when he says that "deliberate listening" may be a self-contradiction and a misnomer — and that "empathetic listening" may be a redundancy.

> To the extent that one is deliberating (mentally criticizing, summarizing, concluding, preparing reports, etc.) he is *not listening*, but formulating his own ideas. Listening by its very nature has to be empathic; a person understands what he has heard, only to the extent that he (she) can share in the meaning, spirit, or feeling of what the communicator has said.[10]

When listeners concentrate on the words being expressed or on their preconceived impressions of the speaker, they are thinking *about* the speaker. By trying to find solutions to problems before the speaker has concluded, they are thinking *for* the speaker. By summarizing or drawing conclusions before the speaker has concluded, they are thinking *ahead* of the speaker. By being empathetic listeners, they are thinking *with* the speakers. They are not anticipating, judging, analyzing — they are just listening.

In order to demonstrate the characteristics of active listening, you must first be an empathetic listener. You must be motivated to listen to the speaker because you have a genuine concern for what he/she is feeling as well as saying. You must temporarily eliminate old impressions and momentarily suspend judgment. Only then can you begin to fully concentrate your energies on looking, listening, and recording the verbal and nonverbal messages of the speaker.

Active Listening Includes the Following Components:

1. Blocking out external stimuli.
2. Attending carefully to both the verbal and nonverbal messages of the speaker.
3. Differentiating between the intellectual and emotional content of a message.
4. Making inferences regarding the feelings experienced by the speaker.

Below are the critical steps involved in developing the skill of active listening. The three basic components include: (1) personal inventory, (2) attending skills, and (3) identifying feelings.

Step 1. Personal Inventory. Effective listening requires that you be aware of your own feelings, prejudices, and expectations about the speaker.

You need to inventory your motivation for being involved with him or her. Ask yourself:

1. How do I feel about the speaker and the topic being discussed?
2. Do I really want to hear what that person is saying? What is my role? Am I here to act as critic? As a problem solver?
3. Do I genuinely want to help the speaker if he/she presents a problem?

4. Can I accept the feelings and attitudes of the speaker even if they are different than my own?
5. Can I accept the speaker as someone separate from myself — a unique person?

Even though the spontaneous nature of most conversations may make such a self-inventory seem impossible, if the interpersonal communication is to be open and honest, you must train yourself to answer the above questions at the onset of an encounter. If your answers are positive, you can then say: "I have accounted for my personal feelings regarding this speaker, and I can now block them out of my mind and concentrate on the intellectual and the emotional content of the messages being conveyed."

Dealing with people's feelings, attitudes, and values is a sensitive matter. Unlike dealing with a topic such as weather, it requires not only highly specialized skills like active listening — but also personal honesty about your motivation and commitment to the communication process.

Step 2. Attending Skills.   At this point, your *attending skills* become important. Establish eye contact, relax, and listen. Attend directly to both the *verbal* and *nonverbal* cues of the speaker. What messages are being delivered? What is the tone and pitch of the speaker's voice? Is he/she speaking loudly or softly; rapidly or slowly? What are the hand and body movements saying? This is a "doubly difficult" task. It requires you to look and listen simultaneously.

Those specialists involved in the study of interpersonal communication often differentiate between the actual words used in conversation and the manner in which those words are delivered. They apply the term *verbal* in describing the actual words being spoken and the term *vocal* in describing the volume, note, tone, pitch, and inflection of the words being expressed.[11] Usually, a speaker's emotions have a direct bearing on both the verbal and vocal messages. For example, Joel Davitz[12] concludes that when someone is feeling angry, he or she may communicate through blaring timbre, fast rate, high pitch, and loud delivery. Conversely, when someone is feeling bored, he or she may speak at a slower rate, lower pitch, and with less amplitude. If you wish to attend to the speaker's affect, you will need to listen for these vocal cues.

Step 3. Identifying the Speaker's Feelings.   As the conversation proceeds, try and make private inferences about what the speaker is *feeling*. Is he or she sending congruent messages? In other words, are the verbal and nonverbal messages consistent with each other? An incongruent message is easy to spot. It is like looking at a child whose body is rigid, whose hands are clenched, and who says to you with stuttering words, "Everything is c-c-cool!" Try to answer the question "How does this person feel toward the topic being discussed?" (Finding the right "feeling" words to describe the speaker's messages may initially present some difficulty, since emotions have not traditionally been viewed as a topic of open discussion and, consequently, most people suffer from the lack of an appropriate "feeling" vocabulary.)

At this point, you have probably received a great deal of information that you would like to pull together and test out for yourself. Try the following review exercise.

Scene I:

You are seated at your desk, after school, organizing your materials. Suddenly you look up and see Bruce, one of your fifth grade students, seated at his desk. He's been moody all day and you sense that he has something on his mind. As he approaches you, you begin to: (check one)

_____ 1. Inventory your motivation for listening.

_____ 2. Quickly gather up your books and prepare for an immediate exit.

_____ 3. Ask him to do an errand for you.

If you checked number one, what types of questions would you ask yourself?

1. _____

2. _____

3. _____

Did you ask yourself how you felt toward Bruce and if you really wanted to listen to him? Did you determine what your role would be in the ensuing dialogue? (yes or no)

Are you going to be a: (check one)

_____ 1. deliberate listener

_____ 2. empathic listener

What criteria did you use in determining your role?

If you chose the latter, you have committed yourself to both listening to and observing Bruce's affective or feeling messages, as well as becoming actively involved in the conversation by demonstrating effective attending skills.

Scene II:

Sure enough, true to your instinct, Bruce says: "Do you have a couple of seconds?" Slowly, he begins to talk about the upcoming math test. He drops his eyes to the floor and quietly says, "You know, this stuff is really silly." You may consider Bruce's past performance in math and think to yourself, "Now, he is usually an excellent student. I wonder what he is trying to say."

Based on both Bruce's verbal cues ("this stuff is silly") and his nonverbal cues (head and voice drop), what do you imagine he is feeling? What inferences can you make?

1. _____

2. _____

3. _____

Perhaps he is saying:

"I feel *scared* about the test."

"I'm not prepared."

"I don't understand it."

Or,

"I'm feeling *bored* with this material. It's too easy."

"If I get 100 on the test tomorrow, everyone will make fun of me."

Can you think of any other affect messages that may be transmitted? Let's stop at this point.

Remember, not every message may have an emotional overtone, so don't exhaust yourself trying to "hear" one. But, if a student does respond with such emotions, attend to them. Interestingly enough, some teachers have noted that the absence of emotional reaction from a student when circumstances would warrant one (i.e., a fight or some other highly emotional experience) often alert them to listen more actively and intently.

Summary of active listening

1. Inventory your personal motivation for listening. Put aside preconceived expectations. Suspend judgment.
2. Attend to speaker's (a) verbal cues and vocal cues and (b) nonverbal cues.
3. Begin making private inferences concerning the speaker's feelings. Tune into incongruent messages if any are apparent.

Mastery Test

OBJECTIVE 2 To differentiate between the intellectual and the emotional content of messages (active listening).

Read each statement and try to differentiate between the intellectual (cognitive) content and the emotional (affective) content being transmitted. Sometimes it helps to read the statements aloud. Each time you read one put the accent on a different word. Does it communicate a different emotional message? In the right-hand columns record both the intellectual message and the emotional message. Some of the statements may contain several different emotions. List them all. When you have finished, compare your list with those in the Answer Key. In order to pass this test, you must receive a total score of at least 85. If you disagree with any of the answers listed, ask friends for their reactions. What messages do they receive?

Statements	Intellectual (Cognitive) (I'm Saying)	Emotional (Affective) (I'm Feeling)
1. "I don't need any help. I'm old enough to do it myself."		
2. "Just go away and leave me alone. I don't want to talk to you or anyone else."		
3. "I couldn't believe it. Imagine me, getting an A on that paper."		
4. "I tried to do it three times and I still don't understand it."		
5. "No matter what I do, I can't seem to please him."		
6. "I don't feel that I have to answer that. It's none of your business."		
7. "Every place I turn, you are always there, standing over me."		
8. "Just trust me."		
9. "Cool it, I'll do it when I'm good and ready."		
10. "Just give me a chance, I know I can do it."		

ANSWER KEY

Mastery Test, Objective 2

Give yourself 3 points for each item which matches those on the key. Give yourself 2 points for those items where your choices only partially match. (There is some similarity between the responses.) Give yourself 0 points if you missed altogether. If you received below 85, reread the preceding Learning Activity. Also share these statements with a friend and compare your perceptions.

Intellectual (Cognitive) *(I'm Saying)*	*Emotional (Affective)* *(I'm Feeling)*
1. I can do it myself.	I feel — angry frustrated annoyed belittled cocky independent
2. I don't want to talk to anyone.	I feel — angry depressed upset withdrawn isolated
3. I got an A.	I feel — surprised amazed delighted
4. I can't do it.	I feel — frustrated confused tired
5. I can't please him.	I feel — frustrated manipulated controlled pressured
6. I won't answer that.	I feel — confronted angry annoyed irritated obstinate arrogant
7. Stop following me around.	I feel — annoyed put upon cornered
8. Trust me.	I feel — confident secure afraid worried manipulating

Intellectual (Cognitive) (I'm Saying) (cont'd)	Emotional (Affective) (I'm Feeling) (cont'd)
9. I'll do it later.	I feel — harried annoyed angry flippant
10. Let me try it.	I feel — eager confident desperate

Objective 3

To differentiate among the three types of reflecting — word messages, behaviors, inferences.

LEARNING ACTIVITY 3

Take a few moments to review objectives 1 and 2. Hopefully, these eliciting behaviors will help provide an environment that is conducive to sharing and self-disclosure. By first attending to your students' nonverbal and verbal cues and then differentiating between the intellectual and the emotional content of their messages, you say to them: "I see you, and I am listening carefully to what you are saying and doing."

Suppose a student expresses an emotional reaction that you wish to respond to. What do you do? What do you say? Consider the following situation and then write down your responses to the students' comments.

Attending to Students

You notice that a student is seated at his desk, with his math book opened. He has been staring into space for several minutes and can't seem to concentrate on his work. He is playing with the pages of the book. You go over to his desk and he suddenly says:

Actively Listening to Students

"Math is dumb. I don't want to do any of this stuff."

Depending upon your past information regarding this student, you may decode the message as:

Content: Math is hard, dumb, boring, etc.

Affect: 1. "I'm *frustrated.* I need help."
(or)   2. "I'm feeling *tired*, and I don't want to work."
(or)   3. "I'm dumb. I can't do it."
(or)   4. "I'm feeling bored. This stuff is too easy."

How would you respond to this student?

1. _____

2. _____

3. _____

Obviously there are numerous approaches a teacher could take in responding to this student. One appropriate way would be to use the skill of *reflecting*. You could reflect at any one of three levels: (1) You might choose to pick up on the student's *words* and try to capture and reflect back the gist of the verbal message; (2) You could respond to the student's nonverbal or body cues by describing his or her actions; or (3) You could make an inference regarding the emotions being transmitted and share this inference with the student.

The effective use of reflecting behavior by the teacher can communicate to the student: "I have listened carefully to what you have said, and I would like to share my observations with you." Following are sentence stems that often begin reflections on each of these three levels.

"I heard you say . . .   (reflecting the student's words, the verbal content of the message)

"I saw you do . . .   (reflecting the student's actions, the nonverbal behavior)

"I imagine you're
feeling . . .   (reflecting the student's feelings that may underlie the verbal and nonverbal behavior)

The teacher's response, in effect, serves as a mirror for the student's words, feelings, and behaviors, thus providing direct feedback regarding the success of the student's communication. Additionally, effective reflecting behavior often facilitates self-exploration, since it provides speakers with an opportunity to ponder their listeners' feedback before reorganizing and clarifying their messages. Reflection can also provide an opportunity for teachers and students to clarify any misinterpretations that may block the process of communication.

The skill of reflecting is comprised of successive behaviors ranging from simply paraphrasing the speaker's words to describing the speaker's body cues or behaviors to reflecting the speaker's affective or feeling messages in order to make inferences or interpretations.

Reflecting Word Messages (paraphrasing)

To reflect word messages, a teacher repeats or paraphrases the essence of the thought (words) just communicated. No attempt is made to reflect the feelings being conveyed or the nonverbal cues or behaviors being displayed. Sometimes hearing an exact repetition or paraphrase of what was just said can be a clarifying experience for both the speaker and the listener.

Look again at the dialogue at the beginning of Learning Activity 3. To reflect the student's word message, the teacher could respond to the student by saying: "So you think that the math is dumb," or, "You don't want to do your math today." Even though such a response may sound trite and mechanical, practice using it for a while — it will not only help to develop your own listening skills, but it will also serve as a means for clarifying the speaker's messages. A teacher may choose to use such a simple response before deciding whether to continue the interaction by reflecting the emotional messages that appear to underlie the verbal content. Reflecting word messages thus serves several purposes: (1) It initiates dialogue between the teacher and students; (2) It provides some "lead time" for the teacher to decide whether to continue the discussion; (3) It may motivate the student to provide additional information regarding his or her thoughts and feelings.

Such a response is reflecting rather than confrontative; it does not force the student to respond. Simply letting a student know that you are listening may be all that is needed to stimulate further dialogue.

Reflecting Nonverbal Messages (behavior description)

The second component of reflecting requires you to describe the physical behaviors of the speaker. When reflecting nonverbal messages, only use the visible behavioral evidence. Following are some of the ways you might begin a response to reflect a student's nonverbal messages.

I noticed that when you did . . . ,	your face . . . .
When you did . . . ,	your body . . . .
	your hands . . . .

Referring again to the interaction at the beginning of Learning Activity 3, if the teacher had chosen to reflect the student's nonverbal message, he or she might have said: "I see you sitting here, staring into space, and playing with your math book. What's up?" Usually the behavior description is followed by a question that will open up some dialogue. You observe, give some feedback by describing the behavior, and then check it out by asking a question.

By describing specific, observed behaviors, you provide insight to the speaker about how he or she is "coming across" or being perceived. Such responses are descriptive and nonevaluative. They do *not* include accusations or inferences about the other person's motives, attitudes, or personality traits. Telling a child that he or she is rude is offering an accusation rather than a description of specific behavior. Often young children have a difficult time differentiating between themselves and their actions. Are they, as human beings, rude people, or are their *actions* inappropriate to the situation? Remember, describe specific *actions* only.

Reflecting in Order to Make Inferences or Interpretations

This third level of reflecting incorporates the skills described in the two preceding behaviors. However, it goes beyond the paraphrasing of words and beyond the reflection of nonverbal cues. It represents an attempt on the part of the teacher to summarize what he or she saw and heard and to "check out" those observations by sharing some inferences regarding the speaker's feelings. Did the listener's perceptions match the original intentions of the speaker; was the speaker really "in touch" with his or her own messages? In the earlier interaction concerning the student who seemed to have problems with his math, the teacher might have responded at this level as follows: "I see you sitting there, playing with the math book (reflecting behavior), saying that math is dumb (reflecting the word messages). Are you feeling frustrated by the problems?" (interpretation of the student's feelings).

Effective reflecting behavior is not a semantic game or a way of putting the other person's ideas in new terms. Rather, it comes from a genuine desire to understand exactly what the student is expressing and feeling both verbally and nonverbally. You are never expected to play the role of a mind reader. You do not have to try to guess what the speaker is thinking or feeling. After summarizing what you saw (behavior description) and what you heard (reflection of content), you share your inference about whatever thoughts or feelings you associate with such a response. In short, "check out" your interpretations with a question. How accurate were your inferences? Did they match the speaker's intentions?

Introductions which can be helpful in checking out your interpretations are:

"It seems to me that what you were saying was . . . ."

"Could it be that . . . ?"

"Were you trying to say . . . ?"

These introductions differ from those used in reflecting word messages in that you go beyond restating the gist of the words by adding an inference of your own. For example, a student says to you: "He makes me sick." You respond by saying: "Are you trying to say that he made you angry when he stole third base?" In this example, you added your own interpretation.

You may also choose to use lead-in sentences that incorporate behavior description and/or paraphrasing.

"I saw you do . . . and I imagine that you are thinking . . . ."

"I noticed that you did . . . and I imagine that you were thinking . . . ."

"I noticed that you did . . . and I imagine that you were feeling . . . ."

"I heard you say . . . . Were you thinking . . . feeling . . . ?"

For additional clarification you could also ask questions at the end of each statement of inference. For example:

"Does that sound accurate to you?"

"Does that seem right to you?"

"Did I perceive (hear, see) that correctly?"

Both the *timing* and the *number* of reflected statements are critical elements in practicing this skill. It can be just as ineffective to reflect too much as too little. It becomes annoying to the speaker to have his or her verbal or nonverbal communications reflected and interpreted constantly. It can often cause students to doubt that you really are seeking clarification. They may suspect that you are trying to manipulate them by putting your own thoughts and values in their mouths. Communication then becomes unbalanced and strained.

Frequent reflecting seems especially appropriate under two conditions: (1) when mistakes could be very costly and, consequently, accuracy becomes vital; and (2) when strong feelings in either the sender or the receiver increase the probability of misunderstanding. In such cases, reflecting becomes crucial as a way of ensuring that the message comes through undistorted. The next time you are having a disagreement with someone, try reflecting what has been said until he or she corroborates your understanding. Note what effect this has on the other person's feelings and also your own.

When used effectively, reflecting enhances the development of a nonthreatening environment in which learners can feel free to express themselves. Reflections should never be judgmental, advisory, challenging, or ridiculing in nature. Rather, they should be *questioning* and exploratory.

Summary of effective reflecting behavior

1. Become aware of any preconceived thoughts or feelings you may have regarding the speaker and/or the topic being discussed. Will they hinder communication? If so, how?
2. Attend carefully to both the verbal and nonverbal messages of the speaker. *Observe.*
3. Make a mental note of the exact words being spoken and the specific behaviors being demonstrated. *Look, listen, and record.*
4. Differentiate between the verbal messages and the emotional messages being delivered. What is the speaker saying? What feelings are associated with the words? *Look, listen, record, and infer.*
5. Respond to the student by:
   (a) Paraphrasing the words. *Reflect words.*
   (b) Describing the specific observed behaviors of the speaker. *Describe.*
   (c) Share your inferences concerning the student's thoughts and feelings that may underlie verbal and nonverbal behavior. *Interpret.*
6. Be aware of the tone of voice you use. Avoid sarcasm, judgment, reprimand.
7. Ask for clarification to assess the accuracy of your perceptions. *Clarify.*

In this listing, the hierarchical nature of the interpersonal skills taxonomy becomes obvious, for, in order to reflect, you must also attend and listen actively.

You have now read descriptions of the three levels of reflecting behavior, and, through a brief classroom dialogue, you have seen how a teacher may utilize these three different types of reflection. Now turn to the Mastery Test and try your luck at coding these three different types of reflection.

Mastery Test

OBJECTIVE 3   To differentiate among the three types of reflecting — word messages, behaviors, inferences.

Code each of the following responses to determine which of the three types of reflecting behavior is being exhibited. Use the following abbreviations: WM = reflecting word messages, B = reflecting behavior, I = interpretive reflections. To pass this test successfully, you must accurately code at least 9 of the 10 responses.

_____ 1. *Student*   (twisting in seat, biting pencil): "I don't like creative writing. I'm no good at writing."

   Teacher: "You don't care for the writing assignments, and you don't feel you have much talent as a writer. What do you find the most difficult about writing?"

_____ 2. *Student*   (smiling broadly and displaying a medal): "Look at the medal I just won. I took first prize in the swimming competition."

   Teacher: "It looks to me as though you're really proud and happy to have done so well."

_____ 3. *Student*   (frowning and slumped in chair): "I don't want to go to the school dance. I hate standing in a line hoping some dumb boy will ask me to dance."

   Teacher: "It sounds like you feel awkward or maybe left out and as if you're standing alone while your friends are dancing. Is that true?"

_____ 4. *Student*   (with his hands in his pockets and shrugging his shoulders): "You know my father. He is really big on sports. He played football, so I have to play football."

   Teacher: "It sounds as if you feel resentful. Is that true?"

_____ 5. *Student:*   "That was a stupid thing for him to do. I told him he'd probably get caught."

   Teacher: "So you warned him."

_____ 6. *Student:*   "I can do that as well as any boy can. Why can't I try it?"

   Teacher: "Are you saying that you feel like you're being discriminated against?"

_____ 7. *Student*   (running across the room, almost knocking over the fish tanks)

   Teacher: "When you run across the room like that, you could easily knock over the tanks."

_____ 8. *Student*   (seated under a tree, reading a book, while the rest of the class is playing kickball)

   Teacher: "Are you sitting here because you would rather read or because you didn't get picked for the team?"

_____ 9. *Student*   (seated under a tree, reading a book, while the rest of the class is playing kickball)

   Teacher: "I see you sitting here reading instead of playing with the class. What's happening?"

_____ 10. *Student*   (seated under a tree, reading a book, while the rest of the class is playing kickball): "I'd rather read than play kickball. I have to finish this book by fourth period."

   Teacher: "Oh, you didn't finish your assignment?"

ANSWER KEY
Mastery Test, Objective 3

1. WM 2. I 3. I 4. I 5. WM 6. I 7. B 8. I 9. B 10. WM

Objective 4

Given written classroom dialogues, to construct the three types of reflection (word messages, behaviors, and inferences).

LEARNING ACTIVITY 4

Remember, the goal of reflecting behavior is to communicate to your students that you have received both their verbal and nonverbal messages and that you would like to share some personal observations with them. In essence, you are reflecting their thoughts by restating their words, their actions by describing specific behaviors, and their feelings by interpreting their words and behaviors. You may choose to reflect such messages by using sentences such as:

"I heard you say . . . ." (thoughts)

"I saw you do . . . ." (actions)

"I imagine you are feeling . . . ." (feelings)

A brief review of the three types of reflecting behavior follows. As you read each description, list sample introductory sentences that would be appropriate to that type of reflecting. Such a review will be helpful in preparing for the activity that follows.

Reflecting Word Messages

This type of reflection captures the essence of the words the student has just used. You can repeat or paraphrase the student's message. Remember, no attempt is made to reflect either the feelings or the nonverbal behaviors of the student. Concentrate on just the words. Let the student hear them again. Reflecting word messages: (1) initiates dialogue; (2) provides you with "lead time" to consider whether you want to continue the discussion; (3) may generate more information from the student regarding his or her thoughts and feelings.

List some sample introductory sentences.

1. _____

2. _____

3. _____

Sample sentences might begin with:

"Did you say . . . ?"

"I heard you say . . . ."
"You said . . . ."

Reflecting Nonverbal Messages

This type of reflecting requires you to describe the specific physical behaviors of the speaker. Use only visable behavioral evidence. Avoid any evaluative statements, accusations, or generalizations.
List some sample introductory sentences.

1. _____

2. _____

3. _____

Sample sentences might begin with:

"I noticed that you did . . . ."
"When you did . . . , ..."
"When you said . . . , your face . . . ."
(combination of both reflecting verbal messages and nonverbal messages)

Reflecting in Order to Make Inferences or Interpretations

This type of reflecting incorporates both verbal messages and behavioral messages. However, it goes beyond such messages and includes the observer's perceptions of what the speaker may be feeling. It represents an attempt on the part of the listener to "check out" his or her observations and to clarify any misperceptions. Such reflections often help the speaker (1) to gain insight concerning how he or she is coming across to others and (2) to become aware of certain feelings that he or she may not have been aware of before.
List some sample introductory sentences.

1. _____

2. _____

3. _____

Sentences like "Were you trying to say . . . ?" go beyond mere paraphrasing. Such reflections may communicate to the speaker: "This is my interpretation of what you just said"; or "Could I infer this from what you just said?"
Sentences like "I saw you do . . . and I imagine you are thinking . . . ."; or "I heard you say . . . and I imagine that you are feeling . . . ." leave plenty of room for clarification. They are not accusatory. Such sentences communicate to the speaker: "Let me check this out with you."

Your Turn

USING REFLECTING TO CONSTRUCT RESPONSES

Try your hand with the following exercise. Included in the exercise are three separate classroom vignettes. The first paragraph in each unit describes the vignette. Each successive paragraph extends the dialogue in a sequential manner.

Working either alone or with a partner, read each brief vignette and the dialogue that follows. Then write a response incorporating one of the three types of reflecting requested in parentheses. Write down a possible response or, if a partner is available, quiz one another spontaneously. (*Caution:* Each response described in the Answer Key that follows represents just one possible response. It should be obvious that there is *no one correct response*. The goal of this activity is to place you in a semistructured situation where you can construct specific responses incorporating one of the three types of reflecting behavior. Your own sense of comfort and the reactions of others will give you feedback concerning your ability to use reflecting effectively.)

One experience that may be helpful is to examine how comfortable and/or natural it was for you to use some of the sample introductory sentences described above. Even though they may initially sound phony, they do serve as a beginning vehicle for developing your own ability to reflect.

VIGNETTE 1

Teri, at the age of eight, still has difficulty in sharing her materials with other children. She often begins fighting with them when they "borrow" her materials, even when she is not working with them. Cheri innocently picks up one of her games, which is lying on the table. Teri immediately runs up to her and grabs it away.

(a) The teacher walks over to the table and says to Teri:

_____

(reflecting behavior)

(b) Teri is screaming: "It's my game and she can't play with it. Tell her to give it back to me."

The teacher says: _____

(reflecting word message)

(c) Teri, red in the face, seems very angry. She says: "It's mine and she didn't ask if she could borrow it."

The teacher says: _____

(interpretive reflection)

(d) *Teri:* "She'll probably just break it anyways."

Teacher: _____

(interpretive reflection)

(e) Cheri, getting very flustered and her eyes filling with tears, says: "I didn't know it was yours. Stop pulling at my arm."

Teacher: _____

(reflecting behavior)

(f) Cheri pulls the game away from Teri and puts it back on the table. She looks at the teacher and says: "Can I play with it?"

Teacher: _____

(open response)

VIGNETTE 2

For the big History Fair, the class has decided to recreate the landing on the moon by the first astronaut. The students are to decide among themselves who will play the astronaut. The selection process has turned into a big popularity contest between two students, Mike and Frank. They both seem to be "battling" with each other.

(a) Frank gets red in the face and quite defensive. He says, "I even look like the guy. I should be it."

Teacher: _____

(reflecting behavior)

(b) *Frank* (still demanding): "So what's the big deal? Just let me play the bit."

Teacher: _____

(reflecting word message)

(c) Mike, equally agitated, shouts: "Just wait one big minute — let me say something."

Teacher: _____

(interpretive reflection)

(d) *Mike:* "Damn right I'm angry. What happens to the big democratic thing we were supposed to have here?"

Teacher: _____

(reflecting word messages)

(e) *Frank:* "Why don't we both read the part and let the kids decide?"

Teacher: _____

(interpretive reflection)

(f) *Mike:* "That will probably turn out to be one big game . . . a popularity contest."

Teacher: _____

(reflecting word message)

VIGNETTE 3

Half of the class is gathered together for a class meeting. There have been several incidents of stealing in the lockers lately, and the teacher thinks that it is necessary to discuss it openly.

(a) *Judy:* "What difference does it make who's taking all the stuff. Let's just put guards out in the hall and keep a lookout for the thief."

Teacher: _____

(reflecting word messages)

(b) *Kenny:* "That doesn't make sense to me. Let's just set a reward system. Give money to anyone who knows anything about it."

Teacher: _____

(reflecting word messages)

(c) *Dorie* (seated quietly in her chair, suddenly blurts out): "That's *crazy.*"

Teacher: _____

(interpretive reflection)

(d) Donald opens his eyes wide and nods his head.

Teacher: _____

(reflecting behavior)

(e) *Donald:* "Boy, we are *assuming* a lot. How do we know that there is just one thief?"

Teacher: _____

(reflecting word messages)

(f) *Melissa:* "Wait a minute. Why don't we just give the thief a chance to return everything before we start a big hunt team."

Teacher: _____

(interpretive reflection)

ANSWER KEY

Your Turn: Using Reflecting to Construct Responses

Remember: The responses that follow are just one group of possible responses. There is no one correct response to an activity like this.

Vignette 1
(a) "I saw you pull that box away from Cheri. What's happening?"
(reflecting behavior)
(b) "It's yours and no one else can play with it."
(reflecting word message)
(c) "Your face is getting red . . . I imagine that you are angry because Cheri didn't ask you if she could borrow it. Is that true?"
(interpretive reflection)
(d) "Are you worried that if someone borrows your game they will break it?"
(interpretive reflection)
(e) "I can see that you are about to cry. Calm down."
(reflecting behavior)
(f) open response

Vignette 2
(a) "Your face is getting red."
(reflecting behavior)

(b) "So you think it's not such a big issue and that you should play the role."
(reflecting word messages)
(c) "You look angry. Do you feel like you haven't had a chance to speak?"
(interpretive reflection)
(d) "You don't think that the selection process is fair? democratic?"
(reflecting word messages)
(e) "You think the kids will be fair judges. Is it because you think that they will vote for you?"
(interpretive reflection)
(f) "You think the kids will vote for the most popular? Do you have any other suggestions?"
(reflecting word messages)

Vignette 3
(a) "You think a guard system is a way to deal with the problem."
(reflecting word messages)
(b) "So you are suggesting a reward system."
(reflecting word messages)
(c) "You obviously disagree with those two ideas. Is it because they seem unfair to you?"
(interpretive reflection)

(d) "I see you nodding your head. Is it because you think they are unfair?"
(reflecting behavior)

(e) "You think we are assuming a lot . . . that maybe there is more than one thief."
(reflecting word messages)

(f) "When you used the term 'hunt team,' I imagine you thought that there was something inhuman or scary about the process of finding the thief. Is that true?"
(interpretive reflection)

Mastery Test

OBJECTIVE 4
Given written classroom dialogues, to construct the three types of reflection (word messages, behaviors, and inferences).

In order to pass this Mastery Test, seven of the eight reflecting responses you construct to the following vignette must satisfy the criteria presented in the Answer Key that follows.

All the students were experiencing the same anxiety regarding the college board examinations that were to be given the following day. David was flipping through the pages of the encyclopedia, which was lying on the back table. Mrs. Clarke walked over to him and said:

1. "_____" (reflecting behavior)

or

2. "_____" (interpretive reflection)
(Write both responses.)

David turns around and says, "I bet I'd have to know everything in this book in order to pass that exam. I'm no genius."

3. "_____" (reflecting word message)

4. "_____" (interpretive reflection)

"My parents really want me to go to college. The pressure is really on."

5. "_____" (reflecting word message)

6. "_____" (interpretive reflection)

David shrugs his shoulders.

7. "_____" (reflecting behavior)

8. "_____" (interpretive reflection)

ANSWER KEY

Mastery Test, Objective 4

It is almost impossible to match the sample responses described in this key. Therefore in scoring your responses, use the following guidelines.
1. In attempting to reflect verbal messages, did you capture the gist of the content? That is, when you say the two sentences aloud, do they connote the same message? Check it with a friend. If so, consider it correct.
2. In attempting to reflect nonverbal messages, did you describe the *specific* behaviors mentioned in the vignette without adding any judgments? If so, consider it correct.
3. In attempting to reflect with inferences or interpretations, did you first include the student's verbal and/or nonverbal messages and then make a personal statement concerning the student's feelings? Did you use such lead-in sentences as "I heard you say . . . ." or "I saw you do . . . ."? If so, you are probably "right-on" in your ability to reflect at this step.

Sample responses might be:
1. "I see you flipping through the pages of the encyclopedia."
2. "Are you thinking about the college boards tomorrow?" (Or: "Are you nervous about the college boards tomorrow?")
3. "You think only geniuses can pass the college boards."
4. "When you say that you would need to know everything in the encyclopedia to pass, I imagine you are quite apprehensive about the exam." (Or: "I imagine that you don't feel bright enough to pass.")
5. "Your parents are really pressuring you."
6. "I would imagine that all that pressure would make you feel uptight."
7. "I see you shrugging your shoulders." (Or: "When you shrug your shoulders like that, . . .)
8. (add) I imagine that you feel that there is nothing more you can do at this point."

Objective 5

To differentiate among inventory questions that (1) describe responses, (2) identify response patterns, and (3) identify the consequences of responses.

LEARNING ACTIVITY 5

Let's take a few moments and review the development of the interpersonal communication skills taxonomy thus far. The skills involved in the first cluster, entitled *Eliciting Students' Expressions of Feelings*, are mood behaviors that stimulate teacher and student interaction and enhance the potential for effective interpersonal communication. When you model attending and active listening behaviors, you are communicating to your students that you have put aside other business and are ready to listen and interact with them.

By effectively attending to your students, you have communicated that you can see them, hear them, and even touch them. Your body posture reflects a comfort level that puts others at ease. By observing *their* facial expressions and body postures and by listening to the pitch and tone of their voices, as well as to their actual words, you are listening actively and differentiating between feeling and word messages. The Cluster II skills, *Clarifying Students' Expressions of Feelings*, teach you how to respond to students in very specific ways. By paraphrasing your students' verbal messages, you allow them to hear their own words, and in doing so, you help clarify any misinterpretations. By describing their behaviors, you help them become more aware of the physical reactions that accompany their verbal dialogue.

By adding interpretation to these descriptions, you share your perceptions of why they may be speaking or acting in a certain manner. Such interpretations can provide additional insights regarding the connection between their thoughts, feelings, and behaviors.

At any of these three levels of reflecting, your students are given the opportunity to accept or reject your reactions and perceptions. Mutual feedback will enable both of you to gain valuable information regarding one another. Such interpersonal interactions will help students become more aware of their own thoughts, feelings, and resulting behaviors. At this point they may begin to see the effects of their actions on other persons.

Inventory questions may now be appropriate. Such questions will enable your students to clarify specific aspects of their behavior further. Too often, people simply take their style of behavior for granted and give little thought as to whether it serves them productively or unproductively. Inventorying one's behavior pattern is a necessary condition for growth, one that is prerequisite to the search for alternative response patterns.

Inventory Questions

If people are to become aware of their thoughts and feelings, they must have an opportunity for looking inside themselves, an opportunity for introspection. Furthermore, once they have gained an awareness of these internal states they must assess their behavioral consequences. Questions that cause people (1) to probe into their thoughts, feelings, and resulting behaviors and (2) to assess the effectiveness of their behaviors are called *inventory questions*. Such questions, when used effectively, allow students to "get inside themselves and evaluate what they see."

Weinstein (1975)[13] states that the product of self-knowledge is to create more "response-ability," or more choice in the way people act. Once they understand how their thoughts and feelings affect their behavior, they can begin predicting, analyzing, and modifying that behavior. In short, the better people understand the causes and consequences of their behavior, the greater their ability to control their actions and live productive, satisfying lives. According to many humanistic psychologists, mature and healthy persons are able to assess their own behavior, to determine their own sense of productivity, and to modify their behavior accordingly. Maturity is reflective of continuous assessment, alteration, and reassessment.

Before either teachers or students can begin generating alternative modes of behavior, they must first consciously consider or *inventory* their specific reactions (physical, emotional, intellectual) to external stimuli. They must be able to describe what they are thinking, saying, doing, or feeling *now*. They also need to determine whether these reactions are typical of their pattern of behavior and whether the consequences of such behavior patterns are productive for themselves and others.

There are three levels of inventory questions. Read carefully the following descriptions.

Level 1. Describing Feelings, Thoughts, and Actions. As a teacher you will need to ask inventory questions that (1) elicit students' expressions of feelings; (2) have students consider the thoughts accompanying their feelings; or (3) help students consider the actions that may accompany certain feelings and emotions.

Questions you might ask in order to elicit students' expressions of *feelings* are:

1. What are you feeling?
2. What sensations and/or feelings are you experiencing?
3. Describe what you are feeling inside.

On the surface, such questions may seem obvious and trite, but the response pattern uncovered is often quite fascinating. Have you ever asked young children to describe what they were *feeling*? Most often, they respond with polarities such as: "I'm feeling good/bad; happy/sad," and they exhibit little ability to describe the various emotional states that lie behind their responses. One reason for such a response pattern may be the fact that children, like most adults, simply lack a "feeling vocabulary." Check your spelling lists. How many weekly vocabulary lists include "feeling words"? Still further, when was the last time someone asked you how something makes you feel? How often do you ask such a question of others?

To help students consider the *thoughts* that accompany their feelings, you might ask:

1. What are you thinking?
2. What were you saying to yourself (as you felt this)?
3. What sentences were (are) running through your head?
4. What were you thinking about?

Finally, to help students consider their actions relative to such thoughts and feelings, you might initiate a dialogue by asking:

1. What are you doing?
2. What did you do with your body?
3. What expression was on your face?
4. How did you behave? How did you physically act or react?
5. What was your body "saying" during the conversation?
6. What were (are) you saying?

Inventory questions are not meant to be analytical, for teachers are not therapists. The purpose of such questions is simply to help students consciously recognize what they are thinking, feeling, or doing in response to an outside stimulus or event.

You may have noticed that none of the above questions ask students *why* they feel, think, or act the way that they do. They merely ask them to describe *what* they are thinking, feeling, and doing. Answering the question "why" often requires the student to analyze or intellectualize about his/her behavior, and this can be counterproductive to spontaneous teacher–student interaction. Furthermore, analytical questions can divert attention away from real, immediate feelings to the business of creating rational defenses for these feelings. Remember, inventory questions encourage individuals to reflect upon "their behavior and their inner experiences with a minimum of obstructive self-judging, defensiveness, or ambitious striving for results."[14]

Level 2. Identifying Patterns. The questions included at this level help students to clarify their style of responding further by identifying typical behavior patterns. Examples of inventory questions that ask students to identify patterns are:

1. How was your response typical of your behavior?
2. How do you usually react in this type of situation?
3. What ways have you reacted before in similar situations?
4. What conditions usually make you act this way?

The objective of these questions is to help your students look for consistent patterns in their behavior and for the stimuli that usually trigger those responses. According to humanistic psychology, if people can learn to observe and describe their reactions to external stimuli and to discover patterns in their behavior, they can learn to control their environment rather than be controlled by it.

Level 3. Identifying Consequences. The most critical step in the inventory process is the determination of how specific actions serve us. Specific questions which a teacher can ask to help students to identify the consequences of behaviors are:

1. How does it serve you to act this way?
2. What does responding this way do for you?
3. How does responding this way help you attain positive consequences? How does this pattern protect you from or help you avoid negative consequences?
4. What price do you pay for responding this way?

By effectively using such inventorying questions, you will enable your students to describe their thoughts, feelings, and behaviors; to identify specific behavior patterns; and to assess the effectiveness of their behavior by determining whether their actions serve them productively or unproductively.

Your Turn

DIFFERENTIATING THE THREE LEVELS OF INVENTORY QUESTIONS

Read the following vignette, and in the blank spaces provided, code the type of inventory questions according to the following categories: D = describing (thoughts, feelings, actions), P = identifying patterns, and C = identifying consequences.

As Mrs. Peterson walks down the hall, she overhears Mindy and Lisa arguing:

Mindy: "Why did you tell me yesterday that you would go?"
Lisa: "I forgot that I already promised Sue that I would go with her."
Mindy: "Thanks a lot, FRIEND."

As Lisa walks into the resource room, her eyes are filling with tears. She looks upset and preoccupied.

Mrs. Peterson: "What's up, Lisa? Your eyes are filled with tears and you look sad."
Lisa: "Nothing . . . ."
Mrs. Peterson: "Does it have anything to do with your conversation with Mindy?"
Lisa: "Yeah. Mindy is mad at me because I can't go to the show with her tomorrow."
Mrs. Peterson: "Want to talk? What happened?"
Lisa: "It's all so stupid . . . . I promised her I'd go to the show with her . . . . I forgot that I had already made plans to go with Sue."

_____ 1. *Mrs. Peterson:* *"So how are you feeling about the confusion?"*
Lisa: "Bad I guess. I don't want Mindy to be mad . . . ."
Mrs. Peterson: "Did you tell Mindy that?"
Lisa: "I meant to . . . but she got so mad and walked away."

_____ 2. *Mrs. Peterson:* *"What are you thinking about now?"*
Lisa: "That I shouldn't have made two sets of plans again."

_____ 3. *Mrs. Peterson:* "Again? *Is this typical of you?*"
Lisa: "Yeah. Last week I did the same thing."

_____ 4. *Mrs. Peterson:* "So you make two different sets of plans with two different friends. What usually happens? *What does it get you in the end?*"
Lisa: "I guess one friend ends up getting mad at me. Why don't I think sometimes, instead of just absentmindedly saying yes."

ANSWER KEY

Your Turn: Differentiating the Three Levels of Inventory Questions

1. D   2. D   3. P   4. C

(*Note:* Reread this dialogue. Do you notice any other interpersonal communication skill being used? If you said "reflecting behavior," you are right. Look at Mrs. Peterson's first sentence: "Your eyes are filling with tears" (behavior description). Look also at her last sentence: "So you make two different sets of plans with two different friends" (reflecting word messages). Remember, the skills are hierarchical in nature. Each successive skill includes components of the preceding ones. Dialogues using inventory questions are more effective when they include reflection. They give students further feedback and increase their insights regarding their behavior.)

Notice the teacher began the conversation by asking the student to *describe* her feelings (1) and thoughts (2) associated with specific behavior. After bringing these thoughts and feelings to a level of consciousness, the teacher helped her student *identify how the present behavior was reflective of a general pattern of behavior* (3). Last, one brief question (4) helped the student to *identify the consequences* of her behavior and to consider how such patterns of behavior serve her, productively or unproductively.

This dialogue was brief. One or two questions from each of the three types of inventory questions were enough. Remember, the teacher's questions merely *guide* the personal inquiry process. It is not our place to probe or analyze. (If this dialogue had continued, the teacher could have asked the student to think of other alternative actions that might be more productive to both herself and other people.)

The inventory process is a continuous and somewhat complicated process. It requires patient, supportive, and sensitive teachers who have mastered a series of specific, focused questions that they can use spontaneously. The entire interactive process necessitates a sensitivity in attending to students' nonverbal cues, sensing when to stop — stop questioning, stop probing. Teachers must protect their students from getting hurt, mocked, or ostracized by others.

Growth is often difficult, and frequently it involves a bit of pain. It often necessitates giving up old response patterns that are comfortable but ineffective. It involves experimenting with new and perhaps "foreign" behavior. While this process is difficult, it is critical if you and your students are to continue growing in healthy and productive ways.

Mastery Test

OBJECTIVE 5   To differentiate among inventory questions that (1) describe responses, (2) identify response patterns, and (3) identify the consequences of responses.

Read the following dialogue and code the underlined sentences according to the three different levels of inventory questions: D = describing, P = identifying patterns, and C = identifying consequences. To successfully complete this test, you must accurately code all six inventory questions.

Mr. Cotter explained the rules of the game and then asked the students to divide themselves into four equally numbered teams. As they were selecting their teams, Mr. Cotter noticed Julia slipping quietly out of the back door. She didn't return until all the teams were selected and the game was under way. Mr. Cotter motioned to Julia to meet him in the hall. Once outside he said:

"I noticed that you left the room as soon as the kids started to select their teams, and you didn't come back until the game started. What made you leave?"

Julia: "I didn't want to stay."

_____ 1. *Mr. C:* "Can you remember what you were thinking about before you left?"

Julia: "That probably no one was going to pick me for a team."

_____ 2. *Mr. C:* "What other thoughts were going through your head?"

Julia: "I never get picked for any team — like yesterday when we had to play kickball, I probably would have been the last one picked . . . . Just because I'm new here nobody picks me."

_____ 3. *Mr. C:* "How did you act then?"

Julia: "I told Mr. Gold that I had to go to the lavatory."

Mr. C: "So when the class is dividing themselves into teams, you usually leave before you get picked."

Julia: "I guess so."

_____ 4. *Mr. C:* "Tell me Julia, what does running away get you? How does it serve you?"

        Julia: "Well, if I can't stick around, then I don't have to be the last one picked."

_____ 5. *Mr. C:* "What are some other consequences?"

        Julia: "I guess I just end up sitting and watching the others play."

_____ 6. *Mr. C:* "Try to describe how you feel inside right now when you see all the kids are inside playing . . . ."

        Julia: "Well . . . I guess I feel 'left out'."

        Mr. C: "So you leave before you can get picked and then feel 'left out' when you have to sit back and watch."

ANSWER KEY

Mastery Test, Objective 5

1. D   2. D   3. D   4. C   5. C   6. D

Objective 6

Given written classroom dialogues, to construct inventory questions that (1) describe responses, (2) identify response patterns, and (3) identify consequences.

LEARNING ACTIVITY 6

The purpose of inventory questions is to help people gain an awareness of their thoughts and feelings and, further, to determine how these internal states affect their behavior. Remember, one of the goals of the personal growth process is to create more choices for effective behavior. Teachers can enhance this process by asking students: (1) to describe their present thoughts, feelings, and actions; (2) to recognize any patterns of behavior that may exist; and (3) to analyze the consequences of their actions upon themselves and other people. Once students see and accept the fact that some of their behaviors are counterproductive, they must assume the responsibility for change. Teachers, peers, and friends can suggest alternative modes of behavior, but each individual must assimilate and internalize the change by him/herself.

A brief review of the three levels of inventory questions follows. As you read each description, list sample types of questions that would be appropriate to that level of questioning. Such a review will be helpful in preparing for the final task of this chapter — constructing your own inventorying questions.

Level 1. Describing Feelings, Thoughts, and Actions. Although it is often difficult to differentiate between one's thoughts and emotions, specific, guided inventory questions, practiced over a period of time, may be helpful.

Questions at this level help students to describe what they are thinking and feeling at a particular moment, as well as to consider how and when they respond to specific stimuli.

List some questions that may elicit students' expressions of feelings:

1. _____
2. _____
3. _____

Students' expressions of thoughts:

1. _____
2. _____
3. _____

Students' expressions of actions:

1. _____
2. _____
3. _____

Which of the following questions sound most natural to you?

Describing feelings
1. What are you feeling?
2. What sensations are you experiencing now?
3. Describe what you are feeling inside your body now.

Describing thoughts
1. What are you saying to yourself?
2. What are you thinking?
3. What sentences are going through your head?

Describing actions
1. How did you act? React?
2. What expression was on your face?
3. What did you do with your body?
4. What were (are) you saying?

What other questions did you list? Compare them with your friends. Do they achieve the same goal?

Level 2. Identifying Patterns.   Questions at this level help students to clarify their style of responding further, by identifying typical patterns of behavior and the stimuli that usually trigger those responses.

List some questions that could elicit this type of information.

1. _____

2. _____

3. _____

4. _____

Did you list any of the following?

1. How was this response typical of your behavior?
2. How do you usually react in this type of situation?
3. What ways have you reacted in similar situations?
4. What conditions usually make you act this way?
5. What factors usually trigger this type of behavior?

Level 3. Identifying Consequences.   This last level of questioning is the most critical to the inventory process, because it helps students to determine the consequences of their actions and to assess the effectiveness of their own behavior.

List some questions that would help students identify the consequences of their actions.

1. _____

2. _____

3. _____

4. _____

Did you list any of the following?

1. How does it serve you to act this way?
2. What is the payoff?
3. What usually happens when you act this way?
4. What does acting this way do for you?
5. What does this behavior protect you from?
6. What are the consequences of your actions?

Your Turn

THE VENTING GAME

The following strategy, entitled the *Venting Game*, includes three separate vignettes. The first paragraph in each unit describes the situation, and each successive paragraph extends the dialogue in a sequential manner.

Step 1. Working alone, read each brief vignette and the dialogue that follows. Then write an inventory question corresponding to the level that is written in parentheses. Appropriate questions are listed in the Answer Key that follows. Judge for yourself how similar your questions are to those described. Complete all three vignettes.

Step 2. Working with a partner, select one of the three vignettes. Read the vignette aloud and ask your partner to role play the situation with you. If possible, tape-record the conversation. Try to be spontaneous in asking inventory questions at each of the three levels. Replay the tape and list the inventory questions you asked. How similar were they to those questions you originally wrote during the first part of the game? Was it easier or more difficult for you to write them or to ask them aloud? How comfortable did your partner feel? Which of the three levels of questions was difficult for you?

VIGNETTE 1

Julie has been carrying her bulging shoulder bag all morning and is unwilling to put it down. You imagine that there is something of importance or worth in it. It is time for Julie to take her physical education final, and she asks her friend if she would watch her pocketbook while she is gone. Julie leaves her possessions with her friend, and the class begins. As the class is about to end, Julie returns and opens her friend's desk to retrieve her bag. It is obviously a lot less bulky — something is missing!

(a) Julie starts yelling and accuses her friend of stealing.

   Julie: "I asked you to please watch my bag. What did you do with the black box that was inside?"
   Friend: "I'm sorry Julie, I got so involved with the game, I forgot. I didn't take anything."

   As the fighting continues, you walk over to Julie and ask:

   Teacher: _____
                                               (describing feelings, thoughts)

(b) *Julie:* "She took something of mine. I just know she did."

   Teacher: _____
                                               (describing actions)

(c) *Julie:* "Maybe I am accusing her without knowing the facts. But . . . . ."

   Teacher: _____
                                               (identifying patterns)

(d) *Julie:* "Well sometimes, like yesterday, I just fly off the handle too fast — but that box is very important to me."

   Teacher: _____
                                               (identifying consequences)

(e) *Julie:* "I guess this isn't going to get us anywhere at this point; all I care about is that box. Do you know what happened to it?"

   The teacher turns to the friend and asks:

   _____
                                               (describe feelings or thoughts)

(f) *Friend:* "I feel so badly. I guess I really let you down. I didn't take it, honestly. Let me help you look for it."

VIGNETTE 2

The topics for the social studies workshops have been presented to the class, and the students are beginning to divide themselves into task groups. Danny picks up the atlas and says to the group: "Okay guys, let's do this first and then we can . . . ." The other members of the group start to protest, and a loud hassle ensues.

(a) You call Danny over to your desk and ask:

Teacher: _____

(describing thoughts or actions)

(b) *Danny:* "Well I guess I thought someone needed to step in and start the project, so why not me?"

Teacher: _____

(identifying patterns)

(c) *Danny:* "Listen, I'm good at organizing things. You know I'm president of the Debating Club."

Teacher: _____

(describe feelings, thoughts, or actions)

(d) *Danny:* "Everyone in the club acts the same way."

Teacher: _____

(identifying consequences)

VIGNETTE 3

For a class project, you lent a personal copy of one of your classics to Ruth. She promised that she would return it to you several weeks ago. You reminded her at least three times. Now she wishes to borrow another book. You refuse to lend her any more of your materials. Her eyes fill up with tears, and she begins to walk away. You call her back to your desk:

(a) *Teacher:* _____

(describe thoughts or feelings)

(b) *Ruth:* "I'm sorry that I keep forgetting your book."

Teacher: _____

(identifying patterns)

(c) *Ruth:* "I don't know what's wrong with me. I guess I'm just forgetful."

Teacher: _____

(identifying patterns)

(d) *Ruth:* "I had to pay fifty cents to the library yesterday for late books."

Teacher: _____

(identifying thoughts or feelings)

(e) *Ruth:* "I really felt dumb."

Teacher: _____

(identifying consequences)

ANSWER KEY

Your Turn: The Venting Game

Remember: The responses that follow are just one group of possible responses. There is no one correct response to an activity like this.

Vignette 1
(a) 1. "What are you thinking right now?"
   2. "What are you feeling now?"
(b) 1. "How are you acting now?"
(c) 1. "Is this a typical way of acting for you?"
   2. "Is this the way you usually react?"
(d) 1. "What are the consequences of acting that way?"
   2. "How does it serve you to act that way?"
(e) 1. "What are you thinking?"
   2. "What thoughts are going through your head now?"
   3. "How are you feeling now?"

Vignette 2
(a) 1. "What thoughts are going through your head now?"
   2. "How did you behave (in the group just now)?"
(b) 1. "Is this typical of your behavior?"
   2. "How do you usually react (in this type of group situation)?"

3. "In what other situations have you acted like this?"
(c) 1. "What kind of thoughts go through your head (when you are in that situation)?"
   2. "How do you usually act in that situation?"
   3. "How do you feel when you are in that situation?"
(d) 1. "What are the consequences when you act that way?"
   2. "How does it serve you to act that way?"
   3. "What does it get you in the end?"

Vignette 3
(a) 1. "What are you feeling now?"
   2. "What are you thinking about now?"
(b) 1. "Is this typical of you?"
   2. "Do you usually act this way?"
(c) 1. "Can you think of any other times you acted this way?"
(d) 1. "How did you feel then?"
   2. "What thoughts were going through your head then?"
(e) 1. "So what's the payoff for acting that way?"
   2. "How does it serve you to act that way?"

Mastery Test

OBJECTIVE 6　Given written classroom dialogues, to construct inventory questions that (1) describe responses, (2) identify response patterns, and (3) identify consequences.

Read the following vignette and then write down the level of inventory questions as indicated. Again, there are several different questions that you could ask at each of the levels. Any of the questions listed on the Answer Key are acceptable. You must complete six of the seven responses in order to pass this test.

Karen has asked you for extra help in her geometry in preparation for the midterm, which is to be given tomorrow. You are surprised that she would ask you for help, for her past behavior has been one of ambivalence and disinterest. You agree to meet her in your class at the end of the school day. You have waited nearly forty minutes, and you are getting ready to leave when she comes rushing into the room.

   Karen: "I'm sorry I'm late, but I ran into an old friend and I just stopped to say hello."
   Teacher: "Well Karen, we had an appointment, and I waited over half an hour for you. Frankly, I've had it. I'm going home."
Karen's face grows red, she drops her head, and whispers: "I just don't know what's wrong with me."

1. *Teacher:* _____

   (describing thoughts or feelings)

   Karen: "I'm really embarrassed. I'm sorry. Sometimes I just forget the appointments I make."

2. *Teacher:* _____

   (identifying patterns)

   Karen: "Either I just forget or I come late."

3. *Teacher:* _____

   (identifying patterns)

   Karen: "The other day I made an appointment with Mr. Orton for help in chemistry, and I forgot that one too."

   Teacher: "What happened then?"
   Karen: "I ran into Eric, an old boyfriend of mine."

4. *Teacher:* _____

   (describing thoughts)

   Karen: "I guess I just wanted to talk for a second or two and got carried away."
   Teacher: "So it seems that meeting an old boyfriend distracts you from your appointments."

5. *Teacher:* _____

   (identifying consequences)

   Karen: "The people that I'm supposed to meet get angry."

6. *Teacher:* _____

   (identifying consequences)

   Karen: "I obviously get in trouble."

7. *Teacher:* _____

   (describing thoughts or feelings)

   Karen: "I feel so stupid."

ANSWER KEY

Mastery Test, Objective 6

1. "What are you thinking right now?"
   "What are you feeling?"
   "What thoughts are going through your head?"
   "What are you saying to yourself now?"
2. "Is this a typical way of acting for you?"
   "Is this a pattern of behavior?"
3. "What other times have you acted this way?"
   "How do you usually react in this situation (when you make an appointment)?"
4. "What were you thinking (at that time)?"
   "What thoughts were going through your head when you met Eric? When you knew you had missed your appointment?"
5. "What's the payoff in the end (for being late or missing your appointment)?"
   "What are the consequences (for being late or missing your appointment)?"
   "What does this type of behavior help you to avoid?"
   "What does this type of behavior protect you from?"
6. Any of the above (question 5)
7. "What are you thinking now?"
   "What are you feeling now?"
   "What thoughts are going through your head?"

SUMMARY

At this point it is time to rest and to reflect upon all you have read. You have been given the opportunity to describe four interpersonal communication skills and to construct dialogues that incorporate each of the skills. The ultimate measure, though, of effective interpersonal communication is to assimilate the information and then to actively demonstrate such skills as part of your behavioral repertoire. You may choose to supplement your learning process by reading any of the resources listed in the following bibliography. It is interesting to note how humanistic psychologists and educators have incorporated such behaviors into their own writings and use such behaviors as criteria for assessing personal effectiveness.

NOTES

1. Gerald A. Weinstein and Mario F. Fantini, *Toward Humanistic Education: A Curriculum of Affect* (New York: Praeger, 1970).

2. Alfred Alschuler, Judith Evans, Gerald Weinstein, and Roy Tamashiro, "Search for Self-Knowledge," *Me Forum* (Spring 1975). University of Massachusetts Press.

3. *Ibid.*

4. J. E. Weigand, ed., *Developing Teacher Competencies* (Englewood Cliffs, New Jersey: Prentice-Hall, 1971), p. 247.

5. Carl Rodgers, *On Becoming a Person* (Boston: Houghton Mifflin, 1961).

6. A. Mehrabian and M. Wiener, "Non-immediacy between communication and object of communication in a verbal message," *Journal of Consulting Psychology* 30 (1966).

7. A. Mehrabian, "Significance of Posture and Position in the Communication of Attitude and Status Relationships," *Psychological Bulletin* 71 (1969): 359–372.

8. Edward T. Hall, *The Hidden Dimensions* (Garden City, New York: Doubleday, 1966), p. 108.

9. Charles Kelley, *Journal of Humanistic Psychology* 14 (1974).

10. *Ibid.*

11. Gerald Miller, *Speech Communication: A Behavioral Approach* (Indianapolis: Bobbs-Merrill, 1966), p. 73.

12. Joel Davitz, ed., *The Communication of Emotional Meaning* (New York: McGraw-Hill, 1964), p. 195.

13. Gerald Weinstein, "Introduction" in *Discovering Your Teaching Self: Humanistic Approaches to Effective Teaching* by Richard Curwin and Barbara Fuhrmann (Englewood Cliffs, New Jersey: Prentice-Hall, 1975), p. xix.

14. Daniel Malamud and Solomon Machover, *Toward Self-Understanding: Group Techniques in Self-Confrontation* (Springfield, Illinois: Charles C Thomas, 1970).

ADDITIONAL READINGS

Combs, Arthur. *The Professional Education of Teachers.* Boston: Allyn and Bacon, 1965.

Gazda, George. *Human Relations Development.* Boston: Allyn and Bacon, 1973.

Glasser, William. *Reality Therapy. A New Approach to Psychiatry.* New York: Harper and Row, 1965.

Glasser, William. *Schools Without Failure.* New York: Harper and Row, 1969.

Horney, Karen. *Self-Analysis.* New York: W. W. Norton, 1942.

Luft, Joseph. *Group Process: An Introduction to Group Dynamics*, 2nd ed. Palo Alto, California: National Press Books, 1970.

Maslow, Abraham H. *The Farther Reaches of Human Nature.* New York: Viking Press, 1971.

Maslow, Abraham H. *Toward A Psychology of Being.* New York: Van Nostrand Reinhold Co., 1968.

McClelland, David. *The Achieving Society.* Princeton: D. Van Nostrand, 1961.

Montagu, Ashley. *The Humanization of Man.* Cleveland, Ohio: World Publishing Co., 1962.

Moustakas, Clark E., ed. *The Self: Explorations in Personal Growth.* New York: Harper and Row, 1956.

Purkey, William. *Self Concept and School Achievement.* Englewood Cliffs, New Jersey: Prentice-Hall, 1970.

Rogers, Carl. *Client-Centered Therapy.* Boston: Houghton Mifflin, 1951.

Rogers, Carl. *Humanistic Psychology.* Columbus, Ohio: Charles E. Merrill, 1971.

Schutz, William. *Firo: A Three-Dimensional Theory of Interpersonal Behavior.* New York: Rinehart and Winston, 1958.

Schutz, William. *Joy: Expanding Human Awareness.* New York: Grove Press, 1967.

Sokolove, Sandra. *A Competency-Based Approach to Humanizing Education.* Ed.D. dissertation. University of Massachusetts, 1975.

Stanford, Gene, and Albert E. Roark. *Human Interaction in Education.* Boston: Allyn and Bacon, 1974.

Ed Keren, Institute of Open Education.

WILFORD A. WEBER

Classroom Management

Objectives

1 To define classroom management, to differentiate it from the instructional dimension of teaching, and to describe its importance.

2 To differentiate between classroom instructional problems and classroom management problems.

3 To differentiate between individual and group classroom management problems.

4 To identify inappropriate classroom management strategies.

5 To describe the nature and dynamics of the behavior-modification approach to classroom management.

6 To describe the nature and dynamics of the socioemotional-climate approach to classroom management.

7 To describe the nature and dynamics of the group-process approach to classroom management.

8 To classify the type of classroom management approach used in given problem situations.

9 To assess the potential effectiveness of the classroom management approach used in given problem situations.

No other aspect of teaching is so often cited as a major concern by prospective, beginning, and experienced teachers as classroom management. No other aspect of teaching is more frequently discussed in the professional literature — or the faculty lounge. The reason is quite simple. Classroom management is a complex set of behaviors the teacher uses to establish and maintain classroom conditions that will enable students to achieve their instructional objectives efficiently — that will enable them to learn. Thus, effective classroom management is the major prerequisite to effective instruction. Classroom management may be considered the most fundamental — and the most difficult — task the teacher performs.

The teacher's competence in classroom management is largely a function of his or her understanding of the dynamics of effective classroom management. Therefore, the purpose of this chapter is to enable you to cope more effectively with classroom management problems by helping you to understand the management dimension of teaching more fully. More specifically, because no one "best" approach to classroom management has been found, three somewhat different approaches will be discussed: the behavior-modification approach, the socioemotional-climate approach, and the group-process approach. You should be more effective in your own teaching if you understand the full range of managerial behaviors implied by each of these approaches and are able to select and apply those specific managerial behaviors most appropriate to particular situations.

Objective 1

To define classroom management, to differentiate it from the instructional dimension of teaching, and to describe its importance.

LEARNING ACTIVITY 1

Definitions

While it is something of an oversimplification, a search of the literature on teaching reveals five rather different definitions of the term "classroom management." Each of the five is different because it represents a particular philosophical position regarding classroom management.

One of these positions — the authoritarian approach — views classroom management as the process of controlling student behavior. The role of the teacher is to establish and to maintain order in the classroom. Primary emphasis is on preserving order and maintaining control through the use of discipline. Indeed, often discipline and classroom management are seen as synonymous terms by advocates of this approach. Typical of the definitions that reflect this position is the following: Classroom management is that set of activities by which the teacher establishes and maintains order in the classroom.

A second position — one directly contrary to the authoritarian approach — is the permissive approach. Advocates of this approach take the view that the role of the teacher is to maximize student freedom — to help students feel free to do what they want whenever they want. To do otherwise, it is claimed, is to inhibit their natural development. A definition that reflects this viewpoint might be stated as follows: Classroom management is that set of activities by which the teacher maximizes student freedom. Indeed, some advocates of this approach find the notion of "management" contradictory to their philosophy of schooling.

While it is clear that both the authoritarian approach and the permissive approach have their advocates, and their practitioners, it is the view here that neither is an effective or responsible approach. The authoritarian approach is inhumane; the permissive approach is unrealistic. Although philosophically defensible, we do not consider either approach useful. This position is examined more fully in Learning Activity 4, where you are encouraged to identify inappropriate classroom management strategies and to look for another approach that would be effective.

The principles of behavior modification provide the basis for a third position. This position views classroom management as the process of *modifying student behavior*. The role of the teacher is to foster desirable student behavior and to eliminate undesirable behavior. In short, the teacher helps the student learn appropriate behavior by applying principles derived from theories of reinforcement. A definition that reflects this viewpoint might take the following form: Classroom management is that set of activities by which the teacher promotes appropriate student behavior and eliminates inappropriate student behavior.

A fourth position views classroom management as the process of *creating a positive socioemotional climate* in the classroom. The assumption of this position is that learning is maximized in a positive classroom climate, which, in turn, stems from good interpersonal relationships — both teacher–student and student–student relationships. It is also assumed that the teacher is the key to those relationships. Therefore, the teacher's role is to develop a positive socioemotional classroom climate through the establishment of healthy interpersonal relationships. The following definition reflects this position: Classroom management is that set of activities by which the teacher develops good interpersonal relationships and a positive socioemotional classroom climate.

A fifth viewpoint conceives the classroom to be a social system in which group processes are of major importance. The basic assumption is that instruction takes place within a group context. Therefore, the nature and behavior of the classroom group are viewed as having a significant effect on learning, even though learning is seen as an individual process. The role of the teacher is to *foster the development and operation of an effective classroom system*. The following definition is one which represents this viewpoint: Classroom management is that set of activities by which the teacher establishes and maintains an effective classroom organization.

Each of the last three definitions presented above represents a different but defensible position concerning classroom management. Because none has been proved best, you are encouraged to develop a pluralistic operational definition in your position toward classroom management. The teacher who adopts such a definition is committed to use those behaviors which are most appropriate to a particular situation; he or she is not tied to only one approach in establishing and maintaining conditions in which students can learn. The advantage of this position seems clear. Additionally, the teacher who would take a pluralistic approach to classroom management would find it impossible, even contradictory, to reconcile the authoritarian and permissive approaches with the other three — the behavior-modification, socioemotional-climate, and group-process approaches. Therefore, in the remainder of this chapter, only these latter three positions are discussed, for only they appear useful, potentially effective approaches. A pluralistic definition which takes these three approaches into account might state: Classroom management is that set of activities by which the teacher promotes appropriate student behavior and eliminates inappropriate student behavior, develops good interpersonal relationships and a positive socioemotional climate, and establishes and maintains an effective and productive classroom organization.

Instruction and Management

Teaching consists of two major sets of activities: instruction and management. Instructional activities are intended to facilitate the student's achievement of specific educational objectives directly. Diagnosing learner needs, planning lessons, presenting information, asking questions, and evaluating learner progress are examples of instructional activities. Managerial activities are intended to create and maintain conditions in which instruction can take place effectively and efficiently. Rewarding promptness, developing teacher–student rapport, and establishing productive group norms are examples of managerial activities. Admittedly, it is often difficult to decide whether a particular teaching behavior is instructional or managerial, because the two are usually intertwined. It is important, however, to try to make this distinction when faced with classroom problems.

Inasmuch as teaching consists of instructional and managerial activities, it follows that the teacher faces both types of problems. The effective teacher must be able to distinguish between instructional problems that require instructional solutions and managerial problems that require managerial solutions. Too often, teachers attempt to solve managerial problems with instructional solutions. (The reverse is also true but occurs with somewhat less frequency.) For example, making the lesson more interesting — a commonly suggested instructional remedy — is not likely to solve the problem of children who are withdrawn because they have not been accepted by their classmates. Nonacceptance and withdrawal are management problems and require a managerial solution.

Importance

If instruction is that set of activities intended to facilitate the student's achievement of educational objectives directly and if management is that set intended to create conditions in which instruction can take place, it follows that effective management is a critical prerequisite to effective instruction. Thus, simple logic supports the notion that effective classroom management is an important aspect of the teaching–learning process.

In addition to the logical argument that can be made for the importance of effective classroom management, an increasingly strong case can be made on the basis of results from teacher effectiveness research. A growing body of research suggests that there is a positive relationship between certain teacher classroom management behaviors and desirable learner outcomes including student achievement and attitudes. For example, the literature indicates that behavior modification is effective, that "reality therapy" — a socioemotional-climate strategy — is effective, and that certain group-process approaches are effective. The Additional Readings section of this chapter lists a number of sources which make a case for one or another of these approaches.

Approaches

Unlike the five classroom management approaches touched upon earlier, which each rely on a definite philosophical position, a sixth approach, the "bag-of-tricks" approach, is not derived from a philosophical or psychological base. Instead, it is an ill-fitting combination of common sense, old wives' tales, and folklore. Descriptions of the "bag-of-tricks" approach usually consist of a list of things a teacher should do — or should not do — when confronted with various types of classroom management problems. These lists of "do's" and "don't's" are commonly found in articles with titles like "Thirty Ways to Improve Student Behavior." Because these lists often have the appearance of being quick and easy recipes, this approach is also known as the "cookbook" approach. The following are typical of the kinds of statements one might find on such a list:

Always reprimand a pupil in private.

Never raise your voice when admonishing a student.

Always be firm and fair when dealing with students.

Never play favorites when rewarding students.

Always be sure a student is guilty before punishing him or her.

Always be sure that all students know all your rules and regulations.

Always be consistent in enforcing your rules.

Because the "bag-of-tricks" approach is not derived from a well-conceptualized base, it lacks consistency. Even though many suggestions put forward by advocates of the "bag-of-tricks" approach make a great deal of sense, there is no set of principles that permits the teacher to generalize to other problems. Additionally, the "bag-of-tricks" approach tends to cause a teacher to be *reactive* in dealing with classroom management. In other words, the teacher who uses a "bag-of-tricks" approach usually is reacting to specific problems and using short-range solutions. It is more effective to be *proactive*, to anticipate problems, and to use long-range solutions. The "bag-of-tricks" approach does not foster this type of teaching behavior, which attempts to deal with possible problems before they actually surface in the classroom.

A last difficulty caused by acceptance of the "bag-of-tricks" approach is that when the specific prescription fails to achieve its intended goal, the teacher is left without recourse. That is, the teacher cannot analyze the situation and posit alternatives because the "bag-of-tricks" approach deals in absolutes. If "such-and-such" happens, the teacher does "so-and-so." On the other hand, advocates of a pluralistic approach can take the position: If "such-and-such" happens, the teacher can do "this" or "this" or "this." And, if one of those fails to work, it is simply a matter of reanalyzing the situation and selecting from a variety of equally attractive alternatives. Teachers who operate from a "bag-of-tricks" framework disadvantage themselves and are unlikely to be effective classroom managers.

Unlike the "bag-of-tricks" approach, the behavior-modification approach is founded on a sound basis — the tenets of behavioral psychology. In simple terms, it is based on the assumption that all behavior — both appropriate and inappropriate behavior — is learned. Those who strictly adhere to the principles of behavior modification assume that (1) a few basic processes such as positive reinforcement, negative reinforcement, punishment, and extinction account for learning at all age levels and under all conditions; and (2) learning is controlled largely, if not entirely, by events in the environment.

The basic premise is that the acquisition of a particular behavior is contingent upon learning that its performance will be rewarded; that is, performance of that behavior will produce a form of reinforcement. Reinforcement is viewed as an event which enhances the possibility that a behavior will be repeated — the behavior is strengthened. The behavior being strengthened by reinforcement may be either appropriate or inappropriate. However, if either type of behavior is rewarded, it is likely to continue.

Reinforcement itself may take different forms. Usually, reinforcement is seen as a reward given to a student who behaves appropriately in the hope that the behavior would be continued. Giving a reward for the purpose of maintaining an already acquired behavior is called *positive reinforcement. Negative reinforcement,* on the other hand, is the strengthening of a behavior through the removal of an unpleasant stimulus.

Punishment is the use of an unpleasant stimulus to eliminate an undesirable behavior. Although punishment is not as effective in dealing with students as was historically thought, neither is it viewed by behavior-modification advocates as completely unacceptable as a means of managing the classroom. Punishment is seen as having the advantage of immediately stopping the undesirable behavior and giving the teacher time to implement a reinforcement system for strengthening more acceptable patterns of behavior. With regard to punishment, there is clearly less than universal agreement concerning its effectiveness and, thus, punishment remains a topic of controversy.

Although punishment and various types of reinforcement have been advocated as having a place in managing the classroom, the behavior-modification literature suggests that (1) ignoring inappropriate student behavior and showing approval of appropriate behavior are very effective in achieving better classroom behavior; and (2) showing approval for appropriate behavior is probably the key to effective classroom management. The references in the Additional Readings section that describe the behavioral-modification approach support this position.

The *socioemotional-climate* approach is built on the premise that effective classroom management is a function of good teacher–student and student–student relationships. Advocates argue that teachers need to recognize that the facilitation of learning rests upon the following attitudinal qualities in the personal relationship between the learner and the teacher: (1) *realness* in the teacher, (2) teacher *acceptance and trust* of the student, and (3) teacher *empathy* regarding the student.

The teacher who uses an interpersonal approach is also guided by the fact that love and self-worth are the two basic needs which must be met for the student to develop a "success" identity. A student needs to experience success; therefore, a teacher must provide the student with an opportunity to achieve success. Furthermore, because the student acts on his or her perceptions of self, if the student is to view himself or herself as worthy of respect, he or she must be treated with respect. Thus, the concerned teacher must treat students with respect.

Advocates of the socioemotional-climate approach also claim that a teacher must be committed to helping students avoid failure. They argue that failure kills motivation, creates a negative self-image, increases anxiety, and leads to misbehavior. The classroom must be made to be a place where the student feels safe and secure, a place where the student has the opportunity to take risks and to fail without excessive sanction.

The socioemotional-climate approach is rooted in a philosophy that stresses empathy and acceptance in teacher–student relationships. It holds foremost that the classroom climate influences learning and that the teacher greatly influences the nature of that climate. Thus, advocates of this approach emphasize the importance of teacher behaviors that cause the student to perceive the teacher as involved and caring. When the student behaves inappropriately, the teacher is encouraged to "separate the sin from the sinner," to accept the student while rejecting the behavior of the student. In all cases, the primary function is to establish positive relationships with each student.

The implications of a socioemotional-climate approach to classroom management suggest that there is a concern with the development of the "whole child," not just the academic learner.

The use of *group processes* for classroom management is derived from the principles of social psychology and group dynamics. It is based on the assumptions that (1) schooling takes place within a group context, and (2) the classroom is a social system with the characteristics of other social systems. Emphasis is given to the characteristics of the classroom group and the interrelationships of its members. The central role of the teacher is seen as the establishment and maintenance of a cohesive, productive, task-oriented classroom group.

In this light, the first task of the teacher is to create a cohesive group. Advocates of the group-process approach stress the need for the teacher to foster group attractiveness and cohesion by directing praise and encouragement to an entire class and by encouraging adequate communication among members of that group. The second task is to help students develop group norms that are productive and satisfying. This would include, for example, the development of acceptable work standards. Once a cohesive, productive group is established, it is a continuing task of the teacher to maintain that unity and those norms.

In solving problems, the rationale for utilizing group processes is based on the belief that misbehavior is not an individual affair that just happens to take place in a group context but is, indeed, a social affair contingent upon the nature of the group. A chief goal of the teacher in the case of misbehavior is to help the group become responsible for its own actions and for its own management. An effectively functioning group exercises great control over its members.

Mastery Test

OBJECTIVE 1   To define classroom management, to differentiate it from the instructional dimension of teaching, and to describe its importance.

Answer each of the following questions in the spaces provided. When finished, check your responses with the Answer Key that follows.

1. You have read several definitions of the term "classroom management." Each is somewhat different from the others because of the philosophical position it represents. Write a brief operational definition of the term "classroom management" that you feel would be useful to you as you think about the concept.

_____

_____

_____

2. Contrast the managerial and the instructional dimensions of teaching through: (a) a comparison of their respective purposes; (b) a description of their chief characteristics; and (c) the presentation of several examples of each.

_____

_____

_____

_____

_____

_____

_____

_____

_____

3. In this chapter, only three approaches to classroom management are viewed as useful: (a) the behavior-modification approach; (b) the socioemotional-climate approach; and (c) the group-process approach. Write out your conception of each, including the philosophical viewpoint on which it is based.

Behavior-Modification Approach

_____

_____

_____

_____

_____

_____

_____

_____
_____

Socioemotional-Climate Approach

_____
_____
_____
_____
_____
_____
_____
_____

Group-Process Approach

_____
_____
_____
_____
_____
_____
_____
_____
_____
_____

4. As noted earlier, there are two major viewpoints which stress the importance of effective classroom management. The first of these was described as being based on logic; the second was described as being based on research. Try to restate each argument in your own words. You might find this a more interesting exercise if you role-play a bit in responding. In the first case, you might write as if you were an experienced teacher attempting to explain "the facts of life" to a teacher-education student. And in the second case, you might write as if you were an educational researcher summarizing research findings in a scholarly paper.

Logical Viewpoint

_____
_____
_____
_____

_____
_____
_____
_____

Research Viewpoint

_____
_____
_____
_____
_____
_____
_____
_____
_____

ANSWER KEY
Mastery Test, Objective 1

The following are suggested responses that might have been given to the questions asked above. Because the questions tend to be rather open-ended, your answers may not be identical, but they should be similar. In those cases where they are not, compare the two sets of responses and try to account for any large discrepancies. If it appears that you may have misunderstood some aspect of the information presented so far, you may want to reread certain parts of Learning Activity 1 or the appropriate resource materials listed in the Additional Readings.

1. An operational definition of the term "classroom management" should be a pluralistic definition — one which embraces several viewpoints — because no one viewpoint has been proven best. The following definition is suggested: Classroom management is that set of teaching behaviors by which the teacher promotes appropriate student behavior and eliminates inappropriate student behavior, develops good interpersonal relationships and a positive socioemotional climate, and establishes and maintains an effective and productive classroom organization. Your definition may not be identical to this one, but it should incorporate these two notions: (1) Classroom management is a set of teaching behaviors or activities performed by

the teacher; that is, classroom management is something the teacher does; and (2) Classroom management — to be effective — is pluralistic; that is, the teacher employs a variety of approaches rather than relying on a single approach.

2. The distinction between management and instructional teaching behaviors is very often not an easy one to make because they tend to be intertwined. However, in simple terms, the purpose of instructional activities is to facilitate student achievement relevant to specific educational objectives, while the purpose of managerial activities is to establish and maintain conditions in which instruction can take place effectively and efficiently. Instructional activities are characterized by teacher behavior intended to facilitate achievement of specific student outcomes directly. Managerial activities are characterized by teacher behavior that creates conditions in which instructional activities can take place. Diagnosing learner needs, planning lessons, presenting information, asking questions, and evaluating learner progress are examples of instructional activities given in Learning Activity 1. Rewarding promptness, developing teacher-student rapport, and establishing productive group norms are examples of managerial activi-

ties presented in Learning Activity 1. (You might have given many other examples.)

3. The *behavior-modification approach* is founded on the principles of behavioral psychology and is based on the assumption that all behavior — both appropriate and inappropriate behavior — is learned. In simplest terms, the basic premise of the behavior-modification approach is that the rewarded behavior is likely to be repeated.

The *socioemotional-climate approach* is derived from the principles of counseling psychology. It views effective classroom management as a function of good teacher–student and student–student relationships. This approach argues that the teacher is the major determiner of classroom climate and that the establishment of a positive socioemotional classroom climate is the result of a teacher displaying realness, acceptance, and empathy in relating to students.

The *group-process approach* is based on the principles of social psychology and group dynamics. The basic assumption is that schooling takes place within a group context and that the classroom is a social system with the charac-

teristics of other social systems. It is assumed that the major role of the teacher is to create and maintain an effectively functioning social system.

4. Logic suggests that effective classroom management is an important aspect of the teaching–learning process because effective management is prerequisite to effective instruction. If the goal of instruction — and of schooling — is to foster student achievement, this goal cannot be realized in the absence of effective classroom management. Thus, effective classroom management is of crucial importance.

A growing body of teacher effectiveness research suggests that there is a positive relationship between certain teacher classroom management behaviors and desirable learner outcomes. While this research has not shown one particular classroom management approach to be superior, it has shown that certain of those teaching behaviors that belong to the behavior-modification, socioemotional-climate, and group-process approaches are effective. Thus, it can be claimed that the appropriate use of those behaviors is important in fostering desirable student outcomes.

Objective 2

To differentiate between classroom instructional problems and classroom management problems.

LEARNING ACTIVITY 2

The previous section presented a very brief discussion of the view that teaching consists of two major sets of activities — instruction and management. The purpose of this section is to expand on that view and to facilitate your achievement of objective 2. Thus, this section is based on three interrelated assumptions:

1. Because teaching consists of two dimensions — instruction and management — classroom problems are of two kinds — instructional problems and managerial problems.
2. Managerial problems require management solutions and are not solved by instructional solutions; instructional problems require instructional solutions and are not solved by management solutions.
3. Effective classroom management is highly dependent on the teacher's ability to identify classroom problems correctly as instructional or managerial in nature and to act accordingly.

Clearly, the first step in solving classroom management problems is being able to identify accurately those problems which are instructional and those which are managerial. The section that follows provides some guided practice in making those kinds of distinctions. Several typical classroom problems are described; some are instructional problems and some are managerial problems. Read each description carefully and decide whether you believe the problem to be instructional or managerial. Indicate your decision by placing a check in the appropriate space. Then briefly note the reason for your decision in the space provided. Because instructional and managerial problems are so often intertwined, in making your decision be sure to go to the cause of the problem, not its symptoms. A discussion of each problem is presented immediately after the spaces provided for your responses.

---

1. Johnny is a sixth grade boy of low-average ability. His academic record is very poor; in reading, for example, he is two years below grade level and nearly a year below any of his peers. His teacher, Mrs. Miller, describes him as "the worst kid in the class," for he seems to be misbehaving continuously. Johnny refuses to do his own assignments and frequently disrupts others in the class while they are doing their assignments. Mrs. Miller feels that he could do the same work the other children do if he would simply apply himself.

   Instructional Problem__✓____   Managerial Problem_____

   Comment _____

   _____

   _____

   _____

   Discussion. Although on the surface this may appear to be a managerial problem, the underlying problem here is instructional. Because Johnny is unable to be successful in his academic work, he is frustrated. His frustration manifests itself in the form of misbehavior. Expecting Johnny to be able to do the same kind and quality of work as his classmates is probably an unrealistic expectation. The teacher will need to provide instruction which is appropriate to Johnny's level of ability and achievement if he is to be successful. It is likely that success would eliminate Johnny's need to misbehave.

2. Although it is now eight weeks since she transferred to her new school, Barbara is still the "new kid in class." She transferred in midyear when her family moved to the city but has not yet become an accepted member of her fourth grade class. She appears to be shy and withdrawn. Barbara's teacher, Mr. Johnson, has made numerous attempts to "bring her out of her shell." He has formed small groups to work on social studies projects and has placed Barbara with a group of three particularly friendly girls.

   Instructional Problem_____   Managerial Problem__✓____

   Comment _____

   _____

   _____

   _____

   Discussion. This is a managerial problem. If Barbara is to become a fully participating, active member of the classroom group, her teacher will have to help her perceive the group as attractive and its members as accepting. Certain kinds of instructional activities — such as small group work — may facilitate this process, but the problem is essentially managerial, not instructional.

3. Mrs. Parker claims that her tenth grade English class is one of the best she has ever had. She finds them to be well behaved and capable — a delight to teach. On the other hand, Mr. Bradley, who has this same group for

American history, finds them to be quite average in achievement and rather poor in conduct. Indeed, on several occasions he has felt that they were close to overt hostility. Although this class, as a whole, has done well in social studies and other subjects in previous years, Mr. Bradley feels that the problem lies in their dislike of the subject.

Instructional Problem_____   Managerial Problem___✓_____

Comment _____

_____

_____

_____

Discussion. This is a management problem. Since the group has done well previously and is presently doing well in another course, one would have to conclude that the problem results from the relationship between the teacher and the class. Because he has had conduct problems and, on several occasions, the class was close to overt hostility, one would suspect that his management style, not his instructional style, is the cause of this problem. In any event, the solution lies in building a positive relationship between the teacher and the students.

4. Ms. Roth enters her fourth grade classroom to find Billie and Steve scuffling on the floor. Their classmates have gathered in a circle around them; they quickly notice Ms. Roth and take their seats. "Stop it this minute!" she calls to the fighting boys. They jump up, surprised that she is there.

Instructional Problem_____   Managerial Problem___✓_____

Comment _____

_____

_____

_____

Discussion. This is clearly a managerial problem. Indeed, it is one of those few problems which is exclusively managerial. In addition, it is an interesting case because there are really two problems — one which is very apparent and one which is not. The obvious problem is that two members of the class are fighting. The second problem — one often overlooked — is that the classroom group sanctioned their behavior. Group norms had not developed to the point where the class would stop the fighting because it was violating their rules of how to behave in the classroom. The teacher will need to deal with both the conflict between the boys and the lack of productive norms within the classroom group.

5. Compared to her eighth grade classmates, Lisa is a rather slow student. She tries very hard but is often unsuccessful academically. Mathematics is a particularly difficult subject for her. During mathematics class, Mr. Bronson, the teacher, sends Lisa and seven other students to the board to work a relatively simple problem — a problem of the kind the class has been working for several weeks. On the basis of her recent work, Mr. Bronson expected that Lisa would have no difficulty. Indeed, he felt that success of a public nature would be good for her. Unfortunately, while the other students get the correct answer, Lisa does not. Upon noticing her rather obvious error, many of the other students begin to giggle and poke fun at Lisa. She is terribly embarrassed and ashamed.

Instructional Problem___✓_____   Managerial Problem_____

Comment _____

_____

_____

_____

Discussion. While at first glance this may appear to be an instructional problem — and there is that element in as much as Lisa does have an instructional problem — the more serious problem is the negative attitude of the class toward Lisa. That is a managerial problem. Of course the teacher must help Lisa with her mathematics, but he must also build a better relationship between Lisa and her classmates.

Mastery Test

OBJECTIVE 2   To differentiate between classroom instructional problems and classroom management problems.

You will be given brief descriptions of 10 typical classroom problems; some are management problems and some are instructional problems. Read each description carefully and indicate whether you believe a particular problem is managerial or instructional by placing a check in the appropriate space. Also indicate the reason for your decision by writing a brief comment in the space provided. In making your decision, try to go to the cause of the problem, not the problem's symptoms. For example, instructional problems very often lead to management problems. You should point out "clues" that made you identify the problems as you did. When you have responded to all 10 descriptions, compare your responses to those in the Answer Key that follows.

1. Bill has accused Tom of stealing his pencil; he has done so in a rather loud voice. He demands that Tom return it immediately. Tom argues that he found the pencil and that since it does not have Bill's name on it, he has no intention of giving it to Bill.

   Instructional Problem_____   Managerial Problem___✓___

   Comment _____

   _____

   _____

   _____

2. No matter what the nature of the task, Mary seems to be done far more quickly than her classmates. Although this happens with some frequency, Mary seldom will elect to engage in a quiet learning activity of her own choice. Rather, she annoys the students around her by talking to them and disrupting their efforts. The students complain to the teacher that Mary is "bothering" them.

   Instructional Problem___✓___   Managerial Problem_____

   Comment _____

   _____

   _____

   _____

3. Nancy is the "new kid," having become a part of the fourth grade class in February. Now, in April, the teacher sees that Nancy is still not an accepted member of the class even though she is bright and attractive; her attempts to "make friends" are to no avail.

   Instructional Problem_____   Managerial Problem___✓___

   Comment _____

   _____

   _____

   _____

   _____

4. No matter who is speaking, teacher or student, John is always interrupting with some sort of "wise-crack." He is quite witty and his comments usually evoke the laughs of his classmates. Only very rarely do his comments have substantive value. The teacher views the comments as disruptive.

Instructional Problem_____   Managerial Problem___✓___

Comment _____

_____

_____

_____

5. The chemistry class sessions in the laboratory are chaotic; disorder seems to be the rule. Most students appear to be unclear about their assignments, the appropriate materials and equipment are often unavailable at the start of the class period, and the work procedures seem to be ill defined. Time and time again, the teacher has admonished the class for being unprepared. On numerous occasions he has given them ample directions and has established rules he feels should have resulted in bringing order out of chaos. Yet the situation remains chaotic.

Instructional Problem_____   Managerial Problem___✓___

Comment _____

_____

_____

_____

6. Jimmy is a rather shy, quiet sixth grader who is something of a "loner." He is prone to daydream and to be inattentive. His grades are generally below average. In spite of many attempts, his teacher has not been able to find an area in which Jimmy will express more than casual interest, nor has she been able to get him to work or play with his classmates.

Instructional Problem___✓___   Managerial Problem_____

Comment _____

_____

_____

_____

7. By the third month of the school year, it is obvious to the teacher that five or six cliques have developed in a class of 30 sixth grade students. The teacher believes that instructional effectiveness and efficiency have been hindered by the existence of the cliques and the lack of communication and cooperation which they have fostered. That the students in one clique have very little to do with the students in another clique is all too clear.

Instructional Problem_____   Managerial Problem___✓___

Comment _____

_____

_____

_____

8. The teacher has returned the midterm examinations to his eleventh grade history class. Although the class is one of above-average ability, test scores are low and grades are poor. The teacher feels it was a tough but fair examination and it covered only the content that had been assigned. However, the students feel that it was a "nit-picking" examination and that it was unfair because it dealt with content that had been in the assigned reading but had not been discussed in class. Many of the students are quite vocal in their criticism of the teacher and the examination when the whole class discusses the examination with the teacher.

Instructional Problem_____ Managerial Problem_____

Comment _____

_____

_____

_____

9. Brad and Paul have always been the best of friends. They live on the same block, have the same friends, and like the same sorts of things. Both are fourteen years old. However, the teacher notices that for several days they have avoided each other in her class even though they sit next to one another and have been working together on a joint project which is due within the next few days. The teacher approaches the boys and inquires about their progress on the project. Paul quickly responds that it is at a standstill because Brad is not doing his share of the work. Brad responds by saying that he has done more than his share of the work and that it is Paul's turn to carry the ball. The boys get into a rather heated discussion in which each blames the other for the impasse.

Instructional Problem_____ Managerial Problem_____

Comment _____

_____

_____

_____

10. Mark, a tenth grader of high ability, has the reputation of being an excellent student. He carries an A average in every one of his courses except American history, in which he received a D for both the first and second report periods. He is outspoken about his dislike of the teacher. He claims that he cannot stand her boring lectures and so he simply "turns her off." Other students in the class are not doing well, but they are not experiencing the dramatic difficulties that Mark is having. Mark likes the study of history, but he does not like his teacher.

Instructional Problem_____ Managerial Problem_____

Comment _____

_____

_____

_____

ANSWER KEY

Mastery Test, Objective 2

Compare your responses with those provided below. If at least 9 of your 10 responses agree with those suggested here, you can feel quite confident about your ability to identify and distinguish between instructional and managerial problems. On the other hand, if you find a larger number of discrepancies, you may wish to analyze your responses so that you might better understand the reasoning behind your decisions. If you feel that you need additional help in this regard, you might find it useful to either: (1) reread Learning Activity 1 and/or Learning Activity 2 or (2) study any of those resources listed for objective 2 in the Additional Readings at the end of the chapter. A discussion of each of the case studies follows.

1. The conflict between Bill and Tom is a managerial problem. In dealing with this problem, the teacher will not be attempting to facilitate the achievement of a particular student outcome. Rather, the teacher will be attempting to establish conditions within which Bill and Tom can benefit from instruction. Thus, it is a managerial problem which requires a managerial solution.

2. This is an instructional problem and requires an instructional solution. It appears that the teacher is not providing Mary with sufficiently challenging assignments, nor is the teacher giving her enrichment assignments that would keep her occupied while the other students are working. In dealing with this problem, the teacher will need to individualize instruction so that Mary is provided with assignments appropriate to her ability.

3. This is a managerial problem very much like one of the examples presented in the previous learning activity. The task of the teacher will be to help Nancy become an accepted member of the classroom group. Managerial strategies are required to accomplish this objective.

4. The problem here is managerial. Indeed, there are two managerial problems: (1) an individual problem — John's disruptive behavior; and (2) a group problem — the group's sanctioning of John's behavior. Both require managerial solutions. In simple terms, the teacher's task will be to help the group establish more productive group norms and to help John accept these norms.

5. This problem appears to be primarily instructional and requires an instructional solution. Laboratory sessions must be particularly well organized if they are to run smoothly; that does not seem to be the case here. To solve this problem, it will be necessary for the teacher to do a more thorough job of planning and organizing his laboratory sessions.

6. The problem described is managerial. The teacher's efforts should be directed toward helping Jimmy become an accepted member of the classroom group, a solution that is managerial.

7. The existence of cliques described in this situation is a managerial problem and requires a managerial solution. The task of the teacher will be to facilitate group cohesiveness. As a beginning, the teacher will have to help the students perceive that full membership in the classroom group is more attractive than membership in a clique.

8. Although both instructional and managerial, the problem here is largely instructional. If the teacher is to solve the problem, he or she will need to engage the students in an analysis of the examination. Together they will have to decide whether the examination was fair (as claimed by the teacher) or unfair (as claimed by the students). If they decide it was fair, they will have to examine their relationship; if they decide it was unfair, the teacher will have to provide the students with another examination.

9. This is a case where instruction and management are very much intertwined. However, the situation calls for the teacher to reestablish a friendly, working relationship between Brad and Paul. This would be a managerial solution. If the teacher is successful in this regard, it is highly likely that the instructional problem will also be solved.

10. This problem is also one in which instruction and management are intertwined. It may well be that poor instruction has resulted in a very negative relationship between Mark and his teacher. However, at this point it is not likely that more interesting lectures — an instructional solution — would solve this problem. It is more likely that what is required is an effort on the part of the teacher to establish a positive relationship with Mark — and his classmates. This is a managerial solution.

Objective 3

To differentiate between individual and group classroom management problems.

LEARNING ACTIVITY 3

If a teacher is to be effective in solving classroom management problems, he or she must be able: (1) to identify various types of individual and group classroom management problems correctly; (2) to understand what teaching behavior and classroom management approaches are appropriate and what ones are inappropriate for particular types of problems; and (3) to select and apply those teaching behaviors and classroom management approaches that are most effective in particular problem situations. The first part of this section focuses on the ability to identify various types of classroom management problems; the second part deals with the ability to understand which teacher behaviors are appropriate — and which are inappropriate — in solving the various types of classroom management problems.

There are two major categories of classroom management problems: individual problems and group problems. This is a somewhat risky classification because individual problems and group problems — as with instructional problems and managerial problems — are often intertwined. However, the classification is a useful one for the teacher who recognizes and appreciates their interrelationship.

Although there are numerous descriptions of both individual and group classroom management problems, we will limit ourselves to two sources, the work of Dreikurs and Cassel[1] for individual problem categories and the work of Johnson and Bany[2] for group problems. These two books are among the soundest available and, in addition, they are among the most easily understood and readily applied because of their relative simplicity.

Individual Problems

Dreikurs and Cassel's categorization of individual classroom management problems derives from their assumption that human behavior is purposive and goal-seeking. Each individual has a fundamental need to belong and to feel worthwhile. When the individual is frustrated in developing a feeling of belonging and a sense of self-worth through socially acceptable means, he or she behaves inappropriately, that is, misbehaves. The authors identify four types of misbehavior: (1) attention-getting behaviors, (2) power-seeking behaviors, (3) revenge-seeking behaviors, and (4) behaviors that are displays of inadequacy. These misbehaviors are given in order of increasing severity. For example, the attention-seeking child who fails to gain attention may become a power-seeker.

The student who is unable to gain status in a socially acceptable manner usually seeks it through either active or passive *attention-getting behaviors*. The active form of destructive attention-getting is found in the show-off, the clown, the mischief maker, the brat, the incessant questioner; the nuisance, in a word. The passive form of destructive attention-getting is found in the lazy or inept student who attempts to get others to pay attention to him or her by requiring constant help.

Power-seeking behaviors are similar to but more intense than those of destructive attention-getting. The active power-seeker argues, lies, contradicts, has temper tantrums, refuses to do what he or she is told to do, and is openly disobedient. The passive power-seeker is one whose laziness is so pronounced that he or she usually accomplishes no work at all. Such a student is forgetful, stubborn, and passively disobedient.

The *revenge-seeking* student is so deeply frustrated and confused that he or she seeks success through hurting others. Vicious, openly defiant behavior is common, and physical attacks (scratching, biting, kicking) against fellow students, authority figures, and animals are not uncommon. He or she is a sore loser and poor sport. Usually the revenge-seeking child is active rather than passive. The active revenge-seeking child is described as vicious and revengeful. The passive revenge-seeking child is described as sullen and defiant.

The student who displays *inadequacy* is one who has become so deeply discouraged in attempting to achieve a feeling of belonging that he or she has given up any hope of succeeding and expects only continued failure. Feelings of hopelessness and helplessness accompany the withdrawal or dropout behavior of such a student, who equates participation with further failure. Such displays of inadequacy always take a passive form.

The table[3] at the top of the next page presents a description of the four types of individual problems.

In addition to describing these four types of individual classroom management problems, Dreikurs and Cassel suggest a rather simple technique by which the teacher can identify the nature of the problem. They suggest that (1) if the teacher feels *annoyed* by the child's behavior, it is probable that the child's goal is attention-getting; (2) if the teacher feels *defeated or threatened*, the child's goal is probably power-seeking; (3) if the teacher feels *deeply hurt*, the child's goal is likely revenge-seeking; and (4) if the teacher feels *helpless*, the child's goal is likely a display of inadequacy. Dreikurs and Cassel assert that the teacher must correctly identify and understand the goals of the student's misbehavior to be effective in dealing with it.

Group Problems

Johnson and Bany, advocates of the group-process approach, identify seven group classroom management problems: (1) lack of unity; (2) nonadherence to behavioral standards and work procedures; (3) negative reactions to individual members; (4) class approval of misbehavior; (5) being prone to distraction, work stoppage, and imitative behavior; (6) low morale and hostile, resistant, or aggressive reactions; and (7) inability to adjust to environmental change.

A *lack of unity* is characterized by conflicts between individuals and subgroups. Examples include conflicts between students of one sex or race and students of the other sex or race. The classroom climate in such situations is marked by conflict, hostility, and tension. Students are dissatisfied with the group and find it unattractive. Students fail to support one another.

When the classroom group exhibits inappropriate behavior in situations where there are clearly established norms, it is categorized as *nonadherence* to behavioral standards. Examples include noisy, disor-

IDENTIFYING THE GOALS OF CHILDREN'S MISBEHAVIOR

INCREASED SOCIAL INTEREST ←——→ DIMINISHED SOCIAL INTEREST

MINOR DISCOURAGEMENT ←——→ DEEP DISCOURAGEMENT

Useful and Socially Acceptable Behavior		Useless and Unacceptable Behavior		Goals
Active Constructive	*Passive Constructive*	*Active Destructive*	*Passive Destructive*	
"success" cute remarks excellence for praise and recognition performing for attention stunts for attention being especially good being industrious being reliable (may seem to be "ideal" student but goal is self-elevation, not cooperation)	"charm" excess pleasantness "model" child bright sayings exaggerated conscientiousness excess charm "Southern belle" (often are teacher's pets)	"nuisance" the show-off the clown walking question mark "enfant terrible" instability acts "tough" makes minor mischief	"laziness" bashfulness lack of ability instability lack of stamina fearfulness speech impediments untidiness self-indulgence frivolity anxiety eating difficulties performance difficulties	GOAL 1 ATTENTION-GETTING Seeks proof of his approval or status (almost universal in preschool children) Will cease when reprimanded or given attention
		a "rebel" argues contradicts continues forbidden acts temper tantrums bad habits untruthfulness dawdling	"stubborn" laziness disobedience forgetting	GOAL 2 POWER Similar to destructive attention-getting, but more intense Reprimand intensifies misbehavior
		"vicious" stealing bed wetting violent and brutal (leader of juvenile delinquent gangs)	"violent passivity" sullen defiant	GOAL 3 REVENGE Does things to hurt others Makes self hated Retaliates
			"hopeless" stupidity (pseudofeebleminded) indolence ineptitude inferiority complex	GOAL 4 DISPLAY OF INADEQUACY Assumes real or imagined deficiency to safeguard prestige

SOURCE: Rudolph Dreikurs and Pearl Cassel, *Discipline Without Tears* (New York: Hawthorn Books, 1972), p. 33. Reprinted by permission.

derly behavior at times when students are expected to be quiet and well behaved. Loud talking and disruptive behavior while students are supposed to be engaged in quiet work at their seats is a typical example. Pushing and shoving in the cafeteria line is another.

Negative reactions to individual members of the class are characterized by expressions of hostility toward persons who are not accepted by the group, who deviate from the group's norms, or who hinder the group's efforts. Typical of this type of problem are instances in which the classroom group picks on the student they consider different. The group's efforts are directed toward getting the individual to conform.

Class approval of misbehavior occurs when the group encourages and supports an individual who is behaving in a socially unacceptable way. The most common example is classroom support for the "class clown." If such misbehavior is advocated by the class, it is both a group and an individual problem. The group problem, however, is the more serious of the two.

A problem exists when the group is easily *distracted or prone to work stoppage*. The group overreacts to minor distractions and allows minor problems to interfere with productivity. The instance in which the class refuses to work because they perceive the teacher as having been unfair is a typical example. Such situations are marked by uncertainty and anxiety.

When the class engages in covert or overt *acts of protest and resistance*, causing work slowdowns or stoppage, it is a most difficult group problem. The expressions of resistance are generally very subtle. Repeated requests for clarity regarding assignments, lost pencils, forgotten homework, and petty grievances are typical. However, overt, hostile, aggressive behavior is relatively uncommon.

Classroom groups who react inappropriately when there is a new rule, an emergency situation, a change in group membership, a schedule interruption, or a substitute teacher are exhibiting an *inability to adjust to environmental change*. Generally, such groups are reacting to stress; they perceive the change as a threat to group unity. The most common example is the normally well-behaved class that behaves very badly with a substitute teacher.

A table describing the seven types of group classroom management problems[4] is presented below. The table is followed by a series of exercises which are intended to give you an opportunity to test your ability to identify various types of classroom management problems. Learning Activity 6 describes group-process teaching behaviors intended to solve these types of problems.

GROUP CLASSROOM MANAGEMENT PROBLEMS AND THEIR BEHAVIORAL DESCRIPTIONS

Distinguishing Characteristics	*Behavior Descriptions*
1. Lack of unity	The class lacks unity, and conflicts occur between individuals and subgroups, as: (a) when groups split, become argumentative over competitive situations such as games, or boys side against girls; (b) when groups split by cliques or minority groups; (c) when group takes sides on issues or breaks into subgroups; when hostility and conflict constantly arise among members and create an unpleasant atmosphere.
2. Nonadherence to behavioral standards and work procedures	The class responds with noisy, talkative, disorderly behavior to situations which have established standards for behaving, as: (a) when group is entering or leaving room or changing activities, lining up, cleaning up, or going to auditorium; (b) when group is working in ability groups or engaging in committee work; (c) when group is completing study assignments, receiving assignments, correcting papers, or handling work materials; (d) when group is engaged in discussion, sharing, or planning.
3. Negative reactions to individual members	The class becomes vocal or actively hostile toward one or more class members, as: (a) when group does not accept individuals and derides, ignores, or ridicules members who are different; (b) when group reacts negatively to members who deviate from group code or who thwart group's progress; when a member's behavior upsets or puzzles members of the class.
4. Class approval of misbehavior	The class approves and supports individuals, as: (a) when they talk out of turn, act in ways which disrupt the normal work procedures, or engage in clowning or rebellious activities.
5. Being prone to distraction, work stoppage, and imitative behavior	The group reacts with upset, excited, or disorderly behavior to interruptions, distractions, or constant grievances, as: (a) when group is interrupted by monitors, visitors, or a change in weather; (b) when members constantly have grievances relating to others, lessons, rules, policies, or practices they believe are unfair and when settlements are demanded before work proceeds.

Distinguishing Characteristics	Behavior Descriptions
6. Low morale and hostile, resistant, or aggressive reactions	The class members engage in subtle, hostile, aggressive behavior, creating slowdowns and work stoppages, as: (a) when materials are misplaced, pencils break, or chairs are upset; (b) when books, money, or lunches are temporarily lost; (c) when there are constant requests for assignments to be repeated and explained; (d) when students constantly complain about behavior of others with no apparent loss of friendship; (e) when children accuse authority figures of unfair practices and delay classwork with their claims.
7. Inability to adjust to environmental change	The class reacts inappropriately to such situations, as: (a) when a substitute takes over; (b) when normal routines are changed; (c) when new members transfer into the class; (d) when stress situations cause inappropriate reactions.

SOURCE: Adapted with permission of Macmillan Publishing Co., Inc. from *Classroom Management: Theory and Skill Training*, by Lois V. Johnson and Mary A. Bany. Copyright © 1970 by Macmillan Publishing Co., Inc.

Mastery Test

OBJECTIVE 3   To differentiate between individual and group classroom management problems.

The following section presents 15 brief descriptions of classroom management problems. Your task is to identify the general type of problem (individual or group) and then to identify the particular version of individual or group problem according to the lists below.

Individual Problem (Dreikurs and Cassel)
1. Attention-getting
2. Power-seeking
3. Revenge-seeking
4. Display of inadequacy

Group Problem (Johnson and Bany)
1. Lack of unity
2. Nonadherence to behavioral standards and work procedures
3. Negative reactions to individual members
4. Class approval of misbehavior
5. Being prone to distraction, work stoppage, and imitative behavior
6. Low morale and hostile, resistant, or aggressive reactions
7. Inability to adjust to environmental change

1. Michael has displayed the ability to disrupt Ms. Hamilton's mathematics lessons. He constantly interrupts her with criticisms. He argues about assignments he is given. He refuses to do what he is told to do even if reprimanded. Ms. Hamilton is afraid he may have the upper hand.

Individual Problem _____   Group Problem _____

Type of Problem _____

2. Mr. Clarkson's eighth grade algebra class is usually very well behaved and hard working. However, Ms. Felder, their substitute teacher, finds that they refuse to work and are quite sullen and defiant, even though she is following Mr. Clarkson's lesson plans to the letter.

Individual Problem _____   Group Problem __✓__

Type of Problem ____*env change*_____

3. Mrs. Appleton finds Barry to be a very annoying child. He is always into one or another form of mischief. His misbehavior is relatively minor but, nonetheless, rather obnoxious.

Individual Problem __✓__   Group Problem _____

Type of Problem _____*attn getting*_____

4. In his twenty-five years of teaching Mr. Ramiriz had never experienced a class which was so defiant as his eleventh grade auto body repair class. The students were constantly complaining about something. Indeed, it appeared to Mr. Ramiriz that they were too busy complaining to get any work done.

Individual Problem _____   Group Problem __✓__

Type of Problem _____

5. Miss Franklin felt that Susan was the most disruptive child in her fifth grade class. She was argumentative and defiant. This in itself concerned Miss Franklin, but of even greater concern was the way in which the other children encouraged this misbehavior. Susan knew that she was acting with the full approval of her peers.

Individual Problem __✓__ *power seeking*   Group Problem __✓__

Type of Problem _____*eng of image behav*_____

6. Manny spends most of his time in Mr. Bishop's class daydreaming and looking out of the window. He plays with his pencil and doodles. He takes no part in the discussions and is oblivious to the teacher. Mr. Bishop is at a loss at trying to get Manny to take an active part in class sessions.

Individual Problem __✓__   Group Problem _____

Type of Problem ___*inad*_____

7. Mrs. Paxton is quite distressed by the behavior of her fourth grade class. In spite of her many attempts to individualize instruction, she finds that six children who are quite a bit brighter than the others always seem to do much better work than the other children. This has resulted in resentment, hostility, and conflict between those six students and the rest of the class.

Individual Problem _____   Group Problem __✓__

Type of Problem _____*inch fbnty*_____

8. Although a student of better than average ability, Mary Ann is always asking for help from Ms. Greenville. Ms. Greenville finds this bothersome, because Mary Ann seems to monopolize her time. Ms. Greenville believes Mary Ann often asks for help she really does not need.

Individual Problem __✓__   Group Problem _____

Type of Problem _____*attn getting*_____

9. Mr. Simpson's room is next to the cafeteria. He is concerned because he cannot seem to accomplish anything with his 11:30 class; they are bothered by the noise in the hall as other students go to lunch.

He cannot seem to hold their interest even with lessons that are highly effective with other classes. They just do not stick to the task.

Individual Problem _____   Group Problem __✓__

Type of Problem ___*prone to workshops*_____

10. A group of third graders are sharing a table and working with finger paints. Margie accidentally smears a bit of blue paint on Philip's paper. He screams at her, accusing her of having ruined his drawing. He grabs her paper and tears it into little pieces. The rest of the class is horrified.

Individual Problem __✓__   Group Problem _____

Type of Problem ___*tantrums*_____

11. Although all the students know that running in the hall is against school rules, the students in Mr. Houston's class continue to run when going to the cafeteria.

Individual Problem _____   Group Problem __✓__

Type of Problem ___*non adherence to school statutes*_____

12. Upon returning the examinations, Mrs. Klein is surprised to hear Danny accuse her of having given an unfair examination. He hurls verbal abuse at Mrs. Klein, accusing her of having lied about what the examination would cover. While the other students do not join in Danny's attack, it is clear that they approve of his behavior.

Individual Problem __✓__   Group Problem __✓__

Type of Problem ___*power seeking*_____

13. Clayton and Alex seem to be enjoying a quiet game of checkers during recess on a rainy day. Suddenly, Clayton picks up the board and throws it to the floor. Checkers fly in every direction as he yells: "You cheated, Alex! There's no way a creep like you can beat me!" He gives Alex a very hard shove, turns, and walks away.

Individual Problem __✓__   Group Problem _____

Type of Problem ___*revenge*_____

14. The class has reached the point where it will no longer tolerate Bob's abuse of Ms. Vincente. His attacking behavior only disrupts the class and keeps the other students from their work. So when Bob "goes into his act" for the umpteenth time, Clark tells him to shut up and sit down. The rest of the class nods in agreement.

Individual Problem _____   Group Problem __✓__

Type of Problem ___*they mention disbelief members*_____

15. No matter what she does, Miss Brennan feels that Ron and she are at odds with one another. If she asks him to be neater in his work, he becomes even sloppier. If she asks him to be less talkative, he becomes even more noisy and disruptive. He is stubborn and ill tempered.

Individual Problem __✓__   Group Problem _____

Type of Problem ___*power seeking*_____

ANSWER KEY

Mastery Test, Objective 3

The following is a list of the responses recommended for the preceding exercise. Compare your responses to them. You should not be satisfied with your performance unless you have correctly identified at least 14 out of 15 as individual or group problems. You should get at least 12 correct responses with regard to the specific type of problem.

1. Individual problem: power-seeking.
2. Group problem: inability to adjust to environmental change.
3. Individual problem: attention-getting.
4. Group problem: low morale and hostile, resistant, or aggressive reactions.
5. Group problem: class approval of misbehavior; and individual problem: power-seeking.
6. Individual problem: display of inadequacy.
7. Group problem: lack of unity.
8. Individual problem: attention-getting.
9. Group problem: being prone to distraction, work stoppage, and imitative behavior.
10. Individual problem: revenge-seeking.
11. Group problem: nonadherence to behavioral standards and work procedures.
12. Group problem: class approval of misbehavior; and individual problem: power-seeking.
13. Individual problem: revenge-seeking.
14. Group problem: negative reactions to individual members; and individual problem: power-seeking.
15. Individual problem: power-seeking.

In questions 5, 12, and 14, the group problems described are viewed as having greater importance than the individual problems. You should recognize, however, that there are conflicting views in this regard. Some argue that resolution of the group problem will solve the individual problem. Others argue that resolution of the individual problem will solve the group problem. Still others argue that they are two separate and distinctly different problems, both of which require attention. You will need to reach your own conclusions about this issue.

Objective 4

To identify inappropriate classroom management strategies.

LEARNING ACTIVITY 4

In addition to describing various types of classroom management problems and the group-process approach used in their solution, Johnson and Bany also describe three inappropriate approaches to classroom management problems: punitive or threatening practices; divertive or ignoring practices; and dominative or pressuring practices. While there is some disagreement about their position, it is one advocated here. The table[5] that follows describes each practice in more detail.

Limitations of space preclude a lengthy discussion of these approaches. However, several observations presented by Johnson and Bany are worth noting:

1. Punitive and threatening practices change only the surface behavior for the moment; this is usually followed by undesirable behaviors, including hostility.
2. Divertive and ignoring practices often result in low morale, unrest, scapegoating, aggression, and hostility.
3. Dominative and pressuring practices often result in surface submission, further frustration, underlying resentment, and hostility.

For the most part, then, these approaches to classroom management are ineffective. Their use usually results in temporary solutions followed by even greater problems, the most serious of which is hostility. At the very best, these approaches deal only with the problem's symptoms and not the problem itself. The Mastery Test that follows gives you an opportunity to practice categorizing teacher behaviors as punitive or threatening, divertive or ignoring, and dominative or pressuring. In the Final Mastery Test, you will be given further opportunity to practice this ability and to judge the effectiveness of these approaches.

INAPPROPRIATE PRACTICES USED TO CONTROL CLASSROOM BEHAVIOR PROBLEMS

1. Punitive or Threatening Practices
   (a) Punishing by force, restraint, or expulsion.
   (b) Using threats or imposing restrictions.
   (c) Using sarcasm or ridicule.
   (d) Punishing an individual as an example.
   (e) Forcing apologies or using other means.

2. Divertive or Ignoring Practices
   (a) Overlooking behavior or doing nothing.
   (b) Changing composition of group by removing members.
   (c) Shifting responsibility for group behavior to a member.
   (d) Switching activities to avoid behavior.
   (e) Diverting behavior by other means.

3. Dominative or Pressuring Practices
   (a) Commanding, scolding, or reproaching group.
   (b) Utilizing pressure of authority persons (parents, principal).
   (c) Singling out individuals for expressions of disapproval.
   (d) Expressing disapproval of group by words, looks, action.
   (e) Coercing, making conditional promises.
   (f) Utilizing praise as comparison as means of pressure.
   (g) Delegating power to pupils to impose control.
   (h) Appealing, cajoling, moralizing, or other means.

SOURCE: Adapted with permission of Macmillan Publishing Co., Inc. from *Classroom Management: Theory and Skill Training*, by Lois V. Johnson and Mary A. Bany. Copyright © 1970 by Macmillan Publishing Co., Inc.

Mastery Test

OBJECTIVE 4   To identify inappropriate classroom management strategies.

In each case the approach described is assumed to be ineffective. As you examine these situations, you might question whether you would come to that conclusion also. You may want to consider the reasoning behind your decision. An Answer Key of recommended responses is given at the end of this section. If you correctly identify at least 9 of the 10 solutions, you can be pleased with your ability to identify inappropriate classroom management approaches.

1. Mrs. Kingman enters her fourth grade classroom just in time to see Billy kick Marty. She says sternly: "Billy, I saw that! You know that kind of behavior isn't allowed in here. You're grounded! You will not be

allowed to go outside for recess for two weeks. I'll find something to keep you busy while everyone else is enjoying themselves outside."

Type of Approach _____

2. Since receiving a failing grade on her mathematics examination, Barbara has been sullen and defiant. She has refused to do any work and spends most of her time finding ways to defy the teacher, Ms. Roth. Having made numerous efforts to get Barbara out of her bad mood, Ms. Roth says to her: "Barbara, your work during the past two weeks has been terrible. If it doesn't improve over the next few days, I will have to talk to your parents about your attitude. I'm sure they want you to do well in school."

Type of Approach _____

3. Mr. Baker has organized his class into six small groups of five members each and has assigned a project to each group. He is pleased to find that five of the groups are doing very well but is disappointed that one of the groups does not appear to be working very well. Students in that group do not cooperate with one another. He decides that this is a problem they will have to work out for themselves. Given enough time, he thinks, they will learn to work together.

Type of Approach _____ *ug* _____

4. Having completed a task that required her to leave the classroom for a few minutes, Mrs. Hollis returns and finds her students out of their seats and talking loudly with one another, rather than working quietly as she had directed them to do. She says: "I'm very disappointed in you! Tenth graders don't act this way! This is the behavior of two year olds! From now on, when I leave the room one of you will be assigned to take charge. Let's see if that works."

Type of Approach _____ *dom & pres,* _____

5. The class had been restless and anxious for reasons unknown to the teacher, Mr. Barlow. No one seemed to be participating in the discussion. There were no raised hands, no willingness to answer questions or make comments, and no expressions of eagerness to participate. In short, Mr. Barlow felt he was pulling teeth. He poses another question and asks Steven to answer it. Steve shrugs his shoulders and says: "I don't know." Mr. Barlow replies: "Steve, I'm good and tired of your attitude and that of the class. Since you don't know the answer, look it up and write the question and the answer five hundred times by tomorrow morning. Anyone else who gives me a hard time will get the same."

Type of Approach _____ *pun & threat* _____

6. Because art supplies are limited, it is necessary for Mrs. Allen's fifth graders to share them. Two students, Art and Juan, begin to argue over a crayon. Before she can intevene, Art says: "That's my crayon, you wetback!" Mrs. Allen looks at Art sternly and says: "Art, that was not a nice thing to call Juan. I want you to tell him you're sorry."

Type of Approach _____ *pun & threat* _____

7. Mr. Snyder's seventh grade geography class is having a terrible time with their small group projects. It is obvious to Mr. Synder that few of his students knew how to work in a small group. After repeated attempts to encourage cooperation and productivity, he says: "Class, it is clear to me that you're not getting anything done in small groups. Therefore, I want each of you to do your own project. I want you to work alone so you can get something done. That way I'll be able to see exactly what each of you has accomplished."

Type of Approach _____ *ug* _____

8. On the whole, Ms. Johnson's third grade is well behaved. From time to time, there are minor infractions of the rules and a bit of mischief but nothing really serious except for one student, Howie. Howie was described by his second grade teacher as a holy terror. Ms. Johnson has found that he has lived up to his billing. After his fifth temper tantrum of the day, she says to him: "Howie, this would be a very good class if you would start to behave yourself. Everyone else behaves so nicely and you behave so badly. If the entire class — and that includes you, Howie — if the entire class can be well behaved this week, on Friday afternoon we'll have a little party to celebrate. I'll bring cookies and read all of you a story from a book the class picks."

Type of Approach

9. Repeated failure has caused Sarah to be an extremely withdrawn child. Most of her time is spent daydreaming. She undertakes no work and participates only when absolutely necessary. Mrs. Michaels believes that the best thing to do is to leave her alone. She is entitled to behave as she wishes as long as she doesn't disturb anyone else.

Type of Approach

10. Andy is the class clown. He is always ready with a joke or a prank to entertain his classmates. His behavior is not vicious, but it is annoying both to the class and to the teacher. Mr. Bowman decides to fight fire with fire. While holding a bright wig in one hand and a makeup kit in the other, he says: "Andy, as long as you're going to act like a clown, you might as well look like one. Here, why don't you paint your face and put on this wig I've brought you?"

Type of Approach _____

ANSWER KEY

Mastery Test, Objective 4

1. Punitive or threatening.
2. Dominative or pressuring.
3. Divertive or ignoring.
4. Dominative or pressuring.
5. Punitive or threatening.

6. Punitive or threatening.
7. Divertive or ignoring.
8. Dominative or pressuring.
9. Divertive or ignoring.
10. Punitive or threatening.

Objective 5

To describe the nature and dynamics of the behavior-modification approach to classroom management.

LEARNING ACTIVITY 5

As discussed earlier, the behavior-modification approach is based on principles from behavioral psychology. The major principle underlying this approach is that all behavior is learned. This applies both to appropriate and to inappropriate behavior. Advocates of the behavior-modification approach contend that a student misbehaves for one of two reasons: (1) The student has learned to behave inappropriately; or (2) The student has not learned to behave appropriately.

The behavior-modification approach is built on two assumptions: (1) There are four basic processes that account for learning at all age levels and under all conditions; and (2) Learning is controlled largely, if not entirely, by events in the environment. Thus, the major task of the teacher is to master and apply the four basic principles of learning that behaviorists have identified as controlling all human behavior. They are: positive reinforcement, punishment, extinction, and negative reinforcement.

Terrence Piper[6] provides an easily understood explanation of the four basic processes. He suggests that when a student behaves, his or her behavior is followed by a consequence. Furthermore, he argues that there are only four basic categories of consequences: (1) when a reward is introduced; (2) when a punishment is introduced; (3) when a reward is removed; or (4) when a punishment is removed. The introduction of a reward is called *positive reinforcement*, and the introduction of a punishment is simply called *punishment*. The removal of a reward is called either *extinction* or *time out*, depending upon the situation. The removal of a punishment is called *negative reinforcement*.

Piper assumes that the frequency of a particular behavior is contingent (depends) upon the nature of the consequence that follows the behavior. Positive reinforcement, the introduction of a reward after a behavior, causes the reinforced behavior to increase in frequency. Rewarded behavior is thus strengthened and is repeated again in the future.

Example

Brad prepares a neatly written paper, which he submits to the teacher (student behavior). The teacher praises Brad's work and comments that neatly written papers are more easily read than those which are sloppy (positive reinforcement). In subsequent papers, Brad takes great care to write neatly (the frequency of the reinforced behavior is increased).

Punishment introduces an undesirable or aversive stimulus (punishment) after a behavior and causes the punished behavior to decrease in frequency. Punished behavior tends to be discontinued.

Example

Jim prepares a rather sloppily written paper, which he submits to the teacher (student behavior). The teacher rebukes Jim for failing to be neat, informs him that sloppily written papers are difficult to read, and tells him to rewrite and resubmit the paper (punishment). In subsequent papers, Jim writes less sloppily (the frequency of the punished behavior is decreased).

Extinction is the withholding of an anticipated reward (the withholding of positive reinforcement) in an instance where that behavior was previously rewarded. Extinction results in the decreased frequency of the previously rewarded behavior.

Example

Susie, whose neat work has always been praised by the teacher, prepares a neatly written paper, which she submits to the teacher (student behavior previously reinforced by the teacher). The teacher accepts and subsequently returns the paper without comment (withholding of positive reinforcement). Susie becomes less neat in subsequent papers (the frequency of the previously reinforced behavior decreases).

Time out is the removal of a reward from the student or the removal of the student from the reward; it reduces the frequency of reinforcement and causes the behavior to become less frequent.

Example

The students in Ms. Clark's English class have come to expect that she will give them an opportunity to play a word game if their work is satisfactory. This is an activity they all enjoy. Ms. Clark notes that all their papers were neatly done except Jim's paper. She tells Jim that he will not be allowed to participate in the class game and must, instead, sit apart from the group (removal of the student from the reward). Subsequently, Jim writes less sloppily (the frequency of the behavior decreases).

Negative reinforcement is the removal of an undesirable or aversive stimulus (punishment) after a behavior, and it causes the frequency of the behavior to be increased. The removal of the punishment serves to strengthen the behavior and increase its tendency to be repeated.

Example

Jim is the one student in the class who consistently presents the teacher with sloppy papers. Despite the teacher's constant nagging of Jim, his work becomes no neater. For no apparent reason, Jim submits a rather neat paper. Ms. Clark accepts it without comment — and without the usual nagging (the removal of punishment). Subsequently, Jim's work becomes neater (the frequency of the behavior is increased).

In summary, then, the teacher can encourage appropriate student behavior by using: positive reinforcement — the introduction of a reward; and negative reinforcement — the removal of a punishment. The teacher can discourage inappropriate student behavior by using: punishment — the introduction of an undesirable stimulus; extinction — the withholding of an anticipated reward; and time out — the removal of the student from the reward. It must be remembered that these consequences exert influence on student behavior in accordance with established behavioral principles. If the teacher rewards misbehavior, it is likely to be continued; if the teacher punishes appropriate behavior, it is likely to be discontinued.

According to Buckley and Walker,[7] timing and frequency of reinforcement and punishment are among the most important principles in behavior modification. Student behavior that the teacher wishes to encourage should be reinforced immediately after it occurs; student behavior that the teacher wishes to discourage should be punished immediately after it occurs. Behavior that is not reinforced at once tends to be weakened; behavior that is not punished at once tends to be strengthened. Thus, the teacher's timing of rewards and punishment is important. "The sooner the better" should be the watchword of those teachers who would maximize their management effectiveness.

Of equal importance is the frequency with which a behavior is reinforced. Continuous reinforcement, reinforcement which follows each instance of the behavior, results in learning that behavior more rapidly. Thus, if a teacher wishes to strengthen a particular student behavior, he or she should reward it each time it occurs. While continuous reinforcement is particularly effective in the early stages of acquiring a specific behavior, once the behavior has been established, it is more effective to reinforce intermittently.

There are two approaches to intermittent reinforcement: an interval schedule and a ratio schedule. An *interval schedule* is one in which the teacher reinforces the student after a specified period of time. For example, a teacher using an interval schedule might reinforce a student every hour. A *ratio schedule* is one in which the teacher reinforces the student after the behavior has occurred a certain number of times. For example, a teacher using a ratio schedule might reinforce the student after every fourth occurrence of the behavior. For the most part, an interval schedule is best for maintaining a consistent behavior over time, while a ratio schedule is best for producing more frequent occurrence of a behavior.

Positive reinforcement has been defined as the introduction of a reward; extinction and time out have been defined as the removal of a reward. Punishment has been defined as the introduction of a punishment; negative reinforcement has been defined as the removal of a punishment. In other words, behavioral consequences have been discussed as either the introduction or the removal of rewards or the introduction or removal of punishment. Therefore, let's take a closer look at the notions of reward and punishment.

By definition, a reward or reinforcer is any stimulus which increases the frequency of the behavior that preceded it; and, by definition, a punishment (or aversive stimulus) is anything which decreases the frequency of the behavior that preceded it.

Different authors classify reinforcers differently. The behavior-modification literature is replete with labels. There is general agreement, however, that reinforcers may be classified in two major categories: (1) *primary reinforcers*, which are not learned and which are necessary to sustain life (food, water, and warmth are examples); and (2) *conditioned reinforcers*, which are learned (praise, affection, and money are examples).

Conditioned reinforcers are of several distinct types including: (a) *social reinforcers* — rewarding behavior by other individuals within a social context (praise or applause); (b) *token reinforcers* — intrinsically nonrewarding objects, which may be exchanged at a later time for tangible reinforcers (money or a system of check marks that can be traded in for free time or school supplies); and (c) *activity reinforcers* — rewarding activities offered the student (outdoor play, free reading time, or being allowed to choose the next song).

Space limitations preclude a complete description of how various types of unconditioned and conditioned reinforcers can be used by the teacher to manage student behavior effectively. Many of the resources listed in the Additional Readings do that quite well. However, it is important to emphasize one point here: a reward is defined in terms of its ability to increase the frequency of the rewarded behavior. Thus, reward (and punishment) can be understood only in terms of an individual student. One student's reward may be another student's punishment. A response that the teacher intended to be rewarding may be punishing, and a response intended to be punishing may be rewarding. The latter is very often the case. A very common example occurs when a student misbehaves in order to get attention. The teacher's subsequent scolding actually rewards rather than punishes the attention-hungry student and, consequently, the student continues to misbehave in order to get the attention he or she seeks.

The above example suggests that the teacher must take great care in selecting a reinforcer that is appropriate to a particular student. While this is true, the selection process need not be difficult. Because reinforcers are idiosyncratic to the individual student, the student is in the best position to designate them. Thus, the best reinforcer is one selected by the student. Givener and Graubard[8] suggest three methods by which to identify individually oriented reinforcers: (1) obtain clues concerning potential reinforcers by observing what the student likes to do; (2) obtain additional clues by observing what follows specific student behaviors; that is, try to determine what teacher and peer behaviors seem to reinforce his or her behavior; and (3) obtain additional clues by simply asking students what they would like to do with free time, what they would like to have, and what they would like to work for.

Having briefly discussed the use of rewards, let us now turn to the thorniest of dilemmas faced by advocates of the behavior-modification approach — the use of punishment to eliminate inappropriate behavior. This is a subject of great controversy, controversy which is far from resolution. While it appears that every author has a somewhat different opinion, three major viewpoints seem most prominent: (1) the appropriate use of punishment is highly effective in eliminating student misbehavior; (2) the judicious use of punishment in limited types of situations can have desirable immediate, short-term effects on student misbehavior, but the risk of negative side effects requires its use to be carefully monitored; and (3) the use of punishment should be avoided completely, because student misbehavior can be dealt with just as effectively with other techniques that do not have the potential negative side effects of punishment.

Few authors present a viewpoint other than their own. However, Sulzer and Mayer[9] do help the reader examine the advantages and disadvantages of using punishment. They identify the following advantages: (1) Punishment does stop the punished student behavior immediately, and it reduces the occurrence of that behavior for a long period of time; (2) Punishment is informative to students because it helps students to discriminate rapidly between acceptable and unacceptable behaviors; and (3) Punishment is instructive to other students because it may reduce the probability that other class members will imitate the punished behaviors.

Disadvantages include: (1) Punishment may be misinterpreted. Sometimes a specific, punished behavior is generalized to other behaviors; for example, the student who is punished for talking out of turn may stop responding even when appropriate to do so; (2) Punishment may cause the punished student to withdraw altogether; (3)

Punishment may cause the punished student to become aggressive; (4) Punishment may produce negative peer reactions; for example, students may exhibit undesirable behaviors (ridicule or sympathy) toward the punished student; and (5) Punishment may cause the punished student to become negative about himself or herself or about the situation; for example, punishment may diminish feelings of self-worth or produce a negative attitude toward school.

In weighing the advantages and disadvantages of using punishment, Sulzer and Mayer conclude that alternative procedures for reducing student behaviors should always be considered. Furthermore, they contend that once a punishment procedure is selected, it should be employed with the utmost caution and its effects should be carefully monitored. They also suggest that the teacher anticipate and be prepared to handle any negative consequences that might arise. Finally, they recommend that teachers find desirable behaviors to reinforce at the same time they are withholding reinforcement or punishing undesirable behavior.

Our earlier discussion of the behavior-modification approach noted that behavioral research has reached these conclusions: (1) Ignoring inappropriate student behavior and showing approval of appropriate behavior are very effective in achieving better classroom behavior; and (2) Showing approval for appropriate behavior is probably the key to effective classroom management. Given the discussion in this section, that earlier conclusion is best modified to read: (1) Rewarding appropriate student behavior and withholding the rewarding of inappropriate behavior are very effective in achieving better classroom behavior; (2) Punishing inappropriate student behavior may eliminate that behavior but may have serious negative side effects; and (3) Rewarding appropriate behavior is probably the key to effective classroom management.

Mastery Test

OBJECTIVE 5   To describe the nature and dynamics of the behavior-modification approach to classroom management.

The following exercise was designed to give you an opportunity to assess your understanding of the information in this section. Please check each statement which represents the behavior-modification approach to classroom management.

_____ 1. The teacher should use positive reinforcement to encourage the continuance of appropriate student behavior.

_____ 2. The teacher should recognize that the failure to reward a behavior tends to weaken that behavior.

_____ 3. The teacher should avoid punishing appropriate student behavior.

_____ 4. The teacher should understand that punishment and negative reinforcement are synonymous terms.

_____ 5. During the early stages of the student's acquisition of a desirable behavior, the teacher should reinforce that behavior immediately after it occurs.

_____ 6. The teacher should know that a ratio schedule of reinforcement is one in which the teacher reinforces the student's behavior after a certain number of occurrences of that behavior.

_____ 7. The teacher should ignore appropriate student behavior and promptly punish inappropriate student behavior.

_____ 8. The teacher should recognize that extinction is the withholding of an anticipated reward after a behavior occurs.

_____ 9. The teacher should understand that the use of negative reinforcement tends to increase the frequency of the behavior which caused the removal of the aversive stimulus.

_____ 10. The teacher should be aware that those things he or she perceives as rewards may not be perceived as rewards by students.

_____ 11. The teacher should avoid reinforcing student misbehavior.

_____ 12. The teacher should use the same rewards for all students so as to be perceived as fair.

_____ 13. The teacher should recognize that intermittent reinforcement is useful for strengthening desirable behaviors the student has learned.

_____ 14. The teacher should operate on the assumption that all student behavior is learned.

_____ 15. The teacher should recognize that the use of token reinforcers is inappropriate because it is nothing more than bribery.

_____ 16. The teacher should always consider alternatives to using punishment to eliminate unacceptable student behavior.

_____ 17. The teacher should understand that there are many types of reinforcers that may be effectively and appropriately used in the classroom.

_____ 18. The teacher should recognize that different students have different — often conflicting — perceptions regarding those things they view as rewarding.

_____ 19. The teacher should use an interval schedule of reinforcement when attempting to maintain a consistent behavior over an extended period of time.

_____ 20. The teacher should never fail to reward appropriate student behavior.

_____ 21. The teacher should recognize that the effectiveness of a token system is enhanced because it allows students to select their own rewards.

_____ 22. The teacher should understand that all behaviors have consequences, including behaviors which are ignored.

_____ 23. The teacher should know that continuous reinforcement is reinforcement which follows each occurrence of a particular behavior.

_____ 24. The teacher should reward only exceptional student behavior because typical behavior does not deserve special attention.

_____ 25. The teacher should recognize that the sole use of teacher attention as a reinforcer tends to increase student dependency.

_____ 26. The teacher should recognize that the timing and frequency of reinforcement influence its effectiveness.

_____ 27. The teacher should view ignoring student behavior as having the potential of being perceived as withholding reward or withholding punishment.

_____ 28. The teacher should reward acceptable student behavior and avoid rewarding inappropriate student behavior.

_____ 29. The teacher should recognize that ignoring student misbehavior is the same as approving of that behavior.

_____ 30. The teacher should understand that rewards are unique to the individual student.

_____ 31. The teacher should recognize that even the careful and judicious use of punishment may bring about serious negative side effects.

_____ 32. The teacher should always carefully monitor the effects of using punishment.

_____ 33. The teacher should view a well-managed token system as a means of promoting appropriate student behavior.

_____ 34. The teacher should anticipate and be prepared to deal with the possible negative effects of using punishment.

_____ 35. The teacher should observe and/or question students to obtain clues concerning potential rewards.

ANSWER KEY

Mastery Test, Objective 5

The listing below presents the numbers of those statements suggested here as representative of the behavior-modification approach. You can feel that you have a good grasp of the information in this section if at least 30 of your responses are in agreement with those listed. Should you feel uncomfortable with the results, reread the materials in the learning activity and/or study those resources listed for objective 3 in the Additional Readings. Statements that reflect the behavior-modification approach are: 1, 2, 3, 5, 6, 8, 9, 10, 11, 13, 14, 16, 17, 18, 19, 21, 22, 23, 25, 26, 27, 28, 30, 31, 32, 33, 34, and 35; 4, 7, 12, 15, 20, 24, and 29 should be blank.

Objective 6

To describe the nature and dynamics of the socioemotional-climate approach to classroom management.

LEARNING ACTIVITY 6

The socioemotional-climate approach to classroom management has its roots in counseling and clinical psychology and, consequently, places great importance on interpersonal relationships. It builds on the assumption that effective classroom management — and effective instruction — is largely a function of positive teacher–student and student–student relationships. Advocates of the socioemotional-climate approach emphasize that the teacher is the major determiner of interpersonal relationships and classroom climate. Consequently, the central managerial task of the teacher is to build positive interpersonal relationships and to promote a positive socioemotional climate.

Many of the ideas that characterize the socioemotional-climate approach may be traced to the work of Carl Rogers.[10] His major premise is that the facilitation of significant learning is largely a function of certain attitudinal qualities that exist in the interpersonal relationship between the teacher (the facilitator) and the student (the learner). Rogers has identified several attitudes that he believes are essential if the teacher is to have maximum effect in facilitating learning: realness, genuineness, and congruence; acceptance, prizing, caring, and trust; and empathic understanding.

Realness is viewed by Rogers as the most important attitude the teacher can display in facilitating learning. Realness is an expression of the teacher being himself or herself. That is, the teacher is aware of his or her feelings, accepts and acts on them, and is able to communicate them when appropriate. The teacher's behavior is congruent with his or her feelings. In other words, the teacher is genuine. Rogers suggests that realness allows the teacher to be perceived by students as a real person, a person with whom they can relate. Thus, the establishment of positive interpersonal relationships and of a positive socioemotional climate is enhanced by the teacher's ability to display realness. Sincere expressions of enthusiasm or boredom are typical examples of realness.

Acceptance is the second attitude which Rogers views as important to teachers who would be successful in facilitating learning. Acceptance indicates that the teacher views the student as a person of worth. It is nonpossessive caring for the learner. It is an expression of basic trust — a belief that the student is trustworthy. Accepting behaviors are those which make the student feel trusted and respected, those which enhance his or her self-worth. Through acceptance, the teacher displays confidence and trust in the ability and potential of the student. Consequently, the teacher who cares, prizes, and trusts the student has a far greater chance of creating a socioemotional climate which promotes learning than does the teacher who fails to do so.

Empathic understanding is an expression of the teacher's ability to understand the student from the student's point of view. It is a sensitive awareness of the student's feelings and is nonevaluative and nonjudgmental. Expressions of empathy are all too rare in the classroom. When they occur, the student feels that the teacher understands what he or she is thinking and feeling. Rogers argues that clearly communicated, sensitively accurate, empathic understanding greatly increases the probability that positive interpersonal relationships, a positive socioemotional climate, and significant learning will occur.

In summary, then, Rogers suggests that there are certain conditions which facilitate learning and most prominent among these is the attitudinal quality of the interpersonal relationship between the teacher and the student. He has identified three attitudes which are crucial to this process: realness, acceptance, and empathy.

Ginott[11] has presented views which are similar to those of Rogers. His writings also stress the importance of congruence, acceptance, and empathy and give numerous examples of how these attitudes may be manifested by the teacher. In addition, Ginott has emphasized the importance of effective communication in promoting good teacher–student relationships. How the teacher communicates is viewed as being of decisive importance.

Ginott has written that the cardinal principle of communication is that the teacher talk to the situation, not to the personality and character of the student. When confronted with undesirable student behavior, the teacher is advised to: describe what he or she sees; describe what he or she feels; and describe what needs to be done. In addition, Ginott has provided a long list of recommendations describing ways in which the teacher might communicate effectively. While a lengthy explanation of each is not possible here, a summary of these recommendations follows:

1. Address the student's situation. Do not judge his or her character and personality, because this can be demeaning.

2. Describe the situation, express feelings about the situation, and clarify expectations concerning the situation.

3. Express authentic and genuine feelings that promote student understanding.

4. Diminish hostility by inviting cooperation and providing students with opportunities to experience independence.

5. Decrease defiance by avoiding commands and demands which provoke defensive responses.

6. Recognize, accept, and respect the student's ideas and feelings in ways which increase his or her feelings of self-worth.

7. Avoid diagnosis and prognosis, which result in labeling the student, because this may be disabling.

8. Describe processes and do not judge products or persons. Provide guidance, not criticism.

9. Avoid questions and comments that are likely to incite resentment and invite resistance.

10. Avoid the use of sarcasm, because this may diminish the student's self-esteem.

11. Resist the temptation to provide the student with hastily offered solutions; take the time to give the student the guidance needed to solve his or her own problem. Encourage autonomy.

12. Attempt to be brief; avoid preaching and nagging, which is not motivating.

13. Monitor and be aware of the impact one's words are having on students.

14. Use appreciative praise, because it is productive; avoid judgmental praise, because it is destructive.

15. Listen to students and encourage them to express their ideas and feelings.

The list above cannot do justice to Ginott's views. The reader who desires a fuller explanation of these recommendations and who wishes to examine examples which support Ginott's suggestions is encouraged to refer to his last book, *Teacher and Child.*

A third viewpoint that might be classified as a socioemotional approach is that of Glasser.[12] Although an advocate of teacher realness, acceptance, and empathy, Glasser does not give these primary emphasis. Rather, he stresses the importance of teacher involvement.

Glasser asserts that the single basic need that people have is the need for identity — feelings of distinctiveness and worthiness. He argues that in order to achieve a "success" identity in the school context, one must develop social responsibility and feelings of self-worth. Social responsibility and self-worth are the result of the student developing a good relationship with others — both peers and adults.

Thus, it is involvement which is crucial to the development of a success identity. Glasser argues that student misbehavior is the result of the student's failure to develop a success identity. He proposes an eight-step process which the teacher should use to help the student change his behavior; he suggests that the teacher should:

1. Become personally involved with the student; accept the student but not the student's misbehavior; indicate a willingness to help the student in the solution of his or her behavior problem.

2. Elicit a description of the student's present behavior; deal with the problem, do not evaluate or judge the student.

3. Assist the student in making a value judgment about the problem behavior; focus on what the student is doing which is contributing to the problem and to his or her failure.

4. Help the student plan a better course of action; if necessary, suggest alternatives; help the student reach his or her own decision based on his or her evaluation, thereby fostering self-responsibility.

5. Guide the student in making a commitment to the course of action he or she has selected.

6. Reinforce the student as he or she follows the plan and keeps the commitment; be sure to let the student know that you are aware that progress is being made.

7. Accept no excuses if the student fails to follow through with his or her commitment; help the student understand that he or she is responsible for his or her own behavior; alert the student of the need for a better plan; acceptance of an excuse communicates a lack of caring.

8. Allow the student to suffer the natural and realistic consequences of misbehavior, but do not punish the student; help the student try again to develop a better plan and expect him or her to make a commitment to it.

Glasser views the above process as effective for the teacher who wishes to help the misbehaving student develop more productive behavior. In addition, Glasser proposes a process for helping a whole class deal with individual and group behavior problems — the socio–problem-solving classroom meeting.

Many behavior problems are best addressed through the use of the class as a problem-solving group under the guidance of the teacher. If each student can be helped to realize that he or she is a member of a working, problem-solving group and that he or she has both individual and group responsibilities, it is likely that discussions of group and individual problems will lead to the resolution of those problems. Without such help students tend to evade problems, depend on others to solve their problems, or withdraw. The social–problem-solving meeting is intended to provide the assistance students need in this regard. It is a viewpoint shared by advocates of the group-process approach.

Glasser suggests three guidelines to enhance the potential effectiveness of social–problem-solving classroom meetings:

1. Any individual or group problem may be discussed; a problem may be introduced by a student or the teacher.

2. The discussion should be directed toward solving the problem; the atmosphere should be nonjudgmental and nonpunitive; the solution should not include punishment or fault finding.

3. The meeting should be conducted with the teacher and students seated in a tight circle; meetings should be held often; meetings should not exceed 30 to 45 minutes, depending upon the age of the students.

The reader who wishes to be more fully informed about these views should refer to Glasser's book, *Schools Without Failure*.

A fourth and final viewpoint which might be seen as a socioemotional-climate approach is that of Dreikurs.[13] While it is true that works by Dreikurs and his colleagues contain many ideas that have important implications for effective classroom management, there are two which stand out from the others: (1) an emphasis on the democratic classroom in which the students and the teacher share responsibility for both process and progress; and (2) a recognition of the impact which natural and logical consequences have on the behavior — and misbehavior — of students.

A dominant theme in this approach is the assumption that student conduct and achievement are facilitated in a democratic classroom. The autocratic classroom is one in which the teacher uses force, pressure, competition, punishment, and the threat of punishment to control student behavior. The laissez-faire classroom is one in which the teacher provides little, if any, leadership and is overly permissive. Both the autocratic classroom and the laissez-faire classroom lead to student frustration, hostility, and/or withdrawal; both result in a devastating lack of productivity. True productivity can occur only in a democratic classroom — one in which the teacher shares responsibility with students. It is in a democratic atmosphere that students expect to be treated and are treated as responsible, worthwhile individuals capable of intelligent decision making and problem solving. And it is the democratic classroom that fosters mutual trust between the teacher and the students and among students.

The teacher who attempts to establish a democratic classroom atmosphere must not abdicate his or her responsibilities as a leader. The effective teacher is not an autocrat, but neither is he or she an anarchist. The democratic teacher guides; the autocratic teacher dominates; and the laissez-faire teacher abdicates. The democratic teacher teaches responsibility by sharing responsibility.

The key to a democratic classroom organization is regular and frank group discussions. Here the teacher — acting the role of leader — guides the group in group discussions that focus on problems of concern. Three products of that process have been identified: (1) the teacher and the students have an opportunity to express themselves in a way that is sure to be heard; (2) the teacher and the students have an opportunity to get to know and understand one another better; and (3) the teacher and the student are provided with an opportunity to help one another. He notes that an essential by-product of such group discussions is the opportunity the teacher has to influence those values of his or her students that may differ from those considered more productive.

Although there is an emphasis on the importance of the teacher's developing a democratic socioemotional classroom climate, you will see in the next learning activity that these views on the value of shared leadership and group discussions are very similar to those of the advocates of the group-process approach.

The second major emphasis concerns the impact of consequences on student behavior. In the classroom setting, natural consequences are those that are solely the result of the student's own behavior. Logical consequences are those which are more or less arranged by the teacher. The natural consequence of the student's grasping a hot test tube is that he or she will burn his or her hand. The logical consequence of breaking the test tube is that the student will have to pay the cost of replacing it. In order to be considered a logical consequence, however, the student must view the consequence as logical. If it is viewed as punishment, the positive effect is lost. Dreikurs and Grey suggest five criteria they view as useful in distinguishing logical consequences from punishment:

1. Logical consequences express the reality of the social order, not of the person; punishment expresses the power of a personal authority; a logical consequence results from a violation of an accepted social rule.

2. Logical consequences are logically related to the misbehavior; punishment rarely is logically related; the student sees the relationship between the misbehavior and its consequences.

3. Logical consequences involve no element of moral judgment; punishment inevitably does; the student's misbehavior is viewed as a mistake, not a sin.

4. Logical consequences are concerned only with what will happen next; punishment is in the past; the focus is on the future.

5. Logical consequences are involved in a friendly manner; punishment involves either open or concealed anger; the teacher should try to disengage himself or herself from the consequence.

In summary, then, logical consequences: express the reality of the social order; are intrinsically related to the misbehavior; involve no element of moral judgment; and are concerned only with what will happen next. On the other hand, punishment: expresses the power of personal authority; is not logically related to the misbehavior; involves moral judgment; and deals with the past. As Glasser does, Dreikurs stresses the importance of the positive effect which the application of logical consequences has on the behavior of students. Both argue it is crucial that teachers help students understand the logical relationship between their behavior and the consequences of that behavior. Both also argue that it is important that the teacher be able to use logical consequences appropriately — and avoid punishment — in helping students change their behaviors to those that are more desirable.

Mastery Test

OBJECTIVE 6   To describe the nature and dynamics of the socioemotional-climate approach to classroom management.

The following exercise is designed to assist you in determining the extent to which you understand the information presented in this section. Check each statement you feel represents the views of the socioemotional-climate approach to classroom management.

_____ 1. A teacher should allow students to suffer the natural and logical consequences of their behavior unless these consequences involve physical danger.

_____ 2. A teacher should recognize that the social–problem-solving classroom meeting is a powerful tool for dealing with both individual and group problems.

_____ 3. A teacher should accept no excuses from the student who fails to follow the behavior change plan to which he or she has made a commitment.

_____ 4. A teacher should help the student identify and describe the behavior problem rather than evaluate the student.

_____ 5. A teacher should recognize that the acceptance of the student implies approval of his or her behavior.

_____ 6. A teacher should direct attention toward solving behavior problems rather than finding fault or assigning blame.

_____ 7. A teacher should help students identify group problems, assign blame, and fix the appropriate punishment.

_____ 8. A teacher should never express feelings not congruent with those he or she is experiencing.

_____ 9. A teacher should address the student's situation, not the student's character or personality.

_____ 10. A teacher should remain aloof and businesslike in dealing with students.

_____ 11. A teacher should recognize that the autocratic classroom and the laissez-faire classroom are unproductive.

_____ 12. A teacher should recognize that he or she cannot abdicate his or her responsibility if a democratic classroom climate is to be achieved.

_____ 13. A teacher should help the student understand the logical relationship between the misbehavior and the consequence.

_____ 14. A teacher should recognize that students view teacher expressions of emotion as a sign of weakness.

_____ 15. A teacher should encourage and accept the expression of student ideas and feelings.

_____ 16. A teacher should understand that effective management is the result of the teacher assuming an authoritarian posture and maintaining control.

_____ 17. A teacher should promote a nonjudgmental, nonevaluative climate when guiding a social–problem-solving classroom meeting.

_____ 18. A teacher should recognize that even well-led group discussions are little more than bull sessions of questionable value.

_____ 19. A teacher should understand that effective communication is essential to positive interpersonal relationships.

_____ 20. A teacher should express empathy toward students so that they feel he or she understands them and their feelings.

_____ 21. A teacher should avoid sarcasm, because this tends to demean the student and decrease his or her feelings of self-worth.

_____ 22. A teacher should avoid becoming overly involved with students and their nonschool problems.

_____ 23. A teacher should understand that the nature of the interpersonal relationship between the teacher and the students is a function of the student behaviors.

_____ 24. A teacher should recognize that social–problem-solving classroom meetings are most effective when relatively brief and frequent.

_____ 25. A teacher should view acceptance as a belief that the student is worthy.

_____ 26. A teacher should know that empathic understanding is an expression of the teacher's ability to understand the student from the student's point of view.

_____ 27. A teacher should recognize that the manner in which the teacher communicates is decisively important.

_____ 28. A teacher should consider a student's behavior as a reflection of his personality and character.

_____ 29. A teacher should understand that certain teacher behaviors increase student hostility and defiance.

_____ 30. A teacher should use behaviors that are likely to promote cooperation and avoid those that are likely to promote competition.

_____ 31. A teacher should always be sure that he or she has correctly diagnosed the student's misbehavior before labeling the problem.

_____ 32. A teacher should be brief and avoid preaching and nagging.

_____ 33. A teacher should not tolerate and should carefully control student expressions of feelings, especially expressions of hostility and defiance.

_____ 34. The teacher should commit himself or herself to helping the student develop self-responsibility and feelings of self-worth.

_____ 35. The teacher should use sarcasm very carefully and only after good interpersonal relationships have been established.

ANSWER KEY

Mastery Test, Objective 6

The list below contains the numbers of the statements viewed here as representative of the socioemotional-climate approach to classroom management. Compare your responses to these. You can consider that you have done well if you disagree on no more than five statements. If you feel the need to review this topic, reread this learning activity or study any of the resources listed for objective 6 in the Additional Readings. The representative statements are: 1, 2, 3, 4, 6, 8, 9, 11, 12, 13, 15, 17, 19, 20, 21, 24, 25, 26, 27, 29, 30, 32, and 34.

Objective 7

To describe the nature and dynamics of the group-process approach to classroom management.

LEARNING ACTIVITY 7

As noted in Learning Activity 1, the group-process approach — also known as the sociopsychological approach — is based on principles from social psychology and group dynamics. The major premise underlying the group-process approach is based on the following assumptions: (1) Schooling takes place within a group context — the classroom group; (2) The central task of the teacher is to establish and maintain an effective, productive classroom group; (3) The classroom group is a social system containing properties common to all social systems. The effective, productive classroom group is characterized by certain conditions that are compatible with those properties; and (4) The classroom management task of the teacher is to establish and maintain such conditions. While there is some disagreement concerning the conditions which characterize the effective, productive classroom group, you will examine the conditions presented in three sources: the work of Schmuck and Schmuck, Johnson and Bany, and Kounin.

First let us focus on six properties identified by Schmuck and Schmuck[14] regarding classroom management: expectations, leadership, attraction, norms, communication, and cohesiveness.

Expectations are those perceptions that the teacher and the students hold regarding their relationships to one another. They are individual predictions of how self and others will behave. Therefore, expectations about how members of the group will behave greatly influence how the teacher and the students behave in relation to one another. The effective classroom group is one in which expectations are accurate, realistic, and clearly understood. The behavior of the teacher communicates to students what behavior the teacher expects of them, and the students, in turn, tend to conform to those expectations. Thus, if students feel the teacher expects them to misbehave, it is likely that they will misbehave; if students feel the teacher expects them to behave appropriately, it is likely that they will behave appropriately.

Leadership is best thought of as those behaviors that help the group move toward the accomplishment of its objectives. Thus, leadership behaviors consist of actions by group members; included are actions which aid in setting group norms, which move the group toward its goals, which improve the quality of interaction between group members, and which build group cohesiveness. By virtue of their role, teachers have the greatest potential for leadership. However, in an effective classroom group, leadership functions are performed by both the students and the teacher. An effective classroom group is one in which the leadership functions are well distributed and where all group members can feel power and self-worth in accomplishing academic tasks and in working together. When students share classroom leadership with the teacher, they are far more likely to be self-regulating and responsible for their own behavior. Thus, the effective teacher is one who creates a climate in which students perform leadership functions. The teacher improves the quality of group interaction and productivity by training students to perform goal-directed leadership functions and by dispersing leadership throughout the group.

Attraction refers to the friendship patterns in the classroom group. Attraction can be described as the level of friendship that exists among members of the classroom group. The level of attraction is dependent upon the degree to which positive interpersonal relationships have been developed. It is clear that a positive relationship exists between level of attraction and student academic performance. Thus, the effective classroom manager is one who fosters positive interpersonal relationships among group members. For example, the teacher attempts to promote the acceptance of rejected students and new members.

Norms are shared expectations of how group members should think, feel, and behave. Norms greatly influence interpersonal relationships because they provide guidelines that help members understand what is expected of them and what they should expect from others. Productive group norms are essential to group effectiveness. Therefore, one important task of the teacher is to help the group establish, accept, and maintain productive group norms. Such norms provide a frame of reference which guides the behavior of members. The group, not the teacher, regulates behavior by exerting pressure on members to adhere to the group's norms. It is crucial that the teacher assist the group in the development of productive norms. This is a difficult task. Advocates of the group-process approach argue that productive norms can be developed — and unproductive norms changed — through the concerted, collaborative efforts of the teacher and the students using group discussion methods.

Communication — both verbal and nonverbal — is dialogue between group members. It involves the uniquely human capability to understand one another's ideas and feelings. Thus, communication is the vehicle through which the meaningful interaction of members takes place and through which group processes in the classroom occur. Effective communication means the receiver correctly interprets the message that the sender intends to communicate. Therefore, a twofold task of the teacher is to open the channels of communication so that all students express their thoughts and feelings freely and, frequently, to accept student thoughts and feelings. In addition, the teacher should help students develop certain communication skills — paraphrasing, perception checking, and feedback, for example (see Chapter 7, "Interpersonal Communication Skills").

Cohesiveness is concerned with the collective feeling that the class members have about the classroom group — the sum of the individual members' feelings about the group. Unlike the notion of attraction, cohesiveness emphasizes the individual's relation to the group as a whole instead of to individuals within the group. Schmuck and Schmuck note that groups are cohesive for a variety of reasons: (1) because the members like one another; (2) because there is high interest in a task; and (3) because the group offers prestige to its members. Thus, a classroom group is cohesive when most of its members, including the teacher, are highly attracted to the group as a whole.

Cohesiveness occurs to the extent to which individual needs are satisfied by group membership. Schmuck and Schmuck assert that cohesiveness is a result of the dynamics of interpersonal expectations, leadership style, attraction patterns, and the flow of communication.

The teacher can create cohesive classroom groups by open discussions of expectations, by dispersion of leadership, by the development of several friendship clusters, and by the frequent use of two-way communication. Cohesiveness is essential to group productivity. Cohesive groups possess clearly established group norms — strong norms, not necessarily norms that are productive. Thus, the effective classroom manager is one who creates a cohesive group that possesses goal-directed norms.

To summarize the position taken by Schmuck and Schmuck, then, it can be said that they give major importance to the teacher's ability to create and manage an effectively functioning, goal-directed classroom group. The implications of their position are, as they suggest, the following:

1. The teacher should work with students to clarify the interpersonal expectations held by individuals in the group; recognize the expectations he or she holds for each individual student and for the group; modify his or her expectations on the basis of new information; foster expectations that emphasize student strengths rather than weaknesses; and make a deliberate effort to accept and support each student.

2. The teacher should exert goal-directed influences by exhibiting appropriate leadership behaviors; help students develop leadership skills; and disperse leadership by sharing leadership functions with students and by encouraging and supporting the leadership activities of students.

3. The teacher should display empathy toward students and help them develop an empathic understanding of one another; accept all students and encourage them to accept one another; provide opportunities for students to work collaboratively; and facilitate the development of student friendships and teacher–student rapport.

4. The teacher should help students resolve conflicts between institutional rules, group norms, and/or individual attitudes; use various problem-solving techniques and group discussion methods to help students develop productive, goal-directed norms; and encourage students to be responsible for their own behavior.

5. The teacher should exhibit effective communication skills and help students develop effective communication skills; foster open channels of communication which encourage students to express their ideas and feelings freely and constructively; promote student interaction, which allows students to work with and get to know one another; and provide opportunities for students to discuss openly the group's processes.

6. The teacher should foster cohesiveness by establishing and maintaining a classroom group that is characterized by: clearly understood expectations; shared, goal-directed leadership; high levels of empathy, acceptance, and friendship; and open channels of communication.

Although the views held by Johnson and Bany[15] are, in many ways, similar to those of Schmuck and Schmuck, they represent a contribution which warrants their examination here. Johnson and Bany describe two major types of classroom management activities — facilitation and maintenance. Facilitation refers to those management behaviors that improve conditions within the classroom; maintenance refers to those management behaviors that restore or maintain effective conditions. The teacher who manages the classroom effectively exhibits both facilitation and maintenance management behaviors.

Johnson and Bany have identified four kinds of facilitation behavior: (1) achieving unity and cooperation; (2) establishing standards and coordinating work procedures; (3) using problem solving to improve conditions; and (4) changing established patterns of group behavior. They have identified three kinds of maintenance behavior: (1) maintaining and restoring morale; (2) handling conflict; and (3) minimizing management problems. Although we cannot give a full description of these managerial behaviors — Johnson and Bany used over four hundred pages in doing that — a very brief explanation of each behavior is presented here.

Achieving classroom group unity and cooperation (cohesiveness) is a worthy and necessary goal if the teacher is to help the group to be maximally effective. Because cohesiveness is largely dependent on group members liking one another and liking the group, the task of the teacher is to make group membership attractive and satisfying. Johnson and Bany assert that cohesiveness is dependent on the amount and frequency of student interaction and communication, the kind of structure which exists within the group, and the extent to which motives and goals are shared. It follows, then, that the teacher should: encourage student interaction and communication by providing opportunities for students to work with one another and to discuss their ideas and feelings; accept and support all students while creating a structure within which each student develops a strong sense of belonging; and help students develop and recognize shared goals.

Establishing standards and coordinating work procedures are among the most important — and the most difficult — of the teacher's responsibilities. Standards of conduct specify appropriate behaviors in given situations; work procedures are those standards that apply to interactive instructional processes. For example, a behavioral standard might involve the behavior prescribed for students as they stand in the cafeteria line or as they pass out of the classroom during a fire drill. A work procedure might refer to the behavior expected of students when they are finished with seatwork assignments or when they wish to ask the teacher a question. Clearly, effective instruction is dependent upon the extent to which the teacher is able to establish appropriate standards and the extent to which the teacher is able to facilitate student adherence to those standards. Johnson and Bany emphasize the importance of group decision methods as a means of establishing behavioral standards and gaining adherence to those standards. Standards which are accepted by the group become group norms. In a cohesive group, there is a great deal of pressure on members to conform to those norms. Thus, the effective classroom group is one in which desirable standards and work procedures are accepted group norms.

The use of group problem-solving discussions to improve classroom conditions is a strategy highly recommended by advocates of the group-process approach. The problem-solving process is viewed somewhat differently by different authors but, for the most part, may be thought of as consisting of: (1) identifying the problem; (2) analyzing the problem; (3) evaluating alternative solutions; (4) selecting and implementing a solution; and (5) obtaining feedback and evaluating the solution. The basic premise underlying this strategy is that students, given the opportunity, skills, and guidance necessary, can and will make good, responsible decisions regarding their classroom behavior. This premise suggests that the teacher should provide students with the opportunity to engage in group problem-solving discussions; should foster the development of student problem-solving skills; and should guide students in the problem-solving process.

Changing established patterns of group behavior involves the use of planned-change techniques similar to those of group problem solving. However, the difference is that the purpose of the problem-solving process is to find a solution to a problem, while the purpose of the planned-change process is to gain acceptance of an already determined solution. Thus, the planned-change process is one of improving conditions by substituting appropriate goals for inappropriate goals. The notion is that group goals exert a strong influence upon the behavior of group members, and when group goals are in conflict with those of instruction, students behave inappropriately. Therefore, it is necessary for the teacher to help the group replace inappropriate goals and behaviors with more appropriate ones, goals that satisfy group needs and that are consistent with those of the school.

Johnson and Bany argue that group planning is the best process to use for changing inappropriate goals and behaviors to more appropriate ones. Their viewpoint is based on the assumption that such changes are much more likely to be accomplished and accepted if members of the group have participated in the decision to change. This suggests that the role of the teacher is to help students understand the goal to be achieved; to involve students in discussions that result in an examination of various plans for achieving the goals, selecting a plan, and identifying tasks that need to be performed; to implement the plan and perform the necessary tasks; and to assess the plan's effectiveness. During the planned-change process, the teacher encourages group acceptance of externally established goals. Students are engaged in decisions regarding the strategies to be used in achieving those goals.

Simply put, then, the facilitation management behaviors of the teacher consist of: (1) encouraging the development of group cohesiveness; (2) promoting the acceptance of productive standards of conduct; (3) facilitating the resolution of problems through the use of group problem-solving processes; and (4) fostering appropriate group goals, norms, and behaviors. The intent of these facilitative management behaviors is the improvement of those classroom conditions which promote effective instruction. Maintenance management behaviors are intended to restore and maintain those classroom conditions. Descriptions of the three types identified by Johnson and Bany follow.

The ability to *maintain and restore morale* is important because the level of classroom group morale greatly influences group productivity. A group with high morale is far more likely to be productive than a group with low morale. Facilitation behaviors build morale. However, the effective teacher recognizes that many factors can cause morale to fluctuate. Thus, the teacher should understand the factors that influence morale and exhibit those behaviors that preserve high morale. Johnson and Bany note that morale is affected by the level of cohesiveness, the amount of interaction and communication, the extent to which members have shared goals, the extent to which the group's goal-directed efforts are hindered, and environmental conditions that cause anxiety and stress or otherwise affect the group adversely.

Thus, the task of the teacher may be viewed as twofold: (1) The teacher should act to rebuild morale; this includes fostering cohesiveness, encouraging increased interaction and communication, and promoting shared goals. (2) The teacher should act to reduce anxiety and relieve stress; this includes fostering cooperation rather than competition, exhibiting shared leadership, eliminating extremely frustrating and threatening situations, neutralizing disruptive influences, and clarifying stress situations through discussion. Crucial to the teacher's effectiveness is the extent to which the teacher is accepted and trusted by the students. The teacher cannot hope to be successful in restoring morale if students perceive him or her as part of the problem or if his or her behavior creates new problems. The use of punishment is an all too common example of the latter.

Handling conflict in the classroom group is among the most difficult tasks a teacher faces. Hostile, aggressive student behaviors are emotion laden, disruptive, and irritating, especially when directed toward the teacher. But conflict and hostility must be viewed as a normal result of the interactive processes that occur in the classroom. It is not realistic to expect otherwise. Indeed, in the initial phases of a group's development, it is not unusual and can be constructive.

There are many causes of conflict. Primary among them is frustration. When the group is hindered or blocked in achieving its goal, the result is frustration. Feelings of frustration manifest themselves as hostility and aggression — or as withdrawal and apathy. The effective teacher should be able to recognize and deal with such problems quickly.

Johnson and Bany suggest a process for resolving a conflict: (1) set guidelines for discussion; (2) clarify what happened; (3) explore differences in points of view; (4) identify the cause or causes of the conflict; (5) develop agreements regarding the cause or causes of the conflict and regarding resolution of the conflict; (6) specify a plan of action; and (7) make a positive appraisal of group efforts. To prevent conflict, the teacher is encouraged to reduce frustrations as much as possible by making it possible for the group to set and reach reasonable goals.

If they are to minimize problems, teachers must understand their classroom group and must be able to anticipate the influence various environmental factors will have on that group. In minimizing management problems, the effective teacher utilizes two major strategies: (1) to use facilitation and maintenance behaviors to establish and maintain an effectively functioning, goal-directed classroom group; and (2) to diagnose and analyze the health of the classroom group continuously and to act on the basis of that diagnosis. For example, symptoms of disunity call for teacher behaviors intended to promote group cohesiveness. Symptoms of inappropriate norms call for teacher behaviors intended to change those norms to more appropriate ones. In addition, certain types of problems — the new student and the substitute teacher — can and should be anticipated. The teacher should help the class prepare for such possibilities.

Effective classroom management, according to Johnson and Bany, involves the ability of the teacher to establish the conditions that enable the classroom group to be productive — and the ability to maintain those conditions. The latter involves the ability to maintain a high level of morale, to resolve conflict, and to minimize management problems. Implicit is the need to build good communication, to establish positive interpersonal relationships, and to satisfy both individual and group needs. The overriding emphasis is on the ability of the teacher to use group methods of management, for these behaviors determine the effectiveness of the group and the success of instruction.

So far in this section we have presented two somewhat different viewpoints regarding the group-process approach to classroom management — the views of Schmuck and Schmuck and the ideas of Johnson and Bany. A brief examination of the work of Kounin[16] completes the viewpoints presented in this section.

Jacob Kounin's ideas are the products of extensive research efforts he conducted in the management dimension of teaching. A brief summary of his findings is presented in the list below.

1. *Desist behaviors* are those behaviors the teacher uses in an effort to stop student misbehavior. Kounin concluded that the type of desist behavior used by the teacher is not a significant determinant of managerial success. He suggests that the teacher's desist techniques do not make a difference in how students behave. Indeed, it may be said that different types of teacher behaviors intended to stop student misbehavior are equally effective — or, more correctly, equally ineffective.

2. *Withitness behaviors* are those behaviors by which the teacher communicates to students that he or she knows what is going on, that he or she is very much aware of what students are doing — or not doing. Kounin concluded that withitness is significantly related to managerial success. That is, teachers who demonstrated withitness are more likely to have fewer and less serious student misbehaviors.

3. *Overlapping behaviors* are those behaviors by which the teacher indicates that he or she is attending to more than one issue when there is more than one issue to deal with at a particular time. Kounin suggests that overlapping — when combined with withitness — is related to managerial success. The teacher who is able to pay attention to more than one issue at a time is more likely to be effective than the teacher who is unable to do so.

4. *Target mistakes* consist of the teacher stopping the wrong student or desisting a less serious deviancy. *Timing mistakes* consist of the teacher desisting misbehavior too late; that is, the deviancy has spread or has increased in seriousness before it is stopped. Kounin found that the teacher who displays withitness and overlapping is less likely to make either target or timing mistakes. He argues that handling the correct deviant on time is more important than the method used in handling the deviancy.

5. *Movement management behaviors* are those behaviors which the teacher uses to initiate, sustain, or terminate a classroom activity. Kounin identified two dimensions of movement management: smoothness (and its counterpart, jerkiness) and momentum (and its counterpart, slowdowns). Smoothness refers to the flow of activities; jerkiness is caused by teacher

actions that interfere with the smoothness of activities. Momentum refers to the pace of activities; slowdowns are caused by teacher actions that impede the momentum of activities. Kounin concluded that movement management — including both smoothness and momentum — is related to managerial effectiveness and that it is especially important for the teacher to maintain momentum. He also suggested that techniques of movement management are more significant in preventing and controlling misbehavior than are techniques of deviancy management.

6. *Group-focus behaviors* are those behaviors teachers use to maintain a focus on the group — rather than on an individual student — during individual recitations. Kounin identified two aspects of group-focus behaviors: *group alerting*, which refers to the extent to which the teacher involves nonreciting students (maintains their attention and "keeps them on their toes"); and *accountability*, which refers to the extent to which the teacher holds students accountable and responsible for their task performances during recitations. Kounin found that group alerting and accountability are related to student behavior. He suggests that teachers who maintain a group focus are more successful in promoting student goal-directed behavior and in preventing student misbehavior than are teachers who do not.

In summarizing his studies, Kounin asserts that his findings suggest there are certain teaching behaviors — withitness, overlapping, movement management, and group-focus behaviors — that are related to managerial success. He also notes that these techniques of classroom management apply to the classroom group and not merely to individual students. Thus, Kounin may be described as a staunch advocate of group management — a most interesting dimension of the group-process approach to classroom management.

Mastery Test

OBJECTIVE 7   To describe the nature and dynamics of the group-process approach to classroom management.

The exercise below is intended to provide you with an opportunity to assess your understanding of the information presented in this section. Place a check mark in front of each statement that is representative of the group-process approach to classroom management. Check your responses in the Answer Key that follows.

_____ 1. The teacher should demonstrate the ability to attend to more than one issue at a time.

_____ 2. The teacher should help students establish productive norms.

_____ 3. The teacher should reward the student whose accomplishments are of an exceptional nature.

_____ 4. The teacher should use group problem-solving discussions to solve management problems.

_____ 5. The teacher should create open channels of communication in which students are able to express their ideas and feelings freely.

_____ 6. The teacher should emphasize the importance of following school rules and regulations.

_____ 7. The teacher should foster group cohesiveness by helping students perceive membership as attractive and satisfying.

_____ 8. The teacher should encourage competition that enables all students to compete on a fair basis.

_____ 9. The teacher should help students develop communication, leadership, and group problem-solving skills.

_____ 10. The teacher should make it clear that conflict is unproductive and, therefore, cannot be tolerated.

_____ 11. The teacher should recognize that change is more readily accepted if individuals participate in the decision to change.

_____ 12. The teacher should encourage student interaction and communication.

_____ 13. The teacher should attempt to maintain smoothness and momentum in managing activities.

_____ 14. The teacher should behave in ways that let students know the teacher knows what is going on.

_____ 15. The teacher should recognize that the ability to deal with individual student misbehavior is more important than the ability to deal with group problems.

_____ 16. The teacher should help students clarify their interpersonal expectations.

_____ 17. The teacher should share leadership with students.

_____ 18. The teacher should understand that effective management begins with his or her ability to control each individual within the group.

_____ 19. The teacher should recognize that hostility and conflict are among the normal and natural consequences of human interaction.

_____ 20. The teacher should attempt to anticipate conditions that might evoke a high level of anxiety or frustration for students so that these might be avoided.

_____ 21. The teacher should help students display empathy and acceptance for one another.

_____ 22. The teacher should focus on the group through group alerting and accountability during recitations.

_____ 23. The teacher should recognize that peer group norms are powerful determinants of member behavior.

_____ 24. The teacher should understand that even in a highly cohesive group, morale fluctuates, requires constant monitoring, and needs restoration from time to time.

_____ 25. The teacher should avoid activities that give students an opportunity to voice opposition to school policies and classroom regulations.

_____ 26. The teacher should understand that the behavior of each individual is greatly influenced by the nature of the classroom group and its properties.

_____ 27. The teacher should recognize that the effective management of problem behavior is based on fully understanding individual behavior and its causes.

_____ 28. The teacher should help students establish behavioral standards that are productive.

_____ 29. The teacher should recognize that group management procedures are not compatible with the individualization of instruction.

_____ 30. The teacher should help students identify management problems without assigning blame.

_____ 31. The teacher should encourage teacher–student interaction and discourage student–student interaction.

_____ 32. The teacher should use the planned-change process, not the problem-solving process, when the goal is known and the process is to encourage group acceptance of a commitment to the goal.

_____ 33. The teacher should be able to cope with more than one event simultaneously.

_____ 34. The teacher should recognize that the ability to handle individual student problems precludes the need to be concerned about group management techniques.

_____ 35. The teacher should understand that preventing classroom management problems is at least as important as solving problems.

ANSWER KEY

Mastery Test, Objective 7

The following is a listing of those statements that reflect the group-process point of view accurately. You should feel comfortable with your level of understanding if at least 30 of your responses agree with those suggested here. If you disagree on more than five statements, reread the materials in this learning activity and/or study the resources listed for objective 7 in the Additional Readings. The statements that represent the group-process view are: 1, 2, 4, 5, 7, 9, 11, 12, 13, 14, 16, 17, 19, 20, 21, 22, 23, 24, 26, 28, 30, 32, 33, and 35.

Final Mastery Test

OBJECTIVE 8 To classify the type of classroom management approach used in given problem situations.
OBJECTIVE 9 To assess the potential effectiveness of the classroom management approach used in given problem situations.

Having completed Learning Activities 1 through 7 and the Mastery Tests associated with each of the first seven objectives, you should now be prepared to demonstrate your competence with regard to the final two objectives of the chapter. Inasmuch as these objectives require you to apply the knowledge acquired previously, no learning activity is presented here. Rather, you are asked to complete the Final Mastery Test. A comparison of your responses with those presented in the Answer Key will allow you to determine what, if any, additional study you might want to undertake.

This Final Mastery Test presents a series of 12 case studies in which you are asked to: (1) describe the classroom management problem, (2) classify the type of classroom management approach used by the teacher, and (3) assess its potential effectiveness. In making your decisions regarding the potential effectiveness or ineffectiveness of the teacher's management behaviors, you might consider the extent to which the teacher's behavior: (1) deals with the cause or the symptom, (2) will influence a majority of the class in a positive and productive way, (3) will have long-range or short-range benefit, and (4) is intended to help students grow toward self-responsibility. Use the spaces provided for your responses. In addition, you may find it helpful to write a brief statement explaining why you determined a particular teacher response was potentially effective or ineffective. Then compare your classifications and judgments with those provided in the Answer Key that follows.

1. In reviewing the parts of speech with her seventh grade English class in preparation for a test on the next day, Mrs. Clarke notices that — as has become usual — only a half dozen or so of her students are answering and being attentive. In an effort to get everyone working and involved, she decides to put twenty sentences on the board and have everyone label all the words as to their parts of speech. Having put the sentences on the board, she is called from her room by the head of the department. Upon returning a few minutes later, she finds the class in an uproar. It is immediately obvious that very little work was done while she was gone. Without prompting, Mike — one of the better students in the class — says: "I don't think it was fair for you to make all of us do this busy work. Some of us were working and do know this stuff." Mrs. Clarke responds, "I decide what is and is not fair in here. However, you may have a point. Those of you who can finish the work on the board before the end of the period with 80 percent accuracy will be excused from the test tomorrow. Only those who can't do this work will have to take the exam. And I can guarantee it won't be any too easy."

Problem _____

_____

_____

_____

Type of Approach _____

Potentially Effective _____ Potentially Ineffective _____

Comment _____

_____

_____

2. It is lab day in Mr. Smith's biology class. Each student is at his or her lab table; Mr. Smith has carefully explained what is to be done by each pair of students and where the materials are. After he finishes his explanation, the students move about the room to obtain the materials needed, and all the groups begin to work quietly. Within ten minutes, the room is in an uproar. There is a lot of bickering over which one in the pair is to do the experiment and which one is to observe and do the written part of the assignment. Voices get louder and Mr. Smith summons the class's attention: "Since all of you seem so interested in performing this experiment, that's exactly what we'll do. If a person from each table will come and get another set of materials, everyone in the class can do his own experiment."

Problem _____

_____

_____

_____

Type of Approach _____

Potentially Effective _____ Potentially Ineffective _____

Comment _____

_____

_____

_____

3. Miss Vick has her geometry lesson well planned. It is review day before the test tomorrow. The students come in, and Miss Vick asks if everyone understands the past work and if there are any questions. The usual silence prevails, so Miss Vick asks eight students to go to the board. She gives each three problems. Only one student answers all correctly. As she talks to individual students about their mistakes, she notices Johnny clowning around at the side board. She ignores him and continues, but soon Johnny has the attention of the whole class. Quickly Miss Vick switches to Johnny's problems: "Well, Johnny, since you have everyone's attention, please explain to the class why all your problems are wrong." There is silence. "Johnny, look at the first problem. You'd know that can't be right if you just use your brain. The same goes for the second problem. Johnny, what's the matter with you? Has your brain gone on vacation?"

Problem _____

_____

_____

_____

Type of Approach _____

Potentially Effective _____ Potentially Ineffective _____

Comment _____

_____

_____

_____

4. Most of the students in the class like physical education class. Almost everyone hurries to change and to charge onto the field. It is baseball season and the boys really seem fired up about the tournament they have going. Each team grabs their equipment and takes their positions. The instructor wanders through the different games, coaching those who seem to have problems. All of a sudden, there is yelling, shouting, and fists flying as a group of boys gather around two others who are pushing, shoving, and punching. The instructor, Mr. Bryant, separates the two and tells everyone to sit down. He says: "I'm concerned about two things here. First of all, I'd like to know what started all of this. And second, I'd like to know how everyone feels about this kind of behavior. I know that some of you are anxious to get back to your game, but it seems to me that discussing this problem and taking a look at what we want to do about it might be better in the long run."

Problem _____

_____

_____

_____

Type of Approach _____

Potentially Effective _____ Potentially Ineffective _____

Comment _____

_____

_____

_____

5. To Ms. Markhem, it seemed that Joe and Paul were always fighting about something. And it appeared that Joe was nearly always at fault. She was determined that this was not going to be allowed to continue. It had to stop. But Ms. Markhem had no desire to single out Joe — or Paul for that matter. Having given careful thought to her plan of action for her sixth graders, she announced to her class: "Boys and girls, although I think you are usually a very well behaved group, I've noticed that from time to time there is fighting in class. This disrupts what we need to be doing. Starting today, at the end of each day, I'm going to give every one of you who is well behaved a check mark on this chart. When one of you has a total of 10 'good behavior' check marks, he or she ought to get a reward." The students decided that the reward should be a specially written note in which Ms. Markhem would tell that person's parents how well behaved he or she had been. This was the plan Ms. Markhem and the students implemented.

Problem _____

_____

_____

_____

Type of Approach _____

Potentially Effective _____ Potentially Ineffective _____

Comment _____

_____

_____

_____

6. Although just beginning first grade, Don had already gained a reputation — thanks to his long-suffering kindergarten teacher — as being something of a "mess." His favorite activity seemed to be creating eyesores — a sloppy desk, spilled paints, smashed crayons, and disorganized bookshelves, for example. Mrs. Marsh, his first grade teacher, was determined that this wasn't going to be the case in her room. Noticing that his desk and books were in total disarray by the end of only the first week, she said to him: "Don, I am not pleased by the sight of such an untidy desk. It very badly needs to be straightened out. I'm sure it will look better on Monday."

Problem _____

_____

_____

_____

Type of Approach _____

Potentially Effective _____ Potentially Ineffective _____

Comment _____

_____

_____

_____

7. Mrs. Langston's tenth grade English classes are unusually well-behaved groups. She has been quick to compliment them to others. She feels that the secret to her success with them can be attributed to a new strategy she has used this year. From time to time she has what she calls "fun periods." They are not regularly scheduled and are only dependent upon whether the class has behaved appropriately during the regular sessions. Fun periods consist of activities which the students have said would be fun. Much to Mrs. Langston's surprise, listening to rock music and discussing the lyrics — much as one discusses poetry — are among the most popular of those selected.

Problem _____

_____

_____

_____

Type of Approach _____

Potentially Effective _____ Potentially Ineffective _____

Comment _____

_____

_____

_____

8. In their art class, the students are doing their second watercolor painting. Most seem to be enjoying themselves, and the low rumble in the room is quite normal. But, shortly, some snickering from the back of the room becomes audible. Ms. Black strolls to the back only to find Sam looking a lot like the Chief Watercolorer of the Polka Dot tribe. By this time, most of the class is staring, giggling, and pointing at Sam. Dismayed by the actions of this graduating senior, Ms. Black says, "Sam, I really can't say I care much for the medium you have chosen to use, but I must say you've done a nice job with regard to color selection. Perhaps next time you should paint your paper instead of your exterior. I think we would both like that effect much better."

Problem _____

_____

_____

_____

Type of Approach _____

Potentially Effective _____ Potentially Ineffective _____

Comment _____

_____

_____

_____

9. Miss Barnes was doing very well with her "advanced" algebra class, except for Lannie, who constantly misbehaved. She knew he was bright and had been well behaved, because she had taught him math during the previous year. As she thought, she remembered meeting his parents at a P.T.A. meeting and their first comment: "If you have any trouble with Lannie, please call. We'll deal with him at home."

After many fruitless days of working with Lannie, she finally told him, "Lannie, if you don't shape up, I'll have to call your parents and talk to them about this. There's no excuse for your low marks, sullen attitude, or constant rule breaking. I know you're capable of much better work."

Problem _____

_____

_____

_____

Type of Approach _____

Potentially Effective _____ Potentially Ineffective _____

Comment _____

_____

_____

_____

10. Today is "cooking" day in home economics class. The girls usually like these days because they are more or less on their own. As Mrs. Thomas walks across the room to check the tables, she smells something burning. She follows her nose and finds the four girls of Group C reading notes from their boyfriends instead of attending to their cooking. Immediately Mrs. Thomas speaks up, "Girls! I believe your meal is burning!" The girls hurry to remove their meal from the oven. After the confusion has settled down, Mrs. Thomas says: "Class, the girls of Group C have burned their meal. This can happen to any cook. I know it has happened to me. Therefore, let's take this opportunity to see what we can salvage from this mess. Food is too expensive to waste needlessly, and there may be much we can do to save this meal. Let's all gather around this table and take a look at what can be done."

Problem _____

_____

_____

_____

Type of Approach _____

Potentially Effective _____ Potentially Ineffective _____

Comment _____

_____

_____

_____

11. Mr. Chambers had presented the fundamentals of oxidation to his students, and all seemed quickly to understand the basic notions. He decided that he would divide the class in groups of three to work problems and exercises for the next few days. The first two days went without complications, but by the third day, he noticed that the group which contained Jane, Don, and Larry was not doing much of anything. He could tell there was some friction. He decides to talk to all three: "Looks like you're having difficulty. What seems to be the problem?" Larry: "Jane thinks she knows it all and her answers are always right." Jane: "Well, at least I'm not lazy like you guys. I work the problems — while you and Don

sit there talking about football!" Don: "I do my share!" Mr. Chambers: "It seems to me that you ought to take some time to look at how you feel about one another and at what you agree would be appropriate behavior as you work with one another. Unless you find a way to interact productively, you won't profit from the advantages to be gained by working in a small group."

Problem _____

_____

_____

_____

Type of Approach _____

Potentially Effective _____ Potentially Ineffective _____

Comment _____

_____

_____

_____

12. Debate was the new topic to be covered in speech class for the next several weeks, and Mr. Jones decided to have six debate groups with five students in each. The first week's work seemed a bit below par, but Mr. Jones believed it was because the subject was a new one for most of his students. In time, however, squabbles that appeared to be personal conflicts became everyday occurrences in several of the teams as they prepared for their debate. Because he had done the original grouping without any thought to student wishes, Mr. Jones felt that perhaps it would help to reconstitute all of the groups on the basis of student choice. At the beginning of the next class period, he announced: "It is pretty obvious that some of you are not getting along well in the groups you're in, so I've decided to let you take a few minutes today to rearrange your groups if you want to do so. You can form any kind of group you like, but I do want each to have six members — no more, no less."

Problem _____

_____

_____

_____

Type of Approach _____

Potentially Effective _____ Potentially Ineffective _____

Comment _____

_____

_____

_____

When you have responded to each case study, you may want to analyze your responses before looking at the suggestions at the end of this section. This analysis will allow you to get some feel for the kinds of strategies you feel are potentially effective and ineffective. Use the following table to record your opinions about the effectiveness of each strategy you identified for each case study. For example, if you thought that the strategy used in the first case study was a group-process approach and that it was effective, you would place an *E* in the space created by the intersection of the row corresponding to the case study (the Case Study 1 row) and the column corresponding to the type of strategy used (the Group-Process Approach column). If you think the strategy was inappropriate, place an *I* in the intersecting space.

Case Study	Punitive or Threatening Approach	Divertive or Ignoring Approach	Dominative or Pressuring Approach	Instructional Approach	Bag-of-Tricks Approach	Behavior Modification Approach	Socioemotional-Climate Approach	Group-Process Approach	
1									
2									
3									
4									
5									
6									
7									
8									
9									
10									
11									
12									

Analyze your tally sheet to see if there is a pattern of bias or preference in your responses. It is very likely that you always found certain approaches to be effective and others to be ineffective. On the other hand, there may not have been any consistent pattern to your preferences. Consider that issue as you summarize your perceptions in the space below and at the top of the next page.

When you have completed this exercise, examine the recommendations and compare your responses to those suggested in the Answer Key that follows.

ANSWER KEY
Final Mastery Test

The table on the next page is similar to the preceding one; it indicates responses which might have been given to the case studies. In addition, a brief discussion of each case study is presented. Compare your responses with these recommendations. If there is at least 90 percent agreement, you can feel comfortable with what you have accomplished. If you fail to meet the 90 percent criterion, you should either reread the appropriate learning activity in this chapter or the appropriate resource material listed in the Additional Readings.

An examination of the responses given in the table may indicate a wide discrepancy between your classification of the approaches used and those indicated in the chart. If that is the case, do not be alarmed. Many of these distinctions are very difficult to make. As you can see, in some cases two approaches are indicated on the chart because of the difficulty in making a particular distinction. On the other hand, it is a more serious problem if you are in major disagreement concerning the potential effectiveness of the approaches used. There should be a high degree of agreement between your responses and those recommended here with regard to effectiveness, even if your classification of the approaches may be somewhat different from those recommended.

The Answer Key reflects a bias that suggests the punitive or threatening approach, the divertive or ignoring approach, and the dominative or pressuring approach are generally ineffective in solving classroom management problems. Additionally, it reflects the position that the behavioral-modification approach, the socioemotional-climate approach, and the group-process approach generally have the potential of being effective in solving classroom management problems. You may want to analyze the extent to which your responses reflect those biases. You should note whether or not you judged the teacher behaviors you described as punitive, divertive, or dominative approaches as ineffective. In addition, you should also note whether or not you judged the teacher behaviors you described as behavior-modification, socioemotional-climate, or group-process approaches as effective.

1. The problem here seems to be one of negative student reaction to teacher behavior which the students felt was unfair and punitive. In response to the problem, the teacher uses a pressuring approach. That is, she attempts to coerce the students by making a conditional promise. It is unlikely that this approach would be effective because it in no way deals with the very negative feelings being expressed by the students. At best this would be a temporary solution to the problem; thus, the teacher's approach is largely ineffective.
2. The problem in this case study would seem to be an inability of the students to work together cooperatively. Lack of proper direction from

Case Study	Punitive or Threatening Approach	Divertive or Ignoring Approach	Dominative or Pressuring Approach	Instructional Approach	Bag-of-Tricks Approach	Behavior Modification Approach	Socioemotional-Climate Approach	Group-Process Approach
1			I					
2		I						
3	I							
4								E
5					E			
6						E		
7					E			
8						E		
9	I		I					
10				E		E		
11							E	
12		I						

the teacher does not seem to be the problem, because secondary students should be able to decide on the roles each will play without specific instructions from the teacher. Mr. Smith uses a divertive approach in attempting to solve this problem. That is, he changes the nature of the activities in which students are engaged in order to avoid the necessity of student cooperation. While this approach might provide a temporary solution in alleviating the problem's symptoms, it does nothing to help students learn to cooperate with one another and to assume responsibility for organizing themselves with regard to cooperative tasks. Therefore, the teacher's behavior would be judged ineffective.

3. This case study describes the misbehavior of a single student; there is nothing to suggest that the student's misbehavior is sanctioned by the class as a whole. The teacher's strategy is to use sarcasm and ridicule in attempting to solve this problem. Thus, she is using a punitive approach. It is highly unlikely that a punitive approach would be effective in helping the student behave more appropriately. Indeed, it is more likely that such behavior would evoke increased hostility and would result in even greater misbehavior.

4. The problem here is twofold. On the one hand, there is conflict between the two boys who are fighting. On the other hand, there is the problem of the class sanctioning the fighting. Be-

cause the teacher here views this as a problem involving the group, he has used a group-process approach in attempting to solve it. He elicits the assistance of the group in examining and solving the problem. In the process of solving the group problem, it is likely that the interpersonal problem between the two boys will also be dealt with effectively.

5. This case study presents a situation in which an individual student misbehaves. The teacher's approach in solving this problem is to reward appropriate behavior; she uses a behavioral-modification approach. It is likely that this approach would be effective if the reward decided upon by the class is also perceived by the misbehaving student as rewarding. That is, if the student who has been misbehaving perceives the "written notes" as a sufficiently powerful reward, it is likely that he would change his behavior so that he might receive that reward. Thus, it is likely that this approach would be effective.

6. This case study describes the inappropriate behavior of a student. The teacher in this situation uses a socioemotional-climate approach in attempting to change the student's behavior. She is very careful to "separate the sin from the sinner" by describing the situation without placing blame on the student. Additionally, she lets the student know that she is awake, involved, and caring. She attempts to create a socioemotional climate which is positive. This approach is likely to be effective if she can establish a warm, positive relationship with the student.

7. This case study does not present a problem. Rather, it describes how a teacher avoids certain types of classroom management problems through the utilization of rewards for appropriate student behavior. In the case described, the teacher's use of the behavior-modification approach is proving to be effective. It is likely that it would continue to be effective so long as students continue to perceive the "fun period" as rewarding.

8. The problem described in this case study is one of student misbehavior. It is difficult to tell from this description whether there is group sanctioning of the misbehavior. It would seem from the teacher's behavior that she perceives the problem to be an individual, not a group one. Therefore, the teacher's approach in this situation is a socioemotional-climate approach. She describes the behavior as inappropriate without being punitive, and she attempts to maintain a positive relationship with the student. It is likely that this approach would be effective.

9. The misbehavior of an individual student is the problem in this case study. The teacher's approach here is to threaten the student. This behavior might be described as either a threatening approach or a pressuring approach because the teacher threatens the student by invoking the authority of this student's parents; thus, either classification would be appropriate. It is not likely that this classroom management behavior would be effective because it does nothing to improve the interpersonal relationship between teacher and student, to help the student accept and act in accordance with accepted group norms, or to modify his behavior through reinforcement. Indeed, such an approach is likely to lead to increased hostility and continued misconduct.

10. The problem here is a very simple one; the students fail to attend to their assignment. An improper handling of this situation, however, might have generated a much more serious management problem. However, the teacher elected to utilize the situation for instructional purposes. That is, rather than being punitive she used the opportunity to teach her students what to do when faced with a similar situation. Her approach might be described as either an instructional approach or a socioemotional-climate approach. On the one hand, she uses an instructional approach as she attempts to facilitate her students' understanding of what to do in this sort of situation. On the other hand, she uses a socioemotional-climate approach as she attempts to maintain a warm, positive relationship with her students in an instance where criticism could so easily have been evoked.

11. This is another problem depicting the inability of students to work together. Here the approach of the teacher is a group-process approach. He guides the group toward an examination of its behavior in an attempt to help them clarify the problem and generate a viable solution. It is likely that this approach would be effective.

12. This problem is also one of group conflict and an inability to work cooperatively. However, the teacher's approach here is to change the composition of the groups rather than to help the original groups function more effectively. Unlike the previous case in which the group-process approach was used, the teacher here uses a divertive approach. While this might temporarily bring an end to the problem's symptoms, it is unlikely that it would have a long-range positive effect.

NOTES

1. Rudolf Dreikurs and Pearl Cassel, *Discipline Without Tears* (New York: Hawthorn Books, 1972), pp. 31–41.
2. Lois V. Johnson and Mary A. Bany, *Classroom Management: Theory and Skill Training* (New York: Macmillan Co., 1970), pp. 45–59.
3. Dreikurs and Cassel, *Discipline Without Tears*, p. 33.
4. Johnson and Bany, *Classroom Management*, pp. 46–47.
5. Johnson and Bany, *Classroom Management*, p. 106.
6. Terrence Piper, *Classroom Management and Behavioral Objectives: Applications of Behavioral Modification* (Belmont, California: Lear Siegler/ Fearon Publishers, 1974), pp. 10–18.
7. Nancy K. Buckley and Hill M. Walker, *Modifying Classroom Behavior: A Manual of Procedures for Classroom Teachers* (Champaign, Illinois: Research Press Company, 1970), p. 30.
8. Abraham Givener and Paul S. Graubard, *A Handbook of Behavior Modification for the Classroom* (New York: Holt, Rinehart & Winston, 1974), p. 8.
9. Beth Sulzer and G. Roy Mayer, *Behavior Modification Procedures for School Personnel* (Hinsdale, Illinois: Dryden Press, 1972), pp. 174–184.
10. Carl R. Rogers, *Freedom to Learn* (Columbus, Ohio: Charles E. Merrill, 1969).
11. Haim G. Ginott, *Between Parent and Child* (New York: Macmillan Co., 1965); *Between Parent and Teenager* (New York: Macmillan Co., 1969); and *Teacher and Child* (New York: Macmillan Co., 1972).
12. William Glasser, *Schools Without Failure* (New York: Harper and Row, 1969).
13. Rudolf Dreikurs and Loren Grey, *A New Approach to Discipline: Logical Consequences* (New York: Hawthorn Books, 1968); and Rudolf Dreikurs and Pearl Cassel, *Discipline Without Tears* (New York: Hawthorn Books, 1972).
14. Richard A. Schmuck and Patricia A. Schmuck, *Group Processes in the Classroom* (Dubuque, Iowa: William C. Brown, 1975), pp. 25–32.
15. Johnson and Bany, *Classroom Management*, 1970.
16. Jacob S. Kounin, *Discipline and Group Management in Classrooms* (New York: Holt, Rinehart & Winston, 1970).

ADDITIONAL READINGS

Objective 1

Johnson, Lois V., and Mary A. Bany. *Classroom Management: Theory and Skill Training.* New York: Macmillan Co., 1970, pp. 6–31.

Objective 2

Dunkin, Michael J., and Bruce J. Biddle. *The Study of Teaching.* New York: Holt, Rinehart & Winston, 1974, pp. 134–135.
Johnson, Lois V., and Mary A. Bany. *Classroom Management: Theory and Skill Training.* New York: Macmillan Co., 1970, pp. 10–11.

Objective 3

Dunkin, Michael J., and Bruce J. Biddle. *The Study of Teaching.* New York: Holt, Rinehart & Winston, 1974, pp. 134–135.
Johnson, Lois V., and Mary A. Bany. *Classroom Management: Theory and Skill Training.* New York: Macmillan Co., 1970, pp. 3–16.

Objective 4

Dreikurs, Rudolf, and Pearl Cassel. *Discipline Without Tears.* New York: Hawthorn Books, 1972, pp. 30–41 and 85–96.

Johnson, Lois V., and Mary A. Bany. *Classroom Management: Theory and Skill Training.* New York: Macmillan Co., 1970, pp. 45–59.

Objective 5

Beatty, Judith Beal, et al. *The Onion Sandwich Principle (And Other Essays on Classroom Management).* Columbus, Ohio: Charles E. Merrill, 1973.

Blackham, G., and A. Silberman. *Modification of Child and Adolescent Behavior: Principles and Procedures.* Belmont, California: Wadsworth Publishing Co., 1975.

Blackwood, Ralph O. *Operant Control of Behavior: Elimination of Misbehavior and Motivation of Children.* Akron, Ohio: Exordium Press, 1971.

Brown, Duane. *Changing Student Behavior: A New Approach to Discipline.* Dubuque, Iowa: William C. Brown Company, 1971.

Buckley, Nancy K., and Hill M. Walker. *Modifying Classroom Behavior: A Manual of Procedures for Classroom Teachers.* Champaign, Illinois: Research Press Company, 1970.

Clarizio, Harvey F. *Toward Positive Classroom Discipline.* New York: John Wiley & Sons, 1971.

Dollar, Barry. *Humanizing Classroom Discipline: A Behavioral Approach.* New York: Harper and Row, 1972.

Givener, Abraham, and Paul S. Graubard. *A Handbook of Behavior Modification for the Classroom.* New York: Holt, Rinehart & Winston, 1974.

Harris, Mary B., ed. *Classroom Uses of Behavior Modification.* Columbus, Ohio: Charles E. Merrill, 1972.

Madsen, Charles H., Jr., and Clifford K. Madsen. *Teaching–Discipline: A Positive Approach for Educational Development, 2nd ed.* Boston: Allyn and Bacon, 1975.

Nielson, Gary E. *Helping Children Behave: A Handbook of Applied Learning Principles.* Chicago: Nelson–Hall Company, 1974.

Piper, Terrence. *Classroom Management and Behavioral Objectives: Applications of Behavioral Modification.* Belmont, California: Lear Siegler/Fearon Publishers, 1974.

Shipman, Helen, and Elizabeth Foley. *Any Teacher Can . . . A Systematic Approach to Behavior Management and Positive Teaching.* Chicago: Loyola University Press, 1973.

Sulzer, Beth, and G. Roy Mayer. *Behavior Modification Procedures for School Personnel.* Hinsdale, Illinois: Dryden Press, 1972.

Weiner, Daniel N. *Classroom Management and Discipline.* Itasca, Illinois: F. E. Peacock Publishers, 1972.

Objective 6

Dreikurs, Rudolf, and Pearl Cassel. *Discipline Without Tears.* New York: Hawthorn Books, 1972.

Ginnott, Haim G. *Teacher and Child: A Book for Parents and Teachers.* New York: Macmillan Co., 1972.

Glasser, William. *Schools Without Failure.* New York: Harper and Row, 1969.

Grey, Loren. *Discipline Without Fear.* New York: Hawthorn Books, 1974.

Objective 7

Johnson, Lois V., and Mary A. Bany. *Classroom Management: Theory and Skill Training.* New York: Macmillan Co., 1970.

Kounin, Jacob S. *Discipline and Group Management in Classrooms.* New York: Holt, Rinehart & Winston, 1970.

Schmuck, Richard, Mark Chesler, and Ronald Lippitt. *Problem Solving to Improve Classroom Learning*. Chicago: Science Research Associates, 1966.

Schmuck, Richard, and Patricia A. Schmuck. *Group Processes in the Classroom*. Dubuque, Iowa: William C. Brown Company, 1975.

Objectives 8 and 9
See listings under objectives 5, 6, and 7.

Terry McKoy, Institute of Open Education.

JOHN HANSEN

Observation Skills

Objectives

1 To discriminate among (1) valued data, (2) descriptive data, (3) selected data, and (4) reproduced data.

2 To record and analyze teacher questions using selected verbatim data.*

3 To record and analyze teacher verbal responses using selected verbatim data.

4 To record and analyze teacher verbal control statements using selected verbatim data.

5 To record and analyze student talk using selected verbatim data.

6 To record and analyze classroom physical movement data.

7 To record and analyze shadowing data.

8 To record and analyze classroom verbal flow using descriptive data.

9 To record and analyze classroom response behavior using descriptive data.

10 To record and analyze task orientation behavior using descriptive data.

The fact that people are so constantly involved in casual observation makes it difficult for them to observe themselves and others formally in a classroom setting. Teachers must observe so much, so often, and from such a personal perspective that they run the risk of observing everything and recording nothing. They are so used to viewing the behaviors of individuals from a total perspective that it becomes impossible for them to sort out and isolate those specific acts and ideas that sometimes hold the key to solving problems or changing behavior.

* Although this chapter teaches the reader techniques for recording and analyzing data in objectives 2–10, the mastery tests at the end of each subsection test only the ability to analyze such data, not to record it. It is simply impossible to test someone's recording ability without an opportunity to observe.

In this chapter observation will refer to the systematic recording of classroom events by an observer during an instructional activity. The recording may take place electronically or with paper and pencil, but the events will be preserved in some form for later study and analysis.

Since there is no single technique or set of techniques that everyone should use in observing teaching, this chapter will present several techniques that teachers can use to observe both themselves and others. Techniques for the collection, analysis, and presentation of accurate, objective, useful, and "persuasive" data will be given.

Objective 1

To discriminate among (1) valued data, (2) descriptive data, (3) selected data, and (4) reproduced data.

LEARNING ACTIVITY 1

Data (plural), or datum (singular), represent a *class* of concepts with several well-defined subsets. In this chapter, data will be used to refer to the four distinct concepts listed in objective 1.

Data are valuable only to the extent that they are persuasive. They are called "good" or "bad" based on their usefulness, *not* on their intrinsic qualities. There are times when valued data are quite appropriate and when purely objective data are not. The well-trained observer should know what data are appropriate at a given time and be able to make use of the best type.

1. *Valued data* are data that *involve* the judgment of an observer. In a questioning period valued data might be presented in the following manner (see table below).

Question	Appropriate Length		Appropriate to Topic		Appropriate to Student		Appropriate to Class Climate	
	Yes	No	Yes	No	Yes	No	Yes	No
1	X		X			X		X
2	X			X	X			X
3	X		X			X		X
4	X			X	X			X
.		X	X		X		X	
n	X		X		X		X	

In the column headings in the above table, "appropriate" represents a subjective value judgment made by the observer. Valued data could also be taken as anecdotal descriptions of observed behavior. In observing a classroom study period, the observer might write:

1. The teacher didn't move around enough.
2. He didn't help the students who needed help.
3. He spent too much time with Mike.
4. He didn't respond to requests for help.

Such judgmental observations are still data, because they are recorded instances. Valued data, however, are useful only to the extent that the person being observed *trusts* the value judgments of the observer.

2. *Descriptive data* are data that have been organized, categorized, or quantified by an observer but do not involve a value judgment. These data are often referred to as "low inference" data. In a questioning period, descriptive data might be collected by using the questioning techniques proposed in Chapter 5 and presented as they are in the following table.

Question	Knowledge	Application	Analysis	Evaluation
1	X			
2		X		
3			X	
4		X		
.				X
.				
.	X			
n		X		

In a supervised study period, descriptive data might look like the following:

1. He helped 16 students.
2. She helped Mike F. 7 times.
3. It took him 11 minutes to notice that Student 5 had his hand up.
4. She helped students 33 times in 24 minutes.

Such data include a decision by the observer, but the decision is "In what category does the behavior belong?" rather than "What value does the behavior have?" Usually, value judgments can be drawn from descriptive data, but the data themselves do not involve those judgments. The person being observed must trust the knowledge of the observer but may operate within a different system of values.

3. *Selected data* are data that objectively record a specific event without valuing or categorizing the event. Selected data are provided in a form that allows the person being observed to categorize and value his or her own behavior. In a questioning period, selected data would be a list of the actual questions asked, like the following:

1. What cities might have developed due to railroads?
2. What are some of the reasons the Miami area developed?
3. What are some possible reasons why cities die?
4. What kind of city would die of crime?
5. In connection with the economy, what is it that would effect the death of a city?
6. What about large towns? What is it about them that makes them grow?
7. Does anyone else have any other reasons for the development of cities?
8. Where did the people concentrate?
9. Where was the land where they lived? Why would the city develop there?
10. What about when they look for enemies?
11. In what period did New York City have its greatest growth?
12. What could have happened that would have increased it?
13. What about people from Europe?
14. What kept it from developing from the center? How did they spread out? In what way did they develop?

In a "self-help" session selected data might be a record of the physical movement pattern of the instructor. On the following page is the seating chart of a classroom. Each box represents a student.

			Goes to T at 11:15		
6 (28)	X	X	(8) (12) (23) 11:13 *26*	X	X
10:57 Asks for help and raises his hand 11:02 Says "Mr. Meyer" 11:08 Pounds on wall (16) 11:08 (33) 11:21	X		Raises hand at 10:11 (7) 11:00 (11) 11:03 *12* Susan	(9) 11:02 Keith	Raises hand 11:10 (10) 11:02 (24) 11:13 *25*
4	X	11:16 Gets up, walks around and sits down (4) *11*	(5) (6) *15*	Raises hand 11:08 Julie	X
3	X	X	X	*19*	*24*
11:02 Raises hand *2* (17) 11:10	10:58 Goes to #4 until *8* 11:02 11:06 Goes to #4; stops at #2 until 11:09 11:10 Goes to books in back until 11:20 (18)	11:07 Gets a book from shelf in back (1) 10:57 (14) (26) 11:15 (19) (32) (29) Mike F.	11:02 Raises hand (13) 11:05 (22) (27) (30) Donna	11:14 Goes to book shelf *18*	X
Gives current events report 11:07 Gets up and stands to talk to #7 until 11:09 *7* Linda	(15) (31)	Liz	Raises hand 11:08 Goes to T at 11:20 (2) (20) 11:10 Mike	Raises hand 11:07 (21) 11:11 *17*	11:15 Goes to book shelf 11:18 Returns to books (3) 11:21 Goes again (25) Martha

T

LEGEND

(1) teacher–student conference at the student's desk (number indicates sequential order)

X an absent student

10:57 time at which conference 1 took place

6 student 6 (used when names are unknown)

⌒ whispering between two students

The person observed must trust the observer to record behaviors accurately but need not trust either the observer's knowledge or his or her value system.

4. *Reproduced data* are data that are made available when an event is reproduced in video, audio, or total transcript (verbatim) form. They contain not only the targeted behavior but all the other behaviors that occurred during the session. The person observed need only trust the ability of the observer to operate the equipment. Reproduced data are

the only data that have not been processed or manipulated somehow by the observer (i.e., classified, judged, or verbally described). They represent a total reproduction of some event.

Techniques for collection of reproduced data are simple — one merely needs to turn on an audio or video recorder. For this reason we shall not focus our attention on the collection of reproduced data in this chapter. Techniques for the analysis of collected data discussed in the chapter may also be applied to reproduced data. Valued data will not be discussed beyond the initial definition either. Since we collect valued data all the time, it is not necessary to learn any special techniques for recording and analyzing this particular type.

All four forms of data are useful. A well-trained and experienced observer can discern which type of data will be most "persuasive" in a given setting and will provide that type for the person being observed.

The learning activities of this chapter are presented in a sequence that is designed to facilitate your learning. Therefore, objectives relative to selected data are presented first, followed by those related to descriptive data.

Mastery Test

OBJECTIVE 1
To discriminate among (1) valued data, (2) descriptive data, (3) selected data, and (4) reproduced data.

Below are a number of statements which contain data from classroom activities. Please indicate in the appropriate blank whether the data are valued (*V*), descriptive (*D*), or selected (*S*).

_____ 1. Five of the seven questions the teacher asked were appropriate to the student's vocabulary.

_____ 2. Five of the seven questions the teacher asked were knowledge questions.

_____ 3. The teacher spent too much time with Mike.

_____ 4. "What is the distance from Rome to Paris?"

_____ 5. "Billy! Close that mouth of yours!"

_____ 6. The teacher talked with every student during the study period.

_____ 7. "Umm, that was a good idea."

_____ 8. The teacher spent so much time talking with Mike that he couldn't help Bill.

_____ 9. Five of the seven questions asked were followed with a probing question.

_____ 10. Bill was at task seven of the twelve times he was observed.

ANSWER KEY

Mastery Test, Objective 1

If you did not accurately identify eight of the ten examples, reread the section.

1. *V.* The observer must make a judgment to determine "appropriateness."
2. *D.* The observer must be able to recognize knowledge questions and to count them. No judgment or record of the question is necessary.
3. *V.* "Too much time" is a judgment.
4. *S.* A verbatim recording of a question asked.
5. *S.* A verbatim recording of a teacher control statement.
6. *D.* The observer recorded who the teacher talked to — not what was said (selected) or its value.
7. *S.* A verbatim recording of teacher verbal response.
8. *V.* Cause–effect statements (". . . so much time . . . that . . .") are valued data.
9. *D.* The observer described the nature of questions that followed other questions.
10. *D.* The observer categorized the physical behavior of Bill.

SELECTED DATA

Selected data, as discussed earlier, are data that record a specific event without valuing or categorizing that event. In objectives 2–7 you will learn the techniques used to collect and analyze three types of selected data: (1) selective verbatim, (2) physical movement, and (3) shadowing data.

Selective Verbatim Data

Selective verbatim is the name given to those observation techniques in which the observer simply records whatever type of verbal behavior is being studied. For example, if the observer or the instructor is concerned about:

(a) . . . *questioning techniques*, the observer would record the actual *questions* asked.

(b) . . . *behavior control*, the observer would record those statements made in an attempt to *control* behavior.

(c) . . . _____ (the reader will supply the category), the observer will record _____ just as it is said.

The observer simply acts as a sorter, recording the statements that fit the designated category of verbal behavior. Students or instructors can also observe their own behavior with the help of an audio tape recorder. The data, whether recorded by oneself or by an observer, can be interpreted later, either through self-analysis or through conference with the observer.

The process, or technique, used to study behavior involves the following five steps:

> *Selected verbatim observation technique*
> 1. Decide which individual or individuals (teacher, all students, a group of students, a student, etc.) will be observed.
> 2. Decide upon the kind of verbal data you want to study (teacher questions, teacher responses, teacher control statements, student talk, etc.).
> 3. Sit in the classroom (or next to a recorder) where you can hear the conversation.
> 4. Write out the actual words (question, responses, etc.) used by the target individual or group.
> 5. Analyze the data.

Selective Verbatim Categories.   From the data collected using the selective verbatim observation technique it is possible to identify and label a variety of verbal behavior categories. The following categories commonly occur in teacher–student interaction and can be easily identified from a verbatim transcript. This list below is far from exhaustive. It simply represents a cross section of verbal behaviors commonly identified and studied.

Patterns of Teacher Verbal Behavior	*Student Verbal Behavior*
1. Teacher questions.	1. Student responses to instructor questions.
2. Teacher responses to student questions. or statements.	2. Student questions.
3. Teacher directions and assignments.	3. Student-initiated questions.
4. Teacher talk patterns (verbal mannerisms such as "Okay" or "All right," repeated use of phrases or words, self-reference, etc.).	4. Initial responses.
5. Teacher rewards or praise of students.	5. Student "active listening" responses.
6. Teacher criticism of student actions.	
7. Teacher control of student actions.	

The data will form a sequential listing of the particular type of verbal behavior *selected* for study. Its usefulness will lie in its ability to help diagnose that particular type of verbal behavior. Judgments may be made after the analysis, but the data will not, by themselves, indicate a "good" or a "bad" teacher.

In objectives 2–5, techniques for collecting and analyzing teacher questions, verbal responses, verbal control statements, and student talk will be discussed. In each case, an introductory discussion concerning data collection will be followed by suggestions for data analysis, exhibits containing sample data, and analytical exercises based on the exhibits. In every case, however, the basic technique for collecting the data is the same as the selected verbatim observation technique already presented.

Objective 2

To record and analyze teacher questions using selected verbatim data.

LEARNING ACTIVITY 2.1

In research conducted by the author, it was found that teachers ask more than one question every minute in the "average" teacher-led discussion. It is not unusual for a teacher to ask 30–40 questions, only six of which were planned, during the course of a thirty-minute discussion. What do the unplanned questions look like? Many teachers have never listened to and systematically analyzed their questions. Using the selected verbatim technique, the teacher can record all the questions and interrogative statements* he or she asks. The resulting data permit a comparison between "what was wanted" and "what was asked for."

Data Collection

Using an audio tape recorder placed on the desk, the teacher records a discussion.† Following the discussion, the teacher records on paper all the questions and interrogative statements that were made but does not record answers or other statements made during the discussion. The result of this recording is a list of the questions asked. Examples are found in Exhibit 1. If the teacher wants to analyze the answers or the other statements, he or she merely needs to replay the tape and record whatever behavior is of interest.

Data Analysis

Lists of teacher questions show that teachers often have a tendency to ask questions in the same way, to start with the same phrases, and to ask multiple questions.‡ Other lists might indicate questioning style built around short, succinct questions or complex ones demanding multiple answers. Whatever characteristics might be found in a list of questions, they are simply a reflection of what the teacher said during a given classroom discussion. As such, they become persuasive data that the teacher can use to modify his or her questioning style in subsequent classroom discussions.

Questions to ask yourself as you analyze teacher questions include:

---

* Interrogative statements are phrases which sound like a question but for which no answer is expected. In a recent research study conducted by the author over 50 percent of teacher questions were not meant to be answered. Actually they are praise, criticism, directions, lecture, etc.

† Of course, an observer could record the same information while sitting in the classroom.

‡ Multiple questions are questions in which, instead of asking one question, the teacher asks three or four before giving the students an opportunity to respond. In these cases, the first question often relates to the discussion at hand, but the last is the only question that is answered. Often there is little relationship between the first and the last question in such a series. The same teacher probably wonders how the students manage to get off the subject.

1. In how many questions was a student response actually requested?

2. What pattern of questioning was revealed? (Were there repetitious phrases, one-word answers, multiple questions, wordy questions, etc.?)

3. What thought levels were demanded in the response? (The observer could use the ideas from the questioning or concept formation chapters or from any of the other recent writers on questioning, like Sanders, Bloom, Hunkins, etc.)

4. How often does the teacher use (a) the word "what", (b) questions that start with a verb, (c) "Do you think . . . ?", and/or (d) _____ (Fill in appropriate word or phase.)?

5. What is the relationship between lesson content and the questions asked?

6. What is the relationship between lesson objectives and the questions asked?

7. What is the relationship between vocabulary used and the students' verbal ability?

8. Is there a relationship between questions asked and student participation patterns?

Sample Data

Following are three lists of questions recorded by trained observers. Exhibit 1 comes from a 1960 junior high school class that was discussing the U-2 incident in which an American reconnaissance plane was shot down over Russia. Exhibit 2 comes from a Miami, Florida elementary school classroom (grade 5) doing a unit on urban development. Exhibit 3 is a high school sociology discussion of penal reform and penal problems.

For each exhibit (1) read the data through completely; (2) reread them asking yourself the questions suggested above; and (3) summarize your thoughts about the questioning style.

EXHIBIT 1   Teacher Questions to Junior High School Class on U-2 Incident

1. Does anyone know now who gave the orders; do you recall this from your newspaper readings?*
2. Should we have sent this pilot in the first place?
3. Any other thoughts?
4. What would the United States have done in such an instance? Karen? (requested by teacher.)
5. Would you briefly tell us now what has been mentioned so far?
6. Any other thoughts on this?
7. Do you want to stay around this classroom or not?
8. What type of information do you think this aircraft would be seeking anyway?
9. What do you think of that, testing the Russian defenses with an American's life?
10. Now, is this a very good example of leadership? This whole incident, all the facts now that we have? What about the leadership of the United States?

---

* The numbers indicate separate questions, that is, questions for which student responses occurred. If two questions were asked together *without* a student response between them, the observer would record it as shown in question 10.

11. What were the most important things in this particular incident?
12. Why was he there?
13. Why was it done?
14. What could happen?
15. What is going to be the result of this particular incident?
16. Are there any questions on this assignment?

EXHIBIT 2   Teacher Questions to Fifth Grade Class on Urban Development

1. What do you think would be some of the reasons why cities develop?
2. But would that cause them to settle there? (No answer)
3. What about things like weather conditions?
4. What about — what modes of transportation did they have at this time? (Student: What are we talking about?)
5. What would be some of the major cities that developed for some of these reasons? What is a city that developed around water?
6. What other city developed about water?
7. What are possibly some cities that might have developed as trade centers? Think of people moving out west.
8. OK, what happened when people . . . . What would be the importance of cities like St. Louis?
9. What cities might have developed due to railroads?
10. What would be some of the reasons why the Miami area might have developed?
11. What would possibly be some reasons why cities would die?
12. What kind of city would die of crime?
13. In connection with the economy, what is it that would effect the death of a city?
14. What about large towns? What is it about them that makes them grow?
15. Does anyone else have any other reasons for the development of cities?
16. Where did the people concentrate?
17. Where was the land where they lived? Why would the city develop there?
18. What about when they look for enemies?
19. What period did New York have its greatest growth?
20. What could have happened that would have increased it?
21. What about people from Europe?
22. What kept it from developing from the center? How did they spread out? In what way did they develop?

EXHIBIT 3   Teacher Questions to High School Sociology Class on Penal Problems and Reforms

10:05   1. Do you want to close the door?
2. What were we talking about yesterday?
3. Give me something that could help to stop the vicious circle.
4. What else?
5. What do we consider to be the main problems?
6. What is one of the problems that stems from this?
7. Why?
8. What's the word?
9. What does THAT mean?
10. From the word "convict" what comes out?
11. What else?
12. What are they classified as?
10:17   13. What does ostracized mean? (No answer)
14. They immediately lose what?
15. What else?

16. What's a deviant?
17. They become hard core criminals more or less because why?
18. Who do they associate with?
19. What do they receive from this? (Student: I don't understand what you want.)
20. What do they get from these people?
21. What do they get from these people?
22. They get acceptance from whom?
23. Any questions on this? Is it understandable?
24. What other restrictions do they place on them?
25. What shows they aren't considered acceptable?
26. What else?
27. The custodial prison does what?
28. What is the idea behind prison?
29. Wouldn't you agree? (No answer)
30. Who should be giving the criminal leadership?
31. What's going to happen as soon as he gets back?
32. Would that be a good assumption? (No answer)

10:29   33. Would you agree? (Student: Yeah.)
34. Do you know anything _____ ? What do you think?
35. What kind of programs should these be?
36. Where is Marianna? (No answer)
37. Does anyone know where Okeechobee is?
38. What was that?
39. They wouldn't take a guy right after he committed a crime and put him on a job, would they?
40. Do you remember what we talked about yesterday?
41. What happens when he's been ostracized from society when he goes over to the hard core group when he's been pushed so far to one side when a program comes up?
42. Why?
43. So what would be considered if he broke away from his peers which he'd be unlikely to do when he takes advantage of such a program?
44. So what happens when the relationship breaks down when he still has two years to go?
45. How can you do this?
46. Is that your only solution?

10:35   47. Do you want to bet on that?

Mastery Test

OBJECTIVE 2   To record and analyze teacher questions using selected verbatim data.

Write out an analysis of Exhibit 3 using the following questions:

1. In how many questions was a student response not actually requested?

_____

_____

2. What pattern of questioning was revealed? (Were there repetitious phrases, one-word answers, multiple questions, wordy questions, etc.?)

_____

_____

_____

_____

3. What thought levels were demanded in the response? (You can use the ideas from the questioning or concept formation chapters or from any of the other recent writers on questioning, like Sanders, Bloom, Hunkins, etc.)

_____

_____

_____

_____

4. How often does the teacher use (a) the word "what," (b) questions that start with a verb, (c) "Do you think . . . ?", and/or (d) _____ (Fill in appropriate word or phrase.)?

_____

_____

ANSWER KEY

Mastery Test, Objective 2

1. Questions 1 and 29 were not meant to be answered.
2. Several patterns exist:
   (a) Use of pronouns without antecedents: 6, 9, 12, 19–25, 32.
   (b) Indefinite, vague questions (too open-ended): 10, 17, 19, 27, 35, 38, 41, 43, 44, 45.
   (c) Repetitious use of "what" questions and agreement questions (asking for "yes" or "no" responses).
3. Using the categories similar to those in Chapter 5, the questions can be described as:

Knowledge: 21 (2, 3, 8, 9, 10, 12, 13, 14, 15, 18, 19, 20, 21, 22, 24, 34, 35, 36, 37, 38, 40).
Application: 6 (17, 27, 31, 41, 43, 44).
Analysis: 4 (6, 25, 28, 39).
Evaluation: 4 (5, 30, 32, 45).
Procedural: 10 (1, 4, 11, 15, 23, 26, 27, 29, 33, 42, 46, 47).

4. The teacher uses "what" and verbs to start questions too often. He or she probably could find more effective alternatives.

LEARNING ACTIVITY 2.2

Tape-record a discussion you conduct in your classroom or use a tape-recorded discussion available in your media center. Record the questions asked in that discussion on paper. Analyze the questions using the suggested questions for data analysis. Rewrite the questions as you might ask them if you had the opportunity to teach the same lesson.

Objective 3

To record and analyze teacher verbal responses using selected verbatim data.

LEARNING ACTIVITY 3.1

Because individuals derive their self-concepts, in large part, from the verbal responses they receive from other people, teachers should be aware of their own response patterns and use them consciously to effect desired learning outcomes, both cognitive and affective. There-fore, the second selective verbatim technique presented in this chap-ter deals with the initial response of teachers to student comments.

Data Collection

As with all selective verbatim categories, the teacher first records a classroom discussion.* After the lesson, the teacher records on a blank sheet of paper the first sentence or phrase (six to ten words) he or she makes every time a student stops talking.

Let us assume that a teacher asked, "Who has the answer to ques-tion 1?" A student responds with some answer to which the teacher replies, "No, it is not that. John?" (indicating another student). John then gives his answer, and the teacher repeats it, gives additional information, and asks for the answer to question 2. (Neither this nor the other verbal responses offered here are intended to suggest ideal lessons.)

The recording the teacher would have made is as follows:

Teacher: ???
Student:
Teacher: No, it is not that. John?
   John:
Teacher: (repeats answer) . . . ?
  Martha:
Teacher: OK, Spain ruled Cuba and . . . (repeats answer).
   Mary:
Teacher: That's right, like Mary said . . . (repeats answer).

The teacher may choose to write out the repetition or merely

---

* Again, an observer can record the same data in a class while the lesson is being conducted.

indicate that repetition is occurring. (The latter is suggested when "repetition" data is not the target of the observation.) When the teacher talks beyond a single phrase, the rest of what was said is indicated with a series of dots. When the teacher's response ends with a question, the question is indicated with a question mark. When the teacher wants to describe what is happening instead of recording the actual behavior, the description is included within parentheses. When several students talk between teacher comments, their talk is shown in the following manner.:

T: Okay, that's right. What else?
S:
S:
S:
S:
T: Now let's summarize what we know about this . . . .

Thus, by the end of the recording the teacher has compiled a record of how he or she responded to students in a given lesson. As with all selective verbatim categories, this type of observation can be made by a teacher alone with an audio recording just as effectively (some would say even more effectively) as with an observer. On a few occasions (such as a "rapid fire" review or drill) observers will not be able to record all comments without hearing them again (or replaying the tape). In these instances, the teacher must decide whether to record the responses slowly, to record only every third response, or to record those that he or she can. Exhibit 7 is an example of a variation of this technique. The teacher recorded verbatim all praise, acknowledgement, and critical comments and simply described (i.e., "repeated answer," "ignored response," etc.) all other responses. These data were recorded after a discussion on the amount and value of praise being given by the teacher. The data were persuasive.

Data Analysis

There is no ideal response pattern. Each lesson, each teacher, and each group of students will demand different patterns. Each collection of data will have to be analyzed in terms of the desired teacher behaviors, the needs of the students, and the nature of the activity. What is most important is that the data be analyzed, hypotheses formed, and future actions planned and modified accordingly. Teachers should learn to analyze their response patterns with questions such as these:

1. Does a response pattern exist? (Does every response start with the same word or phrase? Is the response meaningful or habitual?)
2. Where several responses are repeated, is there any consistent reason for the repetitions? (Does the correct answer get one response while an incorrect one gets another response? Do "relevant" comments or questions get one response while "irrelevant" ones get another response? Do boys get a different response than girls? Do "good" students get a different response than "bad" students?)
3. Are most responses questions? statements? encouragements? value judgments?

4. Since conclusions must be based upon several observations, does the teacher respond differently to different groups? Does one type of lesson result in different responses from another type? Does a particular student usually get a specific category of response?

5. How often are students' names mentioned?

6. When value judgments are made, are the criteria given?

7. When the response is a statement, is the teacher using the idea of a student or changing the subject?

8. Could the response have been made without students having said anything? (See Exhibit 6.)

9. Does every student comment result in a teacher comment? Can several students talk without the teacher commenting?

After answering each of these questions the teacher must then decide whether to act on the information or gather more data.

Sample Data

Exhibit 4 was made in a junior high school class discussing the U-2 incident. Exhibit 5 was made on two different days to see how a teacher in a sixth grade class responded in a lesson dealing with feeling and opinion (in which he felt he got "good discussion") as compared to a "content" lesson (in which he felt he had to "pull teeth" to get responses). Exhibit 6 was made in a fifth grade class following the reading of a story. Exhibit 7 was made in a rural high school in the classroom of a teacher who wanted more information about her praise.

For Exhibits 4, 5, and 6 (1) read the data through completely; (2) reread them asking yourself the questions suggested above; and (3) summarize your conclusions about response behavior.

EXHIBIT 4   Teacher Responses to Junior High School Class on U-2 Incident

1. Does anyone know now who gave the orders . . .*
2. Well, now the big question seems to be . . .
3. All right, now, this is a good point, Robert has mentioned . . .
4. All right, now, Karen has asked the question . . .
5. All right, now, we've heard several different opinions on this . . .
6. Any other thoughts on this, Sandra?
7. All right, boys, that is enough back there now . . .
8. All right, now, just a minute, Jerry, stand up please . . .
9. All right, let's get your behavior back . . .
10. Well, now, Sandra's brought up a very good point . . .
11. All right, now, this is a good point . . .
12. Now, class, what do you think of that?
13. All right, now, this introduces something else too . . .
14. All right, now, we have heard several points of view on this . . .
15. All right, now, let's put this in a briefer question . . .
16. All right, who would be. I think we could just write down . . .
17. In other words, why was it done?
18. All right, what could happen?

* Once again numbers indicate separate responses which followed student comments. If the teacher continued talking it would be indicated by the use of three dots as in #1, 2, 3, 4, 5 and others. Numbers 6 and 12 indicate that the teacher made that type of statement only twice.

19. All right, now, this is the one point of the discussion . . .
20. This will be due on Monday . . .
21. Now, of course, you're going to be somewhere where . . .
22. Well, now, this is one thing that we will perhaps . . .
23. You certainly could do this. Perhaps your parents . . .

EXHIBIT 5   Teacher Responses in Two Sixth Grade Class Discussions

Day 1	*Day 2*
S	S Protective tariffs
T Any other?	T Protective tariffs . . . ?
S	S The West
T Any other?	T The West . . . ?
S	S The railroads
T Naturally, why do you think so?	T Okay, the Republicans said they wanted railroads, . . .
S	
T Any ideas about how they do it?	S ??
S	T It would help the North and the West . . . .
T Well	
S	S New roads
T The system has made it worthwhile	T " ".
S	S ??
S	T Yeah, roads and other things . . . .
S	S ??
S	T Yeah, the party existed in the South
S	S
T Any comments about that?	T Right, the party was in favor of free lands.
S	
T I know but I am asking you.	S ??
S	T They'd pay taxes as soon as they . . .
S	S No! ??
T Do you think this is black-initiated?	
S	T No!
T I got two opinions, let's talk about them.	S
	S
S	T Right.
S	S Electoral votes
S	T (begins lecture on 1860 election results)
T Any other comments about it?	
S	S
S	T No, that was the Northern Democrats . . .
S	S
S	T No, that was the Northern Democrats.
S	S
T That's good, who can summarize it?	T No, the U.S. Supreme Court had a majority . . . .
S	S Congress
T That's a good question. Class, what do you think about it?	T Right, Congress . . . .
S	S
S	T The South had a majority in Congress . . . .
S	S He would have upheld the free slave law
T Now let's summarize our feelings about . . . ?	T He would have upheld all federal laws . . . .
	S

EXHIBIT 6   Teacher Responses in Fifth Grade Class After Reading Story

1. Betty, will you give us a short summary of the Split Cherry Tree?
2. . . . Betty, what happened?
3. Umm. Good summary of the story, Chris.
4. What were your ideas on the story? Like it? No? Why?
5. Did you like the people that were in it?
6. What did you think about the boy?
7. What did you think about the father?
8. Do you like the ending of the story?
9. Did someone not like the story?
10. The placement of stress? Characters, plot, setting?
11. OK, would you like to tell us why?
12. How many characters? Okay, who?
13. What part did these play in the story?
14. What sort of conflict would we look for?
15. Chris, did you have something to add?
16. What was the conflict in this? What happened after?
17. What caused the conflict? What is different about the background?
18. Do you think there was hasty judgment?

EXHIBIT 7   Teacher Responses in a Rural High School Selected for Analysis of Praise

	S (questions assignment)
11:43	1. T Yes, 565–569 (Goes to board and writes it.) (Class works on timeline exercise and Q-A sheet.) . . . OK, who has what #1 is?
11:50	S
	2. T No, it's not that. John?
	John
	3. T (repeats answer) . . . ?
	Martha
	4. T Okay, Spain ruled . . .
	Mary
	5. T That's right, like Mary said (repeats answer)
	Kim
	6. T No, that's not it.
	S
	7. T Right, Senor D_____ wrote a letter . . .
	S
	8. T Okay, that's right.
	S
	9. T That's right . . . ?
	S
	10. T That's right, Congress declared war . . . .
	S
	11. T (repeats answer)
	S
	12. T All right, that's #6. Does anyone know . . .
	S
	13. T Very good (repeats answer)
	S
	14. T All right. You can read it louder please.
	S
	15. T Okay (repeats answer)
	S
	16. T (repeats answer)
	S

17. T Good, where was Santiago?
    S
18. T Good.
    S (questions)
19. T (responds to student?)
    S
20. T Okay, that's that, here is a handout
    Mary (reads part of handout out loud)
21. T All right, that's enough, thank you . . . ?
    S
22. T (asks clarifying question)
    S
23. T All right (writes response on board)
    S
24. T All right (writes response on board)
    Debby
25. T Very good. Debby said (repeats answer)
    S
26. T All right but I wish you'd said that when we talked about #1 . . . .
    S
12:05 27. T Okay (repeats answer)
    S
28. T That's a good answer (repeats answer)
    S
29. T Okay, any more ideas?
    Diane (a 2-minute response)
30. T That's good, like Diane said (repeats an idea) . . . also, like Diane said
       . . . (5½-minute summary of discussion) . . .
    Link (reads part of handout)
31. T Okay (asks question)
    Mary
32. T (asks clarifying question)
    Mary . . . ?
33. T (responds to Mary)
    Diane (asks question)
34. T (responds to Diane)
    Mary
35. T All right (repeats answer), like Mary said . . . remember what Mary
       said . . . ?
    Kim
36. T I don't think you were listening . . . ?
    S
37. T (gives new information)
    Mary (asks question)
38. T (responds to question)
    S
39. T That's right, it was well organized . . . .
    S (asks question)
40. T (responds to question)
    Kim (questions reason for lesson)
41. T Just do what I want and you'll learn something . . . ?
    S
42. T (repeats answer)
    S
43. T (gives new information)
    S
44. T All right (repeats answer)
    S
45. T (repeats answer) . . . I wish some of you would talk more. We'll have
       another discussion tomorrow. Try to talk more then, if you can.
    (bell rings)

Mastery Test

OBJECTIVE 3   To record and analyze teacher verbal responses using selected verbatim data.

Write out an analysis of Exhibit 7 using the following questions:

1. Does a response pattern exist?

_____

_____

_____

2. Where several responses are repeated, is there any consistent reason for the repetitions?

_____

_____

_____

_____

_____

3. Are most responses questions? statements? encouragements? value judgments?

_____

_____

_____

4. Since conclusions must be based upon several observations, does the teacher respond differently to different groups? Does one type of lesson result in different responses from another type? Does a particular student usually get a specific category of response?

_____

_____

5. How often are students' names mentioned?

_____

_____

_____

6. When value judgments are made, are the criteria given?

_____

_____

_____

7. When the response is a statement, is the teacher using the idea of a student or changing the subject?

_____

_____

8. Could the response have been made without students having said anything?

_____

_____

_____

9. Does every student comment result in a teacher comment? Can several students talk without the teacher commenting?

_____

_____

_____

ANSWER KEY

Mastery Test, Objective 3

1. The teacher uses some habitual responses like "that's right" and "All right." Repeated observations would be useful to determine student response to these habits.
2. (a) Kim is treated brusquely (6, 36, and 41) while Mary and Diane are not (5, 21, 32, 33, 35 and 30, 31). Whether or not these were justified or habitual must be determined in another observation.

   (b) There is a definite implication that (1) there is a right answer; (2) the teacher knows it already; and (3) the students simply need to do what the teacher says. (2, 4, 6, 7–10, 13, 15–17, 36–41)
3. The teacher responds, typically, with a value judgment but shows a variety of other responses at least once — repetitions, clarifying questions, statements, directions, etc.
4. Cannot be determined from available data.
5. Four students' names are mentioned (John, Mary, Debby, Diane; 28 in the class), three of these while praising the student.
6. Value judgments are made repeatedly ("That's right"; "Good"; "No, that's not it"; "Good, that's a good answer"; "All right, that's good"*) without criteria being exposed.
7. Cannot be determined from available data.
8. Definitely not. The responses were tied to students' comments. In several instances the teacher used what students said (3, 11, 13, 14, 16, 19, 25, 30, 35 and others).
9. The teacher controlled the flow of interaction in this discussion. Every student comment was followed by a teacher response.

* "That's right" and "All right" are often habitual responses that have no value attached. They are listed here because the observed teacher indicated she used them to show value. (Their effect might be questioned!)

LEARNING ACTIVITY 3.2

Use the recording you made for Learning Activity 2.2 or tape-record another discussion. Record the first phrase or sentence (6–10 words) you said following each student response on paper. (Every time a student stops talking, write down the first phrase that was said.) Analyze the list using questions from the Mastery Test for objective 3. List those responses (1) you should do more of, (2) you should do less of.

Objective 4

To record and analyze teacher verbal control statements using selected verbatim data.

LEARNING ACTIVITY 4.1

Many teachers use verbal statements as their primary means of controlling student behavior. At times, however, the very statements meant to control the students have the opposite effect. In other cases the statements have no effect. Recording the statements a teacher makes in an effort to control or limit student behavior, thus, provides data that can become the starting point for behavioral changes.

Data Collection

The observer in the classroom or the teacher using a tape recording simply records all statements intended to control or limit the behavior of students made during a lesson. These may be worded as questions, sarcastic remarks, directions, commands, reprimands, etc. All non-control comments made during the lesson are omitted from the record. It is often helpful to record the timing of the statement, any verbal or nonverbal "challenge" or response, and the activity occurring at the time of the statements.

Data Analysis

Each collection of data must be analyzed to determine whether alternative statements or behaviors might have been more effective (e.g., giving students more work, ignoring behavior, naming offenders, etc.). In some cases, what isn't said may be more persuasive than what is said. Audio or video recordings may be necessary when the teacher doesn't perceive a problem. One of several other instruments may be necessary to help a teacher locate the "troublemakers" or the reason for the trouble.

Questions to ask yourself as you analyze verbal control statements include:

1. If I were the student being spoken to, how would the comment affect me? How would it affect others?
2. If I were the teacher, how could I improve my behavior in the next class?

Sample Data

Exhibit 8 is indicative of two consecutive days of a student teacher's attempt to control elementary classroom behavior — notice the slight changes in verbal behavior. Exhibit 9 was recorded in a junior high school class.

For each exhibit (1) read the data presented; (2) reread them asking yourself the questions suggested above; and (3) summarize your thoughts about the verbal control statements used.

EXHIBIT 8 Teacher Verbal Control Statements on Two Consecutive Days in an Elementary Classroom

Day 1

3:03	1.	Girls, please turn around.
3:05	2.	Girls!
3:12	3.	Make sure that you write this down in your notebook.
3:17	4.	Okay, most of you have finished. We will go on.
3:20	5.	Sssssh!
3:20	6.	Ssssh!
3:21	7.	Mac!
3:21	8.	Well, you don't have to listen, do you? (No) Then don't listen.
3:23	9.	Okay. Ssssh! Class! Girls! (One of the girls asks which girls.)
3:24	10.	Girls!
3:25	11.	CLASS!
3:25	12.	Would two boys please pass out the books?
3:27	13.	Okay. Sssssh! Turn to page 465.
3:29	14.	Okay. Would someone please read the introduction? Ssssh!
3:31	15.	Class — You girls back there in the corner.
3:40	16.	SSSH!
3:41	17.	Class! Girls! Leslie!
3:41	18.	CLASS! LESLIE! SSSH!

Day 2

3:03	1.	Class, let's have an orderly discussion today. When you want to talk, please raise your hand and I'll call on you.
3:23	2.	Class! Class!
3:25	3.	Let me see hands! Let me see hands!
3:28	4.	Mac, if you have something to say, raise your hand and I'll call on you.
3:29	5.	Class! Leslie, come sit up here.
3:30	6.	Betty! Mr. Ross!
3:40	7.	Bill, collect the notebooks.

EXHIBIT 9 Teacher Verbal Control Statements in a Junior High School Class

Activity			
	10:19	1.	Berta.
	10:20	2.	Linda, please listen.
	10:21	3.	Roberta, I don't want to hear anything more out of you.
Returning papers	10:21	4.	Bill, come back here right now.
	10:23	5.	Bill, I didn't ask for you to answer.
	10:24	6.	Sshh. Just raise your hand.
	10:24	7.	Would you please be quiet (class)?
	10:26	8.	Answer by raising your hand.
	10:27	9.	You don't need to ask??

	10:27	10. Molly, turn around.
	10:28	11. Molly, wait until you are called on before you talk.
	10:29	12. Bill, you didn't have permission to say anything.
	10:29	13. Scott, if you can't join us, you can leave us.
Doing English	10:30	14. Scott, just be quiet.
exercise	10:32	15. Doug, sit down. Put the dictionary away.
at seat	10:32	16. Ted, did you have permission to talk?
	10:35	17. Scott, until you have permission to talk, please be quiet.
	10:37	18. Pat and Molly. (were not talking)
	10:38	19. Molly, this time it was you.
	10:38	20. Randy, what are you doing? (standing at dictionary)
	10:38	21. Scott, if you want to talk, raise your hand.
	10:38	22. Bill, you're not excluded from this.
	10:39	23. Randy — this goes for all of you — I'm going to stand up here and watch. If you want to talk, raise your hand and I'll give you permission.

Mastery Test

OBJECTIVE 4
To record and analyze teacher verbal control statements using selected verbatim data.

Write out your analysis of Exhibit 8 using the following guidelines:

1. How many students' names were mentioned on Day 1?

_____

_____

2. How was control attempted?

_____

_____

_____

3. What does the teacher mean to do by requesting assistance?

_____

_____

_____

4. What happened when the teacher asks "two boys" or "someone" to do things?

_____

_____

_____

5. Did the teacher use any sarcasm? Was it meant?

_____

_____

_____

6. Are there any positive control statements on Day 1?

_____

_____

_____

_____

_____

7. What was different on Day 2?

_____

_____

_____

ANSWER KEY
Mastery Test, Objective 4

1. On Day 1 only two student names are mentioned.
2. Control is attempted through generalized groups (sssh!, girls, class, boys, someone) rather than specific individuals.
3. Assistance is requested when the teacher really means to direct behavior. What would happen if the response to the 3:25 or 3:29 questions had been "No"?
4. "Two boys" and "someone" probably resulted in six to eight "boys" or "someones" trying to respond. What might have happened if the teacher had said "Bill and John" or "John"?
5. The sarcastic remark at 3:21 on Day 1 really wasn't meant.
6. Only two instances of positive control statements, i.e., statements which direct behavior with no "correction" or "punishment" in mind, exist (3:12 and 3:27). How did students know what to do?
7. Note the use of names (3:28–3:40) and tone setting (3:03) in Day 2.

LEARNING ACTIVITY 4.2

Use the recording you made for Learning Activity 2.2 or tape-record another discussion. Record all direction and control statements made by the teacher on paper. Analyze the list using questions from the Mastery Test for objective 4. List those statements (1) you should give more often; (2) you should give less often.

Objective 5

To record and analyze student talk using selected verbatim data.

LEARNING ACTIVITY 5.1

Most selective verbatim categories select "teacher" verbal behaviors for recording. It is obvious, however, that a substantial portion of classroom talk is done by the student — approximately $\frac{1}{4}$ to $\frac{1}{3}$ of the verbal behavior according to recent research. Thus, in the following section you will be asked to analyze student comments.

Data Collection

Of all the selective verbatim categories (except, perhaps, a teacher lecture), this category is the most difficult to observe in a classroom. Most observations of student comments are made from audio recordings. As in other selective verbatim categories, the teacher records a discussion and, after class, he or she writes out all the student comments, noting the pattern of interaction and any other information considered relevant. Lessons characterized by one-word or short-phrase student responses can be easily done. Lessons with longer student comments are harder to record. When the teacher is interested only in predetermined types of student comments, specific categories such as (1) requests for information, (2) "off the subject" comments, (3) indication of feelings, and (4) student questions should be devised.

Data Analysis

Many of the questions asked in the data analysis section of the teacher question and teacher response material can be applied to student comments when responses or questions are being observed. Special attention should be directed to those students who are giving patterned responses. Does discussion cease after a particular student responds? Is one student usually "off the subject"? Is a particular student able to get the teacher "off the subject"?

Also, student talk can be usefully analyzed with any number of analytical schemes derived from specific models of instruction or models of thinking. For instance, a teacher might analyze student comments following the Taba–Piaget[1] framework, which seeks to classify student thought.

THE TABA–PIAGET FRAMEWORK FOR CLASSIFYING
VERBAL THOUGHT PATTERNS

Description of Student Comment	*Classification of Thought*
1. Specific information is sought with no demand for any action other than presentation.	Seeks information
2. Specific facts are given — mostly one-word answers, dates, unexplained data, lists, etc.	Gives information
3. Naming, classifying, categorizing, and grouping of information is sought.	Seeks labels and groups
4. Specific facts are classified, categorized, or grouped.	Gives labels and groups
5. Requests for responses that explain or organize data already known.	Seeks interrelationships
6. Explanations or organization of information already presented.	Gives interrelationships
7. Asks for comparisons, contrasts, consequences, etc. which demand inclusion of information not already stated.	Seeks inferences and generalizations
8. Provides (specifically or through implications) comparisons, contrasts, consequences, principles, generalizations, etc.	Gives inferences and generalizations
9. Requests to apply known information to situations in order to predict events, outcomes, etc.	Seeks predictions and hypotheses
10. Use of information and deduction to predict unknown facts, events, actions, etc.	Gives predictions and hypotheses

Sample Data

Exhibit 10 is a verbatim transcript of student talk during a fourth grade discussion of the effect technology had on Indians and American pioneers.

EXHIBIT 10   Student Talk About Effect of Technology on Indians and American Pioneers

Noah	1. Well, the tools the rancheros had they got later probably and they made some of their own.
T	
Bruce	2. They both used strips of rawhide to tie pieces of wood together because they didn't have nails.
Richard	3. At the beginning of those two periods I think the missions had more/ because when they started the new missions, the missionaries and the people in Mexico, I don't know.
T	
Richard	4. Spain.
T	
Richard	5. They brought tools for the padres to build the missions.
T	
Claudia	6. They couldn't bring that many out there. Later on . . . they could bring . . .

T		
Sarah	7.	The missions and the padres got tools from the traders.
T		
Jeff	8.	The ranchos had lots of tools, too, because for their cattle they needed branding irons, riotos, and knives . . . and things like that.
T		
Richard	9.	Well, the Indians working at the missions also built some primitive tools
	10.	too. / Later the rancheros might have got some idea how to build tools and maybe on their own they thought of ways of building better tools.
T		
Richard	11.	As time goes by, in that period they weren't as civilized as we are today. /
	12.	As periods go up they make better things.
T		
Leora	13.	Settlers?
T		
Leora	14.	Um.
T		
Ronald	15.	From the eastern . . .
T		
Ronald	16.	The mountains.
T		
Ross	17.	I was going to say that in the ranchos they probably had better tools /
	18.	because more people were coming into them from Spain with things to
	19.	the presidios / and the ranchos started with soldiers coming from the presidios and so they probably brought tools and things from there to start their ranchos with.
T		
Richard	20.	The mission men had more tools / The ranchos had tools but they weren't
	21.	as interested. They were interested in crops but not as much as the missions and they needed a lot of tools, but I don't think quite as much as the missions.
T		
Carrie	22.	In the houses of the missions and ranchos, they would make theirs out of
	23.	adobe bricks / but the missions would make it in greater number of things and different shapes than the ranchos would be because ranchos have to be small and they would be making it in greater numbers.
T		
John	24.	Well, I think there would be little.
T		
John	25.	I don't think there was really. In the mission days I think they used pack mules to carry things in and in the rancho days they used oxen to carry caretos and they were pulled by mules.
T		
Scott	26.	I disagree with John that the caretos were pulled by oxen.
T		
Chris	27.	The horses were used.
T		
Jay	28.	Probably used in the missions too.
T		
Julie	29.	The El Camino Real.
T		
Julie	30.	By foot, usually.
T		
Julie	31.	Mules.
T		
Julie	32.	They used horses more in the rancho period than in the mission days.
T		
Frank	33.	Well, in the rancho period, all the people on the ranchos — they had a lot more skill than the people in the missions because well, like one guy — he had a full glass of water and he had it on a tray and he'd go full speed on a horse and he'd stop and no water would spill out.

T
Richie   34. Well, at the missions, weren't they more interested in teaching the Indians how to plant than teaching them skill in horses? They were interested really in building the mission up and teaching the Indians work, so they weren't so interested in horses and having fun. At the rancho, they already had the houses built so they wanted to have maybe a hobby and in the missions they more wanted to teach Indians and work and build up.

T
Jay   35. In the book that I was looking at, they, the rancheros, didn't like to go on foot. They, like the Spanish, the ranchero had a favorite horse called a cavalier and he took great pride in his own horse, his favorite horse, and he always had a horse out early to ride and he didn't like to walk.

Your Turn

ANALYZING STUDENT TALK

Using the suggested framework, analyze the student comments in Exhibit 10.

1. Without regard to the category of comments, count the number of:

   (a) Student seeks _____

   (b) Student gives _____

2. Without regard to seeking or giving, count the number of times the student said something within each of the following categories:*

   (a) Information _____

   (b) Names, groups, and labels _____

   (c) Interrelationships _____

   (d) Inferences and generalizations _____

   (e) Predictions and hypotheses _____

* Decide what category best describes each student comment and place that number in the margin.

ANSWER KEY

Your Turn: Analyzing Student Talk

1. (a) 1
   (b) 28
2. (a) 18 (4, 6, 7, 9, 13, 15, 16, 17, 20, 22, 24, 26, 27, 28, 29, 30, 31, 35)

(b) —
(c) 10 (1, 2, 3, 5, 8, 10, 18, 25, 32, 33)
(d) 5 (11, 19, 21, 23, 34)
(e) 1 (12)

Mastery Test

OBJECTIVE 5   To record and analyze student talk using selected verbatim data.

Write out an analysis of Exhibit 10 using the following questions as the basis for your work:

1. How many students talked?

_____

_____

2. Did some individuals dominate the discussion? (Sex, race, section of the room, or other descriptors could be substituted for "individuals" in this question.)

_____

_____

_____

_____

3. Were the comments questions or statements? factual or emotional? Or did they have some other common characteristics?

_____

_____

_____

_____

4. Were the comments all at one level of thought?

_____

_____

_____

_____

ANSWER KEY

Mastery Test, Objective 5

1. 17 students talked 29 times (25 students were in class).
2. No particular individuals or characteristics dominated the discussion except that only 5 of the 17 students who talked were female. Richard talked 6 of 29 times. Julie talked 4 times. All who talked did so once or twice.
3. Most student comments were factual statements giving additional data to previous work or interpreting what was already stated. One question was asked, apparently for clarification, by Leora.
4. Using the suggested framework for classifying student thought, most student comments were informational or interpretative. Some comments were inferential or predictive.

LEARNING ACTIVITY 5.2

Use the recording you made for Learning Activity 2.2 or tape-record another discussion. Record all the student comments on paper. Analyze the comments as suggested on page 376.

Objective 6

To record and analyze classroom physical movement data.

LEARNING ACTIVITY 6

Observation techniques that record the visible physical movements of both the teacher and the students during a lesson can prove to be very useful to teachers who want additional information about their behavior, as well as their students' behavior, during a classroom activity. There are as many ways to collect these data as there are observers and teachers. Three different versions, each requiring an observer or a wide-angle video, are illustrated in this chapter.

Data Collection

Technique 1.* An observer sits in an advantageous location in the room and draws a pencil representation of the classroom on a pad of paper. Using a legend like the one suggested below or different colored pencils, the observer records the movement of the teacher and appropriate (as defined by the teacher) student movement. In addition, it is often valuable to record which students have conferences with the teacher. Exhibit 11 is an example of this technique, which can be used in any classroom activity where movement is predicted.

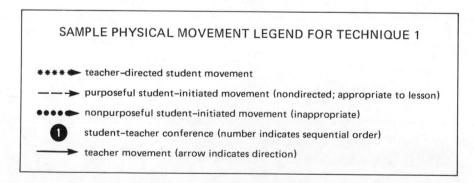

SAMPLE PHYSICAL MOVEMENT LEGEND FOR TECHNIQUE 1

∗∗∗∗➤ teacher–directed student movement

— —➤ purposeful student–initiated movement (nondirected; appropriate to lesson)

●●●●➤ nonpurposeful student–initiated movement (inappropriate)

❶ student–teacher conference (number indicates sequential order)

——➤ teacher movement (arrow indicates direction)

Technique 2. This technique, illustrated in Exhibit 12, is most often used during directed study activities where students are seated individually. Rather than "cluttering up" a seating chart with arrows, lines, and dashes, the observer merely records the teacher's movements by indicating the sequential nature of the conferences.

---

* Use Technique 2 or 3 in any situation where considerable teacher movement is expected.

After work begins, the first conference a teacher has is indicated as **1** 10:57, the second as **2** 10:58, the third as **3** 11:00, etc. The indication is done within the box representing a specific student. An experienced observer will also record in anecdotal form the movements and overt behaviors of students.

Technique 3. This technique is useful when the teacher wants data on classroom traffic and expects a variety of "moves" on his or her part. Exhibit 13 illustrates this technique. In the sample shown, the teacher had four groups "digging through" a pile of newspapers looking for data on the Watergate episode. At intervals a group recorder reported these data to the teacher, who was building a people-and-events flow chart on the chalkboard. The observer drew a representation of the room on one pad and recorded the different *locations* of the teacher each time the teacher changed his or her behavior — either verbal or nonverbal. On another pad the observer wrote a brief narrative description of what the teacher said or did as well as the interaction patterns with each small group.

Data Analysis

Since there is no universally accepted standard of behavior for teacher movement in the classroom, it is easy to relate actual teacher behavior to teacher expectations. The teacher should analyze the data with a number of questions in mind, such as:

1. Was an area of the classroom or a specific student systematically ignored as the teacher moved about the classroom?
2. Were the students who received most of the teacher's attention given undue recognition?
3. Was there a pattern to the teacher's or the students' movements that might be beneficial (i.e., worth repeating) or detrimental (i.e., worth eliminating).
4. How does teacher activity relate to the teacher's instructional goals?
5. How could "results" have been improved through changes in the teacher's or the students' physical behavior?
6. Were these data descriptive of today's behavior only or representative of the "usual" behavior of this teacher?

Sample Data

Exhibit 11 describes a fourth grade individualized study session. Exhibit 12 describes the teacher's movement in a sixth grade social studies work session. Exhibit 13 was made in a high school modern problems class.

For each exhibit (1) read the data through completely; (2) notice the differences between the three techniques; (3) reread each one asking yourself the questions above; and (4) summarize your thoughts about physical movement.

EXHIBIT 11   Observation of Physical Movement Data Using Technique 1

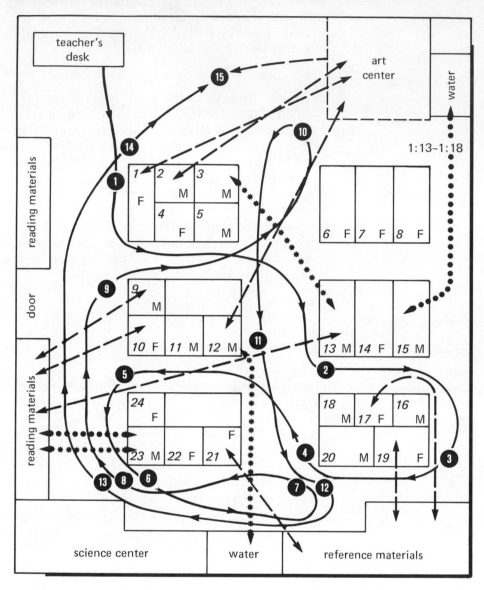

LEGEND

✱✱✱✱➡   teacher–directed student movement

– – –➤   purposeful student–initiated movement (nondirected; appropriate to lesson

●●●●➡   nonpurposeful student–initiated movement (inappropriate)

①   student–teacher conference (number indicates sequential order)

———➤   teacher movement (arrow indicates direction)

EXHIBIT 12   Observation of Physical Movement Data Using Technique 2

6 (28)	X	X	Goes to T at 11:15 (8) (12) (23) 11:13 *26*	X	X
10:57 Asks for help and raises his hand 11:02 Says "Mr. Meyer" 11:08 Pounds on wall (16) 11:08 (33) 11:21	X	*12*	Raises hand at 10:11 (7) 11:00 (11) 11:03 Susan	(9) 11:02 Keith	Raises hand 11:10 (10) 11:02 (24) 11:13 *25*
4	X	11:16 Gets up, walks around and sits down (4) *11*	(5) (6) *15*	Raises hand 11:08 Julie	X
3	X	X	X		*24* *19*
11:02 Raises hand *2* (17) 11:10	10:58 Goes to #4 until 11:02 11:06 Goes to #4; stops at #2 until 11:09 11:10 Goes to books in back until 11:20 *8* (18)	11:07 Gets a book from shelf in back (1) 10:57 (14) (26) 11:15 (19)(32)(29) Mike F.	11:02 Raises hand (13) 11:05 (22) (27) (30) Donna	11:14 Goes to book shelf *18*	X
Gives current events report 11:07 Gets up and stands to talk to #7 until 11:09 *7* Linda		(15) (31) Liz	Raises hand 11:08 Goes to T at 11:20 (2) (20) 11:10 Mike	Raises hand 11:07 (21) 11:11 *17*	11:15 Goes to book shelf 11:18 Returns to books 11:21 Goes again *3* (25) Martha

[T]

LEGEND

(1) teacher–student conference at the student's desk (number indicates sequential order)

X an absent student

10:57 time at which conference 1 took place

6 student 6 (used when names are unknown)

⌒ whispering between two students

EXHIBIT 13 Observation of Physical Movement Data Using Technique 3

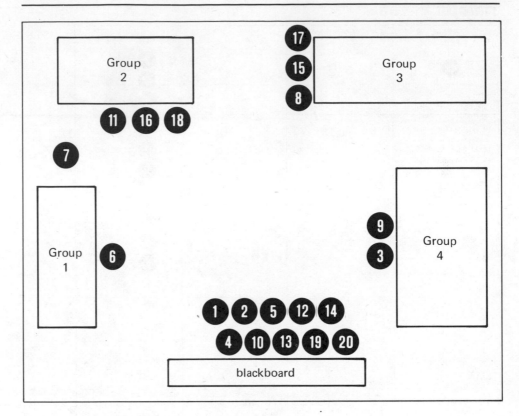

9:57	1. Directs a student who arrived late.
9:57	2. Reinstructs student #1 as to what Group 3 should do.
9:58	3. Reinstructs student #2 as to what Group 4 should do.
9:59	4. Writes line–staff diagram on board.
10:02	5. Surveys groups to see if they were working.
10:02	6. Asks Mike if he was taking notes.
10:03	7. Talks to student who arrived late.
10:04	8. Clarifies Egil Krogh role in Watergate break in to Group 3.
10:05	9. Circles room and stops at Group 4 to admonish them to go to work.
10:06	10. Returns to board and continues writing.
10:08	11. Goes to Group 2 and gets them working together.
10:09	12. Announces to class: I want one person to coordinate all the information gathered and bring it to me; another to keep reading and another to keep writing. I want four people, one from each group, to come to me. Within 5 minutes, I want a group report up here . . .
10:10	13. Returns to board.
10:11	14. Requests information from Group 4. Talks with students from Group 4, Group 3, and Group 1.
10:20	15. Goes to Group 3 and seeks reasons why they're not working. #19 continues with pictures, #18 puts head back on the desk, but others return to work.
	16. Goes to Group 2 and admonishes #4 who says, "When I read, no one listens." (She was right!) Four boys continue working; #4 and #5 continue other work.
10:23	17. Goes back to Group 3 and urges work.
10:23	18. Goes back to Group 2. Stops #5 from other work. She listens.
10:24	19. Returns to front of room to talk with students #1 and #2. Ignores #2 when #1 returns a minute later and interrupts #2 report (#2 reads *Newsweek* while waiting).
10:29	Returns to #2 report.
10:33	20. Okay, people, sit down. Grab a seat. We've got 5 minutes to go over it. What do we know so far? Summarizes information on board.

Mastery Test

OBJECTIVE 6   To record and analyze physical movement data.

1. An observer would use one of the physical movement observation techniques to gather what kinds of information about a classroom?

_____

_____

_____

2. **①   ②   ③   ④   ⑤** on a physical movement chart usually indicate _____

_____

3. Examine the physical movement observation chart below. Mark the statements that follow "T" for true and "F" for false.

_____ (a) The teacher talked with someone at this table three times during the lesson.

_____ (b) There were two interaction patterns in the discussion at this table.

_____ (c) The teacher's interactions with the students at this table were spread out throughout the lesson.

_____ (d) The data do not tell us why the teacher talked at one end of the table three times and only once at the other end.

4. One item which can be learned from physical movement data is whether or not the individuals who get attention are those who really need it (true or false).

5. Reexamine Exhibit 12 and write out your analysis using the questions in the Data Analysis section of this learning activity as a guideline.

_____

_____

_____

_____

_____

_____

_____

_____

_____

_____

_____

_____

_____

_____

ANSWER KEY
Mastery Test, Objective 6

1. An observer would use physical movement data to determine the traffic patterns of the teacher and the students, the degree to which various parts of the room are being used, the students who are getting attention as well as those who are not getting attention, and the "moves" (i.e., separate and discreet instructional activities that a teacher uses, etc.).

2. The sequential order of teacher moves or teacher "stops" for conferences with students are usually indicated by the use of a circle with a number inside. The location of the circle on the seating pattern indicates where the behavior occurred, while the number indicates sequential order of that behavior.

3. (a) F. The teacher stopped four times.
   (b) T. The arrows between the students indicate this.
   (c) T. The teacher's stops were the 7th, 16th, 18th, and the 21st of the lesson. (If this were an unusually long lesson or if the "stops" were rapid or slow, this might not be the case.)
   (d) T. No explanation is given.

4.   T. It doesn't tell you who needs help, but it can tell you whether or not those who need it actually get it.

5. Analysis of Exhibit 12:
   (a) The center two rows got most of the teacher's attention (9 and 13 stops). The side rows and the back corners (see student #5) were ignored.
   (b) Mike F. and Donna got more help than anyone else.
   (c) The teacher moved about the room well but did not help several students (#1, #5, #7, #11, #19, #24).
   (d) Questions 4 and 6 are not answerable from the data given.
   (e) The teacher might have attempted to predict which students would need specific help and to provide that help during the lesson.

Objective 7

To record and analyze shadowing data.

LEARNING ACTIVITY 7

Discipline, it is often said, is not the ability to control thirty students, but the ability to control one student. Many students will learn, will behave, will respond without regard to the behavior of a particular teacher. Unfortunately, most classroom groups have at least one student who does not behave, does not work, and does not respond. The "shadowing" observation technique was devised to provide information about those "problem" students who, for a variety of reasons, fail to live up to the expectations of the teacher.

Data Collection

The observer spends his or her entire time observing and gathering information about a targeted individual. Instead of the normal seating chart, the observer creates an exaggerated version, magnifying the importance of the target person and diminishing the importance of his or her neighbors (see Exhibits 14 and 15; a box is used for the target person and "X" is used for each of the other persons). The observer records comments, movements, behaviors, and reactions as they occur and change during the activity. The behaviors of others as they relate to the targeted individual are also recorded, as are the time, group activities, and patterns of behavior.

The following list summarizes the steps for collecting shadowing data.

1. Select the individual to be observed.
2. Draw exaggerated seating chart (see Exhibits 14 and 15).
3. Sit where the targeted individual can be easily observed.
4. Describe each physical and verbal change of behavior.
5. Describe verbal and physical behaviors of key others (instructor, neighbor, etc.), if appropriate, vis-á-vis the target.
6. Analyze the data.

Data Analysis

The data themselves usually generate questions for analysis. For example, someone examining Exhibits 14 and 15 might be led to question whether or not visible classroom activities (e.g., movement and talk patterns) or physical arrangements (e.g., seating) cause or influence the targeted student's behavior. This is the most common use of shadowing. Questions useful in the analysis of this type of data include:

1. Was the problem real or imagined?
2. Did the targeted student, the instructor, or others exhibit patterned behavior?
3. Could the targeted student's behavior be improved by changing his or her role, role relationships, desk location, the behavior of others, etc.?
4. Does the targeted student have a particular posture, movement, or behavior that precedes misbehavior?
5. Does the targeted student respond to criticism? attention? being ignored?
6. What precipitated unrequested changes in behavior?

Sample Data

The data for Exhibit 14 were obtained in a seventh grade classroom in a Florida middle school. The student being shadowed was a persistent problem for his teacher. Exhibit 15 data were collected in an upper elementary classroom. The targeted individual worked in spurts — he'd work a while, talk and disrupt for a time, and then return to work.

For each exhibit (1) read the data through completely; (2) reread the data using the questions above; and (3) summarize your thoughts on shadowing.

EXHIBIT 14 Shadowing Data from a Seventh Grade Classroom

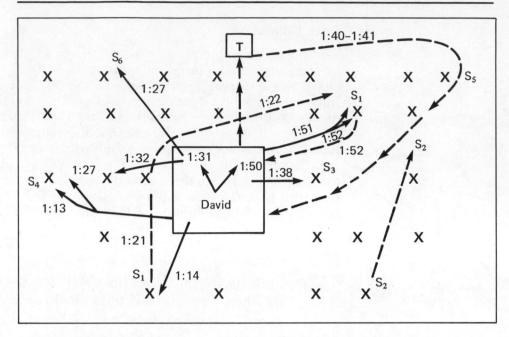

Problem Student (David)	Teacher and Topics
1:17 Head on desk, examining baseball glove.	Discussing divorce rates.
1:20 Laughs exaggeratedly at Group Life joke.	
1:21 S_1 moves his desk to right of David.	Says, "As I was saying, David," to get his attention and moves S_1 to another seat.
1:25 After remark, David remains quiet for 4 minutes, head on desk, examining glove.	
1:27 Begins to play with glove.	Begins group chairperson reports.
1:27 Makes a side remark about S_6's contribution.	Tells Joe not to talk to David.
1:31 Offers "a group of people living together" as a definition of a family.	
1:32 Comments quietly to girl on his left.	Criticizes David's talking.
1:32 Cheers with class at mention of Jews.	
1:32 Returns to head-down, glove-on position.	Discussion of pets as family members.
1:38 Talks to S_3 on his right.	Criticizes him for talking.
1:40 Jumps up and walks around when S_5's money falls.	"David, please sit down!"
1:41 Returns to seat, puts on glove, listens.	
1:44 Puts glove on head and looks around for reactions.	
1:48 Puts glove back on hand, head on desk (no one reacted). Sits quiet for roll call.	Begins roll call while a student passes out test papers.
1:50 Talks to S_1.	
1:50 Raises hand and yells "HERE" to get his paper.	
1:51 Talks to S_1.	
1:52 S_1 comes to him, hits him with a pencil. David complains loudly to anyone listening but does not retaliate.	

EXHIBIT 15 Shadowing Data from an Upper Elementary Classroom

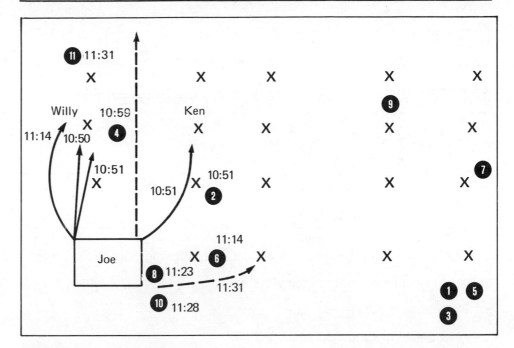

LEGEND

X   students in class

- - - →   student movement

──→   talk between students

●   conference between T and student indicated

2   sequential order of conferences

Student (Joe)	Teacher
10:45 Sitting quietly.	"Joe, turn around and pay attention!"
10:46 "Can we sit in groups? I want to write down what he's getting."	"No." (no response)
10:50 Asked Willy for paper and began doodling.	
10:51 Reprimanded by teacher.	"Don't you want to get to work, Joe?"
10:51 "I can't see the paper."	
10:51 Asked Ken "What chapter?" Talked over assignment with Willy.	
10:54 Began working on assignment (reading but not writing).	
10:59 Stopped reading when T came to respond to ??? of Willy.	
11:00 Return to reading and occasional writing.	
11:14 "Do you want us to . . . ?"	(couldn't hear response)
11:14 Talked to Willy. Complained to T about Willy.	
11:16 Talked with T.	(couldn't hear)
11:23 "I am done with what I'm going to do."	"Do your work!!"
11:28 "Is that in Section 1?"	"If you did your work you'd know!"
11:31 Slid over to talk with girl who came late.	

Mastery Test

OBJECTIVE 7 — To record and analyze shadowing data.

1. What kind of information is shadowing designed to provide?

   _____

   _____

   _____

2. Put the following procedures for collecting shadowing data in sequential order.

   (a) Sit where necessary in the classroom.   _____

   (b) Analyze the collected data.   _____

   (c) Draw an exaggerated seating chart.   _____

   (d) Describe the verbal and physical behavior of "key" others vis-á-vis the
       target student.   _____

   (e) Select the target student.   _____

   (f) Describe each physical and verbal change of behavior of the target
       student during the time allotted.   _____

3. List three questions which you might ask yourself if you were analyzing shadowing data.

   (a) _____

   (b) _____

   (c) _____

4. Write out your analysis of Exhibit 15, using the questions in the section on Data Analysis as guidelines.

   _____

   _____

   _____

   _____

   _____

   _____

   _____

   _____

   _____

   _____

ANSWER KEY

Mastery Test, Objective 7

1. Shadowing is a technique designed to provide information about problem students. Its purpose is to provide a word picture of everything a specific individual says and does during the course of the observation.

2. (a) 3   (b) 6   (c) 2   (d) 5   (e) 1   (f) 4

3. You might have asked any three of the following questions:
   (a) Was the problem real or imagined?
   (b) Did the individual, the instructor, or others exhibit patterned behavior?
   (c) Could the targeted student's behavior be improved by changing his or her role, role relationships, desk location, the behavior of others, etc.?
   (d) Does the individual have a particular posture, movement, or behavior that precedes misbehavior?
   (e) Does the individual respond to criticism? attention? being ignored?
   (f) What precipitated unrequested changes in behavior?

4. (a) The data verify that a problem exists. The student behaved as follows:

Worked	Didn't work
10:45	10:46
10:46–10:50	10:50–10:54
10:54–10:59	10:59
11:00–11:14	11:14
11:15	11:16
11:16–11:23	11:23
11:23–11:28	11:28
11:28–11:31	11:31

   (b) Yes, the student did exhibit patterned behavior. Most of the times when he wasn't working the teacher was nearby.
   (c) Several alternatives could be hypothesized for improving the targeted student's behavior:
      (1) The teacher might stay away from him as much as possible.
      (2) The teacher might quietly give him verbal/nonverbal attention *before* doing other work near him.
      (3) The teacher could ignore his misbehavior, hoping it will go away.
      (4) The teacher could make him aware of his behavior.
   (d) No.
   (e) Data unavailable.
   (f) When the teacher was nearby, the student stopped working.

DESCRIPTIVE DATA

Descriptive data, you will recall from the beginning of the chapter, are data that have been organized, categorized, or compiled by an observer but do not involve a value judgment. Whereas selected data record the specific words, statements, and nonverbal reactions of teachers, students, or groups, descriptive data categorize and organize behavior without trying to preserve it in visible or audible form. Descriptive data can be collected in the classroom setting from tape recordings or from selected data itself.

Three types of descriptive data will be discussed in this section: (1) verbal flow, (2) class response, and (3) task orientation data.

Objective 8

To record and analyze classroom verbal flow using descriptive data.

LEARNING ACTIVITY 8

Teachers must be aware of the verbal and physical interaction patterns in their classrooms. A verbal-flow chart is one way of studying such interaction. Verbal flow is defined as the verbal behavior of students observable during a classroom discussion. This observation technique categorizes and records verbal behavior using a set of symbols that represent the descriptive categories.

Data Collection

1. Select an individual or individuals to be observed.
2. Select an appropriate system of arrows and symbols to be used.
3. Sit where you can note who is talking during a discussion.
4. Using the appropriate arrow or symbol, indicate on the seating chart each time someone speaks.
5. Analyze the data.

A verbal-flow chart simply reflects the involvement of different individuals in a discussion. The basic form for the chart is a representation of the seating pattern (see Exhibit 16). Because seating patterns may take many forms, the observer should probably create the seating chart on a blank pad for each observation, rather than relying on any standard form. The observer can record characteristics such as male, female, socioeconomic background, ethnic or cultural differences . . . in short, any characteristics that might differentiate one individual from another.

Arrows are used as a basic symbol to indicate the categories of behavior. Social comments made between students *not* for the benefit of the entire class and *not* within the context of the ongoing discussion are indicated by a curved tie between two students. Repetition of those social ties can be indicated by a cross bar representative of each repetition, or by recording the time during which they took place. Additional subscripts and other marks can be used to reflect other categories of responses made by individual students. Symbols and categories may be created in response to an expressed need by the teacher for such additional information. For instance, the observer might keep track of when various students responded. This is done by recording either a time or a sequential number next to the arrow. Such data might show that the teacher relies on different students in an obvious pattern, or at different times during a lesson.

A precaution about the data obtained with this technique is in order. A single observation of verbal flow in a classroom discussion is insufficient to use as a basis for drastic changes in behavior. There is no reason to be concerned about how a teacher deals with the front of the room as compared to the back of the room if, on succeeding days, the pattern is reversed. Similarly, there is no reason to be concerned about the difference between the ways males are treated as opposed to females if the pattern is reversed on other days or if, in fact, there is no pattern at all and we *happen to catch one of a continuing series of random treatments.*

Data Analysis

The questions below, as well as those asked earlier in the chapter, can be used to analyze verbal flow data (see questions in the Data Analysis sections of Learning Activities 2.1, 3.1, and 6).

1. How many talked? Who did and who did not?
2. Was there an observable difference between talkers and non-talkers by sex, race, seating pattern, whispering, and/or achievement?
3. Was there an observable difference among those who were directed to respond? those who always gave correct responses and those who gave irrelevant responses? (Use same descriptors as above.)
4. Did an individual or a small group dominate?
5. How did responses differ? statements? questions, etc.?

Sample Data

Exhibit 16 data were collected during an elementary science lesson. Exhibit 17 data were observed in a junior high school home economics discussion.

For each exhibit (1) read the data, familiarizing yourself with the symbols; (2) analyze the data using the above questions; and (3) summarize your thoughts about verbal flow.

EXHIBIT 16   Verbal–Flow Chart of an Elementary Science Lesson

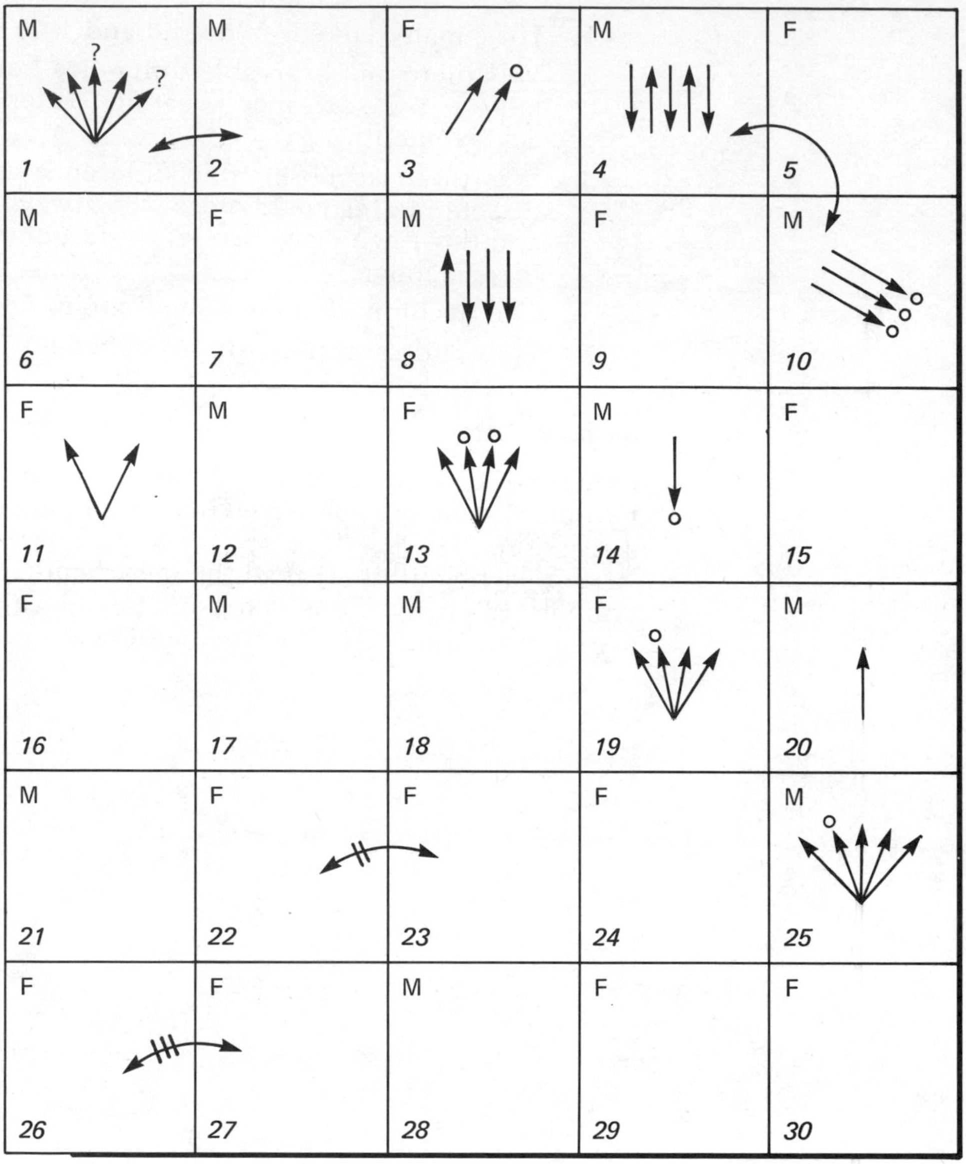

LEGEND

M Male   **F** Female

Student volunteered a relevant or correct response.

Student volunteered an irrelevant or incorrect response.

Student volunteered a question about content.

Student responded to a teacher question appropriately.

Student responded to a teacher question inappropriately.

Students connected by line talked to each other without the teacher's permission.

Student talked to his or her neighbor without permission.

Student talked to his or her neighbor four times without permission.

Student responded to teacher questions five times.

Student volunteered responses five times — one was a question; one was irrelevant or incorrect; three were relevant or correct.

Chapter 9 Observation Skills 395

EXHIBIT 17 Verbal–Flow Chart of a Junior High School Home Economics Discussion

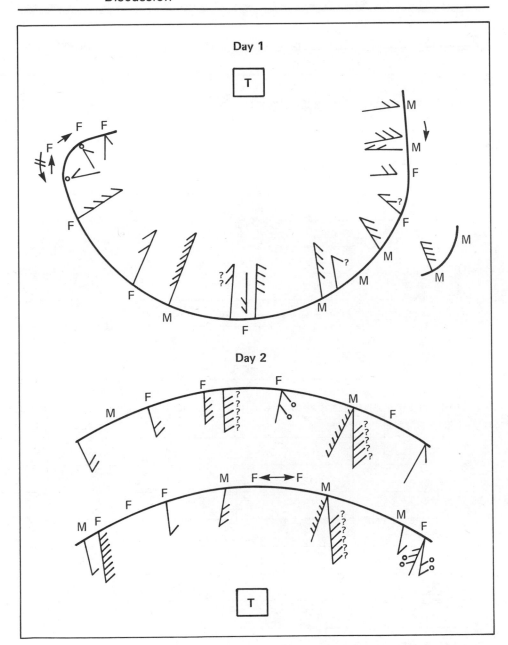

Mastery Test

OBJECTIVE 8   To record and analyze classroom verbal flow using descriptive data.

1. Provide a definition for each symbol listed below.

(a)   **M** _____

(b)   **F** _____

(c)   _____

(d)   _____

(e)   _____

(f)   _____

(g)   _____

(h)   _____

(i)   _____

(j)   _____

2. Write out an analysis of Exhibit 16 using the questions from the Data Analysis section.

_____

_____

_____

_____

_____

_____

_____

_____

_____

_____

_____

_____

_____

_____

_____

ANSWER KEY

Mastery Test, Objective 8

1. (a) Male.
   (b) Female.
   (c) Student volunteered a relevant or correct response.
   (d) Student volunteered an irrelevant or incorrect response.
   (e) Student volunteered a question.
   (f) Student responded to a teacher question appropriately.
   (g) Student responded to a teacher question inappropriately.
   (h) Students connected by line talked to each other without the teacher's permission.
   (i) Student responded to teacher questions three times.
   (j) Student volunteered responses four times: once with a question; once with irrelevant or incorrect information.

2. Analysis of Exhibit 16:
   (a) Eleven students (out of 30) talked a total of 36 times. Four pairs of two students each talked to each other in an inappropriate manner.
   (b) Data not available about most of the descriptors except for:
      (1) Seating pattern: Contributors to the discussion sat in the front three rows rather than the back and the right two rows rather than the left two rows. (It's always interesting to speculate whether a pattern like this results from learned behavior on the students' part or from some other source.)
      (2) Whispering: Of the seven instances of whispering, five were by noninvolved students.
   (c) Only boys were directed to respond. No female was told to respond. Those who did, did so at their own discretion. Student 10 is noteworthy for responding to the teacher's questions inappropriately.
   (d) No student dominated; however, the front and right parts of the room dominated. The most talkative student only spoke five times.
   (e) Data unavailable except that, of the 36 comments by students, only two were questions.

Objective 9

To record and analyze classroom response behavior using descriptive data.

LEARNING ACTIVITY 9

One of the keys to efficient learning is accurate feedback regarding current behavior. To be able to view your responses in realistic (data-based) terms not only helps identify directions for future learning but can also provide the motivational impetus to initiate that learning. Thus, it is incumbent on teachers to help students gather as much information about themselves as possible. Students are continuously providing feedback about themselves, even while instructors are busy sending messages to them. This data collection technique enables an observer to interpret some of those messages and provide some of that feedback.

Data Collection

1. Decide upon the situation to be observed.
2. Select the individual or individuals to be observed.
3. Select an appropriate legend to be used.

4. Sit where necessary to collect data.
5. Write appropriate letter and/or symbol on the seating chart as behavior is exhibited.
6. Analyze the data.

The observer, in a planning conference with the teacher, must determine what types (categories) of response are to be studied. The observer records on a seating chart the behavior of each individual within those categories. Exhibit 18 records seven categories of student response, while Exhibit 19 records seven categories of teacher response. Other categories of response behavior that have been observed in classrooms are: student thought levels, nonverbal communication, negative interaction, and student choices. The most difficult aspect of this data collection technique is the agreement necessary between the teacher and the observer prior to the observation so that the data collected are both accurate and significant.

Data Analysis

The analysis of classroom response data usually revolves around (1) the differences between individual students' response patterns and (2) the differences between expected and actual response patterns. Once existing patterns have been discovered, the teacher must ask the question "So what?" What is the significance of these patterns in terms of future planning and classroom interaction?

It is not possible to provide a predetermined list of questions appropriate to all classroom response studies. The particular type of response being studied determines the questions that must be asked. A few suggestions follow:

1. Questions similar to those from the Data Analysis sections in Learning Activities 2.1 and 8 would be useful in analyzing how students respond to teacher questions or teacher direction.
2. Questions derived from those in the Data Analysis sections of Learning Activities 3.1, 4.1, 5.1, and 6 would be useful in analyzing student talk data.
3. Prior to teaching a lesson, try to predict how the data will look when collected. During analysis compare the actual data with the predictions.
4. Use the questions from the Data Analysis section in Learning Activity 5.1 as a general guide for analysis in addition to specific questions that are aimed at specific categories of response.

Sample Data

Exhibits 18 (student response) and 19 (teacher response) are examples of data collected while classroom discussions were taking place. Exhibit 18 illustrates the nature of student response to teacher questions. Exhibit 19 has *exactly* the same data as is contained in Exhibit 7. So, besides serving as an exhibit of teacher response using descriptive data, it also serves as a good illustration of the difference between selected data (Exhibit 7) and descriptive data (Exhibit 19).

For each exhibit (1) read the data through completely; (2) reread Exhibit 18 (student response) using the questions from the Data Analysis section of Learning Activity 7 as a guideline for analysis; (3) reread Exhibit 19 (teacher response) using the questions from the Data Analysis section of Learning Activity 3.1 as a guideline for analysis; (4) compare the information obtained in Exhibit 7 with the information obtained in Exhibit 19; and (5) summarize your thoughts on class response data.

EXHIBIT 18   Student Responses in a Classroom Discussion Using Descriptive Data

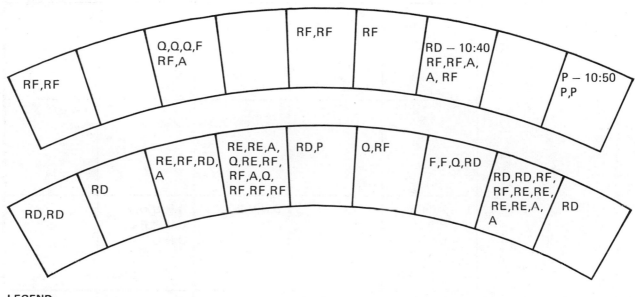

LEGEND

RD   directed to respond to teacher questions
RF   responded freely to teacher questions
A   added to comment of previous student
Q   questioned for information
P   asked procedural question
F   expressed or sought feelings
RE   expanded beyond scope of teacher questions

EXHIBIT 19 Teacher Responses in a Rural High School Using
Descriptive Data for Analysis of Praise

P,P		R,C,C,P,U		U
P	C,C,C Kim		P	
		P,R,I,R		N,N,R
D,R,P,P,R,I, U,P,R,R,U, P,R,R,U Mary		D,N,N,R	D,R,U,U,N, U,U,R,R,D, D,N,U Diane	
D	X	X	P	D

LEGEND

P	praised	**D**	directed to do something
U	idea acknowledged and used	**R**	repeated
I	questioned for information	**N**	teacher changes subject
C	criticized	**X**	an absent student

Mastery Test

OBJECTIVE 9   To record and analyze classroom response behavior using descriptive data.

1. If the observer were recording data concerning the nature of a teacher's response to student comments, what would the following symbols mean?

   (a) N _____

   (b) I _____

   (c) P _____

(d) R _____

(e) U _____

(f) D _____

(g) C _____

2. If you were to use classroom response to observe a teacher's nonverbal responses, what legend would you create?

_____

_____

_____

_____

_____

ANSWER KEY
Mastery Test, Objective 9

1. (a) Teacher changes subject.
   (b) Questioned for information.
   (c) Praised.
   (d) Repeated.
   (e) Idea acknowledged and used.
   (f) Directed to do something.
   (g) Criticized.

2. Any number of legends might be created for this purpose, depending upon the exact nature of the information sought. One of them might look like the following:

G The teacher made a physical gesture toward the student.

S The teacher was obviously pleased with the response and showed it with a smile, grin, etc.

F The teacher was obviously not pleased with the response and showed it with a frown, scowl, etc.

N The teacher made no nonverbal response.

Objective 10

To record and analyze task orientation behavior using descriptive data.

LEARNING ACTIVITY 10

This last descriptive technique was developed in the 1960s as a result of studies at Stanford University. The system used a 35-mm time-lapse camera. From the front corner of the room the camera took a picture of the room every 90 seconds using a wide-angle lens. In the course of a 30-minute discussion, the observer was provided with 20 enlarged pictures showing all the occupants of the room at given moments during the discussion. The observer could then cut up each picture so that he or she had 20 sets of pictures of individual behavior during a discussion.

A variety of results was obtained. Some picture sets looked like the films formerly shown in nickelodeons, where individuals gradually moved from a position of sitting erect in their chairs to a position of sleeping with their heads on their hands, back to a position of sitting and looking attentive. Other collections showed individuals working feverishly on matters that had nothing to do with the task at hand, talking to their neighbors, being vacant from their seats, or engaging in a variety of actions which could be regarded as inappropriate.

The data obtained from the pictures were quite valuable for understanding individual students. The method of collecting data was demanding, expensive, and time-consuming, so experiments were conducted with alternative methods as well. Ultimately, a paper-and-pencil means was developed by the author that provided much the same data as the 35-mm camera. This paper-and-pencil technique has come to be known as "at task."

The intent of an "at task" observation is to provide data that indicate whether or not individuals were engaged in the task or tasks thought to be appropriate for a given activity. Before an observer can use this technique, he or she must be acquainted with what is expected during a given activity. In those activities where one task is expected of all students, there is no observation problem; but in activities calling for a variety of tasks, some preparation is necessary before the observer can use this technique.

"At task" has often been used in public school settings to assess the extent to which students are engaged in expected behavior. When used in that way, a sample legend might contain (see Exhibit 20):

SAMPLE "AT TASK" LEGEND

```
A  at task
B  stalling
C  other work (productive; program-related)
D  out of seat
E  talking
F  other work (non-program-related)
```

An alternative version of "at task" has been developed that focuses entirely on appropriate behaviors exhibited with little attention to inappropriate behavior. (Appropriateness is a judgment one can make later, if desired, when analyzing the data.) Examples of this alternate version can be found in Exhibits 21 and 22.

ALTERNATIVE VERSION OF "AT TASK" LEGEND

Exhibit 21

```
L   listening
N   taking notes
R+  class-related reading
R−  non-class-related reading
T   non-class-related talking
G   out of room
M   miscellaneous other
```

ALTERNATIVE VERSION OF "AT TASK" LEGEND

Exhibit 22	
A	working with manual
B	viewing filmstrip
C	working in "lab"
D	taking assessment measures
E	getting instructor assistance
F	at computer terminal
G_1	not working
G_2	on break
G_3	out of room
H	requesting assistance

Data Collection

At task can be used to provide data about the task orientation/task attentiveness of individuals. It can be used with a videotape replay but, more often than not, it is used by an observer with paper and pencil. The observer follows this sequence:

1. The observer becomes familiar with the variety of tasks that are possible and/or predictable.
2. The observer finds a position in the classroom that permits observation of everyone and eye contact with each.
3. The observer constructs a chart resembling the seating pattern of the group.
4. The observer indicates on the chart the name, sex, and/or identifying characteristics of each individual. (This is particularly important when individuals will be moving about the room.)
5. The observer systematically examines the behavior of each person for a few seconds in order to note the task he or she is engaged in. Using a legend* *created anew* for this particular situation, the observer writes the letter denoting the observed behavior in the box representing that individual. This procedure is repeated for each student.
6. The observer repeats step 5 at convenient time intervals (a trained observer can observe 20 individuals per minute) until he or she has several numbered and lettered observations noted in each box representing the various students (see Exhibits 20–22).

1	C	5	D
2	A	6	A
3	A	7	C
4	A	8	C

Three Precautions. First, remember that the observer is only making judgments about behavior — not about expressions, positions, etc. An individual being observed must be overtly exhibiting behavior that represents the category described. Second, (if "at task" is the

---

* Some legends will emphasize behaviors which are "at task," and others will want detailed "not at task" behavior data.

target) does the behavior being exhibited qualify as an appropriate behavior according to the teacher's definition for that lesson? That is, a student could be out of his seat and talking to his neighbor, but if he is completing the task and doing so within the limits set by the instructor, the observer will record "at task" in the box representing that student. What is important is *not* that he is talking to his neighbor, or that he is out of his seat, but that he is oriented to the task in a manner that the instructor considers acceptable. Third, an observer must be careful to use general categories of "at task" or "not at task" behaviors, so as not to dilute the power of the recording instrument. That is, an observer would seldom have more than ten categories of behavior in any one observation.

Data Analysis

Before at task data can be adequately analyzed, some summarizing is necessary. The observer should construct a matrix with the observed behaviors on the vertical axis and the times of observation on the horizontal one.

Categories	Time Periods 1 2 3 4 5 6 . . . 15
Working with manual	
Viewing filmstrip	
Requesting help	

The observer then tallies the total number of each observed behavior at a given time period. Exhibits 20, 21, and 22 are examples.

The data can then be analyzed in terms of:

1. The variety of behaviors exhibited by the group.
2. The variety of behaviors exhibited by an individual.
3. The variety of behaviors exhibited at any one time.
4. The relationship between behaviors and planned activities.
5. The change of behaviors over time.

Sample Data

Exhibit 20 data were collected in a fourth grade classroom in Eugene, Oregon. Exhibit 21 data were collected in a lecture presentation to an advanced mathematics class. The data in Exhibit 22 were collected in an individualized computer-managed instructional program in a suburban Connecticut school.

For each exhibit (1) read the exhibit and the summary data which follow; (2) analyze the exhibit using the five suggestions above; and (3) summarize your thoughts on at task data.

EXHIBIT 20 At Task Analysis of Fourth Grade Art Class

1		2		3		4		5		6	
1-A	6-A	1-E	6-A	1-E	6-A	1-E	6-D	1-B	6-D	1-A	6-A
2-A	7-A	2-E	7-E	2-A	7-E	2-A	2-D	7-A	7-A	2-A	7-D
3-A	8-D	3-B	8-E	3-A	8-A	3-D	8-A	3-A	8-A	3-A	8-A
4-A	9-A	4-B	9-E	4-A	9-A	4-A	9-A	4-A	9-A	4-A	9-A
5-A	10-D	5-E	10-E	5-A	10-A	5-A	10-E	5-A	10-E	5-A	10-A
	11-D		11-E		11-D		11-E		11-D		11-A

7		8		9		10		11		12	
1-A	6-A	1-A	6-A	1-B	6-A	1-A	6-B	1-A	6-A	1-B	6-A
2-A	7-A	2-A	7-A	2-B	7-A	2-A	7-A	2-A	7-D	2-A	7-D
3-A	8-A	3-A	8-A	3-B	8-A	3-A	8-A	3-A	8-D	3-A	8-C
4-A	9-E	4-A	9-A	4-D	9-D	4-A	9-A	4-D	9-A	4-A	9-A
5-A	10-D	5-A	10-A	5-A	10-A	5-A	10-A	5-A	10-E	5-A	10-A
	11-E		11-A		11-A		11-A		11-F		11-A

13		14		15		16		17		18	
1-B	6-A	1-A	6-A	1-B	6-A	1-A	6-A	1-A	6-A	1-C	6-D
2-A	7-A	2-A	7-A	2-D	7-A	2-A	7-A	2-A	7-A	2-C	7-D
3-D	8-A	3-A	8-A	3-A	8-A	3-A	8-A	3-A	8-A	3-C	8-E
4-A	9-A	4-A	9-D	4-A	9-D	4-A	9-A	4-E	9-A	4-C	9-C
5-A	10-A	5-E	10-E	5-A	10-A	5-A	10-D	5-A	10-A	5-E	10-B
	11-A		11-A		11-D		11-A		11-D		11-D

19		20		21		22		23		24	
1-A	6-A	1-A	6-A	1-A	6-A	1-A	6-A	1-A	6-A	1-D	6-A
2-A	7-E	2-B	7-A	2-A	7-A	2-A	7-A	2-A	7-D	2-A	7-A
3-A	8-E	3-A	8-A	3-E	8-A	3-A	8-E	3-A	8-D	3-A	8-A
4-A	9-A	4-A	9-A	4-A	9-A	4-A	9-A	4-E	9-A	4-A	9-A
5-C	10-E	5-A	10-A	5-A	10-A	5-A	10-A	5-D	10-D	5-A	10-A
	11-E		11-A		11-A		11-A		11-F		11-A

25		26		27		28		29		30	
		1-C	6-D	1-A	6-A	1-A	6-A			1-A	6-A
		2-A	7-A	2-A	7-A	2-A	7-A			2-D	7-A
		3-A	8-A	3-D	8-E	3-A	8-E			3-A	8-A
		4-A	9-E	4-A	9-D	4-A	9-F			4-E	9-A
		5-A	10-A	5-A	10-A	5-A	10-F			5-A	10-A
			11-A		11-A		11-F				11-E

LEGEND

1	10:40	**5**	10:54	**9**	11:10	**A**	at task	**E**	talking to neighbors
2	10:44	**6**	10:58	**10**	11:14	**B**	stalling	**F**	other work (nonproductive)
3	10:48	**7**	11:02	**11**	11:20	**C**	other work (productive)	⟷	student–student conversation
4	10:51	**8**	11:06			**D**	out of seat		

	Times of Observation										
Categories	10:40	10:44	10:48	10:51	10:54	10:58	11:02	11:06	11:10	11:14	11:20
At task	17	21	21	21	23	23	21	18	19	16	14
Stalling	5	2	2	1	—	—	—	—	—	—	—
Other work (productive)	2	1	1	1	1	—	—	1	1	—	—
Out of seat	1	3	3	2	1	5	5	3	4	4	6
Talking	3	1	1	3	3	—	2	6	3	7	5
Other work (nonproductive)	—	—	—	—	—	—	—	—	1	1	3

EXHIBIT 21   At Task Analysis of Student Behavior in Lecture

1		*2*		*3*		*4*	
1–L	6–L	1–T	6–L	1–L	6–L	1–L	6–L
2–L	7–L	2–L	7–L	2–L	7–L	2–L	7–L
3–L	8–L	3–L	8–L	3–L	8–L	3–L	8–L
4–L	9–R+	4–L	9–L	4–L	9–L	4–L	9–R+
5–L	10–R–	5–L	10–L	5–L	10–L	5–L	10–R+

5		*6*		*7*		*8*	
1–N	6–L	1–L	6–L	1–L	6–L	1–L	6–L
2–L	7–L	2–L	7–L	2–L	7–L	2–L	7–L
3–L	8–L	3–L	8–N	3–L	8–L	3–L	8–L
4–L	9–R–	4–L	9–R+	4–L	9–R+	4–L	9–L
5–L	10–N	5–L	10–R+	5–L	10–R+	5–L	10–L

9		*10*		*11*			
1–L	6–L	1–T	6–N	1–L	6–L		
2–L	7–L	2–R–	7–L	2–L	7–L		
3–L	8–L	3–R–	8–G	3–L	8–L		
4–L	9–L	4–L	9–R+	4–L	9–R+		
5–L	10–N	5–L	10–L	5–L	10–N		

LEGEND

1	11:03	**6**	11:12	**L**	listening
2	11:05	**7**	11:14	**N**	taking notes
3	11:07	**8**	11:16	**R+**	reading (class–related)
4	11:08	**9**	11:18	**R–**	reading (non–class–related)
5	11:10	**10**	11:20	**T**	talking (non–class–related)
				G	out of room
				M	miscellaneous

					Time Periods					
Categories	1	2	3	4	5	6	7	8	9	10
L	8	10	10	⑪	⑪	10	⑪	9	4	④
N	1					①		1		3
R+									⑥	3
R–		①	①						1	1
T	②*									
G								①		
M										

* Student 10's behavior is circled.

Behavior Changes per Student

1.	2	5.	3	9.	1
2.	1	6.	2	10.	7
3.	0	7.	1	11.	2
4.	1	8.	0		

EXHIBIT 22 At Task Analysis of a Computer-Managed Class

1

1-A	6-A	11-D
2-A	7-B	12-D
3-B	8-B	13-D
4-B	9-B	14-G_3
5-A	10-A	15-G_2

9

1-A	6-A	11-D
2-A	7-A	12-F
3-A	8-D	13-F
4-A	9-D	14-F
5-E	10-15	15-G_2

15

1-A	6-G	11-B
2-H	7-G	12-B
3-H	8-A	13-B
4-G	9-A	14-A
5-G	10-B	15-A

21

1-F	6-A	11-C
2-F	7-A	12-A
3-A	8-B	13-A
4-A	9-B	14-A
5-A	10-C	15-G_2

2

1-A	6-G_3	11-F
2-A	7-D	12-A
3-D	8-D	13-A
4-D	9-F	14-A
5-G_3	10-F	15-A

10

1-F	6-A	11-G_2
2-F	7-A	12-A
3-F	8-A	13-A
4-G_3	9-G_2	14-A
5-G_3	10-G_2	15-A

16

22

1-G_3	6-D	11-G_2
2-A	7-F	12-G_2
3-A	8-F	13-A
4-A	9-F	14-A
5-D	10-G_2	15-G_3

3

1-H	6-B	11-D
2-H	7-B	12-D
3-H	8-A	13-D
4-E	9-A	14-F
5-B	10-A	15-F

11

1-A	6-A	11-A
2-A	7-A	12-A
3-A	8-A	13-A
4-A	9-A	14-A
5-A	6-A	15-A

17

1-G_1	6-A	11-G_1
2-G_1	7-A	12-G_1
3-G_1	8-B	13-G_1
4-G_1	9-B	14-A
5-A	10-B	15-A

23

1-G_2	6-F	11-H
2-G_2	7-A	12-E
3-D	8-A	13-A
4-D	9-G_1	14-A
5-D	10-G_1	15-A

4

1-G_3	6-A	11-C
2-G_3	7-A	12-C
3-G_3	8-A	13-G_2
4-G_3	9-A	14-G_2
5-G_3	10-A	15-G_2

12

1-B	6-C	11-A
2-B	7-C	12-A
3-B	8-C	13-A
4-C	9-A	14-A
5-C	10-A	15-E

18

1-B	6-F	11-A
2-B	7-A	12-G_2
3-D	8-A	13-G_2
4-D	9-A	14-G_1
5-D	10-A	15-A

24

1-A	6-A	11-A
2-A	7-A	12-A
3-A	8-G_1	13-C
4-G_1	9-G_1	14-C
5-A	10-A	15-C

5

1-B	6-E	11-D
2-B	7-A	12-D
3-C	8-A	13-G_2
4-C	9-A	13-G_2
5-C	10-D	15-G_2

13

19

1-H	6-G_1	11-A
2-E	7-H	12-C
3-A	8-E	13-E
4-A	9-A	14-C
5-A	10-A	15-C

25

1-E	6-A	11-A
2-A	7-H	12-E
3-E	8-E	13-G_2
4-E	9-B	14-E
5-A	10-B	15-A

6

1-E	6-G_1	11-B
2-A	7-A	12-E
3-A	8-A	13-A
4-A	9-B	14-G_1
5-G_1	10-B	15-A

14

1-A	6-F	11-C
2-A	7-E	12-C
3-A	8-B	13-D
4-D	9-B	14-D
5-D	10-C	15-F

20

1-A	6-C	11-A
2-E	7-C	12-A
3-C	8-C	13-D
4-C	9-A	14-D
5-C	10-A	15-D

26

1-G_3	6-D	11-F
2-G_3	7-D	12-A
3-A	8-D	13-A
4-A	9-E	14-A
5-A	10-F	15-A

7

1-A	6-G_1	11-E
2-A	7-A	12-A
3-A	8-A	13-D
4-G_1	9-H	14-D
5-G_1	10-H	15-D

27

1-C	6-D	11-G_2
2-C	7-F	12-G_2
3-C	8-F	13-A
4-C	9-A	14-A
5-D	10-A	15-A

8

1-D	6-A	11-E
2-D	7-A	12-B
3-F	8-A	13-B
4-F	9-A	14-B
5-A	10-H	15-B

28

1-A	6-A	11-B
2-G_2	7-A	12-B
3-G_2	8-G_1	13-B
4-A	9-H	14-B
5-A	10-E	15-B

Terminals		Instructor

LEGEND

1	7:20	**9**	7:52	**A**	working with manual
2	7:24	**10**	7:56	**B**	viewing filmstrip
3	7:28	**11**	8:00	**C**	working in "lab"
4	7:32	**12**	8:04	**D**	taking assessment measures
5	7:36	**13**	8:08	**E**	getting instructor assistance
6	7:40	**14**	8:12	**F**	at computer terminal
7	7:44	**15**	8.16	**G_1**	not working
8	7:48			**G_2**	on break
				G_3	out of room
				H	requesting assistance

Categories	Time Periods														
	1	2	3	4	5	6	7	8	9	10	11	12	13	14	15
Working with manual	10	10	10	8	10	11	14	11	11	10	7	9	10	11	11
Viewing filmstrip	3	3	2	1	1	1	2	5	5	4	3	3	3	2	2
Lab	1	1	3	4	4	2	2	2	—	2	3	3	1	1	1
Assessment	1	1	4	3	5	3	2	3	1	1	4	3	5	3	2
Assistance	2	2	1	2	1	1	1	2	1	1	2	3	1	1	1
Computer	2	2	2	1	—	3	2	2	2	2	2	1	1	1	1
Not at task:															
Not working	1	1	1	4	3	4	1	2	2	1	1	1	1	3	—
On break	1	2	1	—	—	—	—	—	1	2	3	3	4	3	5
Out of room	3	2	1	2	3	1	—	—	—	—	—	—	—	—	1
Requesting help	2	2	2	—	—	—	2	—	2	2	1	—	—	—	—

Mastery Test

OBJECTIVE 10   To record and analyze task orientation behavior using descriptive data.

Categories	Times of Observation										
	10:40	10:44	10:48	10:51	10:54	10:58	11:02	11:06	11:10	11:14	11:20
At task	17	21	21	21	23	23	21	18	19	16	14
Stalling	5	2	2	1	—	—	—	—	—	—	—
Other work (productive)	2	1	1	1	1	—	—	1	1	—	—
Out of seat	1	3	3	2	1	5	5	3	4	4	6
Talking	3	1	1	3	3	—	2	6	3	7	5
Other work (nonproductive)	—	—	—	—	—	—	—	—	1	1	3

From the information in the summary chart above, answer questions 1–6.

1. How many students were in this class? _____

2. How many started to work at the beginning of the lesson? _____

3. How long did it take before everyone was at least prepared to work (no longer stalling)? _____

4. At their most attentive time, how many students were working as the teacher wanted them to? _____

5. At their least attentive time, how many students were working as the teacher wanted them to? _____

6. When the students were not working, what two behaviors were they usually exhibiting? _____

_____

7. What three precautions should an observer keep in mind when planning to study "at task" data?

_____

_____

_____

8. Create an eight-item legend containing four categories of "at task" behavior and four categories of "not at task" behavior.

"At task" behaviors   *"Not at task" behaviors*

1. _____   1. _____

2. _____   2. _____

3. _____   3. _____

4. _____   4. _____

9. Analyze Exhibit 22 using the list of five suggestions in the Data Analysis section as a guideline.

_____

_____

_____

_____

_____

_____

_____

_____

_____

_____

9. *Analysis of Exhibit 22*

A teacher could use the data in Exhibit 22 for the following analyses, interpretation, and plans:

1. The teacher might be satisfied with the pacing of the computer-managed instructional materials — a conclusion drawn from the lack of "bunching" in the lab, at the computer, and so on.
2. The teacher might decide to examine, more closely, the behavior of students 4, 10, and 22, who were away from their work tables more than half of the 60-minute period.
3. The teacher might decide to find a more efficient way of responding to students' needs. He or she might feel that too many students were waiting (students 3, 7, 10, 15, 19, 23, 25, and 28) and too many students had periods of inactivity often associated with waiting (students 6, 7, 15, 19, 23, 24, 28).
4. Since five students were using filmstrips at periods 8 and 9, the teacher might realize that the complement of five sound–filmstrip machines will probably be insufficient and, thus, cause problems at some later date.
5. The teacher might decide to investigate time at the computer. Since the terminal has a 50-second turnaround time and no more than three were there at any one time, there is no reason why students 2, 9, 10, 11, and 22 needed 8–12 minutes at the terminal.

SUMMARY

The observation of classroom behavior is not something that one reads about and files away. Its utility is directly related to the extent to which the reader tries out the techniques in classroom or simulated settings. The reader is encouraged to use these observation techniques with a colleague and compare the data collected for accuracy, utility, and appropriateness. The Workbook, which accompanies this Handbook, has many exercises that should also be helpful.

NOTES

1. James Banks with A. Clegg, *Teaching Strategies for Social Studies* (Reading, Massachusetts: Addison-Wesley, 1973).

ADDITIONAL READINGS

Abramson, Paul. "When Teachers Evaluate Each Other." *Scholastic Teacher* (junior/senior high school teacher's ed.) (September 1972): 24–26.

Acheson, K. A., and J. H. Hansen. *Classroom Observations and Conferences with Teachers.* Tallahassee, Florida: Teachers Inservice Programs and Services, 1974.

Amidon, Peggy. *Nonverbal Interaction Analysis: A Method of Observing and Recording Nonverbal Behavior.* Chicago: Association for Productive Teaching, 1971. 196 pp.

Armstrong, Harold R. *A Teacher's Guide to Teaching Performance Evaluation.* Worthington, Ohio: School Management Institute, 1972. 24 pp.

Beegle, Charles W., and Richard M. Brandt, eds. *Observational Methods in the Classroom.* Washington, D.C.: Association for Supervision and Curriculum Development, 1973. 85 pp.

Flanders, Ned A. *Analyzing Teaching Behavior.* Reading, Mass.: Addison-Wesley, 1970. 448 pp.

Henney, Maribeth, and W. Paul Mortenson. "What Makes a Good Elementary School Teacher?" *Journal of Teacher Education* 24 (Winter 1973): 312–316.

Howard, Clare, and Betty Miles. "The Teacher Rating Game: New Ways To Play It." *Scholastic Teacher* (elementary teacher's ed.) (January 1974): 8–15.

Jacobson, Joan. "Should Students Evaluate Teachers?" *Today's Education* 62 (May 1973): 49.

Lewis, James J. *Appraising Teacher Performance*. West Nyack, New York: Parker Publishing, 1973. 227 pp.

McNeil, John D. *Toward Accountable Teachers: Their Appraisal and Improvement*. New York: Holt, Rinehart & Winston, 1971.

Mueller, Dorothy G. "IIow To Evaluate Teaching." *Journal of Teacher Education* 22 (Summer 1971): 229–244.

Olds, Robert. *Self-Evaluation for Teachers and Administrators*. Worthington, Ohio: School Management Institute, 1973. 64 pp.

Rosenshine, Barak. *Teaching Behaviors and Student Achievement*. IEA Studies no. 1. New York: Humanities Press, 1971. 229 pp.

Sandefur, J. T., and Alex A. Bressler. *Classroom Observation Systems in Preparing School Personnel*. Washington, D.C.: ERIC Clearinghouse on Teacher Education, March 1970. 32 pp.

Simon, Anita, and E. Gil Boyer, eds. *Mirrors for Behavior: An Anthology of Classroom Observation Instruments*. Philadelphia: Research for Better Schools, 1967–1970. Vols. I–XIV and Summary.

Weigand, James, ed. *Developing Teacher Competencies*. Englewood Cliffs, New Jersey: Prentice-Hall, 1971. Chapter 8, "Assessment of Teacher Competencies," by James D. Russell.

Terry McKoy, Institute of Open Education.

TERRY TENBRINK

Evaluation

Objectives

1 To define evaluation and to describe each of the four stages in the evaluation process.

2 To select an appropriate referent.

3 To establish rules for assigning values to individuals.

4 To evaluate, using rules to assign values to individuals.

In your daily life you are an evaluator. You constantly make judgments about the world around you. You judge people as friendly or unfriendly, intelligent or unintelligent, industrious or nonindustrious, and so on. You judge the products you buy, the entertainment you watch, the work you perform, and the degree of "success" you achieve. So, you *can* and *do* form judgments daily. The purpose of this chapter is to help you become more aware of the steps you take when you form judgments and to help you execute those steps well when making educational judgments and decisions.

In education, evaluation usually means judging a student, a teacher, or an educational program. In evaluating students or a program, some testing and grading are often involved, but evaluation is not the same thing as testing. Testing and grading and their relation to evaluation will be discussed later in this chapter. Until then, simply remember that they are not the same. Many good books have been written about testing; very few have been written about using the results of testing and other information-gathering techniques used to evaluate. This chapter should help to fill that gap.

Educational evaluation is useful only to the extent that it helps the educator (administrator, teacher, student) to make sound educational decisions. In this chapter you will be shown how educational evaluation can help you to make better instructional decisions. Then, in the Workbook that accompanies this Handbook, you will learn to make instructional decisions based upon evaluation results.

Objective 1

To define evaluation and to describe each of the four stages in the evaluation process.

LEARNING ACTIVITY 1.1

Stated most simply, to evaluate is to place a value upon — to judge. However, forming a judgment is not an independent action. In order to judge, one must have information. The act of judging depends upon this prerequisite act of obtaining information. Furthermore, the act of forming a judgment is itself prerequisite to an action one step further: decision making. So, evaluation, the process of forming judgments, depends upon information gathering and leads to decision making. Picture it this way:

| obtaining information | → | forming judgments | → | making decisions |

Or, this way:

> Evaluation is the process of obtaining information and using it to form judgments which, in turn, are used in decision making.

The above definition* clearly specifies the interrelatedness among the various stages in the evaluation process; and yet, it also clearly indicates the centrality of forming judgments. If you have not formed a judgment, you have not evaluated. This chapter, therefore, will deal primarily with the procedures for forming judgments.

However, it is important for you to understand the *total* evaluation process. So, let's expand this definition some. So far it is obvious that evaluation involves at least three stages: obtaining information, forming judgments, and using those judgments in decision making. By adding a preparation stage and enlarging a bit on the last stage, we come up with the following four stages:

> *The evaluation process*
>
> *Stage 1:* Preparing for evaluation.
> *Stage 2:* Obtaining needed information.
> *Stage 3:* Forming judgments.
> *Stage 4:* Using judgments in making decisions and preparing evaluation reports.

Let's look at a rather typical teaching–learning situation. Notice how this teacher goes through these four stages as she attempts to make her instruction more effective.

* From *Evaluation: A Practical Guide for Teachers*, by T. D. TenBrink. Copyright ©️ 1974 by McGraw-Hill Book Company. Used with permission.

Stage 1. Preparing for evaluation.

Bonnie, a third grade teacher, has become concerned about Billy. He seems to be having trouble keeping up in reading. Bonnie wonders how long he will be able to function within the reading group he is in. She wonders whether or not she should move him to a slower group. Perhaps there is something she can do to help — some extra work, for example, or some extra attention. She decides she needs more information before she can accurately judge Billy's level of achievement in reading. After determining the kind of information she needs (e.g., information about the kind of errors made when reading orally, information concerning Billy's use of various word attack skills, information about Billy's interests), Bonnie determines when and how to obtain that information.

Stage 2. Obtaining needed information.

Over a period of several days Bonnie obtains a great deal of information about Billy. She gives him a standardized reading test, listens to him read orally, carefully records the kind of errors he makes, and observes him throughout the day watching for patterns of behavior that might indicate particular attitudes toward various subject matters.

Stage 3. Forming judgments.

After analyzing all the information she has obtained, Bonnie comes to the following conclusions:

1. Billy is not capable of reading material written at a third grade level.
2. Billy reads comfortably only that material written on a second grade level or lower.
3. Billy's primary weakness lies in the area of word attack skills.
4. Billy does not have a comprehension problem. He understands what is read to him.
5. Billy likes the children in his reading group.
6. Billy enjoys the stories in the third grade reader.

Stage 4. Using judgments to make decisions and evaluation reports.

On the basis of the above judgments Bonnie decides that she should keep Billy in his present reading group. She further decides to take the following action:

1. Prepare a check list of word attack skills.
2. Systematically teach Billy those skills on a one-to-one basis.
3. Continue to have the stories read to Billy so that he will not fall behind on his comprehension skills.
4. Have Billy check off each word attack skill as he demonstrates competence in using it.

Having made these decisions, Bonnie writes a brief summary of her judgments, noting the actions she anticipates making. She files this in her own files for future reference. She also calls in Billy's parents and shares her findings with them, asking them to cooperate and to give Billy lots of encouragement and praise, supporting him as he struggles to make up the deficiencies she has discovered.

We will refer to the above example several times as we discuss in greater detail each stage of the evaluation process.

STAGE 1

Preparing for Evaluation

The importance of the preparation stage of evaluation cannot be over-emphasized. There are two kinds of errors that arise from a lack of preparation: (1) Judgments are made on the basis of inadequate information; and (2) Information is obtained with no judgments or decisions in mind. The first error is so common that we have an everyday expression for it. It is called a "snap judgment." Snap judgments are usually inaccurate and lead to poorly formed decisions. The second error is especially common in education. All too often tests are administered and scored, only to be filed away in the cumulative folder or in a teacher's record book. If there is no better reason for obtaining information than to accumulate it, perhaps it should not be obtained in the first place.

Notice that our third grade teacher, Bonnie, became aware of the fact that she needed to make a number of judgments about Billy (how well he could read, what his interests were, and so on) so that she could decide on the most appropriate way to teach him. It is only when you know what judgments and decisions you are going to have to make that you can determine what kind of information you will need. And, until you know what kind of information you need, you cannot decide when and how to obtain it.

Three things must be done in the preparation stage of evaluation. First of all, you must determine which judgments and decisions you anticipate making. Second, you must describe the information needed for making those judgments and decisions. Finally, you must determine when and how to obtain the needed information. Each of these will be discussed in turn.

Determining Judgments and Decisions.　Judgments are estimates of present condition or predictions of future condition (e.g., George reads slowly; Emma is the best speller in the class; this book reads well; Peter will do well at the game tonight; this third grade class is far ahead of last year's class; Mary will have a great deal of trouble with first year algebra). A decision, on the other hand, is a choice among alternative courses of action (e.g., I will put Mary in a slower reading group; I will skip lesson 14; Sarah has decided to sign up for "Art for the Beginner"; the English faculty chose the *Handbook of English* as their primary text).

If you can anticipate who or what you will need to make judgments and decisions about, then you can determine more precisely who or what you need information about and the kind of information you will need about them. Fortunately, it is not difficult at all to anticipate the judgments and decisions you will have to make. You simply need to be alert to your own basic curiosity. Notice that the process of evaluation began for Bonnie when she began to wonder how long Billy would be able to function within his current reading group. She wondered whether or not he should be moved to a slower group. She wondered about the kind of work that would help him catch up. Her basic curiosity about Billy and his progress made her raise the questions that ultimately led to judgments and decisions about his future instruction. *Good evaluation always begins with good questions.* The questions that arise out of a curiosity about the instructional process are the kinds of questions that will ultimately lead a teacher to make good decisions for the teacher and the students.

Determining the Kind of Information Needed.   There are three important considerations when trying to determine the kind of information needed. These considerations can be phrased as questions:

1. Who or what is the information about?
2. What characteristics are to be judged about those individuals?
3. How accurate must the information be?

The answer to the first question really comes down to the question of what you are judging and about whom. Are you primarily interested in judging your students, a textbook you used, your own teaching abilities, or the value of the filmstrip you used last month? Obviously, you will need information about those individuals you are about to judge.

What characteristics are about to be judged is particularly important. Most of the judgments and decisions we must make as teachers have to do with how well our students have learned. Consequently, a description of learning outcomes will serve as a useful description of the kinds of behaviors you need information about. A set of well-defined instructional objectives, stated in behavioral terms, will give such a description. (Chapter 3 should teach you how to produce well-written instructional objectives.)

How accurate the information must be can best be answered by deciding how important the judgments and decisions are for which the information will be used. Generally speaking, as the need for accuracy increases, so does the cost of obtaining that information. It takes extended planning, skillful construction of the information-gathering instruments, and careful use of those instruments to obtain really accurate information. More important decisions require information that is as accurate as possible, no matter what the cost. Less important decisions, or decisions that can be reversed easily if you find they are inappropriate, can be made with less accurate information if necessary. But, as a rule of thumb, always obtain information that is as accurate as possible, given your own limitations of time and money.

Determining How and When to Obtain Information.   There are numerous things to be considered in this last part of the preparation stage of evaluation.[1] The most important questions to ask yourself when determining how and when to obtain information are:

1. What techniques should be used to obtain the information needed?
2. What kinds of instruments should be used?
3. Under what conditions should the information be obtained?
4. When will the information be needed?

5. When will conditions be right for getting the needed information?

There are three basic techniques for obtaining information: observation, inquiry, testing. Testing tends to be the most objective technique for obtaining information and is likely to lead to the most reliable information. However, sometimes the kind of information you need will not lend itself readily to testing. You may decide to observe students and/or their products, or you may wish to question students directly through the use of an interview or a questionnaire. When you select among these three techniques, you should choose one that will not only produce accurate information but will also provide you with the kind of information you need about your students. For example, if you need information about how well your students *usually* spell, you will not want to give them a spelling test. Instead, you will observe their spelling over a period of time and across a variety of settings.

Once you have decided on the technique most appropriate for obtaining the needed information, you must determine the type of instrument to be used. For example, having decided to test your students, you must then choose the most appropriate type of test. Will you use a standardized test or make up one yourself? Would a multiple-choice or an essay test be better? Suppose you had chosen to use inquiry as your major information-gathering technique. Would a questionnaire be most appropriate or should you conduct an informal inventory? And, if observation had been chosen, should a rating scale be used or should anecdotal records be kept? These questions must be answered on the basis of how good a particular instrument is for providing you with the kind of information you need. A more detailed explanation of various measurement techniques and/or instruments can be found in any one of a number of good measurement texts presently on the market.*

In deciding on the conditions that should exist during the information-gathering stage, you must consider the following kinds of things: Is maximum performance being measured or am I most interested in the student's typical behavior? Do I want my students to have access to materials like their textbooks or their study notes, or do I expect them to recall from memory? Do I want information obtained in a natural setting or in a carefully controlled setting like a quiet classroom?

To determine when the information will be needed, you must decide when you will need to make the judgments and decisions for which that information will be used. You should always try to obtain your information as close as possible to the time at which the decisions and judgments must be made. For example, suppose you are trying to judge the level of your students' achievement in writing short, descriptive paragraphs. Suppose, further, that you want to make your judgment at the end of the semester. Then, obtain samples of your students' writing near the end of the semester. Any samples of student writing you obtained early in the semester should not be averaged in with those obtained later because the level of achievement at the beginning of the course would obviously be lower than that level reached by the end of the semester.

When are conditions favorable for obtaining information? The an-

---

* See Additional Readings.

swer to this question is important because tests often are administered before the students have really been given opportunity to prepare. Sometimes tests are administered at a time when there is likely to be interference during the testing session (e.g., when a fire drill is expected sometime during that day). And, in spite of what your teachers may have done to you, it is really not appropriate to try to obtain information about your students' maximum level of achievement on the morning following a homecoming dance!

Your Turn

PREPARING FOR EVALUATION

Three was the magic number in this stage. See if you can answer the three, three-part questions that follow.

1. List the three things that need to be done in the preparation stage.

_____

_____

_____

2. List the three questions that need to be answered to determine the kind of information needed.

_____

_____

_____

3. List the three basic techniques used in information gathering.

_____

_____

_____

ANSWER KEY
Your Turn: Preparing for Evaluation

1. (a) Determine judgments and decisions to be made.
   (b) Describe information needed to make those judgments and decisions.
   (c) Determine when and how to obtain needed information.

2. (a) Who or what is the information about?
   (b) What characteristics are to be judged?
   (c) How accurate must the information be?
3. (a) observation
   (b) inquiry
   (c) testing

STAGE 2

Obtaining Needed Information

Simply having the correct instrument for information gathering does not guarantee that you will obtain good information. It is important that you know how to obtain information, how to administer a given test, how to utilize a particular rating scale or other observational technique, and how to be certain that the information you gather will be accurate. There are many suggestions and rules for using each of the various kinds of evaluation instruments. The test and measurement books listed in the Additional Readings at the end of the chapter explain these rules in more detail. You should read them when you get an opportunity to do so. In the meantime, if you follow the four general guidelines given below, you will find that your information-gathering sessions will be more productive and you will be less likely to obtain useless information.

Guidelines for Obtaining Information

1. Be ready.
2. Be consistent.
3. Be fair.
4. Be alert.

1. As you begin any information-gathering session, it is important that you and your students be ready. To prepare yourself, you must make certain that you are familiar with the instruments (for example, a standardized test) that you anticipate using. You should have all the materials (for example, scratch paper, pencils, test booklets, and stopwatch) available and ready for use. You should have worked out in advance any special instructions that the students will need. To prepare your students for an information-gathering session, give them advance warning and indicate what it is you will be obtaining your information about (such as the behavioral objectives for Unit 7). The students should understand the rationale or purpose behind the test so that they are prepared emotionally as well as cognitively. The more positive the students' attitudes toward a test, the better their effort will be and the less likely they are to underperform due to "test anxiety."

2. A cardinal rule of good evaluation is to be consistent. When you are obtaining information about your students, make certain you do so in a way that is consistent — consistent from student to student, from item to item, from observation to observation, and from situation to situation. Do not give credit for information to one child and no credit to another for the same information. In scoring any test, make certain that you have a well-designed scoring key and that you stick to that key. Finally, it is also important to record information in the same format for all your students across various measures. Do not, for example, write down some of the students' scores in letter grades, others in raw score points, and still others in percentage points. Try to find a consistent way of recording your data and stay with that throughout the semester.

3. A common complaint of students is that teachers are "unfair." Many times these complaints are nothing more than the students' attempts to hide their own inadequacies or to rationalize their failure. However, sometimes students have legitimate complaints. Every

teacher is biased in some way; every teacher tends to like some students better than others; and every teacher is subject to the same emotional influences as are other humans. Consequently, during any information-gathering session, you should be alert to those biases so that you can be as objective as possible. It is helpful to develop clearly specified rules for administering and scoring tests (and other information-gathering instruments). Again, the references found in the Additional Readings section at the end of the chapter contain useful information on test construction, administration, and scoring. You may wish to check some of these out and read into this topic more fully.

4. A number of things can occur during an information-gathering session that can introduce error into the information obtained. For example, test results are frequently distorted by disruptions, cheating, students who are sick, students who are filling in the answer sheet incorrectly, etc. If you are alert to these potential sources of error, you can often avoid them or at least take note of them in your judgments.

Your Turn

OBTAINING NEEDED INFORMATION

The four guidelines for obtaining information are listed below. Write a brief (a sentence or two) explanation of each one.

1. *Be ready.*

_____

_____

_____

2. *Be consistent.*

_____

_____

_____

3. *Be fair.*

_____

_____

_____

4. *Be alert.*

_____

_____

_____

ANSWER KEY
Your Turn: Obtaining Needed Information

1. *Be ready.* The teacher should be familiar with the test, know how to administer it, have the materials ready, and have the students prepared.
2. *Be consistent.* Administer and score the same way for each student.

3. *Be fair.* Follow clearly defined objective rules for administering and scoring tests.
4. *Be alert.* Watch what is going on during a test, noting any potential sources of error.

STAGE 3

Forming Judgments

Forming a judgment, or "placing a value," on something is the essence of evaluation. The process involved in forming judgments will be briefly overviewed here, and the rest of the chapter will deal with the process in greater detail. As you read, keep in mind the many kinds of classroom situations where judgments are formed. Each time you attach a grade to an assignment or to a test, you are forming a judgment. Each time you assign a report-card grade, you are summarizing those previous judgments and making a further judgment. Each time you come to a conclusion about the level of achievement and/or the aptitude of a student, you are forming a judgment. Whenever you determine whether your teaching has been good or bad, whether a textbook has been useful or not, or whether a filmstrip or other activity was valuable or not, you are forming a judgment. In each of these situations, the basic process is essentially the same. The three steps involved are previewed below:

A Preview of the Steps Taken in Forming a Judgment

1. Determine the type of judgment to be made.
2. Establish the rules for assigning a value to the individual being judged.
3. Compare the information you have with an appropriate referent and assign a value according to the rules you have established.

Select an Appropriate Referent. Judgments are formed primarily as a result of comparing the information that you have about an individual with other information. We shall refer to that other information as a referent. A *referent* can take the form of a score, a value, or a description of performance, the same type of information that you are likely to have on the individual being evaluated. Obviously, if you have information about an individual in the form of a score, then the referent should also be a score. However, if your information is in the form of the description of a performance, then the appropriate referent would also be one describing a performance. Even more important than the form of the referent is the type of referent used. There are three types of referents corresponding to the three types of judgments that result from their use: norm-referenced judgments, criterion-referenced judgments, and self-referenced judgments.

Norm-referenced judgments are made by comparing the information you have about an individual with the information you have about a group of similar individuals. Whenever you use information about the performance of some group of individuals *on the same task* as a referent, you are making a norm-referenced judgment. If you want to know how well an individual performs in comparison with his peers or in comparison with some other group, then norm-referenced judgments are appropriate.

Criterion-referenced judgments are made by comparing the information you have about an individual with some performance criterion (that is, some description of expected behavior). Criterion-referenced judgments should be made when you are concerned about the level of achievement someone has attained rather than his or her performance in comparison to others. As we shall see later, criterion-referenced judgments are particularly valuable when it is necessary to make decisions about whether students should move on to the next unit of instruction.

Self-referenced judgments are made by comparing information you have about an individual to some other information you have about *that same individual*. Using information you already have about the individual as a referent is especially valuable when you are making judgments about improvements, gains, attitude changes, and so on. Recent advances made in individualized instruction, as well as some of the more recent approaches to education (such as the free school and open classroom), make it imperative that careful records of the *progress* of each individual student are kept. Self-referenced judgments are also valuable for comparing an individual's performance across subject matter areas. We will consider some of these kinds of judgments in the remainder of the chapter, as well as in the accompanying Workbook.

Establish Rules for Assigning Values. When we compare the information we have about an individual to some referent, we will be looking for discrepancies. This means that we will look, first of all, to see whether our information places the student in question below or above the referent. Next, we will want to know *how far* above or below the referent. Suppose, for example, that a student has a spelling test score of 13 correctly spelled words. Comparing this to the class average of 10 correctly spelled words, one can say that the student has scored three points higher than the average score of his or her class. But, what does that mean? What value can we attach to that fact? It is precisely at this point that we need to establish rules for placing particular values on the deviations from the referent. You will learn how to do that in objective 3 of this chapter.

Forming the Judgment. Comparing the information that you have to the appropriate referent and assigning a value according to the rules that you have previously established are relatively simple processes.

At this point, you have an opportunity to make one final review of all the things that lead you to forming a judgment. In objective 4, we will briefly discuss a systematic way to go about forming judgments, and you will be provided with an opportunity to practice making a variety of judgments.

Your Turn

FORMING JUDGMENTS

1. To judge is to _____ .

2. Judging involves _____ information to some _____ .

In questions 3–5, define the following types of judgments and give an example of each type.

3. A norm-referenced judgment

    (a) *Definition:* _____

    _____

    (b) *Example:* _____

    _____

    _____

4. A criterion-referenced judgment

    (a) *Definition:* _____

    _____

    (b) *Example:* _____

    _____

    _____

5. A self-referenced judgment

    (a) *Definition:* _____

    _____

    (b) *Example:* _____

    _____

    _____

ANSWER KEY

Your Turn: Forming Judgments

1. place a value upon
2. comparing; referent
3. *Definition:* A judgment made by comparing the information you have about an individual to information obtained about a group of similar individuals.
   Examples:
   (a) John reads better than his classmates.
   (b) Peter is a low-average reader.
   (c) Mary ranks fifth in her class on academic achievement.
4. *Definition:* A judgment made by comparing the individual to some objective criterion.
   Examples:
   (a) George got 8 out of 10 spelling words correct.
   (b) Sue mastered all but one of the course objectives.
   (c) Nancy has reached a level of achievement in math that makes it possible for her to progress to algebra.
5. *Definition:* A judgment made by comparing the information you have about an individual to other information about the same individual.
   Examples:
   (a) Elmer is better in geography than he is in English.
   (b) Wendy has gained a great deal of confidence since the beginning of the term.
   (c) Sally's writing ability has improved.

STAGE 4

Using Judgments

The real value of evaluation lies not in the formation of judgments, but in the use of those judgments in decision making. Remember, though, that you may not be the only one who will make decisions based on your judgments. Often the judgments you make (about report-card grades, statements of predicted student potential, recommendations, and so on) will be used by others in their decision making. Consequently, in this fourth stage, there are a number of things which you must learn to do.

First of all, you should understand how to verify your judgments and check on their accuracy. Decisions, after all, will never be more accurate than the judgments upon which they are based. Second, you must learn to make decisions based on the judgments you have made. Finally, you must learn to summarize and report those judgments and decisions to others. Parents, teachers, administrators, potential employers, etc., all depend at one time or another on summaries of judgments made by teachers. Using judgments in the evaluation process (including each of the three steps described above) will be treated in greater detail in the Workbook that accompanies this Handbook. In that section of the Workbook, you will be given opportunities to practice using judgments that have been made. In anticipation of these exercises, read the following brief discussion of those steps carefully.

Verifying Judgments. Essentially, there are two things you need to do in order to verify any judgment. First of all, you must make the assumption that your judgment is accurate. Next, with that assumption in mind, try to answer the following general question: "If this judgment is true, what else could be expected?" Your answer should take the form of several hypotheses that can be tested. For example, if we judged Johnny's musical ability to be high, then we might make several hypotheses related to that ability. For example, we might hypothesize that he can learn to read music quickly, that he can accurately identify middle C and other key notes, that he can learn to play any one of a number of musical instruments, etc. A judgment about Johnny's poor reading ability might lead us to hypothesize that he would read poorly in an oral reading situation, that he would score below his grade level on a standardized reading test, and that he would dislike subject matter where he needed to do a lot of reading.

The hypotheses established through the above procedure should follow logically from the judgments that were made, should be stated as expected outcomes, and should be observable and testable. If, upon testing such hypotheses, they are not substantiated, we would suspect our judgment. However, if the majority of the hypotheses formulated for a given judgment are upheld, then that judgment would have been verified.

Making Decisions. All day, day in and day out, each of us makes a multitude of decisions. We decide to go here instead of there, to wear this instead of that, to engage in one activity rather than another. However, when it comes to making instructional decisions, we must learn to be more systematic in our decision making. The following four steps* should assist you in this regard.

Steps in the Decision-Making Process

1. Specify your objective (determine what you want to accomplish).
2. Identify possible alternatives.
3. Consider the consequences of each alternative.
4. Choose the best alternative.

We will discuss these steps in greater detail in the Workbook that accompanies this Handbook, but for now, remember that decision making is essentially a process of selecting, from a number of possible alternatives, the course of action that seems most likely to bring about the desired outcome. Crucial to the selection of an appropriate course of action is the determination of the desired outcome and an identification of the possible alternatives to reaching it.

Reporting Evaluation Results to Others. A good evaluation report should provide all the information needed by those for whom the report is intended and should be clear and easy to understand. The following suggestions should help you to prepare reports that meet these criteria. Look these steps over carefully, thinking about the implications of each suggestion.

Suggestions for Reporting Evaluation Results

1. State clearly what the report is about.
2. Include a guide for interpreting any information contained in the report.
3. State the information to be reported as clearly and concisely as possible.
4. Report the information in a format that will be meaningful to the person receiving the report.
5. When necessary, explain how the information led to the judgments and decisions that were made.

* From *Evaluation: A Practical Guide for Teachers*, by T. D. TenBrink. Copyright © 1974 by McGraw-Hill Book Company. Used with permission.

Your Turn

USING JUDGMENTS

Using judgments involves three steps. List them and describe each one in a sentence or two.

1. _____
   _____
   _____
   _____

2. _____
   _____
   _____

3. _____
   _____
   _____
   _____

ANSWER KEY

Your Turn: Using Judgments

1. Verifying judgments involves testing their truth or accuracy by formulating hypotheses derived from the judgments and trying to substantiate those hypotheses.

2. Making decisions involves selecting from a number of alternative courses of action.
3. Reporting judgments involves stating the judgments made in clear, concise terms and reporting the information that led to the judgments.

LEARNING ACTIVITY 1.2

Talk to a teacher about how he or she decides what to teach, when to teach, and how to teach. Probe for specific answers. Try to identify the various stages in the evaluation process as that teacher explains his or her decision making to you. Could you use the terminology of this chapter to explain what the teacher has done?

LEARNING ACTIVITY 1.3

Ask several teachers to write down for you the questions that came to their minds as they taught on a particular day. Decide how those questions could serve to stimulate evaluation activities. Compare your findings with those of your classmates.

Mastery Test

OBJECTIVE 1 To define evaluation and to describe each of the four stages in the evaluation process.

1. Give a brief definition of evaluation.

   _____

   _____

2. List the four stages in the evaluation process. Describe briefly what goes on in each stage. Use examples from the classroom to clarify your descriptions.

   (a) *Stage 1.* _____

   _____

   _____

   _____

   _____

   _____

   _____

   _____

   (b) *Stage 2.* _____

   _____

   _____

   (c) *Stage 3.* _____

   _____

   _____

   (d) *Stage 4.* _____

   _____

   _____

ANSWER KEY

Mastery Test, Objective 1

1. Evaluation is the process of obtaining information and forming judgments to be used in decision making.
2. (a) *Preparing for evaluation.* In this stage you need to determine the judgments and decisions you anticipate making (e.g., when to begin Unit 2, what assignments to give, where to place Johnny). Next you must decide what information you will need in order to make those judgments and decisions (e.g., how quickly the students are moving through Unit 1, what the students' interests are, how well Johnny reads). Finally, you will decide when and how to obtain the information needed (e.g., weekly, through quizzes; first week of class, using an interest inventory; second week of class, using a standardized test of reading and observing students during oral reading).

(b) *Obtaining needed information.* Involves asking students (inquiry), observing students (watching students setting up an experiment), or testing students (giving a multiple-choice test of history facts).

(c) *Forming judgments.* In this stage you compare the information with some referent and make a value judgment. Grades reflecting achievement and predictions about how well a student might be expected to do are both common examples of classroom judgments.

(d) *Using judgments in decisions and preparing evaluation reports.* Deciding what action to take (e.g., move Johnny to a slower reading group) and reporting the evaluation results that led to that decision comprise the major tasks of the final stage of evaluation. Note that the emphasis is on the *use* of judgments.

Objective 2

To select an appropriate referent.

LEARNING ACTIVITY 2

Earlier in this chapter you were introduced to three kinds of judgments: norm-referenced judgments, criterion-referenced judgments, and self-referenced judgments. When selecting a referent, you must first determine which type of judgment you are going to make. Each has advantages and disadvantages. Each is useful for particular kinds of educational problems. After you determine the kind of judgment you want to make, you will need to select a specific referent, determining where, when, and how that referent will be obtained and what form it should take.

Determining the Kind of Judgment To Be Made

Norm-Referenced Judgments. Norm-referenced judgments are made by comparing information you have about an individual with information you have about a group of similar individuals. Whenever you want to know how well an individual has performed in comparison to his peers, norm-referenced judgments are appropriate. This kind of comparison is particularly valuable when you need to select some individuals out of a group for a certain purpose. Suppose, for example, that you need to choose six students to represent your class in a speech contest. You will want to select those students who will best represent your class, and so you will need to compare each student with his or her classmates to determine which six would be "best." Other selection decisions requiring norm-referenced judgments are illustrated in the following examples. Look these examples over carefully and then see if you can add some examples of your own to the list.

Examples of Selection Decisions Which Require Norm-Referenced Judgments

1. Choosing the "starting five" for the basketball game.
2. Selecting the student who will play first-chair clarinet.
3. Selecting the cheerleading squad.
4. Choosing class valedictorian.
5. Selecting six students for the top reading group.
6. Choosing a student to help those who need extra practice.

There are occasions when you might use norm-referenced judgments to help you decide where to place a student within your program. For example, before you place a student in a particular reading group, you may wish to know how he or she compares with the other students in that group. Predicting the future success of an individual is another situation for which norm-referenced judgments would be helpful. Success (whether in school or on the job) often depends upon how well one can compete with others. If we do want to predict how persons will perform in a competitive situation, we will need to compare their potential with that of their probable competition. That requires norm-referenced judgments.*

Criterion-Referenced Judgments.   Criterion-referenced judgments are made by comparing the information you have about an individual with some performance criteria. These criteria are usually descriptions of expected behavior stated in observable terms (see Chapter 3 on writing instructional objectives). Examine the examples given below. Think about what is being compared in each example.

Examples of Criterion-Referenced Judgments

1. A second grade teacher compares the number of sight vocabulary words to the total number he or she expects the students to be able to pronounce by the end of the year.
2. A typing teacher grades the students on how many words they type per minute. Sixty words/min = A, 50/min = B, etc.
3. An elementary school teacher judged George to be a behavior problem because he had to be corrected more than 15 times in a 30-minute period.
4. A junior high English teacher gives passing grades to all those students who can produce at least six of the ten basic sentence patterns they had been studying.
5. A shop teacher graded one test on the basis of the number of tools the students could correctly identify. A given student's

---

* Predicting college success provides an excellent example of such norm referencing. College aptitude tests are given to large groups of college applicants. Those scoring best (compared to the others) are judged most likely to succeed.

grade depended on how many tools he or she could identify out of the total number tested, not on how that number compared to the number correctly identified by others in the class.

6. A high school history teacher grades students by comparing the number of course objectives they successfully completed with the total number he or she had hoped they would complete.

Notice that, in each of the above examples, information about the students is compared with information concerning the teacher's expectations for these students. None of the judgments required a comparison between a student's performance and the performance of his or her peers. (That kind of comparison would yield a norm-referenced judgment.)

Criterion-referenced judgments are most useful when one is trying to determine as precisely as possible the level of achievement an individual has attained. In fact, a precise measure of level of achievement is just what Glaser had in mind when he first introduced the idea of criterion-referenced measurement:

> Underlying the concept of achievement measurement is the notion of a continuum of knowledge acquisition ranging from no proficiency at all to perfect performance. An individual's achievement level falls at some point on this continuum as indicated by the behaviors he displays during testing. The degree to which his achievement resembles desired performance at any specified level is assessed by criterion-referenced measures of achievement or proficiency. The standard against which a student's performance is compared . . . is the behavior which defines each point along the achievement continuum.[2]

As you can see from Glaser's explanation, the criterion (or referent) used in making criterion-referenced judgments is the behavior defining a point on an achievement continuum.

Self-Referenced Judgments.   Self-referenced judgments are made by comparing the information you have about an individual with other information you have *about that same individual*. One obvious use for this kind of judgment is to check on a student's progress, to find out how much he or she has gained over some designated time period. A teacher who says, "Fred is doing much better in science this marking period," is implying that he or she has compared Fred's performance this marking period with his performance last marking period. A self-referenced judgment is being made.

Another type of self-referenced judgment that is very common is made by comparing an individual's performance on one task with his or her performance on another task (for example, Sam is better at basketball than he is at baseball; Wilma has more ability for English than for math; George doesn't do as well at subtracting fractions as he did at adding fractions). Although these kinds of self-referenced judgments are made quite frequently by teachers, you will soon see that they are difficult to make accurately.

Your Turn

DETERMINING THE KIND OF JUDGMENT TO BE MADE

Read the evaluation problems in this exercise and decide in each case which kind of judgment would be most appropriate. Mark it according to the following key: NRJ = norm-referenced judgment; CRJ = criterion-referenced judgment; SRJ = self-referenced judgment. The first one has been answered for you.

<u>CRJ</u> 1. The school board has decided that too many unprepared students are being allowed to begin advanced algebra. Besides better teaching in Algebra I, they want better evaluation of those students completing the course. Students who do not have the skills needed in order to succeed in Algebra II should be given further training and should not be allowed to go into Algebra II until they are ready.

_____ 2. The teacher in the third grade has decided to give awards to those students who are the most well behaved. She will make the awards once a week on Fridays.

_____ 3. Mrs. Elmone sent a note home to the parents telling them that she felt that each child should be judged as an individual and that the report-card grades would indicate improvement and working up to capacity.

_____ 4. The school district's sports and extracurricular activities committee decides to give a sportsmanship award to the school which demonstrates the most sportsmanlike behavior throughout the basketball season.

_____ 5. The English department used three different textbooks this year in order to determine which one would be most helpful to the students. They wanted to select the best textbok they could find.

_____ 6. "You will be evaluated on your teaching performance this year." This edict from the principal's office was later followed up by a note that indicated the basis for the evaluation. It said, "Each teacher will be judged on the basis of how well his or her students meet the instructional objectives spelled out in the syllabus for each course."

_____ 7. Some schools evaluate their teachers on the basis of student ratings. Those teachers with the highest ratings get the biggest raises; those with next highest ratings, slightly lower raises, etc.

ANSWER KEY

Your Turn: Determining the Kind of Judgment To Be Made

1. CRJ 2. NRJ 3. SRJ 4. NRJ 5. NRJ 6. CRJ 7. NRJ

Selecting a Specific Referent

Once you have decided on the kind of judgment you are going to make, you need to select a specific referent. You will want to decide what form that referent should take and when and how you should obtain it.

Determine the Form of the Referent. A referent, you will recall, is that to which you compare the *information* you have about an individual. Now it makes sense that any meaningful comparison must compare similar kinds of things. Therefore, a referent must be *in the* *form of information* — information about a group of individuals if a norm-referenced judgment is being made; information about the level of expected performance if a criterion-referenced judgment is being made; information about the individual being judged if a self-referenced judgment is being made. The primary forms of information include a score, a value, or a description. Look at the following examples:

Examples of a Score as a Referent

John's spelling score was 8 out of 10 this week, compared to only 2 out of 10 last week.

"Fifteen correct vocabulary words get you a passing grade," said the Latin instructor.

"If you do not get a score of at least 80 on this test, you will need to take it over, so study hard this weekend."

Examples of a Value as a Referent

Peter was doing average work. His score was about the same as the average score of his classmates.

The average grade at OSC was C+. Compared to that value, Sandra's B+ looked very good.

The average value assigned to the sculptures in Mrs. Jardin's art class was B−. That value would be used as a referent for assigning values to the work done by the students in next semester's class.

Example of a Description as a Referent

A set of behavioral objectives describing a good extemporaneous speech was used as a model. Each speaker's performance was judged according to how well it matched the performance described by those objectives.

When determining the form of the referent, the important thing to keep in mind is that the referent must be in the same form as the information you have about the individual being judged. For example, if you have information about the percentage of items missed on a math test, it would not be appropriate to compare that to the average raw score of the class on that test. Rather, it would have to be compared to the class average computed on the basis of percentage of correct scores.

Determine When and How to Obtain a Referent. There is a single, overriding principle that should guide you in determining when and how to obtain a referent: *A referent should be like the information about the individual(s) being judged.* Consequently, the conditions producing information about the referent and the individual should be as similar as possible. This is precisely why standardized tests have such carefully standardized instructions. The referent (usually the average score obtained by a group of individuals like those for whom the test was designed) was obtained under particular test conditions with very specific instructions. Any information which is to be compared to that referent must also be obtained under those same conditions, with those same instructions.

Think for a moment about what this means in terms of practical applications in the classroom. Study each of the procedures described below. They are common classroom practices. Each violates in some way the principle discussed above.

Can you determine how each of the following classroom procedures violates the principle that information and the referent to which it is compared must be alike?

An essay test is given by a history teacher. These are her instructions: "Choose 3 out of the first 5 questions and 2 out of the remaining 3 questions. You will be graded on a curve."

A standardized achievement test was given in the winter. However, the norms accompanying the test were based upon data obtained during the spring of the year.

A third grade teacher decided that the standardized test instructions were not very clear. Consequently he reworded them so that his pupils would not be confused when they took the test.

Three students in Mr. Bollar's class were absent the day of the midterm exam. He gave them the same exam and then compared their scores to the class average.

Notice that in the first classroom procedure the teacher intends to grade "on a curve." In other words, she will make norm-referenced judgments, comparing a student's performance to the group's performance. However, the information obtained differs from student to student. Any comparison of an individual's score to the scores of the other students is inappropriate because the scores are computed on the basis of different sets of items. The information to be compared to the referent and the information the referent is based upon are *not* alike.

In the second example, the referent was based upon information obtained during the spring, while the individuals being evaluated are judged on the basis of information collected during the winter. The norm group could have achieved quite a bit in the interim from winter to spring, and the comparison would be inappropriate.

What did the third grade teacher do wrong? He obtained information about his students under different testing conditions than those under which the referent was obtained (the norm group's directions were different).

Because three of Mr. Bollar's students had more time to study than the rest of the class, it would be inappropriate to compare their performance to the performance of the class. A criterion-referenced judgment would have been better here than a norm-referenced one.

Your Turn

SELECTING A SPECIFIC REFERENT

For each of the following anticipated judgments, describe an appropriate referent.

1. "I want to know how well Sally does in spelling compared to her classmates. She got 16 wrong on the review test."

_____

_____

_____

2. "I want to know how well Sally does in spelling compared to her classmates. She scored 85% on the review test."

_____

_____

_____

3. "I want to know how much Sally has improved in spelling. She got 16 wrong on the review test."

_____

_____

_____

4. You need to know which word attack skills Elmer can use successfully and which ones he cannot use successfully. You have a test measuring each of several word attack skills. You know how many items Elmer missed, and you know which items he missed.

_____

_____

_____

Check your answers to these first four problems. If you missed any, think about why the keyed answer is more appropriate than the one you chose. Now try the rest of these. They are a bit more difficult. If you get most of them right, you will have demonstrated your ability to select appropriate referents. Each answer is explained in the Answer Key.

5. (a) A coach has listed all the plays his team can execute with ease. Describe a referent he could use if he chose to make a norm-referenced judgment about his team.

_____

_____

_____

_____

(b) Now, describe a referent that this coach could use to make criterion-referenced judgments about his team.

_____

_____

_____

6. (a) A teacher wants to predict how well her typing students would function as secretaries in the local businesses. She has information about their typing speed, their clerical speed, their shorthand dictation speed, their ability to answer the phone, etc. She wants to make norm-referenced judgments so she will know how well her students would be able to compete with the secretaries already on the job. Describe the referent she will need if she wants to use scores. How and when would she obtain that referent?

_____

_____

_____

_____

_____

_____

_____

_____

_____

(b) Now suppose she wishes to make criterion-referenced judgments about whether her students would be able to function on the job. Describe the referent(s) which would be appropriate for her to use.

_____

_____

_____

_____

_____

ANSWER KEY

Your Turn: Selecting a Specific Referent

1. The referent should be in the form of a score that would reflect how well the class did (that is, the class average in raw score points). This would be a norm referent.
2. The referent should reflect the class performance in terms of percentage correct (that is, the class average percentage score). This calls for a norm referent.
3. The referent should reflect Sally's previous spelling scores (that is, the number wrong on similar tests taken earlier). This would be a self referent.
4. The referent should be a list of work attack skills. This would be a criterion referent.
5. (a) He could use the average number of plays that other teams could execute with ease. This allows for a comparison between teams (an NRJ).

(b) He could use a list describing the plays to be executed as a referent for making criterion-referenced judgments.

6. (a) She will need a referent that represents an average score in a performance test defined by the secretarial skills she decided were important to success on the job. This referent could be obtained by obtaining scores from the entire class (after the course is about completed) or by obtaining scores from secretaries who are already functioning on the job successfully.

(b) For criterion-referenced judgments, she will need clearly defined, behaviorally stated descriptions of the skills secretaries are known to need in order to succeed on the job.

Mastery Test

OBJECTIVE 2   To select an appropriate referent.

For each of the following statements, determine the type of judgment being made. Answer according to the following key: NRJ = norm-referenced judgments; CRJ = criterion-referenced judgments; and SRJ = self-referenced judgments.

_____ 1. "Are my students ready to go on to the next unit? They seem to be able to add fractions accurately."

_____ 2. George is a high-average reader.

_____ 3. Floyd knows five out of the seven musical scales assigned him.

_____ 4. "The list of objectives for this unit will serve as a basis for your report-card grades. If you accomplish all of them, you will get an 'A.' For each objective you fail to complete, your grade drops one letter grade."

_____ 5. "Jane has more trouble overcoming stage fright than anyone in the class."

_____ 6. "Jane has made a great deal of progress, however. Remember how much she trembled the first day of class?"

The following statements describe evaluation problems not unlike those faced daily by classroom teachers. In each case, decide what kind of judgment would be appropriate using the same key as above.

_____ 7. "You must select the three best students to honor in the assembly tomorrow."

_____ 8. "Has the class as a whole made much progress in self-discipline this month?"

_____ 9. "How much worse are they than last year's class?"

_____ 10. "If only I knew where Leroy was going wrong! He draws so well. Why are his paintings so muddy?"

_____ 11. "Only 10% of you will get A's. Which ones will you be?"

12. A referent can take the form of a _____, a _____, or a _____.

13. In what ways must the referent be like the information that will be compared to it? Why?

_____

_____

Objective 3

To establish rules for assigning values to individuals.

You have some information about an individual (e.g., John's score on the Unit 1 history test was 82.).

You are going to make a norm-referenced judgment, and you have selected an appropriate referent (e.g., The average score of all the students who took the history test was 78.).

Now you compare your information to the referent (e.g., John scored four points above the class average).

But what *value* do you place on that score of 82? Do you assign John a numerical value of +4 because he is 4 points above average? Or, do you assign him a descriptive value such as "average" or "just above average" or "pretty good"? Or, perhaps a letter grade could be used with an "A" meaning "best" or "excellent" and an "F" meaning "worst" or "very poor work." Then, we might give John a C+, meaning "not too bad" or "a bit above average" or "fair work."

The above dilemma is characteristic of what teachers go through almost every time they assign grades to their students. This section is designed to help you cope with this dilemma. After studying it, you should be able to answer questions like those posed above.

LEARNING ACTIVITY 3.1

There are essentially two kinds of rules for determining the values to be assigned to an individual being judged. The first we will call the two-value rule. It is used in forming judgments of mastery learning. The second kind of rule we will call the deviation rule. Let's examine each of these in more detail.

THE TWO-VALUE RULE

The two-value rule is a simple rule. In formal terms, it states that a positive value is associated with information that matches or exceeds the referent and a negative value is associated with information that falls below the referent. A simple example may help: A high school math teacher tells his students that all those who get a score of 85% or better on the test being handed back have done well. However, anyone scoring less than 85% will have to find out where they "goofed" and take the test again the next day.

Notice that the referent is a cutoff score of 85%. It represents a particular level of performance defined in terms of some proportion of correct responses. Therefore, this is a criterion-referenced judgment. All who score below the referent are assigned a "negative" value (that is, they have done poorly and must retake the test). All who score at or above the referent are assigned a positive value. One might see this as a specific example of the pass/fail grading technique, which has become popular recently. Pass/fail grading utilizes a two-value rule.

The two-value rule is not limited to criterion-referenced judgments. All three types of judgments can be made with this kind of rule as you can see from the following examples.

Examples of Judgments Using the Two-Value Rule

Norm-referenced judgment
"The average score of the class was 17 correct. If you scored that high or higher, you did all right and you can go out to recess. If you scored lower than 17, stay inside for a few minutes so that I can explain this type of problem again."

Criterion-referenced judgment
"Anyone who has successfully completed all of the objectives for this unit may take a day off to look at the new library books. The rest of you should keep working until you have completed all the objectives."

Self-referenced judgment
"Those swimmers who have taken 0.5 seconds or more off at least one of their 'best' times had an exceptional meet. Anyone who did not make at least that much improvement must be at practice early tomorrow."

Criterion-referenced judgment
"Tomorrow I will examine your wood finishes. If I find no more than two flaws, you pass. If I find more than two flaws, you fail this unit. However, anyone who has failed this unit will be given another opportunity to pass later on."

It is important to note that the two-value rule is frequently used in situations where a minimum level of performance is expected before the student is allowed to continue on to the next learning activities. The selection of the referent is crucial in these kinds of judgments.* Whenever making these minimum-performance-level judgments, you should have some evidence that the level of performance selected as the referent does indeed represent some minimum level of successful performance. For example, there should be some evidence that students who have in the past performed at that level or higher also were able to function well on the learning activities that followed (in the next unit of study, in the next course, at the next grade level, etc.). Furthermore, those students who had not reached that level would have done poorly at the next level.

---

* Practice for setting minimum performance standards as referents is provided in the Workbook accompanying this Handbook.

Your Turn

THE TWO-VALUE RULE

For each of the three types of judgments, write at least one example illustrating the use of the two-value rule for forming judgments.

1. Criterion-referenced judgments

_____

_____

_____

2. Norm-referenced judgments

_____

_____

_____

3. Self-referenced judgments

_____

_____

_____

ANSWER KEY
Your Turn: The Two-Value Rule

1. *Examples of criterion-referenced judgments:*
   (a) 70% is passing; below 70% is failing.
   (b) If you can make six out of ten free throws, you can join the team.

2. *Examples of norm-referenced judgments:*
   (a) If you score above average, you are in reading group *A*; if you score below average, you are in reading group *B*.
   (b) Admission to the program requires a percentile rank of 80.

3. *Examples of self-referenced judgments:*
   (a) John did worse today than yesterday.
   (b) The class improved its performance this week.

THE DEVIATION RULE

This rule is referred to as the deviation rule because it assigns various values to an individual on the basis of how far the information we have about that individual *deviates* from the referent we have selected. Formally, it establishes a *scale of values* along a negative to positive (or low value to high value) continuum. A numerical grading scale that assigns different values to students depending upon "percentage correct" scores is an example of such a scale:

A Grading Scale Illustrating the Deviation Rule for Forming Judgments:

$$95-100\% = \text{A}$$
$$90-94\% = \text{B}$$
$$80-89\% = \text{C}$$
$$75-79\% = \text{D}$$
$$\text{Below } 75\% = \text{F}$$

The referent in the scale above can be thought of as 100% performance and deviations from that are assigned values ranging from A down to F.* It is interesting to note that letter grades have come to have relatively universal meanings in our society today (A = excellent; B = good; C = average; D = below average; F = failing).

The reason for developing a scale rather than a cutoff point is that most behavior can best be characterized as varying along some continuum. Individual differences can then be viewed in terms of different levels on the performance scale (that makes norm-referenced judgments meaningful). Furthermore, the achievement of a given individual can be described in terms of a specific point on that performance scale (a criterion-referenced judgment). Finally, an individual's progress can be viewed as a movement along that performance scale as measured across time (self-referenced judgments). As we discuss the development of each of these three types of judgments, you will see that developing a deviation scale involves defining points along the scale and assigning values (numerical and/or descriptive) to those points.

Deviation Scales for Norm-Referenced Judgments

The general procedure for developing norm-referenced scales involves deciding on a norm group and then, for each person in that group, determining how far he or she deviates from the referent. Finally, values are assigned to the various degrees of deviation from the referent. For classroom teachers, the appropriate norm group is almost always their own class (or classes if they are teaching several sections of the same class).

Percentile Rank. One of the most useful norm-referenced judgments is based upon a person's rank in the group defined in terms of the *percentage of individuals who score lower* than he does. For example, suppose that an individual has a percentile rank of 87. This means that 87 percent of the individuals in the norm group scored *at the same level or lower than he did.* The steps to take when computing percentile rank are previewed below. Look them over, read through the examples that follow, and then try to work the problems in the exercise that follows.

Computation of Percentile Rank

1. Count the number of individuals in the norm group.
2. Arrange the scores of the norm group in order from lowest to highest.

---

* Of course, any point along this continuum could be designated as the referent. Many teachers would prefer to think of 80% or 85% as the referent. Scores matching that referent are assigned a "C," and deviations above and below that referent are assigned other grades accordingly.

Make the following computations *for each score* that was obtained by at least one individual in the norm group:

3. (a) If only one individual obtained the score, count the number of individuals who scored lower than that score.
   (b) If more than one individual obtained the score, count the number of individuals who scored below that score *plus* one-half of the individuals scoring at that score.
4. Divide the number obtained in step 3 by the total number of individuals taking the test (see step 1).
5. Multiply the result of step 4 by 100.

Let's work through an example. We will use the scores for test A found in Exhibit 1. This exhibit of scores from a hypothetical high school science class will be referred to several times throughout the remainder of this chapter.

EXHIBIT 1

Student	Test A	Test B	Test C	Test D
1. Roger	31	50	50	98
2. Bill	28	47	34	76
3. Sam	34	50	20	93
4. Mary	30	48	38	84
5. Alice	26	52	48	87
6. George	31	49	15	92
7. Sue	29	51	48	72
8. Maurice	17	51	28	63
9. Doug	28	52	51	95
10. Joan	27	50	40	80
11. Mike	25	49	31	75
12. Jill	29	51	52	87
13. Mark	30	48	40	89
14. Nancy	20	52	31	91
15. Dave	24	50	19	96

First, we count the number of individuals in the group. There are 15.

Next, we arrange the scores for test A from lowest to highest: 17, 20, 24, 25, 28, 28, 28, 28, 29, 29, 30, 30, 31, 31, 34.

Now, taking one score at a time, we work through steps 3, 4, and 5.

For example, Roger scored 31 points. One other person also scored 31 points. So following step 3b, we count the number of individuals who scored below 31 (12) and add 1 ($\frac{1}{2}$ of 2). That gives us 13, which we divide by 15 (step 4) and multiply by 100 (step 5): $13 \div 15 = 0.87 \times 100 = 87$. Roger has a percentile rank of 87, which means that 87 percent of the class scored at the same score or lower than he did.

Now let's compute Bill's percentile rank. Six people scored lower than he did. One person scored the same. According to step 3b, that gives us $6 + (2 \div 2) = 6 + 1 = 7$. Next, we divide by 15 and multiply by 100: $7 \div 15 = 0.47 \times 100 = 47$. Bill's percentile rank is 47. That means 47 percent of the class scored at the same level or lower than Bill.

Your Turn

PERCENTILE RANK

Compute the percentile rank for each of the following students on test *A* (Exhibit 1):

Student	Test A Score	Percentile Rank
1. Mary	30	_____
2. Alice	26	_____
3. Maurice	17	_____
4. Nancy	20	_____

ANSWER KEY
Your Turn: Percentile Rank

1. Mary = 73   2. Alice = 26   3. Maurice = 0   4. Nancy = 6

The referent used when computing percentile rank is not immediately obvious. Each person's score is placed on a scale from 0–100 indicating the percentage of persons who score the same as or lower than he or she does. In a sense, this indicates how far an individual deviates from the bottom of the group in terms of the percentage of individuals scoring between him or her and the bottom. The referent, then, is the lowest score. Often, you will want to use the average score of a group to serve as the referent, and a scale of percentile ranks would not be appropriate. The standard score should be used when the group average is used as a referent.

Standard Score. The standard score has been developed to allow you to construct a meaningful numerical scale defined in terms of deviations from the average (that is, from the mean).* The most obvious way to approach this problem is simply to subtract the group's mean from each individual's score. That would give us a scale of deviations from the mean. The problem with this approach is that from test to test the meaning of a given numerical value changes dramatically. For example, Bill (Exhibit 1) scored exactly the same distance (3 points) from the mean on both test *B* and test *C*. However, a deviation of 3 points below the mean on test *B* represents a very poor score (the lowest in the class). That same deviation (3 points) below the mean on test *C* represents a much better score (6 students scored lower). Notice the range of the scores in test *B* (47–52). When all the scores are "bunched together" as in test *B*, a deviation of a few points can be

* The mean is the technical term for the kind of average you are probably most familiar with: the arithmetic average. It is computed by adding up all the scores and dividing that total by the number of scores in the group.

significant, whereas, when the scores are quite "spread out" as in test *C*, a deviation of a few points may not mean much.

As you can see, there is a need for a measure of deviation that takes into account the degree of spread in a set of scores. Such a measure could serve as a standard for determining the meaning of a deviation from the mean. Such a measure has been devised, and it is appropriately called a *standard deviation.* By comparing an individual's deviation from the mean to the standard deviation from the mean, one can make a reasonably meaningful judgment. This kind of comparison yields what is called a *standard score.*

A very basic standard score is called the *z* score. It is essentially a ratio of an individual's deviation from the mean compared to the standard deviation from the mean. A *z* score tells us how many standard deviation units a person's score is above or below the mean. Rarely do people deviate from the mean more than three standard deviation units. Consequently, a scale based upon *z* scores will usually range from −3 to +3 (3 points below the mean to 3 points above the mean). Anyone who scores right at the mean will get a *z* score of 0 because he does not deviate at all (0 deviation) from the mean.

The computation of the *z* score is basically very simple and follows logically from the definition given above. That definition describes a ratio between an individual's deviation from the mean and the standard deviation. Picture it this way:

$$z = \frac{\text{Individual's deviation from the mean}}{\text{Standard deviation}}$$

Replacing the words in the above ratio with "shorthand" symbols, we get the following:

$$z = \frac{X - \bar{X}}{\text{S.D.}}$$

where *z* = standard score, *X* = individual's raw score (number of items correct), $\bar{X}$ = mean or arithmetic average, and S.D. = standard deviation. Shortly, we will see how to compute the standard deviation of a group of scores. But, first let's practice computing the *z* score using the above formula. The mean for test *A* (Exhibit 1) was 27.3 and the standard deviation was 4.3. Given that much information, you should be able to compute each person's standard score for test *A*. For example, Roger scored 31 on test *A* so we compute his standard score as follows:

$$z = \frac{X - \bar{X}}{\text{S.D.}} = \frac{31 - 27.3}{4.3} = \frac{3.7}{4.3} = 0.86$$

Notice that Roger scored above the mean (his *z* score is positive), and he deviated almost one (0.86) standard deviation from the mean. Now let's compute Dave's *z* score. He scored below the mean, so his *z* score should be negative.

$$z = \frac{X - \bar{X}}{\text{S.D.}} = \frac{20 - 27.3}{4.3} = \frac{-7.3}{4.3} = -1.7$$

Dave's *z* score tells us that he scored below the mean (note the negative sign) and that he deviated almost two (1.7) standard deviation units from the mean.

Now let's return to a comparison of Bill's scores on tests B and C. You will remember that his deviation-from-the-mean score was 3 points for both tests. We had decided that he actually had done better on test C, even though he deviated exactly the same number of points from the mean on both tests. Bill's standard score, however, should be different for the two tests. The computation of those scores is as follows:

Bill's Test B z score	Bill's Test C z score
$z = \dfrac{47 - 50}{1.5} = \dfrac{-3}{1.5} = -2$	$z = \dfrac{34 - 37}{12.3} = \dfrac{-3}{12.3} = -0.24$

On test B, Bill scored 2 full standard deviations below the mean. However, on test C, he scored less than $\frac{1}{4}$ (0.24) of a standard deviation below the mean. Bill did indeed do better on test C.

In the next exercise you will be given an opportunity to practice computing z scores. They are not difficult. First, however, let us see how to compute (and how to estimate) the standard deviation of a group of scores. Then you will be able to begin with a set of test scores, compute the mean and the standard deviation, and, finally, figure each person's standard score. That's moving systematically from information about students to norm-referenced judgments about them (in the form of numerical values defined by standard deviation units). ·

The following formula* is used to compute the standard deviation of a set of scores:

$$\text{S.D.} = \sqrt{\frac{\Sigma (X - \bar{X})^2}{N}}$$

where Σ = "sum of," X = scores, and $\bar{X}$ = mean score. The formula reads this way: "The standard deviation is equal to the square root of the sum of the squared deviations from the mean divided by the number of scores." The formula is computed this way:

Students	Scores (X)	$X - \bar{X}$	$(X - \bar{X})^2$
1	7	$7 - 10 = -3$	$-3 \times -3 = 9$
2	9	$9 - 10 = -1$	$-1 \times -1 = 1$
3	11	$11 - 10 = 1$	$1 \times 1 = 1$
4	13	$13 - 10 = 3$	$3 \times 3 = 9$
	$\Sigma X = 40$		$\Sigma(X - \bar{X})^2 = 20$

$$\bar{X} = 40 \div 4 = 10$$

$$\text{S.D.} = \sqrt{\frac{20}{4}} = \sqrt{5} = 2.24$$

* If you have a calculator available, you may find it easier to use the following formula:

$$\text{S.D.} = \sqrt{\frac{\Sigma X^2}{N} - \left(\frac{\Sigma X}{N}\right)^2}$$

If you have a large number of scores and no calculator handy, you may wish to estimate the size of the standard deviation. This can be done quite accurately by a method described by Lathrop.[3] Lathrop's method involves the following three steps:

1. Sum the top one-sixth of the scores and sum the bottom one-sixth of the scores (e.g., if there were 60 scores, you would locate the 10 highest scores and add them up and then locate the 10 lowest scores and add them up).
2. Find the difference between these two sums (i.e., subtract the sum of the lowest scores from the sum of the highest scores).
3. Divide the difference obtained in step 2 by one-half of the *total* scores in the group (not just the total in the top and bottom one-sixths).

Earlier, we indicated that the standard deviation for test A (Exhibit 1) was 4.3. Let's see how close our estimate of the standard deviation would be using the procedure outlined above. There are 15 scores in the group. One-sixth of 15 is 2.5. Rounding this off to 3, we will sum the 3 highest scores ($34 + 31 + 31 = 96$) and the 3 lowest scores ($17 + 20 + 24 = 61$). The difference between these sums is 35 ($96 - 61 = 35$). Now, we divide this difference by one-half of the total number of scores ($35 \div 7.5 = 4.67$). Our estimate is 4.7, which is very close to the actual standard deviation of 4.3.

Your Turn

STANDARD SCORES

For the following questions use the data found in Exhibit 1.

1. Compute z scores for the following individuals on test A. (Remember, in test A: $\overline{X} = 27.3$; S.D. = 4.3.)

   (a) Sue

   (b) Joan

   (c) Dave

(d) Maurice

2. Compute the z scores for Nancy on tests A, B, and C (test A: $\bar{X} = 27.3$; S.D. $= 4.3$; test B: $\bar{X} = 50$; S.D. $= 1.5$; test C: $\bar{X} = 37$; S.D. $= 12.3$).

(a) test A z score

(b) test B z score

(c) test C z score

3. Compute and estimate the standard deviation of test D.

(a) computation

(b) estimate

ANSWER KEY
Your Turn: Standard Scores

1. (a) Sue's z score = 0.395
   (b) Joan's z score = −0.069
   (c) Dave's z score = −0.767
   (d) Maurice's z score = −2.395
2. Test *A* z score for Nancy = −1.697
   Test *B* z score for Nancy = 1.33
   Test *C* z score for Nancy = −0.489

3. (a)
$$\sqrt{\frac{\Sigma X^2}{N} - \left(\frac{\Sigma X}{N}\right)^2} = \sqrt{\frac{110,308}{15} - \left(\frac{1,278}{15}\right)^2}$$
$$= \sqrt{7,353.87 - 7,259.04}$$
$$= \sqrt{94.83}$$
$$= 9.74$$

(b) 98 + 96 + 95 = 289
     75 + 72 + 63 = 210
     289 − 210 = 79
     79 ÷ 7.5 = 10.53

Deviation Scales for Criterion-Referenced Judgments

The referent in criterion-referenced judgments is a level of performance or achievement. That referent is probably most useful if it is in the form of an observable behavior (or set of behaviors). Deviations from that referent will also be most useful if they are described in terms of observable behaviors. Consequently, to develop a criterion-referenced deviation scale, one must first describe the behaviors along an achievement continuum and then assign values to the various levels of achievement defined by that continuum. More specifically, there are three steps to take when producing a criterion-referenced deviation scale:

1. Define the characteristic being judged.
2. Describe the full range of behaviors which are representative of that characteristic.
3. Determine which values will be placed upon which levels of performance.

1. Define the characteristic being judged. It is especially important in criterion-referenced judgments that you define the *characteristic(s)* you are going to be judging. Note well: We do not judge an individual; we judge some characteristic of that individual. For example, we judge that person's weight, height, intelligence, math ability, reading level, problem-solving prowess, etc. Consequently, it is imperative that we know precisely what we are judging before we try to establish the criteria for making that judgment. Usually, criterion-referenced judgments are made in classroom settings so that the teacher can determine the level of achievement of his or her student(s). That means that what is being judged is a student's performance on some desired learning outcome. If that outcome is well defined in observable terms, then step 2 is much easier.[4]

2. Describe the range of behaviors representative of the characteristic being judged. There are two useful approaches to this step. The first involves describing an important learning outcome and the behaviors that are prerequisite to the attainment of the outcome; the second is to describe the extremes of the characteristic being judged and then to specify various points between those extremes.*

Suppose that we wish to evaluate the following learning outcome: "Given a set of raw scores from some test, to convert those scores to z scores with 90 percent accuracy." The ultimate objective is "to compute z scores." That sets the upper end of our continuum:

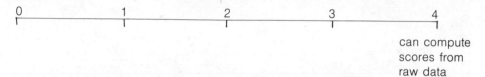

can compute
scores from
raw data

Next we ask the question: "What are the prerequisite behaviors (that is, what must the student know or be able to do) in order to be able to compute z scores from raw data?" As you know, he or she must be able to compute the standard deviation of the scores. Furthermore, in order to do that, the student must be able to compute the mean and the deviations from the mean. If he or she cannot even compute the mean, that person has hardly begun to progress toward the accomplishment of the desired outcome. Placing these prerequisite behaviors along our continuum, it now looks like this:

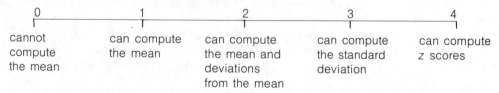

| cannot compute the mean | can compute the mean | can compute the mean and deviations from the mean | can compute the standard deviation | can compute z scores |

Let's try another example. The learning outcome of interest is: "To use addition and subtraction to work out story problems in fourth grade math." Let's arrange the continuum as a vertical scale this time. The ultimate learning outcome is at the top, and the prerequisite behaviors are listed below in order of the expected execution by the students. In this continuum, the prerequisite behaviors cumulate.

5 ⊢ Decides what the problem is asking, determines what information the problem provides, writes a number sentence that fits the problem, and arrives at a correct solution.

4 ⊢ Decides what the problem is asking, determines what information the problem provides, and writes a number sentence that fits the problem, but arrives at an incorrect solution.

3 ⊢ Decides what the problem is asking, determines what information the problem provides, but cannot write a number sentence that fits the problem and arrives at an incorrect solution.

2 ⊢ Decides what the problem is asking, but cannot begin to work toward a solution.

1 ⊢ Cannot even determine what the problem is asking.

* Some of the scales constructed in this section also appear in *Evaluation: A Practical Guide for Teachers*, by T. D. TenBrink. Copyright © 1974 by McGraw-Hill Book Company. Used with permission.

Many learning outcomes require several prerequisite skills that are not necessarily learned by the student in a given order. A scale for determining the level of achievement in these cases might simply indicate the number of prerequisite skills a given student has accomplished at a given point in time. An example of this kind of learning outcome would be: "To use the major reference aids in the public library." A list of the aids would likely include at least the following: (1) *Reader's Guide to Periodic Literature*, (2) *Education Index*, (3) card catalog, (4) bound volumes of journals, and (5) recent, unbound journals.

A criterion-referenced scale for judging a student's level of competency at using these aids might look like this:

0	1	2	3	4	5
uses none of the aids listed	successfully uses one of the five aids	successfully uses two of the five aids	successfully uses three of the five aids	successfully uses four of the five aids	successfully uses all five aids

Not all characteristics teachers are called upon to judge are easily defined in terms of some ultimate outcome. Suppose, for example, that you are trying to judge a student's ability to stay with a task. A useful scale might look like this:

1	2	3	4	5
gives up at the first sign of any trouble	gives up with a minimal amount of struggle	keeps trying even though experiencing difficulties	stays with the task after most would have quit	never quits until told to by the teacher

These kinds of scales are relatively easy to construct if you describe the extreme ends of the continuum first and then fill in the points between those extremes. One way to do that is to think of someone who exemplifies the extreme positive end of the scale and then someone who exemplifies the extreme negative end of the scale. Now, describe each of those persons from the perspective of the characteristic being measured. For example, a scale for judging the quality of a student's speaking voice might look like this:

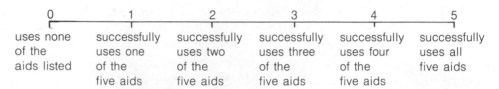

| weak, squeaky, does not carry well | | moderately strong, not full, carries fairly well | | strong, full, carries well |

Or, suppose honesty is the trait to be judged. Using the preacher back home and Uncle Clem as exemplars of the two extremes, we might produce the beginning of a scale that would look like this:

| Uncle Clem always lies, stretches every story out of proportion, exaggerates to his own advantage. | | | | The preacher back home never lies, does not even "hide" the truth or twist it slightly. |

Note that this technique can be applied to the development of a scale for judging products of student performance also. For example, here are the extreme ends of a scale used for judging the quality of a salt-and-flour map:

severely cracked, poorly proportioned, inaccurate topography, sloppy		smooth, well proportioned, excellent accuracy of borders and topography, neat

3. *Assign values to the points along the scale.* The values you assign to the various levels of performance can be defined as letter grades, numbers, or descriptive labels such as excellent, good, fair, etc. It is not easy to determine what values should be assigned to a given level of performance, but the following suggestions should help:

1. Assign highest values to difficult, but attainable, behaviors.
2. Assign lowest values to little or no proficiency.
3. Values should reflect the opinions of other experts (for example, do other high school teachers agree with your assignment of values?).
4. Values should vary according to the grade level of the individuals being judged. (A performance rated excellent for third graders might rate very poor for high school students.)
5. Any minimum standards for passing (mastery) should be reflective of the actual minimum performance possible for continued learning to be a reality.

A final note: Deviation scales probably should include no less than 5 points and no more than 11 points. An A to F letter-grade scale is a 5-point scale unless + and − signs are used, and then it becomes a 12-point scale.

Your Turn

CRITERION-REFERENCED DEVIATION SCALES

1. Construct a scale for judging the following learning outcome: "To be able to distinguish between norm-referenced and criterion-referenced judgments."

2. Describe the extreme ends of a continuum that could be used for judging a student's study habits.

ANSWER KEY

Your Turn: Criterion-Referenced Deviation Scales

1. Your scale should reflect the skills needed to make the discrimination being called for by the outcome. One possible example:

1 — Cannot tell the difference between norm-referenced and criterion-referenced judgments and cannot describe either one.

2 —

3 — Can describe both norm-referenced and criterion-referenced judgments, but cannot identify them correctly when the two kinds are listed together in a group.

4 —

5 — Can describe both norm-referenced and criterion-referenced judgments and can distinguish between them, identifying them correctly when the two kinds are listed together in a group.

2. You would find this easiest if you tried to picture two persons: one with good study habits, one with poor ones. Your extremes might look something like this:

(a) *Poor study habits:* Rarely takes notes, has no schedule for studying, doesn't study until the night before the test, tries to memorize everything instead of trying to understand.

(b) *Good study habits:* Takes good notes, plans study time wisely, works ahead so there is no need for cramming, seeks to understand as well as to commit to memory, uses outside sources to increase understanding.

Deviation Scales for Self-Referenced Judgments

Self-referenced judgments are usually based upon an individual's deviation from a previous performance. The most common use of these judgments is for plotting individual progress. The scale is defined by the potential progress for a particular individual on the characteristic being judged. The values assigned to the positions on that scale will depend upon the judge's (teacher's) knowledge about that individual. Particularly important is his or her understanding of how much progress that individual could reasonably be expected to make in a given time span. High values should be assigned to progress exceeding expectations, and low values to progress failing to meet expectations. Because this procedure for assigning values leans so heavily on the teacher's expectations, it is important for teachers to keep records of student progress over time in a variety of subject matter areas. These records can serve as a useful data base when determining what is "a reasonable amount of progress."

It is important to note that self-referenced scales are often formed on the basis of previously formed norm-referenced or criterion-referenced judgments. One might decide, for example, that an individual has made a great deal of progress because on the last test his or her percentile rank was only 28, but on this test it is 72. (A comparison between two norm-referenced judgments forms the basis for a self-referenced judgment.) Or, take the case where progress along an achievement continuum is judged to be excellent: "Sarah has made excellent progress. In the last week she has moved from almost no proficiency in word attack skills to a moderately high level of proficiency as defined by the continuum defining word attack skills." (A self-referenced judgment based upon a comparison of two criterion-referenced judgments made one week apart.)

Mastery Test

OBJECTIVE 3 To establish rules for assigning values to individuals.

1. Describe the two-value rule for forming judgments. Give at least one example illustrating its use.

_____

_____

_____

_____

_____

2. Describe the deviation rule for forming judgments. Give three examples of such a rule: one where it is being used to make a norm-referenced judgment; one, a criterion-referenced judgment; and one, a self-referenced judgment.

_____

_____

_____

_____

_____

3. Given the scores 1, 3, 3, 8, 10, 15, 22, 23, 25, compute:

   (a) the mean

   (b) the standard deviation

   (c) the z score for a score of 10

4. List the 3 steps to take when producing a criterion-referenced, deviation scale:

(a) _____

_____

(b) _____

_____

(c) _____

_____

5. Most self-referenced judgments are based upon previously formed norm-referenced or criterion-referenced judgments. (true or false)

ANSWER KEY

Mastery Test, Objective 3

1. The two-value rule says that a positive value is to be associated with information matching or exceeding the referent and a negative value is to be associated with information which falls below that referent.
   Examples:
   1. "If you get 8 out of 10 correct on tomorrow's quiz, you do not have to do the extra reading assignment."
   2. All 100 level courses will be graded on a pass–fail basis beginning in the fall 1978 semester.

2. The deviation rule assigns values on the basis of how far the information about an individual deviates from the referent. Formally, it establishes a scale of values along a negative to positive continuum.

Examples of norm-referenced judgments:
1. percentile rank
2. z score

Examples of criterion-referenced judgments:
1. percentage correct scores
2. number of points above the minimum passing score

Examples of self-referenced judgments:
1. improvement or gain scores
2. comparisons across subject matters for the same student

3. (a) 12.22   (b) 8.9   (c) −0.249
4. (a) Define the characteristic being judged.
   (b) Describe the full range of behaviors representing that characteristic.
   (c) Determine the values to be placed on various levels of performance.
5. true

LEARNING ACTIVITY 3.2

Get together with at least two other people and discuss the guidelines for producing criterion-referenced deviation scales. Now, decide on some characteristic of human behavior for which you can build a scale. Have each person develop his or her own scale independently. Next, compare the scales, discussing the similarities and differences. Ask yourselves: "What caused the differences in the scales? Were they serious differences? Would an individual being judged on the characteristic decided upon obtain significantly different ratings depending on the scale used?"

Objective 4

To evaluate, using rules to assign values to individuals.

As you worked through the previous objective, you were given all the tools needed to meet this objective also. In some of the exercises, you were given practice in using the rules as well as in developing them. Consequently, let's simply review the basic process involved in forming a judgment and try some additional practice exercises.

LEARNING ACTIVITY 4.1

To form a judgment is to place a value upon. That is done by comparing information you have obtained about an individual to some other information called a referent. After selecting an appropriate referent, you make the comparison, note the deviation between the information and the referent, and assign a value to the individual based upon a previously established rule.

Just at the point of applying a rule (for example, the formula for computing a z score or the scale defining a set of performance criteria), it is a good idea to check your procedures systematically. The following check list should help you to make sure your judgments are well formed and accurate.

Check List for Evaluating Procedures Used in Forming Judgments

_____   The characteristic being judged is, in fact, the crucial characteristic regarding the decision(s) to be made about the individual being judged.

_____   The information obtained about that individual is accurate and is a measure of the characteristic being judged.

_____   The type of referent is appropriate for the decisions that will be made (for example, do I really want to make a norm-referenced judgment?).

_____   The specific referent selected was obtained under appropriate conditions and is in the same form (for example, a score, description, or value) as the information that will be compared with it.

_____   The rule for assigning values seems like a reasonable rule for the kind of judgment I am making. The values the rule is producing generally match my intuitive feeling about the individual being judged.

LEARNING ACTIVITY 4.2

Gather sample report cards from surrounding school districts. Examine the cards carefully and answer the following questions: What characteristics and/or learning outcomes are the students being judged on? What type of judgments do the grades on the card reflect (NRJ, CRJ, or SRJ)? Is there any indication that the rules for assigning the grades (values) are consistent from grade to grade? teacher to teacher? subject to subject? Should they be? Share your findings with the class.

LEARNING ACTIVITY 4.3

Read some of the recent popular books (or articles) on grading policies.* Talk to teachers, administrators, parents, and students to obtain their opinions about grading. Summarize your findings. Does your understanding of the process of forming judgments help you to formulate your own opinions about grading more clearly? Is a report-card grade a judgment or a summary of judgments? What decisions are likely to be made on the basis of report-card grades?

* See Additional Readings.

Mastery Test

OBJECTIVE 4 To evaluate, using rules to assign values to individuals.

Larry's history test score was 15 out of 25 correct. The test was designed to measure recall of specific facts about the Civil War. The class average was 22 correct, and the standard deviation of the test was 2.4.

1. Compute Larry's percentile rank.

2. Compute Larry's z score.

3. Make a criterion-referenced deviation judgment about Larry's knowledge of facts about the Civil War.

4. What else would you need to know (besides the information provided above) before you could make a self-referenced judgment about Larry's level of achievement in history?

ANSWER KEY
Mastery Test, Objective 4

1. Percentile rank cannot be completed with the information given (the percentage score based on 15 out of 25 can, but that is not the same as percentile rank).

2. $\dfrac{15 - 22}{2.4} = \dfrac{-7}{2.4} = -2.92$

3. Larry received a score of 60%.

4. How well Larry did on previous history tests or how well Larry did on tests in his other classes.

NOTES

1. See T. D. TenBrink, *Evaluation: A Practical Guide for Teachers* (New York: McGraw-Hill Book Company, 1974) for more details.

2. Robert Glaser, "Instructional Technology and the Measurement of Learning Outcomes — Some Questions," *American Psychologist* 18 (1963): 520.

3. Robert L. Lathrop, "A quick but accurate approximation to the standard deviation of a distribution," *Journal of Experimental Education* 6 (1946): 533–536. This estimate assumes a relatively normal distribution of scores.

4. The following discussion is based upon material from TenBrink, *Evaluation*, 1974.

ADDITIONAL READINGS

Bloom, B. S., T. J. Hastings, and G. F. Madaus. *Handbook on Formative and Summative Evaluation of Student Learning.* New York: McGraw-Hill Book Company, 1971.

Gronlund, N. E. *Measurement and Evaluation in Teaching*, 3rd ed. New York: Macmillan Co., 1976.

Lyman, H. B. *Test Scores and What They Mean*, 2nd ed. Englewood Cliffs, New Jersey: Prentice-Hall, 1971.

Stufflebeam, D. I., W. A. Foley, E. G. Gephart, E. G. Guba, R. I. Hammond, H. O. Merriman, and M. M. Provus. *Educational Evaluation and Decision Making.* Itasca, Illinois: F. E. Peacock Publishers, 1971.

TenBrink, T. D. *Evaluation: A Practical Guide for Teachers.* New York: McGraw-Hill Book Company, 1974.

Terwilliger, J. S. *Assigning Grades to Students.* Glenview, Illinois: Scott, Foresman, and Company, 1971.

Wittrock, M. C., and D. E. Wiley, eds. *The Evaluation of Instruction: Issues and Problems.* New York: Holt, Rinehart & Winston, 1970.

APPENDIX A
The Question Master Game

1. Cut out the cards on the following pages and stack them in three piles: Chance Cards, Question About Questions Cards, and Classification Cards.
2. Read the directions.
3. Turn to the game board and begin.

THE QUESTION MASTER

DIRECTIONS

Object: The object of the game is to become the first teacher in your neighborhood to reach that magic circle of the select few (to wit, the Question Master Circle).

Players: 2 to 6

Moves: You move along the board from the space marked "Start" by rolling a die. If you don't have any dice, then simply make and cut out cards numbered from 1 to 6, and each player can select a card from the pile on his or her turn. If you are a professional game player, use your spinner.

Pieces: Use anything that fits on the spaces (different coins, buttons, small pieces of paper with your initials, chess pieces, etc.).

Spaces:

Classification. When you land on a space marked with a C, *another* player selects a card from the pile of Classification Cards and reads the question to you. You must then classify the question on the appropriate level of Bloom's *Taxonomy*. The correct answer is printed on the card. If you are correct, you can stay on that space. If you are *incorrect*, you must go back *three spaces*.

Question. When you land on a space marked with a Q, *another* player selects a card from the pile of Question About Questions Cards. If you answer the question correctly (correct answers are also written on the card), you stay on that space. If you answer incorrectly, you must go back *three spaces*.

Ah, the whims of fortune. If you land on this space, select a card from the Chance pile and follow the instructions.

An arrow signifies a different route that must be followed when you land on this space. The first of these is a shorter route; the second is a longer route.

You lose one turn if you land on this space.

If you land on a space marked Gym, Principal's Office, Lunch Room, or Detention Hall, then you have no questions to answer or classify. You may also be sent to these locations by a Chance Card.

The Question Master: You need *not* land on the last space (Question Master) by exact count.

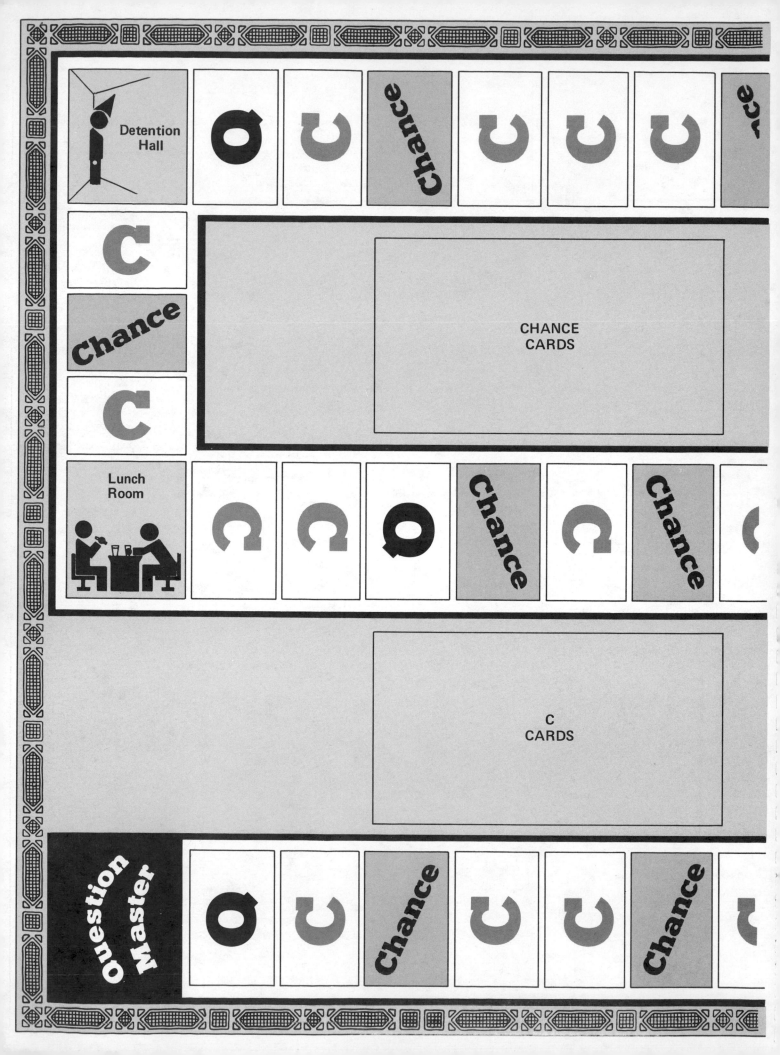

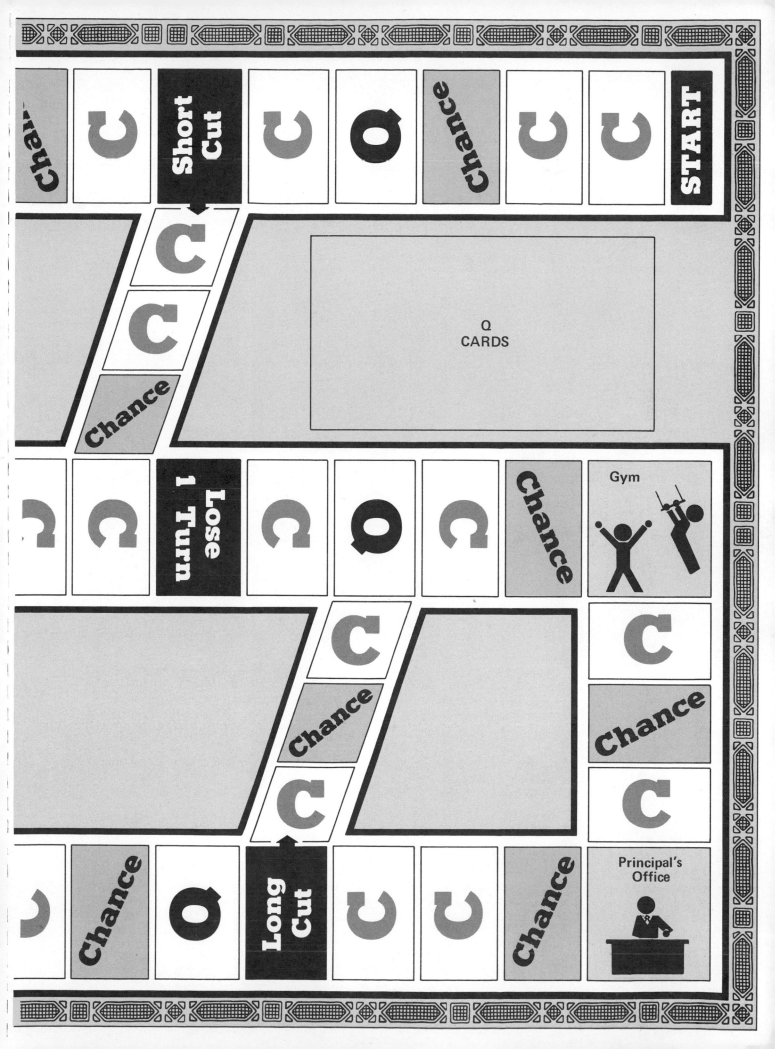

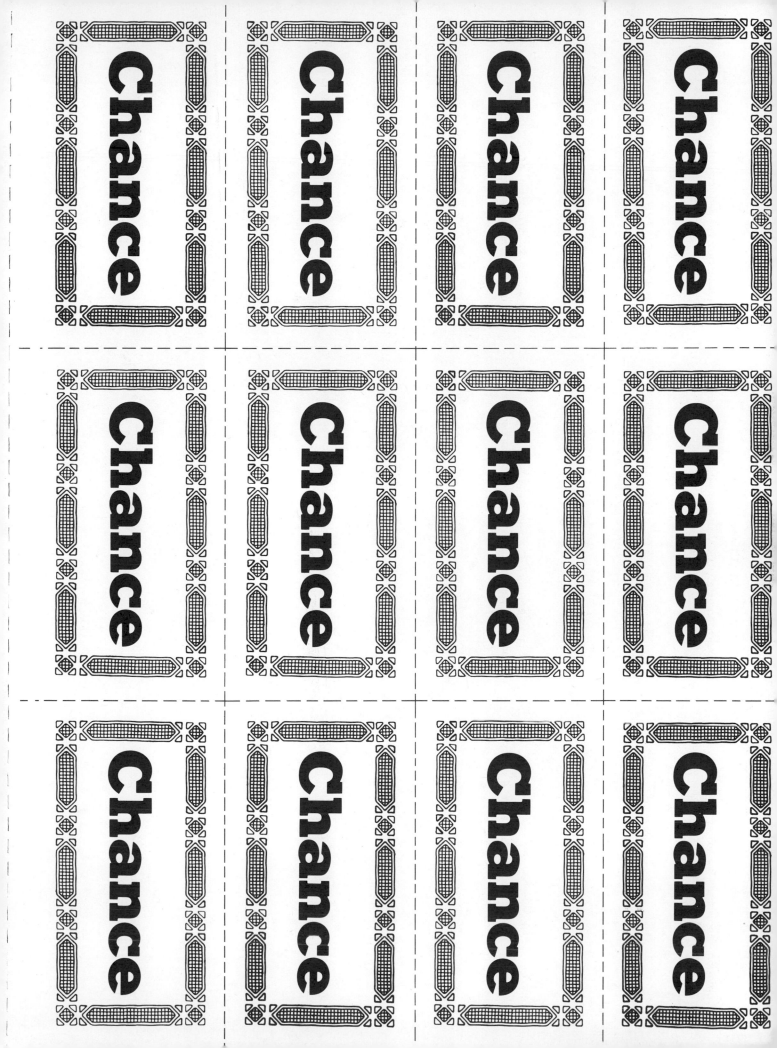

Chance Card

Promotion. Move ahead six spaces if you can re-cite the 6 levels of Bloom's *Taxonomy* backwards within ten seconds. GO.

Chance Card

Teacher of the Year Award. Move ahead 4 spaces.

Chance Card

You've just been passed by for merit. Move back 3 spaces.

Chance Card

The principal smiled at you and said you were doing a fine job. Stay where you are.

Chance Card

You forgot to lock your cabinet, and your prize Hopi Indian Kit is gone. Go back 3 spaces.

Chance Card

You have been using only memory questions in class and your students do not really understand the material. Go back 3 spaces.

Chance Card

Your evaluation report just came back and you will be getting tenure. Live it up. Take another turn.

Chance Card

Your car ran out of gas on your way to work. Lose one turn.

Chance Card

Students just selected you as their best teacher. Roll the dice to determine how many spaces you can move ahead.

Chance Card

Two more students fell asleep when you asked a question. Move back 2 spaces.

Chance Card

You've just been assigned to stay after school with kids who were behavior problems. Go to detention hall.

Chance Card

The principal is coming to observe you and you forgot your lesson plans. Go back 3 spaces.

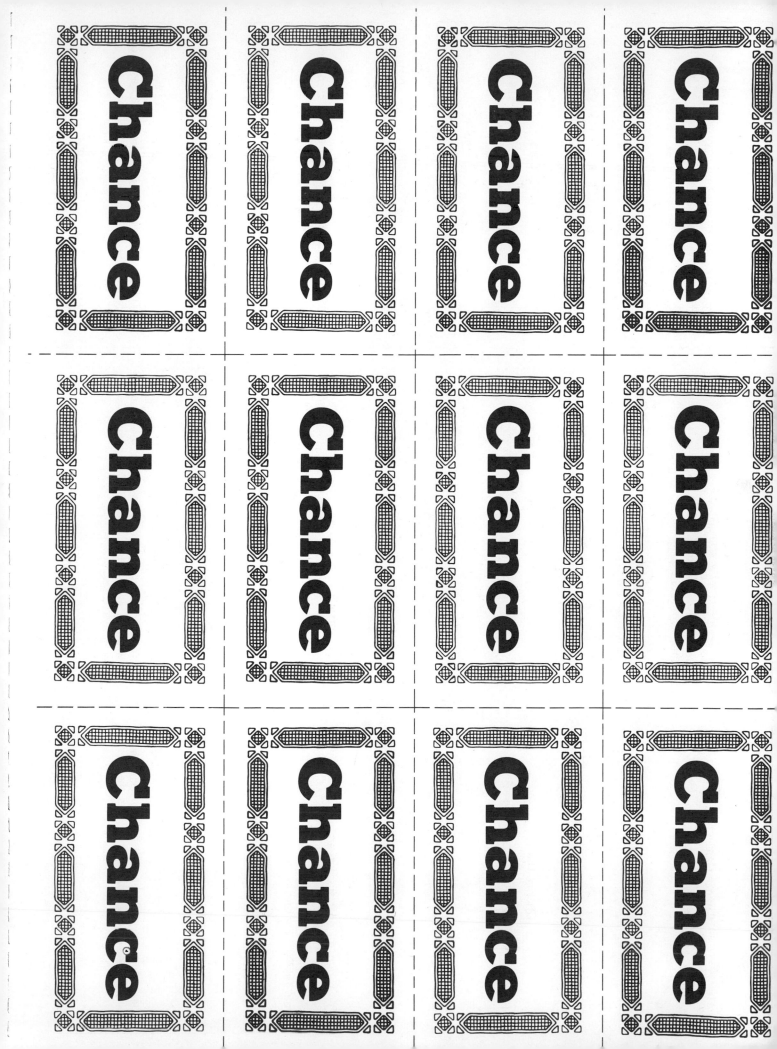

Chance Card

TGIF (Thank God It's Friday). You made it to Friday. Move ahead one space.

Chance Card

You've just been assigned lunch room duty. Move directly to the lunch room.

Chance Card

Christmas Vacation — get your battery recharged. Move ahead 5 spaces.

Chance Card

June is here and everyone has spring fever. Lose one turn.

Chance Card

You are being considered for assistant principal. Go directly to the principal's office and wait — for three turns before going on.

Chance Card

Congratulations! You are now the new basketball coach. Go directly to the gym.

Chance Card

Your attendance reports are missing and the principal would like you to recall who was absent during the last week. Go to the principal's office. Lose two turns.

Chance Card

Your higher order questions are really making a difference and student grades are improving. Go ahead five spaces.

Chance Card

Faculty meeting this afternoon. Lose one turn.

Chance Card

Inservice workshop this afternoon. Go ahead 4 spaces.

Chance Card

The parents of your students are so pleased with your effective classroom questions that they have taken an ad out in the local newspaper thanking you. Take another turn.

Chance Card

You stayed up last night until 2:00 a.m. grading student papers, and you forgot to take them to school this morning. Lose one turn.

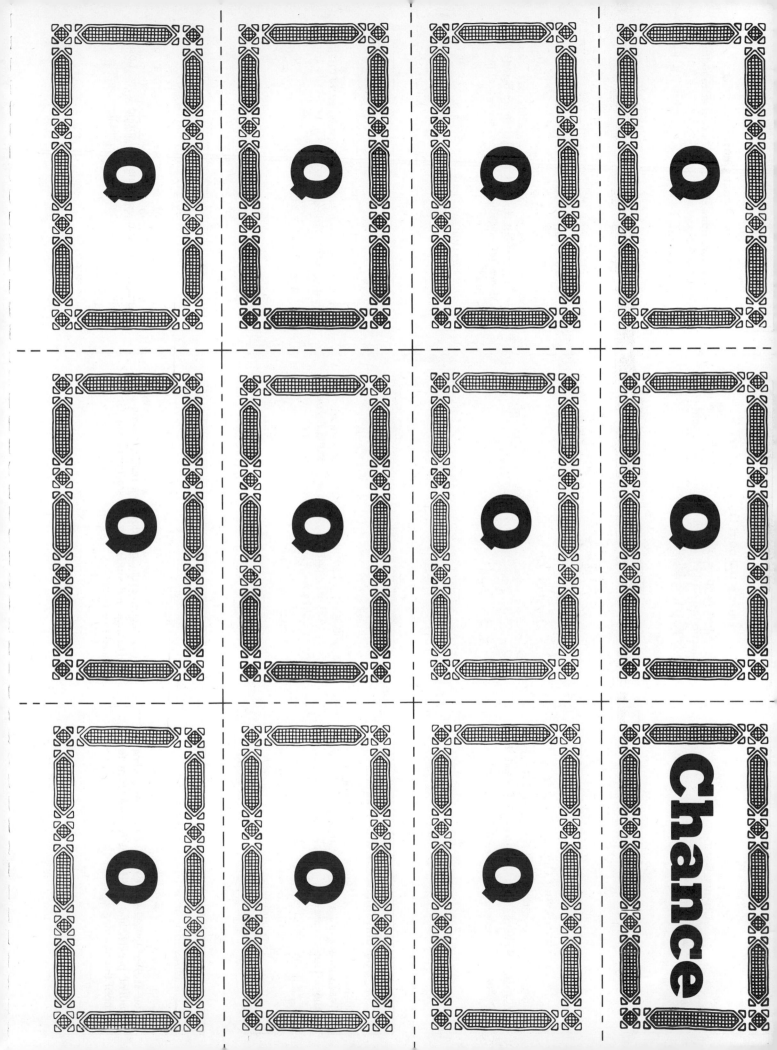

Question About Questions Cards

Analysis questions call for higher order thinking. True or false?

Answer: True

Question About Questions Cards

Which of the following is *not* a process required by analysis questions? (a) identifying evidence to support a statement (b) making a statement based on evidence (c) explaining motives or causes (d) making predictions.

Answer: (d)

Question About Questions Cards

A "why" question suggests a question asked on the analysis level. True or false?

Answer: True

Question About Questions Cards

Synthesis questions require students to do all of the following *except* (a) make predictions (b) solve problems (c) construct original communications (d) evaluate ideas, solutions to problems, and aesthetic works.

Answer: (d)

Question About Questions Cards

A student who is asked to interpret a cartoon is functioning on a (a) knowledge (b) comprehension (c) application (d) analysis level

Answer: (b)

Question About Questions Cards

Application level questions generally have more than one possible answer. True or false?

Answer: False

Question About Questions Cards

If you were asked to use a particular process in order to solve a problem, what level of the *Taxonomy* would you be operating on?

Answer: application

Question About Questions Cards

When you are asked to solve mathematical problems, you are usually working at what level of the *Taxonomy?*

Answer: application

Chance Card

Your use of higher order questions has made this your best year of teaching. Take an extra turn.

Question About Questions Cards

Most of the questions asked by teachers are on what level of thinking?

Answer: Lower order or memory or knowledge level

Question About Questions Card

Memory questions are lower order and not useful. Teachers would be better off if they did not use them. True or false?

Answer: False. Although overused, they are essential for other levels of thinking to occur.

Question About Questions Card

Comprehension questions require students to (a) repeat information exactly (b) make comparisons (c) make judgments (d) offer opinions, beliefs, and values.

Answer: (b)

Classification Card

What is the capital of Maryland?

Answer: knowledge

Classification Card

Who wrote *Romeo and Juliet?*

Answer: knowledge

Classification Card

Who is the governor of Wisconsin?

Answer: knowledge

Classification Card

What did King John say in the next chapter?

Answer: knowledge

Classification Card

Who wrote *Pollution: The Last Chapter?*

Answer: knowledge

Classification Card

How are these two solutions similar?

Answer: comprehension

Classification Card

When was the charter written?

Answer: knowledge

Classification Card

How would you state the main idea of this poem?

Answer: comprehension

Question About Questions Cards

Synthesis questions require original and creative thought from students. True or false?

Answer: True

Question About Questions Cards

Which level of the *Taxonomy* would you be functioning at if you drew a self-portrait?

Answer: synthesis

Question About Questions Cards

What level of the *Taxonomy* is a question that asks you to describe what you think the United States will be like in the year 2000?

Answer: synthesis

Question About Questions Cards

Your new assignment is to judge an all-male beauty contest. You will be asked to decide on a winner. What level of the *Taxonomy* will you be working on?

Answer: evaluation

Classification Card

What does this chart mean?

Answer: comprehension

Classification Card

What is the message of this political cartoon?

Answer: comprehension

Classification Card

How does yesterday's class discussion compare with your textbook account of the American Revolution?

Answer: comprehension

Classification Card

Using the process we discussed yesterday, solve this problem.

Answer: application

Classification Card

How does the geography of Maine compare with the geography of Mexico?

Answer: comprehension

Classification Card

Considering your two reading assignments, what characteristics do Vietnam and Thailand have in common?

Answer: comprehension

Classification Card

In your own words, what were the main ideas in your homework assignment?

Answer: comprehension

Classification Card

Describe yesterday's discussion in your own words.

Answer: comprehension

Classification Card

What is the meaning of democracy? (The students have previously been given the definition.)

Answer: knowledge

Classification Card

How is ecology defined? (The students have previously been given the definition.)

Answer: knowledge

Classification Card

What was the topic of yesterday's discussion?

Answer: knowledge

Classification Card

Give the textbook definition of the feminist movement.

Answer: knowledge

Classification Card

What would society be like if marriage were against the law?

Answer: synthesis

Classification Card

How would people respond if Congress enacted a law that forced people to wear seat belts?

Answer: synthesis

Classification Card

Which song do you prefer?

Answer: evaluation

Classification Card

Should people be allowed to marry at any age?

Answer: evaluation

Classification Card

Should the United States stop foreign aid?

Answer: evaluation

Classification Card

Which solution is best?

Answer: evaluation

Classification Card

Who is your favorite movie star?

Answer: evaluation

Classification Card

Which party do you prefer: Democrats or Republicans?

Answer: evaluation

Classification Card

Who was our greatest President?

Answer: evaluation

Classification Card

Do you believe that he's telling the truth?

Answer: evaluation

Classification Card

Locate Memphis by latitude and longitude on a map.

Answer: application

Classification Card

If Harry takes two hours to mow a lawn and Harriet takes one hour, how long would it take if they both mowed the lawn?

Answer: application

Classification Card

Using any land area in the world, choose a site you consider an ideal location for a city.

Answer: synthesis

Classification Card

What would be the effects of a woman being elected President?

Answer: synthesis

Classification Card

How many answers to this problem can you think of?

Answer: synthesis

Classification Card

Compose a letter to a friend who is having problems in his studies.

Answer: synthesis

Classification Code

Why is New York called "The Empire State"?

Answer: analysis

Classification Card

Why did Myra refuse to give her diary to the publisher?

Answer: analysis

Classification Card

What evidence can you cite to support your argument?

Answer: analysis

Classification Card

What is the tone of the article?

Answer: analysis

Classification Card

Do you like modern art?

Answer: evaluation

Classification Card

Do you prefer Picasso, Chagall, or Miro?

Answer: evaluation

Classification Card

Solve $x^2 + 14 = 18$.

Answer: application

Classification Card

Using the rules of punctuation that we have learned, find the error in the following sentence.

Answer: application

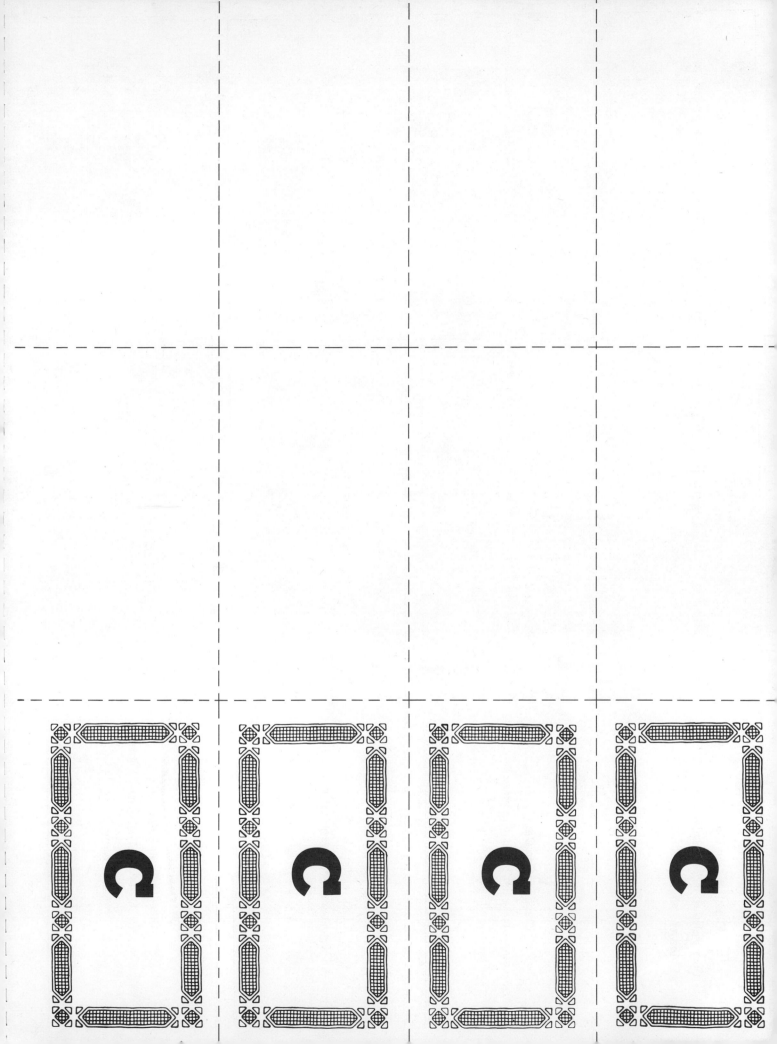

Classification Card

Draw a picture of your favorite building.

Answer: synthesis

Classification Card

How can we make foreign aid more effective?

Answer: synthesis

Classification Card

How can we determine the weight of this object without a standard scale?

Answer: synthesis

Classification Card

What should we call our pet?

Answer: synthesis

APPENDIX B
Concept Cards

soldier	rhythm	haiku
family	translation	set (in mathematics)
love	intensity (in color)	distance
justice	well done (in cooking)	direction
vertebrae	coordination	melody
amoeba	transportation	accent
vowel	heredity	waste
mass media	photosynthesis	airplane

cloud	map	hypotenuse
polygon	symmetry	square feet
moisture	counterpoint	preposition
gravity	hue	adverb
wood	resource	debate
mass	personality	idiomatic phrase
vapor	off key	exercise
democracy	harmony	sprint
slavery	exponent	curve ball
		pocket (in football)

Glossary

Abstract concepts. Those concepts that can be acquired only indirectly through the senses or cannot be perceived directly through the senses.

Active listening. Differentiating between the intellectual and emotional content of a message, and making inferences regarding the feelings experienced by the speaker.

Advance organizers. Informing students of the way in which new information is organized.

Affective objectives. Objectives that deal primarily with emotion and feeling.

Analysis questions. Questions that require the student to break down a communication into its constituent parts such that the relative hierarchy of ideas is made clear and/or the relations between the ideas expressed are made explicit.

Application questions. Questions requiring the student to apply a rule or process to a problem in order to determine the correct answer.

At task observation. An observation technique that provides data indicating whether or not individuals were engaged in tasks thought to be appropriate for a given activity.

Attending behavior. Use of verbal and nonverbal cues by the listener that demonstrate he or she is listening with care and empathy to what is being said.

Attitude. A predisposition to act in a positive or negative way toward persons, ideas, or events.

Attraction. Friendship patterns in the classroom group.

Classroom management. That set of teaching behaviors by which the teacher promotes appropriate student behavior and eliminates inappropriate student behavior, develops good interpersonal relationships and a positive socioemotional climate, and establishes and maintains an effective and productive classroom organization.

Closure. Actions and statements by teachers that are designed to bring a lesson presentation to an appropriate conclusion.

Cohesiveness. The collective feeling that the class members have about the classroom group; the sum of the individual members' feelings about the group.

Comprehension questions. Questions requiring the student to select, organize, and arrange mentally the materials pertinent to answering the question.

Concepts. Categories into which our experiences are organized, and the larger network of intellectual relationships brought about through categorization.

Conclusions. Pieces of information that follow logically from an investigation, formal or informal, and that are presented in the form of a statement.

Concrete concepts. Those concepts that can be perceived directly through one of the five senses.

Conditional reinforcers. Reinforcers that are learned.

Conjunctive concepts. Concepts that have only a single set of qualities or characteristics to learn.

Criterial attributes. The basic characteristics of a concept.

Criterion-referenced judgments. Judgments made by comparing the information you have about an individual with some performance criterion, that is, some description of expected behavior.

Decision. A choice among alternative courses of action.

Descriptive data. Data that have been organized, categorized, or quantified by an observer but do not involve a value judgment.

Desist behaviors. Behaviors the teacher uses in an effort to stop student misbehavior.

Deviation rule. A rule for determining the value assigned to an individual. The rule assigns various values to an individual on the basis of how far the information about the individual deviates from the selected referent.

Diagnostic procedures. Procedures to determine what pupils are capable of doing with respect to given learning tasks.

Disjunctive concepts. Concepts that have two or more sets of alternative conditions under which the concept appears.

Effective teacher. One who is able to bring about intended learning outcomes.

Enactive medium. A representational medium for acquiring concepts by enacting or doing the concept.

Evaluation. The process of obtaining information and using it to form judgments which, in turn, are to be used in decision making.

Evaluation questions. Questions requiring students to use criteria or standards to form a judgment about the value of the topic or phenomena being considered.

Evaluation set. A type of set induction that is used to evaluate previously learned material before moving on to new material.

Expectations. Those perceptions that the teacher and the students hold regarding their relationships to one another.

Extinction. Withholding of an anticipated reward in an instance where that behavior was previously rewarded; results in the decreased frequency of the previously rewarded behavior.

Facts. Well-grounded, clearly established pieces of information.

Feedback. Information about the effects or consequences of actions taken.

Focusing. A stimulus variation technique in which the teacher intentionally controls the direction of student attention.

Generalizations. A special class of conclusions that summarize a collection of wide-ranging, carefully tested facts and have predictive power. A statement of relationship between two or more concepts.

Goals. General statements of purpose.

Group-focus behaviors. Those behaviors teachers use to maintain a focus on the group, rather than on an individual student, during individual recitations.

Iconic medium. A representational medium for acquiring concepts by viewing a picture or image of the concept.

Inference. A conclusion derived from, and bearing some relation to, assumed premises.

Instructional objectives. Statements of desired changes in students' thoughts, actions, or feelings that a particular course or educational program should bring about.

Instructional strategies. Plans for managing the learning environment in order to provide learning opportunities and meet objectives. Strategies involve the methods used, along with concerns for motivating, sequencing, pacing, and grouping.

Interval schedule. A type of intermittent reinforcement in which the teacher reinforces the student after a specified period of time.

Inventory questions. Questions asking individuals to describe their thoughts, feelings, and manifested actions.

Judgments. Estimates of present conditions or predictions of future conditions. Involve comparing information to some referent.

Kinesic variation. A teacher's physical ability to move from one location in the classroom to another to improve communication (a stimulus variation technique).

Knowledge questions. Questions requiring the student to recognize or recall information.

Leadership. Those behaviors that help the group move toward the accomplishment of its objectives.

Movement management behaviors. Those behaviors that the teacher uses to initiate, sustain, or terminate a classroom activity.

Noncriterial attributes. Features that are frequently present in concept illustrations, though they are not an essential part of the concept.

Norm-referenced judgments. Judgments made by comparing the information you have about an individual with information you have about a group of similar individuals.

Norms. Shared expectations of how group members should think, feel, and behave.

Observation. Systematic recording of classroom events by an observer during an instructional activity.

Orientation set. A type of set induction that is used to focus students' attention on the upcoming learning activity.

Overlapping behaviors. Those behaviors by which the teacher indicates that he or she is attending to more than one issue when there is more than one issue to deal with at a particular time.

Pausing. A stimulus variation technique in which silence is deliberately used.

Percentile rank. A person's rank in a group defined in terms of the percentage of individuals who score at the same level or lower than he or she did.

Percepts. Raw impressions that are filtered through any of our five senses.

Primary reinforcers. Reinforcers that are unlearned and that are necessary to sustain life.

Probing questions. Questions following a response that require the respondent to provide more support, to be clearer or more accurate, or to offer greater specificity or originality.

Punishment. Use of an unpleasant stimulus to eliminate an undesirable behavior.

Ratio schedule. A type of intermittent reinforcement in which the teacher reinforces the student after the behavior has occurred a certain number of times.

Referent. That to which you compare the information you have about an individual in order to form a judgment.

Reflection. Giving direct feedback to individuals about the way their verbal and nonverbal messages are being received.

Reinforcement. The process of using reinforcers, in general, any event that increases the strength of a response. A reward for the purpose of maintaining an already acquired behavior is called *positive reinforcement*. Strengthening a behavior through the removal of an unpleasant stimulus is called *negative reinforcement*.

Relational concepts. Concepts that describe relationships between items.

Reproduced data. Data made available when an event is reproduced in video, audio, or total transcript (verbatim) form.

Review closure. A type of closure technique whose main characteristic is an attempt to summarize the major points of a presentation or discussion.

Selected data. Data that objectively record a specific event without valuing or categorizing the event.

Self-referenced judgments. Judgments made by comparing information you have about an individual to some other information you have about that same individual.

Serendipity closure. A type of closure technique wherein the teacher uses spontaneous or "unexpected" opportunities to achieve closure.

Set induction. Actions and statements by the teacher that are designed to relate the experiences of the students to the objectives of the lesson.

Shadowing. An observation technique in which data are gathered about a targeted individual.

Shifting interaction. A stimulus variation technique in which the teacher deliberately varies the three interaction styles: teacher–group; teacher–student; and student–student.

Shifting senses. A stimulus variation technique wherein the teacher requires students to use different senses in order to process information.

Standard deviation. A measure of deviation from the mean score that takes into account the degree of spread in a set of scores.

Standard score. A value placed on an individual using a group average as the referent.

Stimulus variation. Teacher actions that are designed to develop and maintain a high level of student attention during a lesson by varying the presentation.

Symbolic medium. A representational medium for acquiring concepts through symbols such as language.

Synthesis questions. Questions requiring the student to put together elements and parts so as to form a whole. Include producing original communications, making predictions, and solving problems for which a variety of answers are possible.

Systems design. A self-correcting and logical methodology of decision making to be used for the design and development of constructed entities; particularly in this book, instructional systems.

Target mistakes. The teacher stopping the wrong student or desisting a less serious deviancy.

Taxonomy. A classification system; used here in reference to a classification system of educational objectives or skills.

Teaching skill. A distinct set of identifiable behaviors needed to perform teaching functions.

Terminal goals. Goals one can expect to reach at the end of a given learning experience.

Theoretical knowledge. Concepts, facts, and propositions that make up much of the content of the disciplines.

Time out. The removal of a reward from the student or the removal of the student from the reward.

Transfer closure. A type of closure technique that asks students to extend new knowledge from previously learned concepts.

Transition set. A type of set induction that is used to provide a smooth transition from known material to new or unknown material.

Two-value rule. A rule for determining the value assigned to an individual. The rule states that a positive value is associated with information that matches or exceeds the referent and a negative value is associated with information that falls below the referent.

Valued data. Data that involve the judgment of an observer.

Verbal flow. Verbal behavior of students observable during a classroom discussion.

Wait time. The amount of time the teacher waits after asking a question before calling for the answer.

Withitness behaviors. Behaviors by which the teacher communicates to students that he or she knows what is going on.

z score. Ratio of an individual's deviation from the mean compared to the standard deviation from the mean.

Index